GOVERNANCE and OPPORTUNITY in METROPOLITAN AMERICA

Committee on Improving the Future of U.S. Cities
Through Improved Metropolitan Area Governance

Alan Altshuler, William Morrill, Harold Wolman,
and Faith Mitchell, *Editors*

Commission on Behavioral and Social Sciences and Education

Transportation Research Board

National Research Council

NATIONAL ACADEMY PRESS
Washington, D.C.

NATIONAL ACADEMY PRESS   2101 Constitution Avenue, N.W.   Washington, D.C. 20418

NOTICE: The project that is the subject of this report was approved by the Governing Board of the National Research Council, whose members are drawn from the councils of the National Academy of Sciences, the National Academy of Engineering, and the Institute of Medicine. The members of the committee responsible for the report were chosen for their special competences and with regard for appropriate balance.

This study was supported by the National Research Council.

Library of Congress Cataloging-in-Publication Data

Governance and opportunity in Metropolitan America / Alan Altshuler
      [et al.] editors ; Committee on Improving the Future of U.S.
Cities Through Improved Metropolitan Area Governance, Commission on
Behavioral and Social Sciences and Education, National Research
Council.
            p. cm.
      Includes bibliographical references and index.
      ISBN 0-309-06553-4
      1. Metropolitan government—United States. 2. State-local
relations—United States. 3. Cities and towns—United States. I.
Altshuler, Alan A., 1936- II. National Research Council (U.S.).
Committee on Improving the Future of U.S. Cities Through
Metropolitan Area Governance.
      JS422 .G68 1999
      352.14'0973—dc21
                              99-6607

Additional copies of this report are available from National Academy Press, 2101 Constitution Avenue, N.W., Lockbox 285, Washington, D.C. 20055; (800) 624-6242 or (202) 334-3313 (in the Washington metropolitan area); Internet, http://www.nap.edu

iii

Contents

v

PART II: IN-DEPTH PERSPECTIVES

Preface

The Committee on Improving the Future of U.S. Cities Through Improved Metropolitan Area Governance was charged with examining metropolitan problems and their relationship to metropolitan governance. Determining that the future of U.S. cities merited serious attention by the Academy, the Three Presidents' Committee of the National Research Council (NRC), composed of the presidents of the National Academy of Sciences, the National Academy of Engineering, and the Institute of Medicine, provided funds to support the study. The committee gratefully acknowledges additional support received from the Rockefeller Foundation for its information-gathering activities.

The committee's original scope of work and plan of action envisioned a focus on a small number of "problems of metropolitan areas" (transportation, environmental regulation, and residential segregation were suggested); the unifying concern was to be "the extent to which current governance structures contribute to improvements in these areas or exacerbate the problems." The committee's task was thus a logical extension of two previous NRC reports: *Urban Change and Poverty* (1988) was concerned with demographic and economic trends affecting urban areas and their central cities, and *Inner-City Poverty in the United States* (1990) focused more intensively on the extent and location of neighborhood poverty and the question of neighborhood effects.

Following the original charge, the committee began by making clear that its conception of urban was metropolitan in scope, and therefore we took urban problems to mean metropolitan-area problems. Metropolitan problems were defined as problems affecting the entire metropolitan area or significant parts of it or problems caused by the characteristics of metropolitan areas.

vii

It is important to be clear about how the committee formulated its task and what this report attempts and does not attempt to do. The National Research Council provided a general mandate to the committee, with the goal of opening up a new topic for examination that is socially important and could also lay the groundwork for further work in this area. Because the study was internally funded, the committee had considerable flexibility in interpreting this mandate. Charged to develop recommendations directed to the problems of American urban areas in relation to the question of governance, the committee made an early judgment to focus on inequality of opportunity in metropolitan areas, the disparities that result, the causes of these disparities, and the role of governance and the government system in contributing to and, potentially, in solving these problems.

The committee's report addresses these problems of inequality of opportunity in metropolitan areas through a review of existing research and knowledge, an assessment of the logic of alternative strategies that have been proposed, a review of research evaluating those that have been tried, and a set of recommendations for research and policy options that reflect its assessment of existing knowledge. The intended audience is the community of scholars and researchers concerned with urban areas and their functioning and informed policy makers who grapple with these issues.

The committee is composed of scholars and practitioners from a variety of relevant fields, including economics, political science, education, land use, transportation, the environment, and government. To inform its deliberations, the committee commissioned papers, held workshops, and participated in discussions with its Working Group on Race, Civic Consciousness, and Governance.

The committee benefited greatly from a set of papers it commissioned, which served as background for its discussions. These papers, by Ingrid Gould Ellen, William A. Fischel, Keith R. Ihlanfeldt, Michael A. Pagano, and Martin Wachs and Jennifer Dill, constitute the second part of this report.

The committee was also assisted by a number of people who attended its workshops. David Burwell, Rails to Trails Conservancy; Elmer Johnson, Kirkland and Ellis; Roger Parks, Indiana University; and David Walker, University of Connecticut, participated in a workshop held in Woods Hole, Massachusetts. Participants in the two meetings of the Working Group on Race, Civic Consciousness, and Governance included: Camille Cates Barnett, Research Triangle Institute; Sheri Dunn Berry, National Community Building Network; Angela Blackwell, Rockefeller Foundation; Larry Bobo, University of California, Los Angeles; Dayna Cunningham, Rockefeller Foundation; Michael Dawson, University of Chicago; Ingrid Ellen, Brookings Institution; Christopher Gates, National Civic League; Marilyn Gittell, City University of New York; Otis Johnson, Youth Futures Authority; Keith Lawrence, Rockefeller Foundation; Charles Lee, United Church of Christ Commission for Racial Justice; Robert Liberty, 1000 Friends of Oregon; Clyde Murphy, Chicago Lawyers Committee for Civil Rights Under Law; Manuel Pastor, Jr., University of California, Santa Cruz; Eduardo

Reyes, Office of Council Member Mike Hernandez, Los Angeles; Catherine Ross, Georgia Tech University; Todd Swanstrom, State University of New York, Albany; Katherine Tate, Ohio State University; Phil Thompson, Barnard College; and Margaret Weir, Brookings Institution.

This report has been reviewed in draft form by individuals chosen for their diverse perspectives and technical expertise, in accordance with procedures approved by the NRC's Report Review Committee. The purpose of this independent review is to provide candid and critical comments that will assist the institution in making the published report as sound as possible and to ensure that the report meets institutional standards for objectivity, evidence, and responsiveness to the study charge. The content of the review comments and draft manuscript remain confidential to protect the integrity of the deliberative process.

We thank the following individuals for their participation in the review of Part I of this report: John S. Adams, Department of Geography, University of Minnesota; Roy Bahl, School of Policy Studies, Georgia State University; Brian J.L. Berry, School of Social Sciences, University of Texas, Dallas; Ester R. Fuchs, Center for Urban Policy, Barnard College and Columbia University; Royce Hanson, School of Social Sciences, University of Texas, Dallas; Robert P. Inman, Wharton School, University of Pennsylvania; Laurence Lynn, School of Social Services Administration, University of Chicago; Douglas Massey, Population Studies Center, University of Pennsylvania; Elinor Ostrom, Workshop in Political Theory and Policy Analysis, Indiana University; and Clarence N. Stone, Department of Government and Politics, University of Maryland. Although the individuals listed above have provided many constructive comments and suggestions, it must be emphasized that responsibility for the final content of this report rests entirely with the authoring committee and the institution.

Alan Altshuler
William Morrill
Committee Co-Chairs

GOVERNANCE and OPPORTUNITY in
METROPOLITAN
AMERICA

PART I

GOVERNANCE and OPPORTUNITY in
METROPOLITAN
AMERICA

Executive Summary

Socioeconomic inequality—of income, wealth, and opportunity—in the United States is high compared with other developed democracies, and it appears to be growing. A considerable body of scholarship is concerned with measuring inequality and identifying its causes. The Committee on Improving the Future of U.S. Cities Through Improved Metropolitan Area Governance has chosen to revisit the issue of inequality of opportunity in the United States from a perspective not widely explored in scholarly accounts: the perspective of metropolitan governance.

The spatial distribution of inequality, and in particular the increasing isolation of low-income minority populations in central cities and inner suburbs, appears to be a result of mutually reinforcing efforts by working-class and middle-class people to create living arrangements to their liking and by economic actors to locate their activities in a manner that furthers their specific interests. These efforts have become institutionalized in the fragmented, decentralized structures of metropolitan governance, and these structures in turn both exacerbate socioeconomic inequality and effectively stand in the way of policies that might ameliorate or reduce its extent and social costs.

Although the underlying causes of inequality cannot be addressed solely or even primarily by metropolitan governance reforms, in the committee's view it is of utmost importance to document the role that current patterns of metropolitan governance play in exacerbating socioeconomic inequality and in restricting the range of potentially effective ameliorative public policies. Furthermore, acknowledging that patterns of state and local political representation are themselves the product of the forces that have produced the social and economic isolation of

poor minority groups, it is the committee's view that both the scholarly community concerned with inequality and policy makers who recognize its costs to
society as a whole must begin to identify and evaluate state-level policies that
aim to undermine the forces of inequality.

EXTENT OF DISPARITIES
BETWEEN CENTRAL CITIES AND THEIR SUBURBS

Analyses of differences in economic and social conditions in metropolitan
areas are nearly always presented in terms of central-city versus suburban differences, even though there is clearly substantial variation across individual suburbs. In many metropolitan areas, there are inner-ring suburbs or industrial
suburbs whose residents share the same environment and consequent problems as
residents of the central city. However, virtually all of the available research
examines only central-city/suburban differences, and it is that research that we
report.

The extent of central-city/suburban disparities is striking. In 1990, the
poverty rate of central-city households was 18 percent compared with 8 percent
for suburban households. Median household income in the central city was less
than 75 percent that of the suburbs, and the unemployment rate was 70 percent
higher. Disparities in employment and education were somewhat smaller, but
central-city residents appear to be more deprived in these realms as well.

Central-city/suburban disparities vary considerably by region. The disparities appear to be greater in the Northeast and the Midwest and lower in the South
and the West. On average, the per capita income of central-city residents in the
South and the West nearly matched that of their suburban counterparts. In the
average metropolitan area in the Midwest and the Northeast, by contrast, the per
capita income of central-city residents was just 76 and 65 percent, respectively,
of that of suburban residents. Central-city poverty rates are almost 2 times
greater than suburban poverty rates in the West, and they are almost 4 times
greater in the Northeast.

Perhaps more significant than the magnitude of these disparities are their
trends over time. With the exception of education, every measure of change
indicates that the relative status of central-city residents has consistently declined
over the last three decades. Relative to their suburban counterparts, central-city
residents now have lower incomes, higher poverty rates, and lower employment
rates than they did 10, 20, and 30 years ago. The deepening of central-city
disparities over time reflects both the selective migration of better-off people to
the suburbs and the declining fortunes of lower-skilled and low-income groups
who remain in the city.

Disparities among racial and ethnic groups in metropolitan areas remain
pronounced as well. In 1990, the poverty rate for blacks in metropolitan areas
was 28 percent and for Hispanics 25 percent, compared with 8 percent for non-

Hispanic whites. Per capita income of blacks and Hispanics was roughly half that of metropolitan-area non-Hispanic whites, and unemployment rates were nearly 3 times greater for blacks and more than 3.5 times greater for Hispanics than for non-Hispanic whites.

In part, these racial and ethnic gaps in income reflect differences in labor force participation and employment rates. Over 90 percent of non-Hispanic white men of prime working age in metropolitan areas held jobs in 1990, compared with 83 percent of Hispanic men and just 73 percent of black men of similar ages.

Some fraction of the employment gap may be explained by racial and ethnic disparities in educational attainment and skill level. Among men between ages 25 and 34, for instance, nearly 90 percent of non-Hispanic whites have at least a high school diploma. The corresponding proportion for blacks is 76 percent and for Hispanics, 56 percent.

CAUSES OF DISPARITIES IN METROPOLITAN AREAS

There is research evidence for a variety of causes of these disparities in the well-being of people and places in metropolitan areas. Some of the most important causes are unrelated, or related only indirectly, to metropolitan governance. For example, differences in labor market outcomes between blacks and whites and between central-city and suburban residents may be related in part to differences in human capital—the education and skills they bring to the workplace.

In addition, changes in the structure of the national economy and technological change have increased education and skill requirements for jobs in many sectors of the economy, including manufacturing. Well-paid, low-skilled jobs in manufacturing and other sectors have largely disappeared. When combined with differences in the education and skills of prospective employees, the result is a mismatch of skills between labor demand and supply that disadvantages lower-skilled workers in general and black workers, a higher proportion of whom are lower-skilled, in particular.

Other causes, more directly related to metropolitan-level processes, are discussed below.

Spatial Mismatch

The spatial mismatch hypothesis states that there is a disjuncture between jobs that are increasingly found in the suburbs and potential qualified workers who are constrained to live, as a result of low income or housing segregation patterns or both, in central-city neighborhoods. Research, although not conclusive, suggests that a combination of barriers hinders central-city blacks and less-educated whites from obtaining suburban jobs; these barriers include an absence of information on suburban job opportunities, greater hiring discrimination against blacks in suburban areas (reflecting both consumer and employer prejudice), low levels of automobile ownership, and difficulties in commuting from the inner city to suburban employment centers via public transportation.

Concentrated Poverty, Social Isolation, and Neighborhood Effects

Other possible reasons why central-city residents have low employment rates relative to suburban residents are not necessarily related to distance but may nonetheless be related to location and metropolitan structure. One possible set of reasons relates to the social isolation of poor people, particularly blacks, in high-poverty neighborhoods. Residence in such areas, it is argued, imposes "neighborhood effects" on inhabitants, external costs that would not be present if the individual lived elsewhere.

Some neighborhood effects are simply the result of features highly associated with poverty. Since crime and poverty are related, individuals living in high-poverty neighborhoods are more likely to be the victims of crime than would be the case if they were living in some other neighborhood. Some effects have to do with the level of public services and amenities in high-poverty neighborhoods, which tend to be worse than would be the case in other neighborhoods.

Others, however, have to do with more subtle influences of residents on the behavior of each other. Since behaviors considered socially undesirable are more prevalent in poor neighborhoods, people living there are more likely to be influenced to engage in self-destructive or antisocial behavior, from poor school performance to higher rates of crime and teenage pregnancy.

Some neighborhood effects may directly affect employment prospects. Youth growing up in concentrated poverty areas may be cut off from mainstream values and may adopt values of their peers that are not well related to workplace success. The lack of adults in the area with steady employment may also affect the employment prospects of other people in the neighborhood. Also, young people living in a neighborhood of concentrated poverty may know very few people who work. This provides two forms of disadvantage: they are not linked into word-of-mouth job networks, through which many jobs are filled, and they are not exposed to modeling about appropriate job behavior.

Although research evidence increasingly suggests that neighborhood effects exist, the importance of these effects relative to other factors is still uncertain, and little is known about how they operate.

Racial and Economic Segregation

Racial segregation is extremely high in most U.S. metropolitan areas, although it has been declining slightly over time. Segregation by economic class is also prevalent, and, unlike racial segregation, it is growing.

Racial segregation appears to promote concentrations of poverty among low-income blacks; poor black people are much more concentrated in high-poverty areas than poor white people are. This in turn contributes to disparities in measures of well-being between blacks and whites through the neighborhood effects and social isolation mechanisms just mentioned.

In addition, racial segregation, when combined with incomes that are lower for blacks than for whites, may mean that blacks (including middle-income blacks) are more likely than whites to reside in communities with lower tax bases relative to need and thus a lower ability to finance public services from their own resources. As a consequence, segregation contributes to disparities in levels of public services.

Research suggests that racial segregation does contribute to disparities in outcome, but there is little research on the contribution of economic segregation to disparities in outcomes between minority groups and whites, except for the findings on neighborhood effects.

Tax/Service Disparities

Socioeconomic segregation by jurisdiction in metropolitan areas routinely translates into tax and public service disparities. That is, jurisdictions with lower than average tax bases must impose higher tax rates or provide lower levels of public services than their more affluent neighbors. Also, jurisdictions with high concentrations of poverty tend to have higher levels of per capita need than more affluent jurisdictions—for example, larger numbers of at-risk children, higher crime rates, and greater service requirements for commuters who live elsewhere. Such disadvantages in tax base and service need can be overcome by equalization grants from higher levels of government, and in most other developed western nations, they are, to a very considerable extent. Such efforts at equalization in the United States have generally been weak in the past, but the courts of numerous states have recently mandated fiscal equalization policies for elementary and secondary education, and a few states have made substantial progress toward achieving it.

The public service that is most important for human capital development and that has received the most attention in this context is education. The available research suggests that there is little correlation between school spending or resource levels and educational outcomes when more powerful determinants of educational achievement—in particular, family background and peer influences— are held constant. However, some recent studies have found more positive relationships between school spending and educational outcomes and between spending and labor market outcomes.

Metropolitan Governance and Government Structure

The system of metropolitan governance has also been implicated as a contributor to these disparities. The spatial distribution of population that isolates poor people in central cities and stratifies the suburbs by income is not simply the inevitable result of the interaction of individual choice, market forces, and technology; it also reflects the impact of public policies, broadly construed to include choices about the structure of political institutions.

The policies that have given rise to this pattern are state deference to local governments with regard to land use, state laws permitting easy incorporation of municipalities, and a fiscal system that requires municipal governments to finance most services from their own tax base. Local land use regulation and municipal incorporation efforts have been driven to a substantial extent by exclusionary impulses. And the system of local self-reliance has provided localities with a powerful fiscal incentive—over and above social patterns of discrimination and preferences—to exclude low- and moderate-income households, which typically consume public services costing a good deal more than they contribute in local tax payments.

The ease of municipal incorporation permits the creation of many local governments within metropolitan areas. One important motive for incorporation is to exercise land use controls at the local level in order to exert control over the local setting. Although close proximity of residents to land use decisions has many desirable attributes, it also allows those with sufficient resources to influence who their neighbors are by using land use controls to raise the price of housing beyond what lower-income households can afford. In addition, there are fiscal incentives for local governments to keep poor people out, since, as we said, low-income households consume more in public services than they contribute in local taxes.

The resulting fragmented system of local government in metropolitan areas has thus frequently been pointed to as a contributor to unequal opportunity and disparities. Fragmented metropolitan areas, some contend, are likely to be more highly stratified by both income and race; they are also likely to have greater tax/ service disparities among local governments.

To find that local government fragmentation accentuates tendencies toward segregation and fiscal disparities is not the end of the story, however. First, even the least fragmented urban areas display high levels of segregation and inequality. Second, the fragmented system of local government has many positive features—involving efficiency, choice, and grass-roots accountability—that might be lost in a more consolidated system. In short, there may be very real trade-offs between these benefits of a fragmented local government system and the equity gains of a more consolidated system.

Most of the research effort with respect to fragmentation has been directed toward the impact of fragmentation on size of government, as measured by expenditures per capita, or on service delivery and efficiency. This research generally indicates that small-scale (fragmented) local governments are more efficient for many of the public services that local governments provide, particularly for those that are heavily labor-intensive. More consolidated forms of metropolitan government are efficient for more capital-intensive services, since they are able to take advantage of declining costs associated with economies of scale.

The body of literature directed at the effects of government fragmentation on disparities and inequality is smaller and less compelling. The variation in measures of fragmentation and the nature of dependent variables and methodologies used make it difficult to come to overall conclusions.

The Costs of Extreme Disparity

In the committee's view, the costs associated with extreme disparity threaten the future well-being of society. A rough estimate is that, when comparing metropolitan areas that have very high levels of segregation to those that (within the American context) have relatively low levels, the segregation of blacks results in a 3 to 6 percent decline in productivity. In addition to the economic cost of lower productivity and output, there are the social and economic costs of crime, the threat to personal security and social order inherent in a large disadvantaged population that feels it has been denied opportunities, and the long-term debilitating effect on the quality of American democracy, which depends on a well-socialized population with active commitment and participation from its diverse population groups.

The higher unemployment rates and lower incomes resulting from unequal opportunity also impose greater public costs on all levels of government, through higher public expenditures on welfare, medical care, food stamps, social services, housing assistance, police protection, and prisons. These costs are reflected directly in higher taxes paid by taxpayers throughout the nation.

RECOMMENDATIONS FOR RESEARCH

The charge to the committee called for the delineation of specific research priorities and policy considerations of interest to social scientists, urban planners, and policy makers at all levels of government. In this respect, the committee is impressed by both the importance of the task it undertook and by how much remains to be known about it. It is very clear that additional research is needed, both with respect to causal processes and, even more so, with respect to the effects of policies that have been proposed and undertaken to deal with unequal spatial opportunity structures and unequal opportunity in metropolitan areas. The ability to conduct such research depends on the availability of relevant data, many of which can be gathered only by the federal government as a provider of public goods. We strongly urge that the Census Bureau and other related agencies continue to perform their vital role in collecting and providing data on metropolitan areas and their residents and governments. Indeed, such efforts should be expanded. In addition, the committee recommends that research be conducted on the following questions of high priority:

- The spatial distribution of metropolitan population and its determinants.
- The extent and causes of mobility into and out of areas of concentrated poverty and of racial concentration.
- The nature of the "push" factors related to the condition or characteristics of the central city that movers to the suburbs wish to avoid, and their relative importance.
- The pace and extent of suburbanization cross-nationally and its causes. Relatedly, variation among countries in spatial segregation by income and race and in the location of the poor within metropolitan areas.
- The stratification of metropolitan areas by race and income. The broad question from the committee's perspective is why households are sorted in a manner that results in highly stratified areas.
- The effects of recent public efforts to consciously affect the spatial distribution of population through various devices to limit land use controls (e.g., urban growth boundaries and inclusionary zoning policies).
- The variation in tax/service capacity among local governments within metropolitan areas, including changes over time.
- The relationship of metropolitan-area density to disparities in outcomes. There has been virtually no research on the contribution, if any, of density to disparities in outcomes among jurisdictions or among groups.
- The extent to which government structure and particularly fragmentation contributes to differences in outcomes.
- The distinction between the portion of inequality of outcomes that is metropolitan in nature and the portion that is due to broader causes—such as differences in human capital or racial discrimination in employment—that are simply manifested in metropolitan areas because that is where most people live.
- The relationship between unequal spending and outcome disparities in noneducational services (currently most of the research focuses on education). In all cases, including education, we need to know more about the production function or basic processes that are at work by which input resources are transformed into outcomes.
- The effects of recent strategies to reduce inequalities in spatial opportunity structures, such as empowerment zones and community development corporations; worker mobility and reverse commuting programs; Gautreaux-type residential dispersion strategies; housing vouchers; and the equalization of educational expenditures.
- Whether the extent of governmental fragmentation in metropolitan areas affects the degree of inequality of income or racial and economic segregation in those areas.
- The extent to which there is greater equalization of service delivery in more consolidated metropolitan areas, or in metropolitan areas with more "elastic" cities, than in more fragmented areas.

- The nature of effective political coalitions at the state legislative level on behalf of city interests.
- The costs imposed on suburbs and their residents—and on metropolitan areas and the nation—by the decline of central cities.

POLICY OPTIONS

The committee has identified policy options worthy of serious consideration by policy makers. Most of these are directed at the state and local level. Although the research base in many areas is not as strong as we would like, it is the committee's determination that there is sufficient evidence to allow us to identify certain options as making a positive contribution to the reshaping of spatial opportunity structures in metropolitan areas.

The committee considered two alternatives to the existing system of governance in metropolitan areas. Both are counterfactuals, in the sense that they require us to consider how their implementation would result in differences from the current system and to shape our discussion with these in mind. The first is a change in government structure that would reduce reliance on small-scale local governments and move to a system of more consolidated metropolitan government. The second, which is the committee's preference, would largely retain the existing system of nested local governments—smaller units of local government overlain by larger ones that provide broader functions—but would increase the critical role of state government in reducing barriers to equal access and opportunity in metropolitan areas.

The committee supports a restructuring of metropolitan *governance*, focusing particularly on the critical role of state government. In our judgment, more aggressive state government action is fundamental to reducing inequality of opportunity in metropolitan areas and to achieving prosperous metropolitan areas that are less racially and economically stratified. Local governments operate within a framework of state laws and regulations; the state is, after all, the locus of constitutional authority with respect to local governments. State governments thus have both the responsibility and the authority to bring about change in the metropolitan governance system by changing the legal framework within which local governments operate and the set of incentives they respond to.

At a minimum, state governments can stop being an agent for discriminatory action and a barrier to equal opportunity by exercising oversight over the constitutional authority they have devolved to local government with respect to local land use controls. States routinely override local zoning for a raft of purposes—to facilitate the location of power plants, public facilities, group homes, and churches on one hand, and to constrain local development impulses for such reasons as environmental and public health protection on the other. They can do likewise to prevent exclusionary zoning behavior discriminating against low- and moderate-income households. The committee also supports more vigorous efforts to enforce housing antidiscrimination laws in metropolitan areas and to ensure that access to housing credit is available on a nondiscriminatory basis.

The committee recognizes that reducing the ability of jurisdictions to exclude low- and moderate-income households through exclusionary zoning devices may result in some loss of allocative efficiency. If so, that would be a cost that we consider worth incurring as a means of reducing inequality of opportunity in metropolitan areas.

Finally, attention should also be given to the potential for breaking the link between place, income, and quality of life outcomes. Three areas of particular importance are education improvement, providing access to suburban jobs, and reducing fiscal disparities.

1

Introduction

America's metropolitan areas serve as the symbol of its prosperity, dynamism, and innovation. Their economies are powerful engines of national economic growth and well-being. Yet many metropolitan areas are also characterized by a set of problems so severe that some see them as threatening the long-term viability of American society.

Although public concerns focus on the problems of central cities, the problems are metropolitan in scope. And there is public unease that these problems are getting worse. This concern has increased attention on the role of metropolitan governance in creating these problems, in perpetuating them, and in standing as a barrier to their solution.

COMMITTEE'S CHARGE AND PERSPECTIVE
ON METROPOLITAN-AREA PROBLEMS

The Committee on Improving the Future of U.S. Cities Through Improved Metropolitan Area Governance was charged by the National Research Council with developing recommendations directed to the problems of American urban areas in relation to the question of governance. We began by making clear that our conception of *urban* is metropolitan in scope, which means that urban problems are metropolitan-area problems. Metropolitan-area problems are defined as problems affecting the entire metropolitan area or significant parts of it, as well as problems caused by the characteristics of metropolitan areas.

Metropolitan-area problems in this context can include physical and environmental concerns, such as transportation, pollution, and sprawl. Since metropolitan areas are functional labor markets, inadequate economic growth and development are clearly metropolitan-area problems, as are poorly functioning labor and housing markets. Poor relations among the racial and ethnic groups living in metropolitan areas also qualify. The economic, social, physical, and fiscal problems of central cities are metropolitan-area problems to the extent that they affect the surrounding suburbs and the metropolitan area as a whole or are caused, at least in part, by features related to metropolitan-area governance.

Metropolitan-area problems can be characterized in a variety of ways. One very useful distinction is to divide them into those concerned with "life-style" issues and those concerned with "system maintenance" issues (Williams, 1971). Life-style issues involve social access and the interaction of individuals in settings such as neighborhoods and schools. System maintenance issues involve development and maintenance of the metropolitan infrastructure, broadly construed, in such areas as transportation, water and sewer systems, and environmental protection. System maintenance issues are much less controversial.

A related way of classifying these problems is to distinguish between those concerned (or perceived to be concerned) with common-purpose objectives and those involving redistribution, in which values are controversial. Although the latter problems are much more difficult to address effectively, they may well be of greater importance. This is because, in general, problems perceived to involve the redistribution of important resources—income, employment, tax base, social status and values, access to valued locations—are more intrinsically divisive, since they are seen to be "zero-sum" in nature, that is, creating winners and losers. Common-purpose problems have solutions that are perceived to benefit the entire community and are viewed as involving economic efficiency rather than redistribution.

Different metropolitan-area problems vary substantially in terms of their susceptibility to being effectively addressed and solved through the existing system of metropolitan governance. In general, it is the system maintenance and common-purpose problems that are the easiest to solve. Problems involving the redistribution of resources but not necessarily involving changes in social access and interaction are considerably more difficult to address. Problems whose solutions require redistribution of resources *and* redistribution in terms of life-style and social access have proven the most intractable.

The above discussion sets forth how the committee conceptualized the problems facing urban areas. The term "metropolitan governance" also deserves some initial discussion. The committee defined metropolitan governance broadly to include *governmental institutions* within metropolitan areas, *processes* (the way in which groups participate, decisions are made, resources are allocated, and activities undertaken in metropolitan areas), and *policies* that influence the metropolitan area. It also extended its concern to the *spatial structure* that is produced, at least in part, by these institutions, processes, and policies.

The committee thus distinguished between metropolitan *governance* and the set of formal governmental institutions (the metropolitan *government* system) in metropolitan areas. With respect to the latter, the committee began by recognizing that the benefits of the existing system of local government are substantial. Most people are very attached to local government as a concept and, in particular, to their own local government. It provides people, at least those with money, with a range of choices and with the opportunity to "vote with their feet" if they are dissatisfied with their current local government or if attracted by features of others. And, as this report details, such governments appear to be more efficient for some purposes than are larger-scale, more consolidated governments.

In addition, the existing system of metropolitan governance has proven remarkably flexible and effective in addressing system maintenance concerns that cut across local jurisdictional boundaries. To a large extent, it has done so through the creation of region-wide institutions. Region-wide political institutions are common in the areas of transportation, air quality, water and sewer systems, parks, economic development, airports, and other system maintenance areas. Preliminary estimates for 1997 indicate that, in metropolitan areas with more than one county (approximately 60 percent of all metropolitan statistical areas), there were 1,957 multicounty governmental districts within metropolitan areas. The most numerous functions performed by these districts were fire protection (318), water supply (277), soil and water conservation (124), drainage (108), and libraries (108).

Nevertheless, there is a large, interrelated set of problems in urban America that has not been addressed very effectively either by local governments in metropolitan areas or by the broader system of metropolitan governance. The most important feature of these problems, in the context of American values, is the high degree of inequality of opportunity, as evidenced by the striking disparities in measures of well-being among communities in metropolitan areas (and particularly between central cities and their suburbs) and between white and minority residents in these areas.

The problem of substantial inequality of opportunity is perceived to reflect life-style and redistributional concerns rather than system maintenance and common-purpose ones. It has not been addressed effectively by the existing metropolitan governance system or by regional institutions. As Harrigan (1993:371) cogently observes: "Equal access to sewers does not threaten anybody's life-style in the suburbs, but it is essential to maintain the health and safety of the majority of the population. . . . Even in metropolises such as Toronto, Miami, and the Twin Cities, where major metropolitan reorganizations have been achieved, the new governments have been much more effective in the physical-development issues than they have in the social issues where questions of life-style are at stake."

COMMITTEE'S FOCUS:
EQUALITY OF OPPORTUNITY

The committee recognizes that there are serious physical, environmental, land use, and developmental problems facing metropolitan areas. The governance system in metropolitan areas has been reasonably flexible and responsive in addressing many of these system maintenance problems. Our assessment is that, compared with these concerns, there has been much less success at coping with—and, indeed, much less public attention paid to—metropolitan-area problems related to equality of opportunity. These problems involve life-style issues and redistributional and equity concerns. They are therefore inherently difficult to address.

Our primary concern is with the exclusion of a substantial portion of metropolitan-area residents from the overall level of well-being characteristic of an American standard of living and reflecting, to a substantial extent, an unequal structure of opportunity. This is manifested by disparities in important indicators of well-being among residents in metropolitan areas and particularly (1) between residents of central cities and distressed suburbs and residents of the more affluent suburbs and (2) between minorities and whites.

These disparities are quite striking. In 1990, the poverty rate of central-city households was 18 percent compared with 8 percent for suburban households. Median household income in the central city was less than 75 percent that of the suburbs, and the unemployment rate was 70 percent higher. In 1990, the poverty rate for blacks in metropolitan areas was 28 percent and for Hispanics 25 percent, compared with 8 percent for non-Hispanic whites. Per capita income of blacks and Hispanics was roughly half that of metropolitan-area non-Hispanic whites, and unemployment rates were nearly 3 times greater for blacks and more than 3.5 times greater for Hispanics than for non-Hispanic whites.

The disparities do not simply reflect the fact that, for whatever reason, poor people have chosen to live in the cities and wealthier people in the suburbs. They reflect, to a substantial extent, the presence of unequal opportunity structures. Individuals who live in poor communities or high-poverty neighborhoods are disadvantaged *because* they live there; their opportunity structure is more restricted and constrained than that of a similarly endowed person living in a middle-class area.

It is a widely shared belief in American society that individuals should have an equal chance of taking advantage of and developing their inherent talents and capabilities. However, from an early age, people do not face equal opportunity structures. This is partially a result of differences in family background and social environment, but it is also a result of spatial variations in opportunity structures (which, in turn, exaggerate, rather than compensate for, differences in family background and social environment).

Metropolitan-area opportunity structures consist of the set of social networks, public and private institutions, and markets with which individuals interact. It is clear that similarly talented individuals face more favorable opportunity structures if they live in middle-class suburban areas than if they live in poor inner-city areas, because they have access to (among other things) more favorable social networks, educational systems, and employment opportunities. Society's goal should be to equalize access to opportunities throughout the metropolitan area *without regard to where people live.* We are thus concerned with *spatial opportunity structures* as critical components of opportunity structures within metropolitan areas. (For an elaboration of the concept of metropolitan opportunity structure and its relationship to equal opportunity, see Galster and Killen, 1995.)

The variation in spatial opportunity structures can be seen in its most severe form in neighborhoood poverty. Neighborhoods of concentrated poverty—which are defined as census tracts with 40 percent or more of the households with income below the poverty level—accounted for 5 percent of total metropolitan-area population in 1990, but for 17 percent of metropolitan-area blacks and 11 percent of Hispanics (compared with 1 percent of whites). Although only 18 percent of all poor people in metropolitan areas lived in these high-poverty areas, 34 percent of black poor people and 22 percent of Hispanic poor people did so. Growing up in neighborhoods of pervasive poverty imposes substantial penalties on children who live there. They do not experience equal opportunity; they *begin* well behind the starting line.

Difficulty of the Problem

These problems of unequal opportunity exist in an environment that, in several respects, exacerbates them and makes their amelioration more difficult. Globalization of the economy has restructured the role of American cities and has given them specific roles in the international economy. Cities of international significance can be divided into several tiers: the first tier consists of world cities, such as New York, Tokyo, and London; a second tier, with substantial influence over large portions of the world economy, includes the U.S. cities of Los Angeles, Chicago, and Washington, D.C.; a third tier, with more limited or specialized international functions, includes Houston, Miami, and San Francisco; and a fourth tier consists of cities of national importance with some transnational functions, including Boston, Dallas, and Philadelphia (Knox, 1997).

Although other cities do not play roles of international significance, they are still affected by globalization: "The world economy has been inscribed into local economies almost everywhere in one way or another. . . . A few towns do remain primarily export platforms for low-value-added, labor-intensive products made by unskilled cheap labor. Many more, though, have had a traditional industrial core hollowed out and are in the process of restructuring their economies, making higher-value-added items that employ sophisticated technologies" (Knox, 1997:23-24).

The consequences of globalization thus place a premium on labor skills. In a global economy, low-skilled American workers who produce goods for export markets (or goods that are susceptible to competition from imports) can no longer compete with low-skilled workers in developing countries who are paid a fraction of U.S. wages. In all but a few U.S. metropolitan areas, most low-skilled workers can no longer expect to make relatively high wages, if, indeed, they are able to find employment at all. But the consequent new emphasis on education means that unequal opportunity, as it extends to educational opportunities, is reflected more than in the past in unequal incomes.

Three other trends make the problem of unequal opportunity in metropolitan areas more difficult to deal with. First, except for crime and welfare, the problems of cities and their residents have largely fallen off the nation's political agenda, particularly in comparison to the 1960s. Second, the devolution of fiscal responsibilities from the federal government has pushed resources and problem-solving initiatives downward to lower levels of government. At the same time, the need to remain competitive in an international economy has limited the redistributive abilities of cities and metropolitan areas. These factors, combined with the constitutional fact that local governments are creatures of state government, have placed renewed emphasis on states as critical players in addressing unequal opportunities at the metropolitan level. And third, the belief has arisen that government at all levels is irrelevant to these problems and cannot appreciably contribute to their solution. More corrosively, there is a cynicism about even engaging in efforts to do so.

This is unfortunate. This report argues that government is not irrelevant. Public-sector activity bears some responsibility for the creation and persistence of unequal spatial opportunity structures, and public-sector activity will be required in order to bring about solutions. "The process of urban development in the United States is not random nor is it given. It is a process that has been structured politically" (Weiher, 1991:194). Yet, as we have seen, problems of unequal opportunity are viewed as life-style and redistributional issues, issues that are very difficult to address effectively within the existing system of metropolitan governance.

Costs of Unequal Opportunity

In the committee's view, severe inequality of opportunity is a potential threat to the well-being of society. We begin with the most fundamental concern: the deepest values that Americans share about the type of society we are and should be revolve around individualism and equal opportunity. A lack of equal opportunity is thus in the most profound sense a "moral" problem for Americans.

Beyond moral concerns, unequal opportunity imposes very real costs on the nation. Holzer, in a calculation made for the committee (see Chapter 3), estimates that unequal opportunity in the form of the segregation of blacks results in a 3 to 6 percent decline in productivity for metropolitan areas that have high levels of segregation compared with those that have relatively low levels. In addition to the economic cost of lower productivity and output, there are the social and economic costs of crime, the threat to personal security and social order inherent in a large disadvantaged population that perceives that it has been denied opportunities, and the long-term debilitating effect on the quality of American democracy, which depends on a well-socialized population with active commitment and participation from its diverse population groups.

The higher unemployment rates and lower incomes resulting from unequal opportunity also impose greater public costs on all levels of government through higher public expenditures on welfare, medical care, food stamps, social services, housing assistance, police protection, and prisons. These costs are reflected directly in higher taxes paid by taxpayers throughout the nation. The reductions in personal income for those who have experienced unequal opportunity also result in lower tax payments by these residents and, consequently, higher taxes for the rest of the population.

The cost to suburban residents of central-city decline are equally compelling, even if they are not readily recognized. Central-city problems adversely affect the well-being of the surrounding communities and their residents in several ways. Adverse city conditions, such as crime and the impact of poverty on local schools, often spread directly into surrounding suburbs, worsening the quality of life there. Perhaps less well recognized, metropolitan areas are in economic competition with other areas, and those with deteriorating central cities or serious social problems may suffer from competitive disadvantages.

The image of a central city beset by economic, social, and physical distress may adversely affect decisions being made by potential investors and residents about whether they should locate in the region at all; the result may be reduced investment and income throughout the entire region. In addition, the social and physical problems of the central city may induce firms to locate in the suburbs, thus preventing them from taking advantage of "agglomeration economies," which are cost savings resulting from firms and workers locating in close proximity, or from locating in what otherwise would be their optimal location. This places a cost on both firms and consumers.

The fiscal problems of central cities also adversely affect suburbs and their residents when they result in underexpenditure for purposes for which the entire region benefits. Such purposes include maintenance of the components of the city infrastructure that constitute a part of the regional infrastructure system, such as major surface transportation routes, bridges, and water distribution systems; elementary and secondary education, which prepares city residents to be part of the metropolitan area's labor force; and cultural institutions located in and financed at least partly by the central city but that serve a regional function or are regionally utilized, such as museums, zoos, and the main public library.

Suburban residents also suffer in ways that, although unrelated to direct economic or fiscal costs, are just as real and important. For example, their quality of life may diminish if the problems of the central city prevent them from enjoying amenities and recreational opportunities there that they would otherwise take advantage of.

Not only are the problems of central cities and of unequal opportunity serious, but also they are getting worse, which is surely another reason why they should command our attention. In 1990, central-city median income was only 77 percent of suburban median income compared with 89 percent in 1960, and central-city poverty rates were 2.4 times those of suburbs compared with 1.5 times in 1960. Between 1980 and 1990, per capita income for whites in metropolitan areas rose by 19 percent, whereas for blacks it increased by only 13 percent. These data reflect an opportunity structure in metropolitan areas that is getting worse rather than better.

Finally, because the minority groups now concentrated in central cities will form a growing part of the nation's future population, what happens in cities is vital to the future of the entire society. By the year 2020, according to Census Bureau projections, 45 percent of all children in the United States under age 18 will be either black, Hispanic, or Asian. This trend will affect all Americans, including suburban residents.

SCOPE OF THE STUDY

It is important to emphasize what this report attempts and does not attempt to do. Charged to develop recommendations directed to the problems of American urban areas in relation to the question of governance, the committee made an early judgment to focus on inequality of opportunity in metropolitan areas, the disparities that result, the causes of these disparities, and the role of governance and the government system in contributing to and potentially in solving these problems.

The report thus explores the nature and causes of unequal opportunity and disparities in well-being in metropolitan areas, and it explores policy options to address these problems. It does not argue that these problems are solely a product of the system of local governance and government in metropolitan areas. It identifies a variety of causes and attempts to assess the importance of each. With respect to the existing structure of local government, it argues that the present system does contribute to these problems and makes their solution more difficult. But the focus of the report is not on the restructuring of the system of local government in metropolitan areas, and the report does not recommend a major restructuring of the local government system.

Instead, the report attempts to develop a plausible and convincing *counterfactual* with respect to the present governance system. What might a system of governance, *different from that which now exists*, look like? The possibilities for such a construct include the following (or some combination of the following): (1) a regional or metropolitan unitary government, (2) a two-tier or federated metropolitan government system, (3) an expansion of single-purpose regional authorities, (4) increases in informal cooperation by local governments and across the public, private, and voluntary sectors, (5) federal government incentives, sanctions, or mandates to bring about greater metropolitan-area cooperation, and (6) state government activity, including changing the legal framework within which local government operates to reduce its potential for exclusionary action (acting in its constitutional capacity as the regulator of local government activity) and other policies to promote reduction of extreme inequalities of opportunity in metropolitan areas. In each case, the questions are whether the development of the counterfacutual is politically plausible; whether, even if it were to occur, it would address effectively the problem of extreme inequality of opportunity; and, finally, what would be the cost to other important social objectives, such as efficiency, choice, accountability, and local autonomy.

OUTLINE OF THE REPORT

Chapter 2 examines the broad context in which the problem of substantial inequality of opportunity in metropolitan areas occurs and discusses why it is a problem of national concern. It examines the spatial distribution of population in metropolitan areas in the United States, describes the distribution of population between central cities and suburbs and the degree of racial and economic segregation in metropolitan areas, and examines the causes of this pattern of spatial distribution. The chapter ends by examining the extent to which central cities and suburbs are interdependent and whether there is still an economic rationale for the central city.

Chapter 3 begins with the evidence for disparities in important outcomes of well-being between central-city and suburban residents and between whites and minority groups. It goes on to relate these disparities to the spatial opportunity structure in metropolitan areas. The task is to examine the causes of these disparities, assessing the extent to which they are due to metropolitan phenomena and particularly unequal spatial opportunity structures; we also consider the spatial components of causes of unequal opportunity less directly related to metropolitan phenomena. The next section reports calculations prepared at the committee's request on the costs to the nation, and to the suburbs, of the problems of central cities and their residents. Finally, the chapter examines disparities in the fiscal capacities of jurisdictions in the same manner, as special problems created by unequal spatial opportunity structures.

Chapter 4 reviews various strategies that have been tried or proposed to alter the spatial distribution of population, reduce outcome disparities between residents of central cities and suburbs and between non-Hispanic whites and minority groups, reduce tax/service disparities among local jurisdictions within metropolitan areas, and improve metropolitan governance.

Chapter 5 sets forth the committee's recommendations for research and discusses policy choices, based on our review of the literature.

2

Central Cities, Suburbs, and Metropolitan-Area Problems

In this chapter, we outline the spatial distribution of the population of metropolitan areas in broad terms, comparing central cities with suburbs and examining race and income characteristics of metropolitan-area residents. We then discuss the role of local governments in creating and perpetuating this pattern of spatial distribution. Next we consider the role of central cities and whether they retain a competitive advantage for economic growth in metropolitan areas. We then discuss whether the problems of central cities and their residents affect the suburbs and their residents and employers. Finally, we examine strategies for building political support for central cities.

SPATIAL DISTRIBUTION OF POPULATION IN METROPOLITAN AREAS

Metropolitan areas consist of central cities (municipalities of 50,000 or more residents) and surrounding areas (counties) that are economically and socially integrated with these central cities, as determined primarily by commuting flows.[1] Metropolitan areas are thus functional labor markets. In 1990, 78 percent of Americans lived in metropolitan areas, compared with only 26 percent in 1900 and 63 percent in 1960.

Of the increase of nearly 80 million in metropolitan-area population between 1960 and 1990, approximately 42 million was a result of population increase within constant boundaries,[2] and 38 million was a result of the addition of new metropolitan areas (from 212 to 318)[3] and changes in the composition of existing ones (as metropolitan areas added counties on their fringe that previously were not included as part of the area) (U.S. Bureau of the Census, 1995:961-962). Between 1960 and 1990, the total land area in metropolitan areas more than doubled, from 308,000 to 673,000 square miles. In 1990, metropolitan areas comprised more than 16 percent of the total land area in the United States (U.S. Bureau of the Census, 1995:962).

In comparison to similar areas in most other countries, U.S. metropolitan areas are characterized by large numbers of local governments (Weiher, 1991:176). In 1997, the average metropolitan area consisted of 114 local governments: 2 counties, 42 municipalities or towns, and 70 special districts, of which 21 were school districts. There were 18 local governments for every 100,000 people in metropolitan areas.

The variation in the number of governments per metropolitan area is substantial, even after standardizing for population size. Of the 15 largest metropolitan areas, St. Louis and Houston had the largest number of governments per 100,000 people, and New York and Los Angeles had the fewest (see Table 2-1). Chicago had the largest total number of local governments, followed by Boston and Philadelphia; Anaheim, San Diego, and New York had the fewest. The number of

TABLE 2-1   Governments in 15 Largest Primary Metropolitan Statistical Areas, 1997

Metropolitan Area	Total Governments	Governments/ 100,000 Population	General-Purpose Governments/ 100,000 Population
Anaheim	147	6.1	1.3
Atlanta	261	8.8	4.3
Boston[a]	1,000	17.9	7.0
Chicago	1,458	19.7	6.3
Dallas	326	12.2	5.8
Detroit	378	8.9	5.1
Houston	790	23.8	2.6
Los Angeles-Long Beach	354	4.0	1.0
Minneapolis-St. Paul	549	21.6	13.5
New York	213	2.5	1.0
Philadelphia	877	17.8	7.4
Riverside-San Bernadino	309	11.9	1.9
San Diego	181	7.2	0.8
St. Louis	789	31.7	12.5
Washington, D.C.	169	4.0	2.7
Average		11.9	4.4

[a]Boston figures refer not to the Primary Metropolitan Statistical Area but to Boston's New England Consolidated Metropolitan Area.

Source: Census of Governments preliminary estimates, 1997.

local governments per 100,000 residents in metropolitan areas was greater in the Midwest (27) and the Northeast (20) than in the West (15) and the South (13) (U.S. Bureau of the Census, preliminary 1997 estimates.)

There has been a modest amount of research on what accounts for the variation among metropolitan areas in the number of local governments. Not surprisingly, the absolute level of local governments among metropolitan areas is associated with size as well as with age of the area and income level (Hawkins and Dye, 1971). There has also been some research on the geopolitical fragmentation of metropolitan areas (measured by the number of local governments per 10,000 people divided by the percentage of total metropolitan-area population residing in the central city) and the extent to which metropolitan-area government structure is dominated by the central city (with low levels of geopolitical fragmentation indicating central-city dominance). Geopolitical fragmentation was found to vary regionally, with the most fragmented areas concentrated in the Northeast and the North Central regions and the least fragmented (most city-dominated) in the South and the West, where county government dominated (Zeigler and Brunn, 1980).

Central Cities Versus Suburbs

Within metropolitan areas in 1990, approximately 40 percent of residents lived in central cities, and 60 percent lived in suburbs. However, this proportion varied enormously among metropolitan areas: for example; among the 15 largest metropolitan areas in the United States, only 16 percent of Atlanta metropolitan-area residents and 21 percent of Washington, D.C., metropolitan-area residents lived in the central cities, compared with 51 percent in Houston.

The process of suburbanization has characterized metropolitan areas for many decades. In 1950 in metropolitan areas, 59 percent of the population lived in central cities and 41 percent in the suburbs. By 1990, however, this was reversed: almost 60 percent lived in suburbs and only 40 percent in the central city (Table 2-2). In every census since 1930, the suburban-area population has grown at a more rapid rate than the central-city population (Heilbrun, 1987:29). However, the regional variations are substantial. From 1980 to 1990, the central-city population grew by only 3 percent in the East and the Midwest, but it increased by 17 percent in the South and 24 percent in the West. Despite frequent references in the popular press to "back to the city" movements, the movement of people into the city from the suburbs in the mid-1990s continued to be overwhelmed by people moving from the city to the suburbs (Kasarda et al., 1997). This is, of course, not inconsistent with the revival of specific selected neighborhoods in cities.

Despite the slow growth or decline of many of the cities in the Northeast and the Midwest, central cities nationwide have retained their *share* of the U.S. population over a long period of time. Cities accounted for 32.5 percent of the U.S.

TABLE 2-2   U.S. Population Living in Metropolitan Areas and in Their Central Cities and Suburbs, 1900-1990 (percentage)

	U.S. Population Living in:			Metropolitan Population Living in:	
Year	Metropolitan Areas	Central Cities	Suburbs	Central Cities	Suburbs
1900	25.5	19.7	5.8	77.3	22.7
1910	28.3	21.7	6.6	76.7	23.3
1920	34.0	25.3	8.7	74.4	25.6
1930	44.6	30.8	13.8	69.1	30.9
1940	47.8	32.5	15.3	68.0	32.0
1950	56.1	32.8	23.3	58.5	41.5
1960	63.3	32.3	30.9	51.0	49.0
1970	69.0	31.4	37.6	45.5	54.5
1980	74.8	30.0	44.8	40.1	59.9
1990	77.5	31.3	46.2	40.4	59.6

Note: Metropolitan areas as defined at each census since 1910. Data for 1900-1940 exclude Alaska and Hawaii.

Source: U.S. Bureau of the Census (1990b).

population in 1940, 32.3 percent in 1960, and 31.3 percent in 1990. Suburbs of metropolitan areas, in contrast, increased their share from 15 to 31 to 46 percent over the same time periods, almost completely at the expense of nonmetropolitan areas (see Table 2-2).

Race and Income

Metropolitan areas are characterized by substantial spatial clustering with respect to both race and income. Minority populations are particularly concentrated in central cities. Although nationally only 25 percent of non-Hispanic whites lived in central cities in 1990, 57 percent of all blacks and 52 percent of all Hispanics lived in these areas (see Table 2-3). As a consequence, central cities are disproportionately the home of minorities, and suburbs are disproportionately the home of whites. In 1990, 21 percent of central-city residents were black compared with 7 percent in the suburbs; 15 percent were Hispanics compared with 8 percent in the suburbs (Frey, 1995:322). However, there were important variations among metropolitan areas. In the Detroit metropolitan area, for example, 66 percent of the central-city population was black compared with 4 percent in the suburbs; in Los Angeles-Long Beach, 14 percent of the city population was black compared with 9 percent in the suburbs.

Racial segregation is extraordinarily high in most U.S. metropolitan areas. The conventionally used measure of segregation is the dissimilarity index, which

TABLE 2-3   Breakdown of Residence by Race and Ethnicity, 1990 (percentage)

Residence	Total Population	Non-Hispanic Whites	Blacks	Hispanics
Metropolitan Areas	77.5	74.7	83.8	90.4
Central Cities	31.3	24.5	57.3	51.5
Suburbs	46.2	50.3	26.4	37.3
Nonmetropolitan Areas	22.5	25.3	16.2	9.6

Source: U.S. Bureau of the Census (1990a).

measures the percentage of one racial group that would have to move in order for each census tract to have the same percentage of that group as exists in the entire metropolitan area. The average black-white dissimilarity index for 318 metropolitan areas in 1990 was 66 (Jargowsky, 1997). Among the 15 most populous metropolitan areas, the dissimilarity index for 1990 ranged from a high of 87 in Detroit to a low of 56 in Seattle. Since school attendance is largely based on residential patterns, school segregation is also quite high. In 1991-1992, 66 percent of all black students and 73 percent of all Hispanic students attended schools that were predominantly minority, and 34 percent of each group attended schools that were 90 to 100 percent minority (Orfield et al., 1993).

There is general agreement that segregation, as measured by the dissimilarity index, has been declining slightly over time. Examining the 30 metropolitan areas with the largest black populations, one study suggests that black-white segregation declined 8 percent, from an average of 81 in 1970 to 73 in 1990 (Massey and Denton, 1993:Table 8.1). Over the 1980s, another study reports that the average dissimilarity index between blacks and non-Hispanic whites fell from 70 in 1980 to 66 in 1990, and that 260 of the 318 metropolitan areas actually experienced decline in the index over the 1980-1990 period (Jargowsky, 1997). Farley and Frey (1993) report that the average index of dissimilarity for 232 metropolitan areas with significant black populations declined from 69 to 65 over the same period.

Modest declines are reported since 1968 in the proportion of blacks and Hispanics attending predominantly minority schools, and massive drops are reported in the percentage of blacks attending schools that are 90 to 100 percent minority (from 64 percent in 1968 to 34 percent in 1991; however, the percentage of Hispanics attending such schools actually increased from 23 to 34 percent over the same period). Virtually all of the improvement occurred in the early years of that period, and there have been slight increases in the segregation of schools since the late 1980s (Orfield et al., 1993).

Similarly to minority populations, low-income people tend disproportionately to live in central cities rather than suburbs. In 1990, 60 percent of the population of metropolitan areas living in households below the poverty level lived in central cities, compared with 40 percent in suburbs. Economic segregation also exists throughout the entire metropolitan area and, unlike racial segregation, is growing. Using a dissimilarity index as a means of measuring the economic segregation of the poor in metropolitan areas (that is, the proportion of the poor who would have to move in order to achieve an even distribution of poor people by census tracts across the metropolitan area), one study found that the mean value for households with income below the poverty level in the 100 largest metropolitan areas rose from 33 in 1970 to 36 in 1990, an increase of 11 percent (Abramson et al., 1995).

The residential racial segregation of blacks is not simply a by-product of economic segregation. As described by Massey and Denton (1993), the average level of segregation for blacks, as measured by the dissimilarity index, in the 30 metropolitan areas with the largest black population varies hardly at all by black income. High-income blacks live in areas nearly as segregated as do low-income blacks. Massey and Denton note that this pattern contrasts sharply with that of both Hispanic and Asian segregation, which "begins at a relatively modest level among the poor and falls steadily as income rises" (1993:87).

In addition, the level of income segregation is markedly lower than the racial segregation dissimilarity indices. The average racial segregation dissimilarity index for the 204 metropolitan areas examined by Cutler and Glaeser (1997) was 59 percent, and the average income segregation dissimilarity index (measured by examining what percentage of the bottom quartile of the income distribution for all households would have to move in order for each census tract to have the same percentage of low-income people as the entire area) was 22 percent. Likewise, for the 100 largest metropolitan areas, Abramson et al. (1995) found that the mean dissimilarity index for the poor was 36 in 1990, considerably lower than the mean dissimilarity index for blacks of 61.

The unequal distribution of poor people across metropolitan space tells only part of the story; equally important is the issue of concentrated poverty. As of 1990, 5 percent of the total population of metropolitan areas lived in high-poverty areas, an increase from 3.3 percent in 1980 and 3.0 percent in 1970. However, 17 percent of metropolitan-area blacks and 11 percent of Hispanics lived in such areas (Jargowsky, 1997).[4] Jargowsky (1997) documents that the number of high-poverty census tracts more than doubled between 1970 and 1990 (an increase of 132 percent), and the number of people living in them rose by 92 percent over that time period. In 1990, 18 percent of all poor people in metropolitan areas lived in high-poverty areas, but, for the black poor, the figure was 34 percent (compared with 26 percent in 1970) and for Hispanics, 22 percent (slightly down from 24 percent in 1970).

CAUSES OF SUBURBANIZATION

Contrary to much of conventional popular wisdom, suburbanization trends are long-standing. Suburbanization in the United States can be traced back to the 1880s, with the major surge beginning in the 1920s; the decades following World War II were not unusual in their suburbanization trends (Fischel, this volume). This suggests that many of the factors cited as explanations for suburbanization, such as the federal mortgage insurance programs of the 1950s, the interstate highway system of the 1960s, and the racial tensions, fear of crime, and poor city schools of recent decades, can at best be only partial explanations. As Mieszkowski and Mills (1993:135) observe, these "are all postwar phenomena, and are mostly provincial U.S. problems. In reality, the trend toward suburbanization has been prewar as well as postwar, and has been international in scope."

There are two different types of explanation for suburbanization (Mieszkowski and Mills, 1993). The first relies on the standard location model of the urban economist and involves improvements in transportation infrastructure (which reduce the costs of commuting), technological changes that allow employment decentralization, and long-term increases in household income that allow households to act on their preferences for greater space. The second class of explanations stresses "push" factors related to the fiscal and social problems of cities, such as high taxes, inadequate public schools and other government services, racial tensions, crime, and poor city amenities (1993:137).

Clearly the two types of explanation are not mutually exclusive. Margo projected 1980 incomes onto 1950 household location patterns and estimated that 43 percent of suburbanization between 1950 and 1980 was due to rising income (cited in Fischel, this volume). After considering other possible causes, Fischel concludes, "it seems reasonable to guess that perhaps a quarter of Americans' move beyond the limits of central cities may be accounted for by factors other than mostly benign 'natural' economic trends." Fischel believes this residual 25 percent may be due to the second class of explanation given by Mieszkowki and Mills.

There is yet another explanation, unrelated to population out-migration, whether driven by pull or push factors. Danielson (1976:15) argues that "the political separation of city and suburbs is not the product of 'natural' forces which caused the city to cease to expand and independent suburban jurisdictions to grow up around the urban core. Until the last part of the 19th century, outmigration simply resulted in expansion of the city boundaries and was not accompanied by creation of politically independent suburbs. After that time opposition to annexation increased on the part of middle-class neighborhoods at the city's edge, and state laws permitting easy incorporation and making annexation more difficult resulted in an end to city expansion." He concludes (1976:17): "The underlying cause of the end of annexation and the political containment of the city was the universal desire of the periphery for political autonomy from the core. This objective was rooted in class and ethnic conflict and the desire of middle-class areas for local control over their relatively homogeneous communities."

ROLE OF LOCAL GOVERNMENTS IN SPATIAL STRATIFICATION

There is ample evidence that the spatial distribution of the U.S. population is not the inevitable result of market forces and technology, but a reflection of the impact of public policy, broadly construed to include choices about the structure of political institutions. Downs (1997:26) vigorously argues: "the disproportionate concentration of poor households within central cities arises from the fundamental institutional structure of U.S. metropolitan areas and of their growth processes. This structure may seem 'natural' or the result of 'free market forces,' but it is neither. In fact, other structures prevail in most of the world."

Likewise, Fischel (this volume) states that where the poor live relative to the rich within metropolitan areas is an empirical question rather than an inevitable result. Similarly, Danielson (1976:1) argues that "public policies have played a central role in the development of a spatially differentiated metropolis in which blacks are separated from whites, the poor from the more affluent, the disadvantaged from economic and educational opportunity."

The distinctively American political institutions that give rise to spatial patterns of residential location are local control of land use decisions, state laws permitting easy incorporation of municipalities, and a fiscal system that requires municipal governments to finance most of their local services from their local tax base (Danielson, 1976). The ease of municipal incorporation permits the creation of many local governments within metropolitan areas. The motive for incorporation is to exercise land use controls at the local level in order to exert control over the local setting. As a consequence, Americans with sufficient resources are able to influence who their neighbors are by using land use controls to raise the price of housing beyond what lower-income households can afford. In addition, the fiscal system facing local governments in the United States provides incentives to keep poor people out, since low-income households will consume more in public services than they will contribute in local taxes. As Downs describes the process (1994:19):

> In most U.S. metropolitan areas, residents outside the original city's boundaries establish separate communities legally independent of it. These people want separate jurisdictions in part because they do not want certain externalities affecting them that are regulated by some broad government that reflects the interests of persons living throughout the metropolitan area. . . . Many suburban residents also want to live in neighborhoods occupied primarily by households with incomes equal to or higher than their own, similar cultural values and outlooks, and similar racial or ethnic backgrounds. . . . They also fear that the proximity of lower-income households will reduce the market values of their

homes. And a large group of low-income households within their jurisdiction might cause their local governments to raise taxes to provide the services needed by such households.

Local government action permits and facilitates this spatial segmentation, and local control of land use is the critical linchpin that encourages fragmentation and thus results in economic stratification (Danielson, 1976). Although research is sparse, comparative social policy experts frequently observe that the degree of economic segregation in urban areas is much higher in the United States than in many other western nations in which land use controls are not exclusively local (Berry, 1973; Sellars, 1998).

Fischel (this volume) argues that, although income segregation by neighborhood is probably inevitable, it is greatly accentuated by modern zoning. He observes:

> Although I regard neighborhood income segregation as likely to occur under almost any mechanism that operates without a strong dose of coercion, it must be emphasized that income segregation is greatly accentuated by modern zoning. It is one thing to observe that the rich and poor live in different neighborhoods separated by a thoroughfare, a cemetery, or a railroad track. It is something of a greater order of magnitude to observe that they live in entirely different municipalities separated by miles of low-density development or natural preserves. The latter separation surely discourages economic and social interactions that would otherwise be mutually beneficial and that are the cornerstone of a prosperous, democratic society.

But zoning also plays a role in contributing to allocative efficiency in metropolitan areas. Tiebout (1956) and others (Ostrom et al., 1961; Bradford and Oates, 1974; Hamilton, 1975; Hamilton et al., 1975) contend that systems of local government in which large numbers of jurisdictions compete for residents by offering differing packages of public services result in efficient resource use. Each jurisdiction thus attracts a set of residents who have similar preferences for services. As Mills and Oates (1975:5) observe, however, "Once we recognize that the demand for public services is systematically related to income, we see that the Tiebout model implies powerful tendencies toward segregation by income level." Zoning serves as a mechanism for supporting this system. It does so by preventing lower-income residents from moving into higher-income areas with high tax bases, thus enjoying a level of services at a lower tax price than they could otherwise afford and achieving a fiscal subsidy from their wealthier neighbors (Bradford and Oates, 1974; Hamilton, 1975).

There is a variety of means by which local governments are able to use land use regulation to control access to their community and to exclude lower-income and, consequently, many minority households. Exclusionary zoning techniques include requiring a minimum lot size or a minimum number of square feet for any home built on the lot, thus increasing the cost of new housing, and prohibiting multifamily units or apartments with more than two bedrooms. In addition, unreasonably high building code standards and strict subdivision requirements may also raise the cost of housing beyond the means of lower-income families. The recent explosion of residential community associations may also be serving exclusionary purposes.

Weiher (1991:194) contends that exclusionary techniques are one part of a two-part process that results in sorting by income and race. The other part involves the role of political boundaries in providing a proxy for a set of information about the jurisdiction that provides cues to persons making location decisions. He argues that "political boundaries support the recruitment that is the complement to exclusion in urban sorting." He observes (1991:177): "If it is true that the presence of cues generates a peculiar decision-making calculus, there should be differences in the settlement patterns that characterize the United States and those that are found in other countries. Specifically, there should be a higher degree of segregation by salient characteristics in the United States. No definitive work has been done on this subject, but there is anecdotal evidence to support this hypothesis. . . . Berry (1973) comments on the relative lack of segregation by race and class in Britain and Western Europe."

There is evidence that the ease of municipal incorporation promotes the creation of large numbers of local governments, a precondition for income stratification by jurisdiction (Nelson, 1990; Burns, 1994). The existence of more local governments permits households to sort themselves out by income, and research has shown that the number of local governments is associated with more income stratification. Studies by Hamilton et al. (1975) and Eberts and Gronberg (1981) demonstrate that census tracts in metropolitan areas that have numerous governments—and numerous independent zoning authorities—are more homogeneous with respect to income than tracts within metropolitan areas that have fewer governments, although research by Stein (1987) finds that fragmentation leads to residential sorting by race and perhaps education, but not income. (For a review of the empirical research on sorting, see Dowding et al., 1994.)

Burns (1994) contends that since 1950 the desire to segregate by race has been more important than the desire to segregate by income as a factor in explaining the creation of new municipal governments. Employing multivariate analysis to explain variation in the incorporation of new municipalities in a sample of 200 counties, she found that the number of nonwhite people in the county had a significant and more substantial impact on incorporation than did the number of poor people. Weiher (1991) makes a similar argument and found, using analysis of variance, that segregation by race, education, and income over the period 1960-1980 came to be organized more by city than by neighborhoods within cities. He argues (1991:94) that a series of policy changes, primarily through court rulings, have made segregation by race within jurisdictions subject to legal action, but has rendered segregation at jurisdictional boundaries legally secure.

With respect to the actual impact of zoning, Fischel (this volume) concludes that "This is an instance in which the conventional wisdom—that exclusionary zoning is a real issue—is confirmed by the evidence." He cites evidence that high-income communities almost always have more stringent zoning regulations than other communities and observes that "if market forces alone were sufficient to create exclusive communities, one would expect to see zoning standards such as minimum lot sizes to be more uniform among communities."

THE VALUE OF CENTRAL CITIES

Central-city residence has adverse effects in many metropolitan areas in two obvious ways. First, fiscal disparities frequently impose higher tax burdens on residents and provide them with lower-quality services than would be the case if they lived in a suburb with the average area tax capacity. The result is a reduction in the income and well-being of city residents, a penalty for city living. Second, the movement of jobs from the central city to the periphery and the reduction of low-skilled jobs in the city make it more difficult for city residents to gain access to jobs and lead to the problem of spatial mismatch.

A healthy central city affects the well-being of its residents. And, as discussed below, it also affects the well-being of suburban residents and the nation. Central cities have provided the agglomeration economies that have powered metropolitan growth. They have also functioned as the port of entry, socialization, and assimilation for immigrants, providing them with low-cost housing and opportunities for economic advancement. Daniel (1994:i) notes that, of the 8.5 million immigrants who arrived in the United States during the 1980s, 75 percent lived in just 16 large cities in 1990 (nearly 25 percent in Los Angeles alone and an additional 17 percent in New York).

Can central cities continue to perform these traditional functions? Is the central city still viable?

Do Central Cities Still Have a Competitive Advantage?

The traditional rationale for the economic contribution of cities is that agglomeration economies provide a competitive advantage for firms locating in cities; they are seen to be the driving force in the development of the metropolitan economy. Agglomeration economies are cost savings to firms that result from their locating in urban areas. Such economies are of two types. Localization economies are savings that result from a firm locating near other firms in the same or related industries. Urbanization economies are economies that result when the production costs of a firm decline as the aggregate level of economic activity expands within the area. Mills and Lubuele (1997:729) cite Henderson's estimate that metropolitan-area output per unit of input increases 4 to 6 percent for each doubling of its population.

These agglomeration economies traditionally occurred in the central city, primarily in the central business district area. According to Ihlanfeldt (1995), agglomeration economies have three causes: labor market economies, scale economies in the production of intermediate inputs, and communication economies. He observes that the last two of these clearly favor central cities.

There is general agreement that agglomeration economies still exist and provide important advantages to metropolitan economies. But there is the question of whether they can now be achieved at lower densities in the suburbs.

Some researchers argue that suburbanization of office development and the growth of "edge cities" (Garreau, 1991) provide the same opportunity for agglomeration economies that exists in central cities, and thus cities have lost their competitive advantage (Hicks, 1987; Hartshorn and Muller, 1987). Others contend that telecommunications advances will soon make it possible to transact business without the need for face-to-face contact, again eroding the advantage of cities. Danielson and Wolpert (1994:72) argue that a new metropolitan form is emerging in the suburbs that, by implication, reduces the significance of the central city:

> This new metropolis is a new urban form, the latest stage in an evolving process. . . . [T]he spreading suburbs of the new metropolis are diversified, economically robust, and ever less dependent on the city and its central business district. The vibrant world of the new metropolis encompasses corporate headquarters, new industries such as aerospace and electronics, research laboratories and health complexes, massive malls and lesser retail clusters, hotel and convention centers, arenas and stadiums, government offices and university campuses. These developments produce a sprawling landscape of low-density settlement punctuated by nodes of intense activity usually located at major intersections of radial expressways. . . . As the new metropolis evolves, the original central business district becomes one among many centers, with its own specialized activities and market niche.

Muller (1997:44) observes that "globalization forces intensify and accelerate the suburban transformation of the American city. A new urban future is being shaped as fully developed suburbs become the engine driving metropolitan and world city growth."

There are, however, counterarguments. First, as Clapp (1983) argues, even though telecommunication technology may *permit* interaction, people still may enjoy face-to-face interaction more and gain more from it. Indeed, Mills (1992) makes a distinction between ambiguous and unambiguous information, with the former inevitably requiring face-to-face exchange regardless of the state of telecommunications technology.

Ihlanfeldt (1995) has examined evidence on the extent to which central cities retain the advantages of an agglomeration economy, observing that empirical research on this question has been sparse. He nonetheless cites studies indicating that face-to-face contacts continue to be an important determinant of the location of office activity. He also has reviewed evidence on the type of firms that locate in central cities and suburbs and concludes that "information-processing jobs are attracted to central cities, suggesting, at a minimum, that these economies exist within central cities. If not, why would firms be willing to incur the otherwise high production costs associated with a central-city location? Nevertheless, the growth of information-processing employment in the suburbs indicates that central cities may be losing their locational advantage over time" (1995:135).

Indeed, a multivariate analysis of municipalities' share of employment growth for each decade from 1960 to 1990 in the New Jersey suburbs of New York City found that physical proximity to New York was of declining importance in determining employment share (Danielson and Wolpert, 1994). They observed (1994:89) that the initial comparative advantage of the densely settled cities "based upon proximity to New York City, good commuter access, and existing agglomeration of population and employment offered less attraction to firms and residents with a clear preference for lower density sites and highway and road access." These findings are consistent with the retention of agglomeration economies for activities involving face-to-face contact and information processing in central-city locations. A review of the literature by Mills and Lubuele (1997:727) states that "all recent studies conclude that inner cities [central cities] remain important and integral parts of their MSAs."

Interdependence of Central Cities and Suburbs

Many suburban residents appear to believe that their suburbs are functionally independent of the central city and that central-city problems do not affect them at all. This view is shared by some knowledgeable researchers as well. Hartshorn and Muller (1989:1) write: "With surprising speed in the '70s and '80s, suburbs have evolved from loosely-organized 'bedroom community' into a full-fledged 'outer city,' characterized by metropolitan-level employment and activity concentrations and functional shifts that amount to nothing less than the achievement of suburban economic, social, and geographic independence from the nearby central city that spawned these satellite settlements several decades ago."

Others go so far as to argue that it is the central city that is now dependent on the suburb (Bingham and Kalich, 1996). Their evidence for this dependence is the need of the central city to supply qualified workers for its high-skilled jobs. Furthermore, at least in cities that have an income tax, the city is dependent on this suburban workforce for a substantial portion of its revenues.

It can also be argued, however, that suburban residents are dependent on the city for their jobs in the city's central business districts. Indeed, most recent scholarship contends that cities and suburbs are interdependent (Ledebur and Barnes, 1992, 1993; Savitch et al., 1993; Voith, 1992, 1993, 1995; Hill et al., 1995a).

Suburbs and the entire metropolitan area are affected by central cities in a number of ways. Ihlanfeldt (1995:125-26) suggests five sources of interdependence: "First, the fortunes of suburbs may be tied to those of the central cities to the extent that outsiders' perceptions of the region are influenced by conditions prevailing within the core. Second, because of their location or history, central cities may contain amenities that are valued throughout the region. Third, individual cities may provide a 'sense of place' that is valued not only by their residents but also by outsiders. Fourth, the fiscal problems endemic to a declining city may raise tax burdens in suburban areas and thereby retard economic development. Finally, central cities may offer unique agglomeration economies that define an important and specialized role for the central city in the regional economy."

Another argument is that the fiscal problems of cities, caused by low tax capacity and high service needs, result in suboptimal levels of spending on the city's infrastructure, resulting in "deterioration in the public sector's contribution to the production function of private firms throughout the metropolitan area. Suburban firms will be adversely affected in two ways. First, because the central city serves as the hub of many critical infrastructure systems, deterioration in those systems will reduce operating efficiencies. Second, because suburban firms purchase goods and services from firms located in the central city, reductions in the operating efficiency of supplier firms will be reflected in gradual increases in the operating costs of suburban firms" (Hill et al., 1995a:164).

Hill et al. also argue (1995a:165) that central-city fiscal problems can impose costs on the entire region if inadequate spending on education leads to deterioration in the relative quality of public education and lowers the productivity of the workforce, since central-city residents are an important component of the metropolitan labor force.

One study bases its claim for interdependence on positive correlations between central city and suburban per capita income and between central-city office space and downtown office space (Savitch et al., 1993). Another study found positive correlations between both city and suburban income growth and city and suburban population growth during the 1970s and 1980s, but not during the 1960s (Voith, 1992). Voith concludes that cities and suburbs, at least since the 1970s, are complements rather than substitutes for each other—that is, that there is interdependence. Ledebur and Barnes (1992) found that change in median central-city household income between 1979 and 1989 accounted for 82 percent of the variation in change in median suburban household income over the same time period. They also report that metropolitan areas with lower disparities in per capita income between central cities and suburbs had higher employment growth between 1988 and 1991. This finding has been frequently cited with the implication that a causal relationship exists.

Hill and colleagues (1995a), while agreeing that cities and suburbs are interdependent, criticize these findings on a variety of grounds. First, they argue that central cities and suburbs are simply parts of the same whole—the metropolitan economy—and that "to properly use correlational analysis, one must assume that the two phenomena being observed are at least separable, if not independent entities" (1995a:149). Second, they observe the correlations are bivariate and do not control for a range of other factors that might be operating on the entire metropolitan area, causing change in both central-city and suburban income. Finally, they criticize the implication of causality and particularly the interpretation that lower disparities in per capita income between central cities and suburbs lead to higher rates of metropolitan employment growth. They argue instead that economic theory suggests that the causal relationship is likely to work the other way: that metropolitan economic growth, through tightening labor markets and therefore pulling unemployed central-city workers into employment, will lead to lower disparities in per capita income between central cities and suburbs.

A study by Voith (1995) has addressed many of these criticisms through a structural equation model that relates city income growth to suburban income growth, population growth, and house price appreciation. He uses a variety of econometric techniques to deal with the problem that the correlations found in the previous literature could be spurious (the result of factors affecting both city and suburban variables) or simultaneously determined. Voith (1995) found that growth in city income results in higher growth in suburban income, house price appreciation, and population growth and that these effects on suburbs are greater for larger cities than for smaller ones.

Although Ihlanfeldt (1995) questions whether Voith's methodology has adequately solved the problems of controls and causality, he nonetheless observes that, "Despite these shortcomings, Voith's results are the strongest evidence to date in favor of the interdependence hypothesis" (1995:138). Voith closes his paper by contending that (1995:21): "The statistical evidence of complementarity is important because the long-run, gradual nature of the negative effects of urban decline makes it difficult for people to observe casually, let alone mobilize support for policies to prevent urban decline. In particular, the negative impact may be unrecognized by suburban residents because the suburb is performing so much better than its declining central city counterpart. Thus, suburban residents may perceive themselves as relatively better off when compared with their city neighbors, even though their incomes, populations, and house values are adversely affected by the city decline."

Building Viable Political Support for Cities

Addressing the problems of metropolitan areas requires strong political support on behalf of central cities. There are two main strategies for building support for cities. One emphasizes the potential for metropolitan action through the development of broad coalitions that emphasize consensus building at the regional level across cities and suburbs. The other emphasizes the construction of majority coalitions of groups acting through the political process to further their own interests. Central-city interests would be at the core of such coalitions, but to be successful they would have to be extended to encompass the interests of poor and working-class suburbs and some "out-state" areas. Which of these approaches holds the greater prospects for success has been the subject of controversy among advocates for cities.

Consensus Building

Advocates of the consensus-building approach point to the emergence in many metropolitan areas of regional alliances across city and suburban and public-, private-, and nonprofit-sector lines, which incorporate a wide diversity of interests on behalf of regional initiatives; they argue that visible successes are growing (Peirce, 1993; Dodge, 1996). Critics contend that these successes, while desirable, are limited. Successes tend to occur on issues related to regional infrastructure, economic growth, and the environment, for which the primary concern is efficiency and promotion of the common good. Issues that are seen to be redistributive and controversial—that is, that affect the spatial opportunity structure and the disparities in outcomes between city and suburban residents and between whites and minority groups—are seldom dealt with effectively through metropolitan consensus-building efforts.

The proponents of regional consensus building argue that the trust and relationships built by successes on less controversial issues will ultimately translate into the ability to take on more difficult problems.

Political Coalition Building

Others argue that ultimately successful action on behalf of cities will depend not on consensus created at the metropolitan level, but on the construction of majority coalitions in which the winners outvote the losers, particularly at the state legislature level.

For example, Myron Orfield, who is both a researcher and a practitioner, argues for a coalition based on self-interest among state legislators representing central cities, inner suburbs, and outer middle-income residential suburbs with a small commercial or industrial tax base (Orfield, 1997). This grouping could provide the core of a majority coalition on behalf of tax base sharing, regional housing opportunity, increased state aid, and other policy measures beneficial to central cities. Such a coalition, aided at times by cooperation with legislators who may have nothing directly at stake, constitutes a majority of state legislators in Minnesota and, Orfield contends, in other states with large metropolitan areas as well. He writes (1997:12-13):

> Though the notion of building a total win-win regional consensus is appealing in theory, in practice sustained regional reform clearly demands the formation of enduring coalitions that can weather intense opposition and controversy. . . .

[I]t has become clear that Twin Cities suburban communities are not a monolith with common experiences and political needs. The emergence of these patterns has created a metro-majority political coalition between the central cities, which make up one-third of the region's population, and the inner suburbs and middle-class developing suburbs, which make up another third. . . . On the merits, these middle-income, blue-collar suburbs are the largest prospective winners in regional reform. To them, tax base sharing means lower property taxes and better services, particularly better funded schools. Regional housing policy means, over time, fewer units of affordable housing crowding their doorstep.

The appeal of Orfield's argument is that majority political coalitions based on self-interest and built around class-based concerns that will yield favorable returns to cities are politically possible, at least in terms of the numbers involved. The problem is whether the "objective" self-interests that Orfield identifies will be recognized and acknowledged and, even if they are, whether they will be powerful enough to overcome the class- and race-based concerns that exist among the city's potential coalition partners. Even in Minnesota, where enlightened attitudes and the relatively low proportion of minorities in the Twin Cities metropolitan area suggest a highly propitious environment for a self-interest, class-based coalition, the relatively modest success thus far gives pause.

Other types of coalitions beneficial to cities are also possible. In Oregon, the state legislature passed Portland's Urban Growth Boundary with the support of a coalition that included farmers, environmentalists, and urban interests (Abbott, 1997:28-29). The housing element of Oregon's state land use program has been consistently supported at the state level by environmental groups, city interests, and, after initial opposition, business and developer groups (Knapp, 1989).

Efforts to affect the spatial distribution of population in metropolitan areas through breaking down exclusionary zoning or fostering inclusionary zoning are more likely to succeed when contested at the state level than at the metropolitan level (Knapp, 1990). This is because the strength of interests differs significantly at the state and local levels. Residential and homeowner groups are particularly strong at the local level, but less so at the state level. As Knapp observes (1990:44), "Environmentalists and developers, who are outnumbered at the local level, are more effective at the state level, where organized interest groups are more effective and it is difficult to mobilize exclusionary interests." He also admits that "It is difficult . . . to predict whether an environmentalist-developer coalition can be formed in other states."

NOTES

[1] Metropolitan statistical areas (MSAs) are defined as follows: "Each MSA must include at least: (a) one city with 50,000 or more inhabitants, or (b) a Census Bureau-defined urbanized area (of at least 50,000 inhabitants) and a total population of at least 100,000 (75,000 in New England). Under the standards the county (or counties) that contains the largest city becomes the central county

(counties), along with any adjacent counties that have at least 50 percent of their population in the urbanized area surrounding the largest city. Additional 'outlying counties' are included in the MSA if they meet specified requirements of commuting to the central counties and other selected requirements of metropolitan character (such as population density and percent urban) (U.S. Bureau of the Cencus, 1996a:937). An urbanized area is "an area consisting of a central place(s) and adjacent urban fringe that together have a minimum residential population of at least 50,000 people and generally an overall population density of at least 1,000 people per square mile of land area" (U.S. Bureau of the Census, 1994:G-54). Unlike metropolitan areas, which must contain entire counties, urbanized areas are defined with reference to density.

[2] Holding 1960 metropolitan-area boundaries constant, the proportion of the U.S. population living in these areas actually fell slightly, from 63 percent in 1960 to 62 percent in 1990.

[3] Metropolitan areas are divided into primary metropolitan statistical areas (PMSAs) and consolidated metropolitan statistical areas (CMSAs). CMSAs consist of two or more contiguous and closely related PMSAs. As of June 1995, there were 271 metropolitan areas, consisting of 253 PMSAs and 18 CMSAs. The 18 CMSAs contained within them a total of 73 PMSAs. The total number of PMSAs was therefore 326.

[4] Increases in the proportion of the population living in high-poverty areas may result from an increasing number of census tracts being classified as high-poverty areas as nonpoor households move out, from an increasing incidence of poverty, or from an increasing propensity of the poor to move into such areas.

3

Disparities in Outcomes

This chapter examines the state of existing knowledge on the disparities in outcomes experienced by individuals and jurisdictions in metropolitan areas. For individuals and groups, these disparities may be grouped into three categories: income disparities (median family income levels, per capita income levels, and poverty rates); labor market disparities (employment and unemployment rates for working-age men); and educational disparities (high school and college completion rates). These simple measures do not, of course, fully capture the differences among groups in metropolitan areas. Moreover, they reflect outcomes that result from many factors, not simply from inequalities in the metropolitan opportunity structure.

We then go on to consider the extent to which these disparities are caused by differences in the metropolitan opportunity structure; we also consider the spatial components of causes less directly related to metropolitan phenomena. To give an indication of the costs to individuals and groups of these disparities, the committee reports the work of researcher Harry Holzer who calculated at our request the costs of unequal opportunity borne by those most directly affected, as well as by the entire metropolitan area.

Finally, we shift to consider disparities in fiscal capacities among local governments, in terms of taxes and services.

DISPARITIES AMONG INDIVIDUALS

Central-City and Suburban Residents

Analyses of intrametropolitan differences in economic and social conditions are nearly always presented in terms of central-city and suburban differences, even though there is clearly substantial variation across individual suburbs (Danielson and Wolpert, 1992). In many metropolitan areas there are inner-ring suburbs and industrial suburbs whose residents share the same environment and consequent problems as residents of the central city. However, because of the way data are presented, virtually all of the research examines only central-city and suburban differences; for that reason, most of the data and the discussion presented in this chapter focus on the central-city/suburban distinction.

In 1990, central-city residents had incomes that were considerably lower than those of suburban residents (Table 3-1). The median household income of urban residents was only 74 percent of that of their suburban counterparts, their per capita income was 84 percent of suburban per capita income, and their poverty rate was over twice as high. Disparities in employment and education were somewhat smaller, but central-city residents appear to be more deprived in these realms as well. In particular, compared with suburban communities, the unemployment rate of men of prime working age was 1.7 times higher in central cities, and the rate of young men (ages 25-34) who completed high school in central cities was only 94 percent that of the suburbs.

Perhaps more significant than the magnitude of these disparities are their trends over time. Table 3-2 shows, for selected measures, the ratios of suburban to central-city outcomes for the decades from 1960 through 1990. With the

TABLE 3-1   Comparison of Selected Outcomes for Central-City and Suburban Residents, 1990

Outcome	Central City	Non-Central City	Ratio of Central-City to Suburban Outcome
Median household income	$26,727	$36,314	.74
Per capita income	$13,839	$16,527	.84
Poverty rate, families	14.1%	6.0%	2.35
Employed men ages 25-54[a]	83.3%	90.0%	.93
Unemployment rate, men ages 25-54	6.8%	4.0%	1.7
High school graduates, men ages 25-34	80.7%	85.8%	.94

[a]Members of the armed forces are counted as employed.

Source: U.S. Bureau of the Census (1990a).

TABLE 3-2   Ratios of Selected Outcomes for Central-City and Suburban
Residents, 1960-1990

| Outcome | Ratio of Central-City to Suburban Outcome | | | |
	1960	1970	1980	1990
Median family income	.89	.85	.81	.77
Per capita income	NA	.92	.88	.84
Family poverty rate	1.52	1.75	2.08	2.35
Percent employed, men age 16 and older[a]	0.96	0.93	0.92	.91
Unemployment rate, men age 16 and older[a]	1.37	1.33	1.34	1.59
Percent high school graduates, age 25 and older	0.85	0.86	0.9	.94
Percent college graduates, age 25 and older	0.82	0.84	0.94	.96

[a]For 1960, the employment and unemployment rates correspond to men at least 14 years of age.

Source: U.S. Bureau of the Census (1960, 1970, 1980, 1990a).

exception of education, every measure in the table suggests that the relative status
of central-city residents has consistently declined over the last three decades.
Relative to their suburban counterparts, central-city residents now have lower
incomes, higher poverty rates, and lower employment rates than they did 10, 20,
and 30 years ago.[1]

The income differences are particularly stark. In 1960, the income of central-city families was 89 percent of that of suburban families. By 1990, this ratio
had fallen to 77 percent. Per capita income follows a similar pattern, with ratios
falling from .92 in 1970 to .84 in 1990. Poverty is becoming increasingly concentrated in central-city areas. In 1960, poverty was 1.5 times as frequent for
families living in central cities; by 1990, the ratio had risen to 2.4. Finally, in
1960 the unemployment rate in central cities was 1.5 percentage points higher
than the unemployment rate in the suburbs; by 1990 it was 3 percentage points
higher.

These central-city/suburban disparities have grown much more rapidly for
blacks than they have for the population as a whole (Ihlanfeldt, this volume). The
deepening of central-city disparities over time reflects both the selective migration of better-off people to the suburbs and the declining fortunes of lower-skilled
and low-income groups remaining in the city. Their declines in fortune result
from changes in the national economy, referred to earlier, that reduce the relative
earning power of low-skilled workers.

As noted, education is a marked exception to the general trend of continued
central-city decline. Because it is easier to increase the proportion of high school

and college graduates in a population that has fewer of them to start with, the relative fortunes of central-city residents improved as a result of overall societal progress. Between 1960 and 1990, for example, although the high school graduation rate rose by 66 percent in non-central-city areas, it rose by 79 percent in central cities.

These comparisons lump together all suburbs as a single entity, but suburbia is hardly monolithic (Orfield, 1997). Data on neighborhoods within suburban areas provide some sense of their diversity. Although, as noted above, the median household income in suburban America is significantly larger than that in central cities ($36,314 compared with $26,727), in approximately one-fifth of suburban neighborhoods, the median household income is actually less than the central-city median. (And without the commercial tax base of a central business district, these suburbs may be even worse off than their central cities.)

The story is similar with the poverty rate. Nationwide, the poverty rate is 8 percent in the suburbs and 18 percent in central cities. But approximately 10 percent of suburban census tracts had poverty rates of at least 18 percent.

How do these city-suburban disparities vary by region or by size of the metropolitan area? Table 3-3 indicates that the disparities appear to be greater in the Northeast and the Midwest and lower in the South and the West. On average, the per capita income of central-city residents in the South and the West nearly matched that of their suburban counterparts. In the average metropolitan area in the Midwest and the Northeast, by contrast, the per capita income of central-city residents was just 76 and 65 percent, respectively, of that of suburban residents.

A similar geographic pattern applies to the relative poverty rates. In the average metropolitan area in the Midwest, the central-city poverty rate was more than 4 times that of the suburban poverty rate. In the West, central-city poverty was only 1.8 times that of suburban poverty.

In larger metropolitan areas, central-city residents fare worse relative to their suburban counterparts than they do in smaller ones. Table 3-4 shows that in metropolitan areas with over 1 million residents, per capita income in central cities is an average of 80 percent of per capita income in suburban locations. In contrast, in metropolitan areas with under 250,000 residents, the per capita income in central-city and suburban areas is almost identical. Similarly, in metro-

TABLE 3-3   Mean Central-City/Suburban Disparities in 1990 by Region

Region	Per Capita Income	Poverty Rate
Northeast	.65	3.75
South	.96	2.31
Midwest	.76	4.24
West	.94	1.77

Source: Tabulations from U.S. Bureau of Census (1996a).

TABLE 3-4   Mean Central-City/Suburban Disparities in 1990 by Population Size of Metropolitan Statistical Area

| MSA-Size Class | Mean Ratio of Central City to Suburban Outcome in Set of Metropolitan Statistical Areas | | |
	Per Capita Income	Poverty Rate	Employment Rate, Men 16-64
1,000,000 +	.8	3.3	.9
250,000-999,999	.91	2.6	.92
100,000-249,999	.97	2.2	.94
0-99,999	.97	2.2	.94

Source: Tabulations from U.S. Bureau of Census (1996a).

politan areas with over 1 million residents, the central-city poverty rate is more than 3 times larger on average than the suburban rate. In metropolitan areas with under 250,000 residents, the ratio is just over 2. In contrast to income and poverty measures, the difference in employment rates between central-city and non-central-city residents varies only modestly with population size.

Ellen (this volume) has constructed an index of disparity and ranked all metropolitan areas by their degree of city-suburban disparity.[2] Significantly, she found that not all central cities are worse off than their surrounding suburbs. In 1990, central cities were actually as prosperous or more so than their surrounding suburban communities in 101 (31 percent) of metropolitan areas (see also Hill and Wolman, 1997a).

Table 3-5 presents the mean characteristics of selected variables for each of four quartiles of disadvantage. Once again, the regional pattern is pronounced.

TABLE 3-5   Regional Distribution of Central Cities, Ranked by Degree of Central-City Disadvantage (percentage)

| Region | Quartiles of Central-City Disadvantage | | | |
	Q1: Greatest Disadvantage	2nd Quartile	3rd Quartile	Q4: Least Disadvantage
Northeast	43.9	25.6	8.5	3.6
Midwest	31.7	36.6	22.0	10.8
South	20.7	22.0	45.1	60.2
West	3.7	15.9	24.4	25.3
Total	100	100	100	100
Mean Population	934,560	537,981	542,056	277,366

In the quartile with the most disadvantaged central cities, 44 percent are located in the Northeast, 32 percent in the Midwest, 21 percent in the South, and 4 percent in the West. In the quartile with the least disadvantaged central cities, by contrast, just 4 percent are in the Northeast, 11 percent are in the Midwest, 60 percent are in the South, and 25 percent are in the West. With respect to size, the metropolitan areas with greater disparities tend to have larger populations.

Variations across metropolitan areas in income disparities between cities and suburbs are substantial. Table 3-6 displays the ratios between central-city and suburban outcomes for the 15 largest metropolitan areas. The ratio of central-city to suburban per capita income ranges from a low of .56 in Detroit to a high of 1.0 in San Diego and Los Angeles.

The ratios of employment rates range from a low of .74 in Detroit to a high of .98 in San Diego, and high school completion ratios vary from .68 in Anaheim to a high of 1.03 in San Diego. Consistent with the results above, these disparities tend to be larger in the metropolitan areas located in the Northeast and the Midwest and smaller in those in the South and the West. Anaheim is the one

TABLE 3-6   Disparities Between Central-City and Suburban Residents in the 15 Largest Metropolitan Areas, 1990

		Ratio of Central-City to Suburban Outcome		
Metropolitan Statistical Area	Elasticity[a]	Per Capita Income	Employment Rate, Men 16-64	Percent High School Graduates, Men 25-34
Atlanta, GA	.139	.89	.86	.94
Riverside-San Bernadino, CA	.151	.96	.96	.97
Washington, DC	.155	.93	.90	.92
St. Louis, MO	.162	.69	.87	.91
Boston, MA	.2	.79	.91	.94
Anaheim-Santa Ana, CA	.232	.58	.95	.68
Detroit, MI	.235	.56	.74	.81
Minneapolis-St. Paul, MN	.26	.85	.92	.97
Philadelphia, PA	.326	.63	.83	.86
Dallas, TX	.394	.96	.92	.89
Los Angeles-Long Beach, CA	.442	.998	.96	.93
San Diego, CA	.445	1.00	.98	1.03
Chicago, IL	.459	.68	.85	.85
Houston, TX	.494	.89	.93	.87
New York, NY	.857	.68	.89	.90

[a]Elasticity is the proportion of the metropolitan area population that lives in the central-city named in the title of the Primary Metropolitan Statistical Area. (When two central cities are named in the title of the Primary Metropolitan Statistical Area, the population of both are counted as living in the primary central city.)

Source: U.S. Bureau of the Census (1990a).

notable exception, probably because of the high proportion of low-skilled, Hispanic immigrants living in its central city—nearly 50 percent of its central-city population is Hispanic.

There is also a substantial gap in educational performance between children who attend public schools in central cities and children who attend public schools elsewhere. Only 43 percent of fourth graders attending central-city schools scored at a basic or higher level on the 1994 National Assessment of Educational Progress (NAEP) reading test, compared with 63 percent for children attending public schools outside the central city. The difference was essentially the same (42 versus 66 percent) for eighth graders on the NAEP math test, and it was even greater (38 versus 65 percent) for eighth graders on the NAEP science test (*Education Week*, January 8, 1998).

Minorities and Whites

In the last 30 years, racial minorities have gained access to some opportunities previously closed to them. The black middle class has grown (O'Hare and Frey, 1992), racial segregation has declined (albeit modestly), and attitudes about racial prejudice appear to have softened (Farley et al., 1993; Firebaugh and Davis, 1988). Still, racial disparities remain pronounced, especially between African Americans and non-Hispanic whites (Table 3-7).

Income differences are particularly striking: The median income of black households living in a metropolitan area was just 61 percent that of the median

TABLE 3-7　Comparison of Selected Outcomes for Different Racial Groups, 1990

| | Population in Metropolitan Areas | | | | |
| | Outcomes for Different Racial Groups | | | Ratios of Outcomes | |
Outcome	NHW	Black	Hispanic	Black to NHW	Hispanic to NHW
Median household Income	$34,676	$21,247	$25,009	.61	.72
Per capita income	$17,559	$9,414	$8,603	.54	.49
Poverty rate	7.7%	27.5%	24.5%	3.6	3.18
Percent employed, men 25-54	90.3%	72.5%	82.6%	.8	.91
Unemployment rate, men 25-54	3.9%	11.5%	14.1%	2.95	3.62
Percent high school graduates, men 25-34	89.4%	76.0%	55.7%	.85	.62

Note: NHW, non-Hispanic white.

Source: U.S. Bureau of the Census (1990a).

non-Hispanic white household in 1990; the median income of Hispanic households was 72 percent that of non-Hispanic white households. Racial differences in per capita income are even greater, since minority households are larger on average than white households. Finally, 3.6 times as many metropolitan-area blacks and 3.2 times as many Hispanics lived in poverty in 1990 as non-Hispanic whites.

In part, these racial and ethnic gaps in income reflect differences in employment rates. As the table also shows, over 90 percent of prime working-age, non-Hispanic white men in metropolitan locations held jobs in 1990, compared with 83 percent of Hispanic men of prime working-age and just 73 percent of black men of similar ages. There are sharp differences in the numbers of men explicitly looking for work as well. The unemployment rate was 3 times as great for prime working-age black men as for working-age white men, and the disparity between Hispanics and non-Hispanic whites was even greater.

Some fraction of the income gap, as well as the employment gap itself, may be explained by significant racial and ethnic disparities in educational attainment. Among men between the ages of 25 and 34, for example, nearly 90 percent of non-Hispanic whites have at least high school diplomas. The corresponding proportions for African Americans and Hispanics are just 76 and 56 percent, respectively.

As Table 3-8 illustrates, these relationships have generally not changed much over the decade from 1980 to 1990.[3] In general, blacks improved their educational attainment relative to whites, and the poverty gap closed modestly as well. Still, the gains were small, and blacks actually lost ground relative to whites with respect to their labor market success and per capita income.

Racial differences vary both by region and by metropolitan-area size. Table 3-9 illustrates that the gap between black and white per capita income is smaller

TABLE 3-8   Percentage Change in Selected Outcomes by Race, 1980-1990

| | Population in Metropolitan Areas | |
| | Percent Change in Outcome, 1980-1990 | |
Outcome	Whites	Blacks
Median household income (constant dollars)	5.6	6.7
Per capita income (constant dollars)	19.4	13.4
Poverty rate	2.4	−.7
Percent employed, men ages 25-54	−.6	−4.9
Unemployment rate, men ages 25-54	.0	15.0
High school graduates, men age 25 and older	12.0	19.9

Source: U.S. Bureau of the Census (1980, 1990a).

TABLE 3-9   Mean Racial Disparities in Per Capita Income in Metropolitan
Areas in 1990 by Region

| | Mean Ratio of Per Capita Incomes in Set of Metropolitan Statistical Areas[a] | |
Region	Black/Non-Hispanic White	Hispanic /Non-Hispanic White
Northeast	.56	.51
South	.53	.631
Midwest	.544	.602
West	.607	.501

[a]Ratios of black and non-Hispanic white and Hispanic and non-Hispanic white per capita income
were first calculated for each individual metropolitan area. These ratios were then averaged within
the region, weighted by the population of the metropolitan area.

Source: Tabulations from U.S. Bureau of Census (1996a).

in the West than in the other three regions. An examination of the poverty rate
reveals a similar pattern—the poverty rate for African Americans is 1.8 times
higher than the white rate in the Western region of the country, and a full 4 times
greater in the Midwest (Current Population Reports, 1993). For Hispanics, the
income gaps tend to be lower in the South and the Midwest and higher in the
Northeast and the West. Significantly, the regional differences are considerably
larger for the Hispanic-white differentials than for the black-white ones, probably
because of the large differences in background between the Hispanic population
groups living in different areas of the country.

The magnitude of racial disparities appears to vary with the size of a metropolitan area and to be somewhat larger in larger areas (Table 3-10). In metropolitan areas with over 1 million people, per capita income for blacks was just 55
percent of that for white households on average. In metropolitan areas with less
than 100,000 residents, by contrast, black per capita income was, on average, 60
percent of white per capita income. The Hispanic-white disparities in per capita
income followed a similar pattern. The per capita income of Hispanics in metropolitan areas of over 1 million people was an average of 53 percent of that for
non-Hispanic whites; in metropolitan areas with less than 100,000 residents, the
corresponding ratio was just 62 percent. For Hispanics, the difference may be
due to the fact that recent Hispanic immigrants tend to settle in larger metropolitan areas (Bartel, 1989).

These regional and population size averages, of course, conceal considerable
variation across individual metropolitan areas. In certain metropolitan areas,
minority groups appear to do far better than in others, and the extent to which
central-city residents fall behind their suburban counterparts varies a great deal as
well. To give a sense of the range of disparities across metropolitan areas, Tables
3-11 and 3-12 display racial, ethnic, and urban-suburban disparities for the 15

TABLE 3-10   Mean Racial Disparities in Per Capita Income in Metropolitan Areas by Metropolitan Statistical Area Population Size, 1990

Metropolitan Statistical Area Size Class	Mean Ratio of Per Capita Incomes in Set of Metropolitan Statistical Areas[a]	
	Black to Non-Hispanic White	Hispanic to Non-Hispanic White
1,000,000 +	.545	.531
250,000-999,999	.566	.608
100,000-249,999	.577	.616
0-99,999	.603	.624

[a]Ratios of black and non-Hispanic white and Hispanic and non-Hispanic white per capita income were first calculated for each individual metropolitan area. These ratios were then averaged within the size-class, weighted by the population of the metropolitan area.

Source: Tabulations from U.S. Bureau of Census (1996a).

largest metropolitan areas (Nassau County, NY, is omitted since it has no central city), for three outcomes: per capita income, employment rates for men of prime working age (between 25 and 54), and high school completion for men ages 25 to 34.

In Table 3-11, comparing blacks and non-Hispanic whites, the ratio of per capita income ranges from a low of .43 in New York City to a high of .64 in Riverside. Black-white employment ratios meanwhile vary from a low of .70 in Detroit to a high of .95 in Anaheim. Black-white high school graduation rates range from a low of .78 in New York City to a high of .99 in Anaheim. As expected, these disparities generally tend to be greater in the metropolitan areas in the Northeast and the Midwest. The disparities are also larger in the metropolitan areas with larger and more segregated black populations. Indeed, the simple correlation between the segregation index for blacks (measured by the index of dissimilarity) and Ellen's index of disparity (in this volume) is −.91. More work would be useful to try to probe further into the roots of these metropolitan-area differences.

The range in disparities for these three outcomes is even greater for Hispanics and non-Hispanic whites (Table 3-12), consistent with the large cultural variation in the Hispanic population living in the United States. The Hispanic-white ratio of per capita income ranges from a low of .32 in Los Angeles to a high of .77 in St. Louis, and employment ratios range from .79 in Philadelphia to .97 in Washington, DC. High school completion ratios vary from .45 in Dallas to .89 in St. Louis. In general, the disparities are smaller in metropolitan areas, such as St.

TABLE 3-11   Disparities Between Blacks and Non-Hispanic Whites in the 15 Largest Metropolitan Areas, 1990

Metropolitan Statistical Area	Ratio of Black to Non-Hispanic White Outcome		
	Per Capita Income	Employment Rate, Men 16-64	Percent High School Graduates, Men 25-34
Anaheim, CA	.63	.95	.99
Atlanta, GA	.51	.86	.92
Boston, MA	.55	.83	.86
Chicago, IL	.45	.73	.8
Dallas, TX	.44	.83	.89
Detroit, MI	.54	.7	.81
Houston, TX	.44	.82	.86
Los Angeles, CA	.48	.8	.86
Minneapolis, MN	.5	.76	.88
New York, NY	.43	.81	.78
Philadelphia, PA	.53	.76	.81
Riverside, CA	.64	.84	.99
St. Louis, MO	.52	.77	.85
San Diego, CA	.53	.88	.95
Washington, DC	.55	.87	.88

Source: U.S. Bureau of the Census (1980, 1990a).

TABLE 3-12   Disparities Between Hispanics and Non-Hispanic Whites in the 15 Largest Metropolitan Areas, 1990

Metropolitan Statistical Area	Ratio of Hispanic to Non-Hispanic White Outcome		
	Per Capita Income	Employment Rate, Men 16-64	Percent High School Graduates, Men 25-34
Anaheim, CA	.38	.95	.48
Atlanta, GA	.66	.95	.71
Boston, MA	.46	.85	.71
Chicago, IL	.4	.94	.55
Dallas, TX	.39	.94	.45
Detroit, MI	.64	.89	.82
Houston, TX	.38	.95	.47
Los Angeles, CA	.32	.95	.47
Minneapolis, MN	.52	.92	.86
New York, NY	.34	.86	.67
Philadelphia, PA	.43	.79	.66
Riverside, CA	.51	.95	.6
St. Louis, MO	.77	.94	.89
San Diego, CA	.43	.93	.63
Washington, DC	.51	.97	.65

Source: U.S. Bureau of the Census (1980, 1990a).

Louis, that have smaller, more middle-class Hispanic populations. The simple correlation between the standardized mean of these disparities and the index of Hispanic residential segregation is –.91, and the correlation between the mean disparity and the proportion Hispanic in the metropolitan area is –.57.

In summary, large disparities in social and economic outcomes persist between central-city and suburban residents and between minorities and whites. In general, the magnitude of the racial and ethnic disparities has remained fairly constant between 1980 and 1990, and the city-suburban and skills differentials have grown significantly. Nonetheless, there is substantial variation across individual metropolitan areas.

ACCOUNTING FOR THE CAUSES OF OUTCOME DISPARITIES

This section examines the causes of the disparities in outcomes between central-city and suburban residents and between whites and minorities in metropolitan areas. The focus is on factors that relate specifically to metropolitan phenomena and, in particular, to the metropolitan spatial opportunity structure. We consider the ways in which the physical and institutional structure of metropolitan areas affects these disparities. And we distinguish causes of outcome disparities that are metropolitan in nature from causes that are national and are manifested in metropolitan areas simply because these areas constitute such a large share of the U.S. population.

Metropolitan-Related Causes

Spatial Mismatch

The spatial mismatch hypothesis states that there is a disjuncture between the location of jobs (which are increasingly found in the suburbs) and the location of potential qualified workers (who are constrained to live, as a result of low income or housing segregation patterns or both, in central-city neighborhoods). As evidence, proponents of the spatial mismatch hypothesis point to high unemployment rates in many central cities at the same time that metropolitan labor markets are tight and jobs are apparently available in suburbs. Spatial mismatch is thought to reduce the well-being of central-city residents and contribute to city-suburban disparities by making it more difficult for central-city residents to find work, by reducing wage rates in the central city relative to the suburbs, and by increasing the commuting costs of central-city residents (Ihlanfeldt, this volume).

There are several reasons related to distance and metropolitan structure that explain how such a mismatch could exist. The most straightforward of these is that low-income central-city residents lack physical access to suburban jobs as a consequence of low rates of car ownership and poor public transportation services. Another possibility is that information atrophies with distance, and that central-city residents know little about job opportunities in outlying suburban areas. A third related hypothesis is that minorities are apprehensive of hostility in distant suburbs with which they have little experience, whether or not such hostility exists. But reasons unrelated to distance may also play a role. Suburban employers may, in fact, discriminate against minority workers, or against central-city workers regardless of race. And central-city workers may have poor access to information about job opportunities, regardless of distance from their residence, if they are isolated from job information networks.

Earlier research suggested that it was not distance (job accessibility) but race that explained racial differences in youth employment rates (Ellwood, 1986). However, reviewing the recent evidence on the spatial mismatch hypothesis, Ihlanfeldt (this volume) found that distance *does* matter in explaining the large difference in employment rates of black and white youth in metropolitan areas. In a recent review of the literature, Mayer (1996:38) is somewhat less definite but concludes that "commuting times appear to be an important factor in explaining reduced employment for black and Hispanic youth."

Little of the spatial mismatch research has focused on smaller metropolitan areas, where the distance component of spatial mismatch should be reduced. Ihlanfeldt reports (this volume) that, although racial differences in youth employment rates are only modestly lower in smaller than in larger metropolitan areas, the importance of job accessibility as a determinant of these racial employment gaps is directly proportional to metropolitan size and is unimportant for metropolitan areas of less than 1 to 1.5 million people. This, by inference, casts doubt on the importance of the distance factor in larger metropolitan areas as well and suggests that dynamics other than distance, such as lack of connection to job information networks and social isolation, may be important factors at work in explaining employment disparities between black and white youth.

Ihlanfeldt also reports on research that he and colleagues have done on the relative importance of specific barriers that prevent blacks from shifting their labor supply to suburban areas in response to spatial mismatch. This research is of particular importance in terms of its relevance for policy responses. It concludes that a combination of barriers prevents central-city blacks and less-educated whites from obtaining suburban jobs, including an absence of information on suburban job opportunities, greater hiring discrimination against blacks in suburban areas (reflecting both consumer and employer prejudice), and the inability to commute from the inner city to suburban employment centers via public transportation.

Concentrated Poverty, Social Isolation, and Neighborhood Effects

Other possible reasons why central-city residents have low employment rates relative to suburban residents are not necessarily related to distance but may nonetheless be related to location and metropolitan structure. One such possible set of reasons relates to the social isolation of poor people, particularly blacks, in high-poverty neighborhoods. Residence in such areas, it is argued, imposes "neighborhood effects" on inhabitants, external costs that would not be present if the individual lived elsewhere.

Some concentrated-poverty neighborhoods are inevitable and functional parts of every large metropolitan area (Downs, 1997). This is both because poverty exists and such neighborhoods provide low-cost housing for the poor and because newly arriving immigrants tend to concentrate in a small number of specific neighborhoods with low-cost housing in which previous arrivals from their ethnic group have congregated. However, in many American cities, the degree of concentrated poverty, as well as its racial dimensions, make it unusual and clearly dysfunctional.

The extent of concentrated poverty in metropolitan areas—defined as the percentage of the metropolitan-area population living in census tracts with 40 percent or more of the households with income below the poverty level—is largely the result of metropolitan-wide processes of income generation and neighborhood sorting (Jargowsky, 1997). Variation in the level of black neighborhood poverty is related significantly to mean metropolitan household income (the lower the mean income, the greater the neighborhood poverty rate), to income inequality (the higher the degree of income inequality, the greater the neighborhood poverty rate), and to the ratio of black mean household income to metropolitan mean household income in metropolitan areas (the higher the ratio of black mean household income to metropolitan-area mean household income, the lower the neighborhood poverty rate) (Jargowsky, 1997). But it is also positively related to what Jargowsky calls "neighborhood sorting processes" as measured by indices of racial and economic segregation.

The critical question is whether such neighborhoods are simply staging grounds for people who move outward and upward after an initial period of residence, or whether they are permanent ghettos for those who live there, from which movement out is unlikely. If these areas are actually "sinkholes," then the adverse effects of living in them constitute a part of the metropolitan opportunity structure that may contribute to inequity and the disparities we have discussed.

There are very substantial rates of emigration from high-poverty areas. In any one year, 25 percent of all poor white adults leave such areas for other areas. However, only 10 percent of poor black adults do so (Gramlich et al., 1992). Gramlich and colleagues note (1992:246): "This is still a high enough rate of exit to shed doubt on the entrapment hypothesis, but the fact that it is so much lower [for blacks] than for similarly situated whites means that perhaps poor whites and blacks are not similarly situated after all." They also found that the overwhelming majority of leavers from poor areas do not return, although others from nonpoor areas take their place.

These data do not tell us what proportion of the population of high-poverty areas are long-time residents; it is possible that it is substantial. Nor do they provide information on who is moving into these areas (other than information on the areas from which they have come). Weicher (1990:91-92) analyzed movement into and out of poverty neighborhoods (neighborhoods with 20 percent or more of the households below the poverty line) and found most of those moving into these neighborhoods during this period came from elsewhere in the same city.

The impact of living in areas of concentrated poverty may have serious adverse consequences for metropolitan opportunity structures. These effects may vary with stage in the life-cycle, having relatively small impacts on small children, but increasingly more on older children and youth (Ellen and Turner, 1997). Some of these effects may be intergenerational in nature. Corcoran and colleagues (1992:589) found, for example, that the sons of families who lived in neighborhoods with a high proportion of welfare recipients when the son was growing up do significantly worse, for a range of labor market outcomes, than do sons of similarly situated families who lived in areas with a low proportion of welfare recipients. However, the little research that has been done on intergenerational links has, except for the finding just cited, not shown relationships between neighborhood characteristics and economic outcomes. Corcoran et al. (1992) found that other community characteristics—area median income, unemployment rate, and percentage of families that are female headed with children—were unrelated to the economic outcomes of sons, and neighborhood poverty rates were related to future economic outcomes of white men, but not of black men or white women (Corcoran and Adams, 1997). Haveman and Wolfe (1994:250-251) found that the relationship between growing up from ages 6 to 15 in a "bad neighborhood" and economic inactivity at age 24, although positive, was not statistically significant.[4]

Neighborhood effects, broadly construed, are the effects imposed on individuals as a result of living in a specific neighborhood that the same individual (or household) would not experience if living in a different neighborhood. With respect to neighborhoods of high poverty concentration, these effects are overwhelmingly adverse.

Some neighborhood effects are simply the result of features highly associated with poverty. Since crime and poverty are related, individuals living in high-poverty neighborhoods are more likely to be the victims of crime than would be the case if they were living in a nonpoverty neighborhood. Some effects have to do with the level of public services and amenities in high-poverty neighborhoods, which tend to be worse than would be the case in other neighborhoods.

Some effects, however, have to do with more subtle influences of residents of the neighborhood on the behavior of each other. Since behaviors considered socially undesirable according to dominant norms are more prevalent in poor neighborhoods, individuals living there are more likely to be influenced to engage in self-destructive or antisocial behavior themselves (Ihlanfeldt, this volume). Thus, peer effects could result in greater rates of school dropout and poor performance in school (if education is not valued or if high grades are seen as acting "white") or higher rates of teenage pregnancy than would be the case for similarly situated individuals living in nonpoverty areas. Research going back to the original Coleman report on equal opportunity in education has pointed to the importance of peer effects in the classroom on student performance (Coleman et al., 1966).

Some neighborhood effects may be related directly to employment prospects. Youth growing up in neighborhoods of concentrated poverty may be cut off from mainstream values and may adopt a set of peer group "oppositional" values that are not well related to workplace success. The lack of adults in the area with steady employment may also affect the employment prospects of others in the area. Also, young people living in a neighborhood of concentrated poverty may know very few people who work. This provides two forms of disadvantage: they are not linked into word of-mouth job networks through which many jobs are filled, and they are not exposed to modeling about appropriate job behavior.

The theoretical and conceptual literature concerned with neighborhood effects suggests that these effects are nonlinear—that is, that there is some threshold of neighborhood poverty at which negative external effects appear, whereas previously they did not. Thus, an increase in the percentage of poverty households in a neighborhood from 10 to 20 percent might be unlikely to have any of the hypothesized adverse neighborhood effects, whereas an increase from 20 to 40 percent (the conventionally used indicator of high-poverty neighborhoods) might do so (see Quercia and Galster, 1997). Unfortunately, there seems to be no theoretical or empirically derived reason for selecting 40 percent as the threshold above which such effects are likely to occur.

Although there is a growing amount of research on such neighborhood effects, much of it is problematic because of the difficulty in accounting for the possibility of endogenous effects. It is possible, for example, that people who behave in ways society deems undesirable choose to live in neighborhoods of concentrated poverty because they prefer the social environment or other characteristics of such a neighborhood over that of other neighborhoods in which low-income housing might be available, or they are forced to live in such neighborhoods because housing they can afford is unavailable elsewhere. As Ihlanfeldt observes (this volume), "There is always the concern that effects that are attributable to neighborhoods may simply reflect unmeasureable characteristics of individuals or families who end up living in the poorest neighborhoods."

An oft-cited earlier review of the literature by Jencks and Mayer (1990:174) was skeptical of the existence of neighborhood effects. They concluded that "there is no general pattern of neighborhood or school effects that recurs across all outcomes." However, recent research has tended to provide more support for the hypothesis. Ihlanfeldt notes that a study by Case and Katz (1991) is the most convincing, since they explicitly modeled the possibility of endogenous residential location. Case and Katz modeled a variety of behavior for 17- to 24-year-olds, including criminal activity, illegal drug use, alcohol use, church attendance, idleness (neither working nor in school), friendship with gang members, and parenthood outside marriage. For all but the last two behaviors, they found that a youth's involvement is dependent on the extent to which other youth in the same neighborhood engage in the same behavior.

Likewise, three recent reviews found indications of convergence in results with respect to the existence of neighborhood effects (Galster and Killen, 1995; Mayer, 1996; Ellen and Turner, 1997). Galster and Killen observe, for example (1995:35): "Much statistical evidence supports the influence of neighborhood social networks and economic conditions on youth's intellectual development, educational attainment, marriage and fertility, labor market participation and earnings and, to a lesser extent, criminal behavior and drug use. We believe that this evidence is sufficiently convincing that neighborhood effects should be adopted as a working hypothesis."

Ellen and Turner (1997) conclude that the bulk of the empirical studies found that neighborhood effects do exist. Nonetheless, they are more cautious, observing that neighborhood effects tend to be small relative to the importance of family characteristics. Furthermore, they emphasize what we do not know (1997: 834-835): "the existing evidence is inconclusive when it comes to determining *which* neighborhood conditions matter most, *how* neighborhood characteristics influence individual behavior and well-being, or *how* neighborhood effects may differ for families with different characteristics."

A few recent studies have tried to sort out the relative impact of spatial mismatch (job accessibility) and neighborhood effects on labor market outcomes. Cutler and Glaeser (1995) and O'Regan and Quigley (1996) found that both are important but that the strength of the neighborhood effects variables is dominant. Ihlanfeldt (this volume), however, criticizes the measure of job accessibility used in both studies as likely to have underestimated the true effect of this variable.

Finally, Quercia and Galster (1997:11) note that "virtually none" of the literature on neighborhood effects has tested for threshold effects, which, as they note, may differ for different kinds of outcomes and population subgroups.

Racial Segregation

Chapter 2 described the high extent of racial segregation in U.S. metropolitan areas. There is little question that some portion of the residential segregation of blacks is voluntary, representing the tendency for ethnic groups of all types to prefer living in close proximity to those similar to others like themselves. However, in a review of the segregation literature, Massey and Denton (1993), citing the very high dissimilarity indices for blacks compared with those for European-origin ethnic groups, conclude that voluntary segregation can explain very little of the high degree of racial segregation of blacks in urban areas. They note (1993:57) that "not only was the segregation of European ethnic groups lower, it was also temporary. Whereas Europeans' isolation indices began to drop shortly after 1920, the spatial isolation characteristic of blacks had become a permanent feature of the residential structure of large American cities by 1940."

Indeed, a recent survey of the residential preferences of blacks in Atlanta, Boston, Detroit, and Los Angeles (Farley et al., 1997) found that more than half preferred living in a neighborhood that was 50 percent white (although only 8 percent preferred living in a neighborhood that was more than 85 percent white). More than one-third of the blacks interviewed said that they would be willing to be the first black family to move into an all-white neighborhood with attractive and affordable housing (1997:794).

What is the purported relationship of racial segregation to disparities in outcomes? If racial segregation promotes concentrations of poverty among low-income blacks, then it will adversely affect outcomes through the various mechanisms discussed above. Indeed, racial segregation does seem to be linked to concentrations of poverty among low-income blacks; in 1990, 34 percent of poor blacks, but only 6 percent of poor whites, lived in areas of highly concentrated poverty (Jargowsky, 1997). Similarly, to the extent that racial segregation is involuntary and disproportionately confines blacks to central-city residence, then the negative effects of spatial mismatch will contribute to black-white disparities.

In addition, racial segregation, when combined with incomes that are lower for blacks than for whites, may mean that blacks (including middle-income blacks) are more likely than whites to reside in communities with lower tax bases and thus a lower ability to finance public services from their own resources. As a consequence, segregation would contribute to disparities in public service levels and to disparities in labor market and other outcomes, to the extent that inferior education and other public services contribute to such disparities.

Galster (1993:1431) argues that segregation can contribute to intergroup disparities in outcomes between minorities and whites in four ways:

> First, separate informal networks and formal institutions serving the minority community, because they have a narrower scope and base of support, will have fewer financial, informational, and human resources upon which to draw; therefore, they will offer inferior options for the development of human capital and the discovery of alternative employment possibilities. Second, isolation can encourage and permit the development of distinct subcultural attitudes, behaviors, and speech patterns that may impede success in the mainstream world of work, either because they are counterproductive in some objective sense or because they are perceived to be so by prospective white employers. Third, an identifiable, spatial labor market may be formed in the minority community and attract employers offering only irregular, low-paying, dead-end jobs. Fourth, inter-racial competition and suspicions are abetted, encouraging the formation of discriminatory barriers in many markets.

Ihlanfeldt (this volume) cites research on the Gautreaux program in the Chicago area as providing the strongest support that racial segregation adversely affects outcomes for minority groups and contributes to unequal opportunities and disparities. In this program, put in place as a result of a court decision, families residing in public housing in the city of Chicago were given the opportunity of receiving certificates to rent market-rate housing in "revitalized" neighborhoods throughout the Chicago area. Because most participants accepted the first unit offered to them, whether in the city or in suburban areas, this created a quasi-experimental design. A comparison of the results for those who moved to predominantly black, low-income areas in the city of Chicago with those who moved to predominantly white, middle-income neighborhoods in the suburbs found that adult employment was higher for suburban compared with central-city movers, although earnings and hours worked were not. For children, suburban movers were more likely, compared with city movers, to graduate from high school, attend college, and attend a four-year college. For the children of movers who did not attend college, suburban movers were more likely to receive higher wages and better job-related benefits (Rosenbaum, 1995).

Econometric work has also supported the adverse impact of racial segregation on black outcomes. Cutler and Glaeser (1997) examined the level of segregation at the metropolitan level and asked whether it was related to outcomes for blacks throughout the region. They related the level of racial segregation as measured by the dissimilarity index to a variety of outcomes for young people, controlling for other possible determinants of those outcomes, in 204 metropolitan areas for 1990. They conclude that (1997:28-29): "blacks are significantly worse off in segregated communities than they are in non-segregated communities. If we measure success by high school graduation rates, not being idle, earnings, or not becoming a single mother, then integration is intimately associated with success. Our estimates suggest that a one standard deviation reduction in segregation (13 percent) would eliminate one-third of the gap between white and blacks in most of our outcomes."

Jargowsky (1997:Ch. 6) also found that racial segregation is significantly related to level of neighborhood poverty for blacks in both 1980 and 1990 and to the change in levels of neighborhood poverty for blacks between 1980 and 1990. It is thus implicated indirectly in terms of the adverse effects that concentrated poverty has on unequal opportunities and disparities. Galster and Keeney (1988: 104-105) found that residential segregation was related to black-white income differentials in metropolitan areas, although only for metropolitan areas that were characterized by governmental fragmentation.

As mentioned earlier, Ellen (this volume) investigated the link between the extent of racial segregation in metropolitan areas and the extent of central-city suburban disparities as measured by a city-suburban index of disparities. Controlling for region, population size, percentage of blacks and Hispanics in the metropolitan-area population, and poverty rate, she found that both black-white segregation and Hispanic-white segregation are positively related to disparities;

the greater the degree of segregation in a metropolitan area, the greater the disparities between central city and suburb.

Economic Segregation

Residential segregation by income—economic segregation—is also a characteristic of U.S. metropolitan areas, facilitated, as discussed earlier, by the existence of large numbers of local governments in most metropolitan areas, each with control of land use powers. As Downs (1994) notes, although there is some heterogeneity in all communities, in general, neighborhoods in metropolitan areas are sorted out by income level, with the poor living in low-prestige areas with poor housing, because that is all they can afford.

As a result of the migration of middle- and high-income groups to the suburbs and racial segregation, the central city typically (but not always) becomes increasingly low-income. The results of this process in terms of the disparity in income between central cities and suburbs have been described.

The extent to which such segregation by income is inevitable, either at the jurisdictional or at the neighborhood level, is debatable. Fischel (this volume) argues that economic segregation by neighborhood will occur "under any mechanism that operates without a severe dose of coercion" (although, he contends, economic segregation by *jurisdiction* is not inevitable). However, indices of metropolitan-area economic segregation do show substantial variation among metropolitan areas (see Abramson et al., 1995:50-53). In addition, the degree of economic mixing in many European urban areas is widely thought to be substantially greater than is the case in the United States (Berry, 1973; Danielson, 1976:1; Weir, 1995:217; Sellars, 1998).

The logic of the relationship between economic segregation and disparities in outcomes operates in much the same manner as that for race. If there are adverse impacts resulting from the tendency of lower-income individuals to associate in their neighborhood environment primarily with other low-income individuals rather than mixing with those from higher socioeconomic backgrounds, then economic segregation will contribute to them. Of particular concern are the peer effects for children. Similarly, when economic stratification occurs by jurisdiction, as between the typical central city and its middle- and higher-income suburbs, residents of the lower-income jurisdictions will be faced with lower levels of service, or higher tax burdens, or both. Disparities in public service, such as education and public health, may be translated into disparities in outcomes among residents of jurisdictions in terms of future income and employment.

What empirical evidence exists that economic segregation, either by neighborhood or by jurisdiction, does have an adverse impact? At the neighborhood level, we have already reviewed the adverse effects on outcomes caused by areas of highly concentrated poverty. But there is little or no research on the effect on outcomes of the degree of economic stratification among neighborhoods or jurisdictions across the metropolitan area.

Unequal Provision of Public Services

Metropolitan areas are characterized by substantial variations in public service levels. These variations flow from the very structure of U.S. metropolitan areas: a large number of service-providing local districts, stratified by income and race, each primarily dependent on its own local tax base for the ability to finance and provide public services. Since most public services can be considered to a large extent consumption goods, lower levels of public services (or the necessity of accepting a higher tax burden in order to receive equivalent levels) in themselves represent a disparity resulting from metropolitan-area structure that adversely affects the well-being of those who live in jurisdictions with inadequate fiscal capacity.

Although a case can be made for the effects of a variety of public services on human capital development, education is the most obvious area and the one that has received the most attention. The view commonly expressed through the press and by most of the public is that variations in the level of school resources will result in associated variations in the quality of education provided as measured by student performance and other outcomes. However, at least until recently, conventional wisdom, based on social science research dating back to the Coleman report (Coleman et al., 1966), was skeptical. The Coleman study found that differences in a variety of school input measures that reflect increased spending, including class size and teacher quality, had little impact on student achievement, as measured by performance on standardized test scores. A recent review of 377 studies of education production functions counted the number that found significant relationships, as opposed to no relationships or relationships in the unexpected direction, and concluded there was no systematic relationship between teacher-pupil ratios or teacher education on student performance (Hanushek, 1996:54).[5]

However, the conclusion that school inputs are unrelated to outputs is not universally accepted by researchers. Using formal meta-analysis techniques, Hedges and colleagues (1994) and Hedges and Greenwald (1996) reexamined the same set of studies Hanushek examined and found evidence that both teacher-student ratios and teacher education are positively and significantly related to student achievement. In addition, other recent studies have begun to cast doubt on the earlier conclusions and to provide support for the relationship between expenditure differences and variation in student performance. Ferguson (1991) and Ferguson and Ladd (1996) engaged in carefully structured studies that overcome many of the methodological differences of other education production function studies.[6] In their study of Alabama schools, they found that class size, teachers' test scores, and teachers' education all affect student performance and concluded that, since these "all cost money," money matters and money spent for instructional purposes particularly matters (Ferguson and Ladd, 1996).

Card and Krueger (1996) argue that, whatever their effect on test scores, school resources positively affect long-term outcomes such as educational attainment and earnings. They conducted a natural experiment involving two states that spent substantially different amounts on the per pupil education of black children and white children between 1900 and 1960. During that period, North Carolina systematically provided more resources per black students and fewer for white students than did South Carolina. In the state with higher spending on black children (North Carolina), the future wages of blacks were higher than those of blacks educated in South Carolina. In the state with higher spending on white students (South Carolina), the future wages of whites was higher than those of whites educated in North Carolina.

Size and Density

The effects of physical features of metropolitan areas, such as population size, land area, and density (or sprawl), on metropolitan-area opportunity structures and outcome disparities is a question of great interest and controversy, and the empirical evidence is sparse and contradictory.

On one hand, larger metropolitan areas may affect the spatial mismatch problem by increasing distances between the central city and suburban workplaces; they may also intensify the impact of social isolation, since information on labor market opportunities may be more readily available in smaller areas. On the other hand, larger metropolitan areas may provide more opportunity and greater and more complex information linkages, thus increasing the chances that connections will be made to labor market opportunities.

Low-density areas may lead to unequal opportunity by increasing the distance between central-city residents and suburban job opportunities, thereby contributing to spatial mismatch. Low-density development, particularly if supported by exclusionary zoning practices, may also increase the land cost of housing, thus making it more difficult for low- and moderate-income households to reside in suburban areas near areas of growing job opportunity.

Ihlanfeldt observes that the difference in youth employment rates for blacks and whites is only slightly less in metropolitan areas with low population than in those with high population, suggesting that size of area is unlikely to have much effect. However, he cites his own research (1992) as the only work that provides separate estimates for different size metropolitan areas of the impact of job access on both youth job probability and racial employment gaps. He found that the impact of job access measures on these outcomes was directly proportional to metropolitan size, with no importance found for job access measures in metropolitan areas of less than 1 to 1.5 million people.

Cutler and Glaeser (1997) found that metropolitan-area population size is related to differences in college graduation rates between blacks and whites: the larger the metropolitan area, the lower the college graduation rate for blacks relative to whites. However, they also found that large metropolitan areas are associated with higher black earnings relative to whites (suggesting that the negative relationship between relative black earnings and metropolitan-area size presented in Table 3-10 above is reversed in the context of a multivariate analysis in which other variables are controlled for). The rate of single motherhood is also lower for blacks relative to whites in larger metropolitan areas.

Hill and Wolman (1997c) include the log of metropolitan-area population size in a model designed to explain per capita income differentials between suburbs and the central city in metropolitan areas for all metropolitan areas whose central-city population exceeded 250,000. Controlling for region, elasticity, employment structure, and other variables, they found that these differentials were inversely and significantly related to metropolitan-area population size: the larger the metropolitan-area population, the smaller the per capita income difference between suburbs and the central city. However, Ellen (this volume) estimates a multivariate model and found that metropolitan-area population size is not significantly related to an index of city-suburban disparities.

Persky and Wiewel (1998) attempted to calculate the costs and benefits of placing a new electrical equipment plant with 1,000 workers in a "greenfield" [field of undeveloped suburban land] site in the outer suburbs of Chicago rather than a site in the central city. They found low-income groups and city residents to be the biggest losers from locating the plant in the suburbs; their calculations, although based on controversial methodological assumptions, also indicate that there is essentially no difference in efficiency in terms of whether the firm locates in the city or the outer suburbs.

Economic and Population Growth

Conventional wisdom suggests that growth and increased labor market tightness should narrow city-suburban income disparities. The reasoning is straightforward. Since highly skilled labor is likely to be employed throughout the business cycle and tends to reside in suburbs, growth should disproportionately attract lower-skilled individuals into the labor market. Disproportionate numbers of these lower-skilled individuals are likely to live in central cities.

However, examining data for the period 1980-1990, Hill and Wolman (1997b) found that increasing labor market tightness, as measured by either declines in the unemployment rate or by increases in the ratio of employment to the working-age population, was positively correlated with city-suburban disparities: as labor markets tightened, disparities increased.

They then examined central-city/suburban per capita income disparities in a cross-sectional multivariate model, using employment as a percentage of working-age population as a variable to measure labor market tightness and controlling for a variety of variables. They found a nonlinear relationship between tightening of labor markets and city-suburban income disparities. Increasing labor market tightness at first leads to *greater* disparities in city-suburban per capita income, but finally reaches a point (when the ratio of employment to working-age population is 71.9 percent, slightly below the mean of 72 percent for all of the metropolitan areas in the sample) above which further increases begin to reduce disparities. Hill and Wolman note, however, that (1997b:573) "these spatial income gaps do not disappear even in very tight local markets."

They explain their results by observing that employers seeking additional labor in tight labor markets tended to be located disproportionately in the suburbs. This demand was met in the first instance primarily through increases in the suburban labor force as secondary workers—spouses, teenagers, and elders— entered the labor market. Only after this additional source of labor was utilized did employers turn to lower-skilled central-city workers. Hill and Wolman conclude (1997b:577) that "economic growth, bringing about tighter labor markets, is clearly desirable, but it is not a cure for inner-city poverty and will not narrow gaps between central-city and suburban incomes in and of itself."

In related research, Pastor and colleagues (1997:Ch. 3) examined the relationship between metropolitan growth (in per capita income) and poverty between 1980 and 1990, using a simultaneous equation approach. They found no significant relationship between metropolitan growth and change in the city to suburban poverty ratio and conclude (1997:3-13) that "growth itself will not necessarily 'trickle down' to help the central city more than the suburbs."

Danielson and Wolpert (1992, 1994) found evidence that growth widened disparities. Studying the effect of population and employment growth on per capita income disparities among 365 contiguous municipalities in northern New Jersey, they concluded (1992:513): "Our test case of rapid growth in a highly fragmented metropolitan area demonstrates that disparities between richest and poorest communities widened significantly, especially when growth accelerated during the 1980s. Development and jobs shifted to the outer suburbs and rural fringe and bypassed the low-income and minority cities in the region."

Elasticity

It has been argued that fewer city-suburban disparities are found in metropolitan areas with more elastic cities—which are cities that can expand their population either by developing vacant land within existing borders or by annexing areas outside their borders (Rusk, 1993). The explanation, according to Rusk, is the greater control that elastic central cities have over their environment.

The concept of elasticity has proven difficult to operationalize in a satisfying manner. Rusk himself provides a definition that is complex and not clearly related to the concept. He operationalizes it as a variable (1993:53) by multiplying the ranking of a city's density (population per square mile) in 1950 by its ranking for the percentage by which it expanded its boundaries between 1950 and 1990. A seemingly more direct approach would operationalize elasticity by taking central-city population as a percentage of metropolitan-area population.

Using his operational definition described above, Rusk shows that elastic cities comprise a higher proportion of metropolitan-area population than do inelastic cities. He also found (1993:75-82) that city-suburban income gaps are wider in metropolitan areas with inelastic cities than in those with elastic cities. However, this finding is simply a bivariate relationship without any controls.

Contrary evidence is provided by Hill and Wolman (1997c). They use the alternative definition of elasticity described above[7] in a model designed to account for differences in the central-city/suburban per capita income gap across metropolitan areas. Controlling for a variety of factors, including region, metropolitan-area economic structure, tightness of metropolitan-area labor markets, and human capital differences between city and suburban residents, they found no statistically significant effect (at the .05 level or below) for elasticity on city-suburban per capita income differentials.[8]

Ellen (this volume) tested for the effect of elasticity (defined as the population of central cities in a metropolitan statistical area, MSA, as a percentage of MSA population) on her index of city-suburban disparities in a multivariate model that includes region, various metropolitan demographic characteristics, and government structure. She found a nonlinear, "kinked" relationship. When elasticity is below .45 (i.e., when the central-city population is less than 45 percent of the metropolitan-area population), elasticity is negatively and significantly related to the disparity index; as elasticity increases up to the .45 level, central-city/suburban disparities decrease. Above an elasticity level of .45, increases in elasticity have essentially no effect on city-suburban disparities.

Metropolitan Government Structure

Another possible contributor to the degree of disparities among residents within metropolitan areas, both by place and by group, is the nature of the government structure in these areas, particularly the number of local governments and the degree of fragmentation. We consider in what ways political fragmentation might contribute to a spatially determined opportunity structure.

We begin with the basic fact that local governments in the United States finance their services primarily from their own tax base. General-purpose local governments also control local land use decisions. As a consequence, local governments have both the incentives and the means to differentiate themselves with respect to the income, tastes, and tax and service preferences of their residents, and residents have the ability to make choices among local governments based on these same characteristics. Political boundaries thus facilitate sorting, and the more jurisdictions there are, the more effective the sorting process is likely to be (Lewis, 1995).

The logic of this argument is that greater fragmentation will lead to a more differentiated spatial opportunity structure, with more fragmented metropolitan areas experiencing greater disparities among individuals in important outcomes and greater tax/service disparities among local governments. It is not clear whether central-city/suburban differences should be greater in more fragmented areas. Since fragmentation increases the potential for choice and thus sorting, we would also expect fragmentation to be positively related to income segregation in metropolitan areas (Bradford and Oates, 1974; Mills and Oates, 1975) and, since race and income are correlated, to racial segregation.

The concept of fragmentation needs to be distinguished carefully from the concept of elasticity, as discussed above. Elasticity refers to the central city's ability to exercise influence and control over the metropolitan area, and it is best measured by the percentage of metropolitan-area population living in the main central city. Fragmentation, as we define it, relates to the ability of the local government system to engage in sorting behavior through offering a multitude of choices (local governments) with the effective ability to exclude. It should be measured by the number of relevant local governments per capita in a metropolitan area. A relatively elastic metropolitan area may still be fragmented if the remainder of the area is divided into a large number of local governments. Similarly, a relatively inelastic metropolitan area may have little fragmentation if the remainder of the area has few other local jurisdictions with the ability to engage in sorting behavior. This would be the case where the basic unit of local government with land use powers is the county government, as in Maryland and Virginia.

Most of the research effort with respect to fragmentation has been directed toward the impact of fragmentation on size of government, as measured by expenditures per capita or on service delivery and efficiency (see Wagner and Weber, 1975; Sjoquist, 1982; Chicoine and Walzer, 1985; Schneider, 1986, 1989; Dolan, 1990; U.S. Advisory Commission on Intergovernmental Relations, 1991; Boyne, 1992a, 1992b; Foster, 1997:Ch. 3). Boyne (1992b) reviews more than 20 studies of the impact of fragmentation on local government spending. He found that fragmentation leads to lower per capita spending for the system of *multipurpose* government units (i.e., typically municipalities) within metropolitan areas, but higher per capita spending for *single-purpose* units. He explains the difference by noting that fiscal migration is a much more potent threat to multipurpose governments (thus acting as a restraint on spending) than to single-purpose governments and also that many single-purpose governments provide services that are capital-intensive and thus incorporate economies of scale.[9] In another review of the literature, Dowding and colleagues (1994) also conclude that local government fragmentation leads to reduced expenditure. However, they agree that existing research is unable to sort out whether this effect is due to competition or to other causes related to the smaller size of government in fragmented areas, such as fewer opportunities to redistribute among income classes.

The body of literature directed at disparities and inequality is smaller and less compelling, and it is particularly so given the difficulties in constructing a convincing operational measure of fragmentation.[10] The variation in measures of fragmentation and the nature of the dependent variables and methodologies used make it difficult to come to overall conclusions. The seminal research was conducted by Hill (1974), who attempted to account for income inequality among *municipalities* in 63 metropolitan areas (rather than among all households in metropolitan areas). His dependent variable as a measure of intrametropolitan income inequality was the standard deviation in the distribution of median family income among municipalities. In a multivariate analysis, he found that political fragmentation, measured as the number of municipalities per capita, was positively related to his measure of municipal income inequality (but that fragmentation, as measured by the total number of municipal governments, was not).

Ostrom (1983:98) criticizes Hill's methodology, contending that "comparing means or medians of different-sized units can lead to false conclusions about the extent of heterogeneity in a population." Ostrom, however, does not attempt to remedy this by providing additional empirical analysis; indeed, there appears to be no research that relates political fragmentation to income heterogeneity, as she terms it, in the metropolitan-area population.

Other research has examined the impact of fragmentation on the income differential between the central city and its suburbs. Logan and Schneider (1982), Bollens (1986), and Morgan and Mareschal (1996) all fail to find a significant relationship between fragmentation (governments per capita) and city-suburban income differences in metropolitan areas. This is not surprising; it simply suggests that the difference between city and suburban per capita income is not affected by the *number* of suburbs (relative to population) in the metropolitan areas. Ellen (this volume), however, found that fragmentation (number of general-purpose governments per 100,000 people) is negatively and significantly related to an index of disparities in a multivariate model that includes region, metropolitan demographic characteristics, and elasticity: the greater the degree of fragmentation, the lower the disparity between central city and suburbs.

Fragmentation has been implicated as a contributor to some of the other factors that we have shown to be related to unequal outcomes. Cutler and Glaeser (1997) found that the number of municipal and township governments in metropolitan areas is positively related to metropolitan-area racial segregation as measured by the dissimilarity index. However, since their purpose is to use number of governments as an instrument for segregation, they do not develop a fully specified model to estimate the relationship. Hamilton and colleagues (1975) measured the link between income segregation across census tracts in a metropolitan area and metropolitan government structure. They found that income segregation is greater when there is more choice, i.e., when the number of school districts is greater.

Galster and Keeney (1988) found that residential segregation was related to black-white income differentials in metropolitan areas, but only for metropolitan areas that were characterized by high governmental fragmentation (as measured by the number of jurisdictions in the area). They concluded (1988:104-105): "this finding, that SMSAs with more segregation have lower relative black incomes *only* to the extent they are jurisdictionally fragmented, suggests that the direct link . . . [between segregation and black/white income differentials] transpires through interracial differentials in public service packages consumed, presumably education primarily."

Lewis (1996) examined the relationship between fragmentation and spatial mismatch, arguing that there should be greater mismatches between job areas and housing areas in more fragmented metropolitan areas. He found that his fragmentation index was positively and significantly related to average commuting time.[11]

Other Causes With Spatial Components

We now turn to causes of disparities in outcomes between residents of central cities and their suburbs and between minorities and whites that are traditionally conceived of as less related, or unrelated, to metropolitan phenomena. However, as we note, all of them have important spatial components that are affected by the spatial structure of metropolitan areas.

Human Capital

Differences in black-white labor and city-suburban labor market outcomes may be related to differences in human capital—that is, to the skills that prospective employees bring with them to the workplace. These differences, although unrelated to metropolitan phenomena, may nonetheless result, in part, from adverse neighborhood effects or unequal provision of education services, as discussed above. Neal and Johnson (1996) found that differences between blacks and whites in educational attainment and test scores (which are a likely proxy for the quality of education) account for most of the differences in hourly wages, although they account for less of the differences in employment rates. Holzer (1994) emphasizes the point that quality of education must be taken into account as well as educational attainment. He cites literature indicating that reading and numerical skills of blacks are not comparable to those of whites in the same educational categories, and that these differences in scores on reading and math tests account for much of the racial differences between blacks and whites in earnings and in employment probabilities.

Hill and Wolman (1997b:574) found that differences in human capital between central-city and suburban residents (measured by the difference in the percentage of residents with more than a high school education in the two areas) were significantly and strongly related to their differences in per capita income. Each percentage point difference in the percentage of suburban and central-city residents with more than a high school education was associated with a 1.41 percentage point difference in per capita income.

Decline in Demand for Less-Skilled Labor

The national economy has undergone substantial structural change over the past 25 years that has greatly reduced the proportion of employees in manufacturing jobs and increased the proportion in service-sector jobs. In 1970, 26 percent of all U.S. workers were employed in the manufacturing sector, compared with only 16 percent in 1994. In addition, technological change has increased skill requirements in many sectors of the economy, including manufacturing. These changes have shifted labor demand from less-educated to more-educated portions of the workforce. Well-paid, less-skilled jobs in the manufacturing and other sectors have largely disappeared. When combined with differences in human capital on the supply side, the result is a skills mismatch that disadvantages less-skilled workers in general and blacks, a higher proportion of whom are less skilled, in particular (see Wilson, 1987, 1996).

Research results suggest that a skill mismatch exists and that declining manufacturing employment has contributed to black-white disparities by reducing the relative earnings and employment of blacks, with particular impact on the youngest and least educated black males (see Holzer, 1994, for a review of this literature). Holzer emphasizes, however, that substantial earnings and employment gaps between blacks and whites remain even after the decline of manufacturing employment and skill mismatch are taken into account.

Spatial factors also interact with the decline in demand for less-skilled jobs. Kasarda (1995) and Holzer (1996) both found that job growth in the central city has been in sectors that require higher skills, such as finance and business services, than do the sectors of suburban job growth, such as retail trade, personal services, and traditional blue-collar manufacturing. Kasarda (1995) notes that this exchange of goods-processing for information-processing jobs (requiring higher skills) in central cities has meant that central-city jobs are no longer *functionally* accessible to less-educated city residents, even if they are *physically* accessible. Meanwhile, opportunities for the relatively less-skilled jobs that might be appropriate for less-educated city residents are constrained by the spatial mismatch problems discussed earlier.

Racial Discrimination in Employment

Part of the black-white gap in labor market outcomes may simply be due to employer discrimination in labor markets. Indeed, there is very good reason to believe this is the case. Holzer (1994) summarizes recent evidence, which appears in Turner et al. (1991) and is based on an Urban Institute audit study, in which matched pairs of black and white job applicants, with employment histories and skills designed to be exactly comparable, applied to several hundred firms in two major metropolitan areas. Blacks received significantly fewer job offers than did whites (19 versus 29 percent).

Furthermore, there appears to be a spatial element in employer discrimination. Holzer (1996) found that the ratio of black new hires to black applicants is lower in the suburbs than in the central city. He concludes that there is a "relatively lower employer preference for black applicants in suburban areas than elsewhere" (1996:95). In a multivariate analysis, he found that the probability of a firm's hiring blacks is lower for those with mostly white customers, which are more likely to be located in the suburbs. Finally he indicates that the evidence suggests "that discriminatory employers may deliberately choose locations for their firms that make them inaccessible to blacks" (1996:95).

COSTS OF UNEQUAL OPPORTUNITY

The costs of unequal opportunity are clearly borne by those who are most directly affected in terms of lower income, higher unemployment, and constrained choices. But in addition, there are very real costs imposed on the entire metropolitan area as well as on the nation as a whole.

In work undertaken at the request of the committee, Harry Holzer arrived at a rough estimate, for the purposes of this report, of the costs that segregation imposes on young blacks (ages 20-30) in metropolitan areas, as well as on the metropolitan areas overall. He first used regression results from Cutler and Glaeser (1997) to calculate the effects of differences in the levels of segregation across metropolitan areas (as measured by the dissimilarity index) on several major outcomes for young blacks in these areas: high school graduation, college graduation, the probability of not being employed, the log of annual earnings, and the probability of being a single mother. He then linked the costs borne by the young people themselves to their outcomes for the metropolitan areas overall.

Holzer's calculations estimate the impact of segregation by contrasting the most highly segregated metropolitan areas with the least segregated metropolitan areas. He derived two estimates of the effects of segregation on young blacks. The first is based on the difference between high and low segregation *levels* (i.e., dissimilarity indexes of between .70 and .75 at the high end and between .45 and .50 at the low end). Examples of metropolitan areas with high segregation levels include New York and Philadelphia; those with low levels include Phoenix and Raleigh; the difference constitutes a change of two standard deviations in the distribution of segregation levels in metropolitan areas.

The second estimate is based on differences in segregation between the most and the least segregated areas (dissimilarity indexes of between .80 and .90 for the most segregated and between .30 and .40 for the least segregated). Examples of metropolitan areas with the most segregation include Detroit, Chicago, and Gary; those with the least include Albuquerque and San Jose. This difference constitutes a change of four standard deviations in the distribution of segregation levels (almost the entire range).

Using this technique, Holzer found very large negative effects of segregation on blacks when comparing the least segregated to the most segregated metropolitan areas. An increase in segregation from low to high levels caused a drop in high school graduation rates of 6 percentage points. An increase in segregation from the level of the least segregated areas to that of the most segregated reduced high school graduation rates by 12 percentage points. Similar increases in segregation caused college graduation rates of young blacks to drop by 2.5 to 5 percentage points, the percentage of those not employed or in school to increase by 7.5 to 15 points, annual earnings to decline by 20 to 40 percent, and the probability of being a single mother to increase by 10 to 20 percentage points.

Holzer then linked these adverse consequences on individuals to costs for the metropolitan area and beyond. Assuming that worker productivity is proportional to earnings and that blacks are about 15 percent of the population in large metropolitan areas, then, in a steady state over time, a 20 to 40 percent reduction in earnings due to high segregation translates into a 3 to 6 percent decline in productivity for the area as a whole.

Segregation also affects labor turnover through increasing high school dropout rates. Turnover imposes major costs on employers, in the form of fixed costs for recruiting, hiring, and training, as well as in lower productivity from lost accumulation of work experience. Turnover rates are at least 40 percent higher per year among high school dropouts than among high school graduates (Bernhardt et al., 1997). An increase in dropout rates of 6 to 12 percentage points implies increases in dropout rates of 30 to 60 percent (since the dropout rate of blacks in low-segregation cities is about 20 percent). This in turn implies an increase in dropout rates of 4.5 to 9 percent for the metropolitan area as a whole (if blacks constitute 15 percent of the population) and an increase in turnover rates of 2 to 4 percent for area employers.

Finally, Holzer notes that the result in effects on area crime also are substantial. Freeman (1992) has shown that well over 50 percent of black male dropouts between the ages of 16 and 34 are in the criminal justice system, compared with only 10 percent for black male high school graduates. Thus, an increase in black high school dropout rates due to an increase in segregation will lead to huge increases in crime. Assuming young black males account for approximately 30 to 40 percent of serious crime in less-segregated metropolitan areas, Holzer calculated that the impact of moving from low to high segregation levels will increase serious crime in the metropolitan area by 45 to 60 percent. The impact of moving from segregation levels of the least segregated areas to those of the most segregated areas will increase serious crime by 90 to 120 percent.

Holzer's estimates should be taken as rough approximations of the impact of high compared with low degrees of segregation. As such, they are an overstatement of the impact for most metropolitan areas. And, as he cautions, they may also overestimate somewhat the effect on employers of labor turnover (because employers are likely to pay lower wages to employees who have a higher probablity of turnover) and the effect on crime (since the causality may run both ways: high school dropouts may be more likely to engage in crime, but those who have a propensity to engage in crime may be more likely to drop out of school). Nonetheless, they provide an illustrative estimate of the potential costs, both to blacks and to the metropolitan area as an entity, that are imposed by highly segregated areas compared with what would be the case if these areas had very low levels of segregation.

To what extent are these overall costs in metropolitan areas borne by white suburban residents as well as by black inner-city residents? Although it is difficult to make precise estimates, it is very likely that some significant costs are borne by whites as well as blacks.

For instance, the lower earnings of less-educated black workers brought about by unequal opportunity will reduce white income through the multiplier effect, as blacks purchase fewer goods and services throughout the area. In addition, the lower earnings and productivity of these black workers will generate lower tax revenues from them and higher transfer payments to them, both of which are ultimately borne by middle-class taxpayers of both races. Higher poverty rates among blacks will also generate other costs to the white middle class, such as greater expenditures on law enforcement (discussed below) and health care for these groups.

Lower productivity of black employees in a given set of jobs will almost certainly result in lower profits to their employers. Even if their lower productivity could be fully offset through lower wages, the "surplus" that accrues to employers as a result of their efforts will still be reduced. And, to the extent that the lower productivity of these employees generates higher turnover, this results in higher direct costs to their employers (in the form of recruitment, screening, and training costs) as well as foregone output while their jobs are vacant. When labor markets are tight, the costs to employers of attracting and keeping good employees can be especially high.

Finally, the costs of central-city crime to suburban residents are likely to be substantial. The direct costs of administering the criminal justice system (including the building and staffing of prisons) are currently about 2 percent of gross domestic product nationally, or $150 billion, borne entirely by taxpayers. Although the majority of crime victims are themselves minorities who live in high-crime neighborhoods, some urban crime clearly spills over into neighboring suburban areas; a fear of crime often pervades those areas, above and beyond what actually occurs. Even for those who have effectively escaped the risk of crime by residing in outlying suburbs, the loss of enjoyment of urban amenities may entail some real costs.

DISPARITIES IN FISCAL CAPACITY

In turning from disparities in outcomes among individuals or groups of individuals to disparities among *jurisdictions*, we focus on disparities in *fiscal capacity* among local governments. Tax/service disparities—using the term synonymously with fiscal capacity disparities—are an important part of the metropolitan spatial opportunity structure; they themselves contribute to the disparities in outcomes between central-city and suburban residents and between minority and white households.

Tax/Service Disparities

Local governments in metropolitan areas differ, sometimes widely, in the tax burden they impose on their citizens and in the level of services they provide. These observable variations in tax burden and services may be termed *tax/service differences*.[12] They reflect a variety of causes, including variations in public preferences, in local government efficiency, and in tax capacity and expenditure need. The committee's concern, however, is not with these differences per se, but with tax/service *disparities* (sometimes called *fiscal disparities*), which we define as differences *based on factors outside the control of local officials* in the ability of their governments to provide a reasonable level of services with a reasonable tax burden on their residents (Yinger, 1996:1). In the absence of equalizing aid from higher levels of government, residents in local governments with low tax capacity or higher expenditure needs are faced with a difficult choice: they must either pay a higher percentage of their income in taxes than do wealthier communities in order to obtain equal levels of public services, or, if they tax themselves at a comparable rate, they must accept lower levels of public services.

To the extent that tax/service disparities reflect differences in tax capacity and service need rather than preference, the committee considers them undesirable both in terms of their impact on the spatial opportunity structure of metropolitan areas and in terms of equity.[13] The problems stem from the fact that local services are financed largely out of locally raised revenues. In 1991-1992, 62 percent of all local government general revenue (and 72 percent of all municipal government general revenue) was raised from local government's own sources, with the remainder coming from intergovernmental aid (U.S. Bureau of the Census, 1996c). This means that, to the extent that quality of service is related to amount spent, residents of low-income communities face a difficult dilemma. Unless they live in a community with a substantial business tax base, or unless their community is compensated for its low tax base with disproportionate amounts of intergovernmental aid, they will be faced with paying more out of their income in order to receive similar levels of service or, if they do not wish to take on this extra burden, with receiving inferior levels of service. This has particularly severe effects with respect to services, such as education, that are related to life chances. As a consequence, the opportunity structure for residents of low-income communities is spatially constrained.

The equity problem is also serious. Let us consider two similar households, each with an income of $30,000, one residing in community A with a local tax base of $10,000 per capita and the other in community B with a local tax base of $40,000 per capita. For the sake of illustration, assume both communities impose only a tax on income to raise local revenues. In order to spend $2,000 per capita in public services, community A would have to impose a tax rate of 20 percent on income, and community B would have to impose a tax of only 5 percent. The $30,000 household in the lower-income community would thus face a tax of $6,000, and the $30,000 household in the wealthier community would face a tax of only $1,500. This clearly fails the test of horizontal equity.

Now consider a poor household with an income of $15,000 in community A and a middle-class household with an income of $40,000 in community B. In order to receive the same $2,000 of services per capita, the poor household in community A would have to pay $3,000 in taxes, and the wealthier household in community B would have to pay only $2,000. In short, poor people living in lower-income communities must pay a higher proportion of their income, in this example, a larger absolute amount of income, than wealthier people in more prosperous communities in order to receive the same level of spending on services. Thus, the test of vertical equity is also failed.

The fiscal system in metropolitan areas operates either to reduce the income of residents of low-income communities relative to those of wealthier communities, thus contributing to disparities, or to reduce the level of spending on public services financed out of local revenues, with negative effects on life chances.

It is true that the tax/service disparities described above are moderated to some extent by the capitalization of the relative taxes into house values (Oates, 1969; Hamilton, 1975). Thus, the purchase price of a house in a high-tax/low-service area would be lower than that of a similar house in a low-tax/high-service area. However, capitalization of these fiscal factors into house values are unlikely to fully offset tax/service disparities. In addition, they serve to reduce the wealth of existing owners of homes in central cities, most of whom, as the result of selective out-migration, have low and moderate incomes. As the tax burden of central-city residents increases and public services deteriorate, the value of the homes of existing homeowners declines to reflect these changes, thus bringing about a real decline in the value of their capital assets.

There has been relatively little research on intrametropolitan fiscal disparities, although Ladd and Yinger (1991) have shown that fiscal disparities among large cities are substantial. Empirical studies are fraught with difficulty. Obviously gross differences in own-source revenues and spending reflect differences among communities in preferences and in the efficiency with which services are provided, as well as differences in tax capacity and expenditure need. Furthermore, communities may export taxes to those outside the area, so that own-source revenues may not always come from local residents. In addition, disparities due to tax base and expenditure need may be reduced to some extent through aid from higher levels of government. (For a more extensive discussion of this, see Ladd, 1994a, 1994b). Finally, as Pagano points out (this volume), most disparity studies have not taken into account the increasing reliance of local governments on fees and services and the effect of proliferating residential community associations and their "voluntary" contributions on service receipt and taxpayer burden.

One study calculated estimates of fiscal capacity for a sample of general-purpose local governments in the Chicago metropolitan area for 1987 (Rafuse, 1991). Own-source revenue-raising ability was estimated by calculating how much revenue each local government would raise from each of 10 separate categories of revenues (e.g., property tax, sales tax, fees, and charges) if they were to levy rates at the average level for all governments in the area. Representative expenditure need was estimated by calculating what it would cost each local government to provide a standard (average) set of local public services, given the underlying socioeconomic and demographic composition of the community (and assuming the average level of efficiency for local governments in the area. Both the revenue and the expenditure capacity estimates were indexed to the average for the entire metropolitan area, so that the average overall fiscal capacity value was 100. An overall fiscal capacity index was created by dividing the own-source general revenue index for a local government by its index of representative expenditures.

Using this mechanism, the city of Chicago had an own-source general revenue index of 80 and an index of expenditure need of 111; this yielded an overall index of fiscal capacity of 72 (28 percent below the average for the metropolitan area). However, when Rafuse factored in federal and state grants and added them to own-source revenue, Chicago's index of fiscal capacity rose to 87, still 13 percent below the average for local governments in the metropolitan area. By contrast, Evanston's overall index of fiscal capacity (including federal and state grants) was 117, Lake Forest's was 266, and Winnetka's was 207. Several lower-income suburbs had fiscal capacity indexes considerably lower than Chicago's: Maywood's was 54, North Chicago's was 60, and Burbank's was 68.

Unfortunately, similar data are not available for a broad range of metropolitan areas. However, a similar analysis was performed for all municipal governments with populations over 2,500 in the state of Wisconsin for 1987-1991 (Green and Reschovsky, 1994). Using a slightly different methodology, Green and Reschovsky construct a need-expenditure gap similar to Rafuse's fiscal capacity index. The need-capacity gap for the "average" city was set at 0. Milwaukee had a gap between needed expenditures and revenue-raising capacity of $111 per capita after taking into account intergovernmental aid. Some other older suburbs also had very high gaps. These included Cudahy ($148), South Milwaukee ($143), and West Allis ($67). By contrast, many of Milwaukee's suburbs had negative need-capacity gaps: Brookfield (–$249), Glendale (–$198), Menomonee Falls (–$114), Whitefish Bay (–$102), and Wauwatosa (–$47).

Causes of Tax/Service Disparities

Why is there variation among citizens in a metropolitan area with respect to the local tax burden they face and the level and quality of local public services they receive? The first and most obvious reason is because, in virtually all metropolitan areas in the United States, there are many separate local governments, each with its own authority (albeit constrained authority) to make taxing and spending decisions and each highly dependent on its own local tax base for its revenues. As a consequence, residents in different local jurisdictions will naturally face variations in the tax rates they pay and in the level and type of services they receive.

As has been noted, these variations occur for a variety of reasons, including differences in preferences and in local government efficiency as well as differences in fiscal capacity. However, it is the differences in fiscal capacity with which we are here concerned. Fiscal capacity differences can reflect differences in both revenue-raising capacity and in expenditure needs.

Differences in the revenue-raising capacity of local governments (defined as the amount of revenue each local government could raise from various tax bases—the major ones are property, sales, and earnings—if it imposed a standard tax burden on its residents) arise for two reasons, according to Ladd (1994a:238); there are "differences in the average per capita income of residents and differences in the ability of cities to export tax burdens to nonresidents. For example, at the standard tax burden a city with richer residents can raise more revenue per resident from its residents than can a city with poorer residents. And a city with a large proportion of its property tax base in the form of business property, with a large proportion of its retail sales to nonresident commuters or tourists, or with a large proportion of earnings generated in the city accruing to nonresident commuters, can substantially increase its revenues by exporting tax burdens to nonresidents."

Differences in the expenditure needs of local governments (defined as the amount of money local governments must spend in order to achieve a standardized package of public services) reflect differences in the costs they face of providing public services. Costs may vary because of differences in input costs, such as the market-determined costs of attracting workers, and because of environmental factors (Ladd and Yinger, 1991). Environmental factors include both the composition of the population (a local government with a higher proportion of school-age children in the population will have greater expenditure need for education than will one with a lower proportion) and because of the difficulty in providing services (e.g., a local government with social and economic conditions that breed crime will have to spend more on police protection than will a typical upper-middle-class suburban community).

Using regression analysis to determine the impact of various environmental conditions on the cost of providing average levels of public service, Ladd reports that (1994a:239) "poverty, for example, has a big impact on the costs of providing public safety. A city with a poverty rate 1 percentage point higher than that of another city will have police costs that are 5.5 percent higher on average. Furthermore, a city with a poverty rate one standard deviation above the 1982 mean must pay 36.4 percent more for police services than a city with average poverty. The size of a city, as measured by its population, and the amount of its economic activity, as measured by private employment per capita, also increase the costs of public services."

It is clear that, given their population characteristics, central cities are likely to have both low standardized revenue-raising capacity and high expenditure needs. Suburbs may vary, with poorer, inner-core suburbs increasingly resembling central cities with respect to relative fiscal disparities or even being worse off, and with higher-income suburbs at the top end.

The actual fiscal condition of a city reflects not only its standardized revenue-raising capacity and expenditure needs, but the actual set of fiscal institutions it operates under (Ladd and Yinger, 1991). Local governments are constrained by their state with respect to the kinds of taxes they are actually permitted to levy and the rate at which they can levy them (see Pagano, this volume:Table 5, for variations among states in the extent to which they permit local governments to levy income and sales taxes); they may also be constrained by state limitations on the total amount of taxes they can raise or expenditures they can make. As Pagano notes, a city that is prohibited access to an earnings or income tax that can be imposed on nonresident employees who work in the city will find itself in a poorer revenue-generating position than one that is permitted to do so.

State governments also set forth the service responsibilities for local governments. Local governments with a broader range of service responsibilities will have greater expenditure needs than those with a narrower range of responsibility. Although most large city governments do not have responsibility for financing welfare, there are some, such as New York City, that do. The activity of overlying units of local government also affects the actual fiscal condition of a specific local government: the greater the taxes levied by overlying units of government, the less revenue-raising capability exists for the local government. Finally, actual fiscal condition is also affected by the amount of state and federal aid that a local government receives, since such aid makes up, to some extent, for the gap between local revenue-raising capacity and expenditure need.

Ladd and Yinger found substantial variations in actual fiscal health among large cities across metropolitan areas. Some of these variations reflect differences that are likely to be greater *among* metropolitan areas than *within* metropolitan areas, which is our concern. Thus, for example, differences facing local governments in the cost of labor are likely to be smaller within a metropolitan area, and state fiscal rules conditioning local government behavior (taxes allowed, tax and expenditure limits) and defining service responsibilities are likely to vary much less among jurisdictions within a metropolitan area.

Thus, differences in state-imposed fiscal rules may explain the extent of fiscal disparities among local governments across metropolitan areas, particularly the relative fiscal health of cities. Pagano notes (this volume) that only 11 states permit some of their local governments to levy an income tax on nonresidents or a payroll tax on employees, regardless of residence. In most cases, the ability to levy such taxes is severely limited to the very largest municipal governments, although Ohio and Pennsylvania permit large numbers of municipalities access to these taxes.[14]

NOTES

[1] Data from the Current Population Survey presented in Ihlanfeldt (this volume) suggest that the city-suburban disparity in family income continued to rise between 1989 and 1995.

[2] The index is calculated from three ratios of central-city to suburban outcomes: per capita income, employment rate for men between 16 and 64, and the proportion of persons 25 or older who have at least a high school diploma. In order that each of the three measures is weighted equally, they are each standardized to a scale of 0-100, and the standardized ratios are then averaged to create an overall index of disparity. The higher the number, the better off the central city relative to its suburban counterparts. In order to give equal weight to each of the three ratios, they were each standardized to a scale of 0-100 before being averaged. The minimum value was assigned as zero and the maximum value 100. The ratios in between are assigned values between 0 and 100 according to the following formula: $y = (x - x_{min}) / (x_{max} - x_{min})$.

[3] The figures here compare all whites and all blacks, since separate non-Hispanic white estimates were not available for 1980.

[4] A "bad neighborhood" is defined as a neighborhood in which more than 40 percent of teenagers are high school dropouts, more than 40 percent of families are headed by single females, and less than 10 percent of employed persons hold professional or managerial jobs.

[5] Hanushek (1996:59) does not argue that schools or school inputs do not matter. He argues, instead, that, although commonly measured input characteristics, such as class size and teacher education and experience, do not make a difference, there are other unmeasured characteristics of schools and teachers that do.

[6] In particular, they were able to utilize a "value added" approach to track changes in educational performance over time for individual students, to isolate instructional spending from total educational spending, and to utilize measures of actual class size rather than school or district averages of teacher-pupil ratios.

[7] In metropolitan areas in which there is more than one central city, they included the largest central city, but included smaller central cities only if their population was over 100,000.

[8] Blair et al. (1996) examine the effect of elasticity on both city and metropolitan-area growth in population, employment, per capita income, and poverty in 117 metropolitan areas between 1980 and 1990. They found that elasticity is related significantly to growth in all of the variables for central cities (positively for the first three and negatively for poverty). It is significantly related to growth in population and employment, but not for per capita income or poverty for metropolitan areas. However, the only variable controlled for in the analysis was the state change (net of the

metropolitan area) in each of the dependent variables examined. These findings do not address the question of the impact of elasticity on central-city/suburban disparities.

9 The finding that more fragmented systems of government lead to lower per capita spending does not *necessarily* mean they are more efficient, since it is virtually impossible in these studies to separate out expenditure differences that reflect efficiency from those that reflect differences in the quantity or quality of services provided. Indeed, we would expect the demand for services to vary with different sizes of government over which demand is aggregated and with different spillover effects associated with different sizes of government.

10 The most commonly used operational measures is the number of local governments in a metropolitan area or number of local governments per capita. But it is not clear that this is a valid measure of the concept. Should all local governments be counted in fragmentation research? To the extent the research is concerned with coordination difficulties, then perhaps the most commonly used measures are reasonable: the greater the number of local governments (or local governments per capita), the greater the difficulties in arranging coordinated activity across the area. But, if the concern is the "sorting" consequences of fragmentation, as discussed above, perhaps only those local governments that have an important effect on the sorting process, i.e., those with local land use powers (primarily general-purpose units of local government rather than special districts) should be counted. However, it might well be argued that local school districts, although a special district and without land use powers, play such a significant role in the sorting process that they should be included as well.

11 Lewis' measure of fragmentation differs dramatically from previously utilized measures. He constructs a fragmentation index that is equal to TE(1-SSP), in which TE is total expenditures per capita in the metropolitan area and SSP is the sum of the squared percentages of total expenditures accounted for by each local government. The greater the number of governments, each with a lower share of total government expenditure, the greater will be the fragmentation index.

12 Bahl (1994:297) reports on tax/service differences in 35 metropolitan areas between central cities and suburbs in the aggregate. On average in these 35 areas, central cities spent $1.51 per capita for every $1.00 per capita spent by the area's suburbs. (The difference was due to the much higher level of spending by cities on noneducational expenditures; suburban governments spent more per capita on education than did cities.) However, taxes as a percentage of family income (tax burden) were an average of 44 percent higher in the central cities, and Bahl notes (1994:297) that the tax burden disparity is increasing over time.

13 Oakland (1994:7-8) argues, however, that fiscal disparities are not necessarily undesirable and that efforts to reduce or eliminate them could have perverse efficiency consequences.

14 Pagano observes (this volume) that, on the basis of the Ladd and Yinger measures, the cities with the greatest actual revenue-raising capacity are in Ohio, which permits the most progressive earnings taxes on commuters; Cleveland's revenue-raising capacity was 41 percent higher than the average U.S. city and Dayton's 59 percent higher, both substantially above their standardized revenue-raising capacity.

4

Strategies for Reducing Disparities

This chapter reviews a number of strategies to address the unequal spatial opportunity structure of metropolitan areas and the disparities that result, at least in part, from it. It sets forth a range of options that have been suggested and, in many cases, tried in at least a few areas. It discusses the rationale for the strategies and relevant arguments on both sides of the issue. If the strategy has been put into effect, we present available evidence on its effects.

CHANGING THE SPATIAL DISTRIBUTION OF POPULATION

Since large numbers of municipal governments have already been established in most U.S. metropolitan areas, policy options for reducing the sorting process that facilitates stratification by race and income have focused primarily on land use controls. One set of strategies seeks to break down exclusionary zoning practices that help to increase the cost of housing beyond the means of low- and moderate-income households. Another set of strategies is inclusionary, seeking to require local governments or developers to include housing for low- and moderate-income households in the community. Some approaches contain elements of both strategies.

Ending Exclusionary Practices

Ending exclusionary practices inevitably means placing limits on local government's control of decision making about land use. Existing local government control over land use could be eliminated, reduced, or circumscribed in a variety of ways. These include statewide control of local land use decisions and statewide review of local land use decisions to determine their consistency with state guidelines; metropolitan-area-wide control of land use decisions within metropolitan-area boundaries or metropolitan review of local land use decisions; and state regulation of local land use, in particular the prohibition of specific exclusionary zoning practices. Another possibility would give developers the right to sue local jurisdictions that restrict their ability to provide low- and moderate-income housing, as in the Massachusetts Anti-Snob Zoning Law.

Zoning as a mechanism supports the system of small and fragmented local government that facilitates income segregation by jurisdiction (Mills and Oates, 1975). To the extent that such a system is associated with allocative efficiency by permitting the various local governments to respond to the relatively homogeneous preferences of their residents, as Tiebout (1956) and his followers argue, then reducing exclusionary zoning practices will adversely affect efficiency by promoting heterogeneity of preferences among the citizenry. The possibility of a trade-off between achieving optimal levels of allocative efficiency and reducing inequality of opportunity in metropolitan areas must be acknowledged.

State Land Use Plans

Several states—Oregon, Florida, New Jersey, California, and Vermont, among others—have adopted state land use planning laws. Oregon's structure is probably the most elaborate and strongest in terms of the limits it places on traditional local government control of land use. The state has established 19 statewide goals and guidelines, 2 of which are particularly relevant. Goal 10 requires local government plans to provide for land uses that make housing available that meets the needs of households at all income levels. Goal 14 requires all urban areas in the state to designate urban growth boundaries outside of which land cannot be converted to urban use. In effect, all urban growth is to occur within these areas.

Local government plans, which are reviewed by the state land use authority, must conform to these goals. One study found that the state authority does indeed carefully review the plans and require revisions (Knapp, 1990). Indeed, Knapp notes that, of the 53 urban jurisdictions with populations over 5,000, only one plan satisfied the requirements for goals 10 and 14 on its first review. He concludes that Oregon is exercising a consistent policy favoring high-density development and requiring local governments to zone for their fair share of multiple-family and high-density housing and that, furthermore, this policy is not one that local governments would have adopted on their own.

As to the question of whether these developments have actually reduced the cost of housing and opened up the suburbs to low- and moderate-income households, Knapp observed in 1990 that there had been little research on this question. He contended that, although there had been a multifamily housing boom, "there is no evidence that the newly constructed housing is more affordable to the poor" (1990:43).

Two other researchers note the post-1990 rapid rise in housing prices in the Portland area (Abbott, 1997:34-35; Fischel, 1997). This suggests the possibility that the impetus for lower housing costs brought about through higher-density development may have been swamped by the rising cost of land caused by the pressures of recent rapid population growth on the restricted supply of land within the urban growth boundary. Additional research is clearly needed on the Portland experience.

Metropolitan Land Use Plans

Fischel (this volume) argues that lodging land use decisions at the metropolitan level would include those who would otherwise be excluded, and, as a consequence, political pressures would reduce the incidence of exclusionary zoning. He cites research suggesting that big cities tend to be less exclusionary in their zoning than do their suburbs.

Downs (1997) argues that the most logical way of reducing fragmented local government control over land use decisions is to adopt a single metropolitan-area-wide government. However, Downs then succinctly observes, "that tactic has absolutely no political support from either suburban or city residents or officials; hence it will never happen in most metropolitan areas" (1997:47).

A close approximation to metropolitan land use control, at least in its structural form, exists in the Minneapolis-St. Paul region. The Twin Cities Metropolitan Council, under state legislative authorization, established a Development Framework Plan for the region in 1976. All the region's municipalities and townships are required to submit their own comprehensive plans to the metropolitan council for approval. If the local plan is inconsistent with the growth projections of the Development Framework Plan, the council can hold up the plan's approval. Unlike the Oregon state land use plan, there is no specific provision for low- and moderate-income housing required of local governments by the Development Framework Plan. Also unlike the Oregon experience, the process appears to have had very limited impact. Orfield observes (1997:123): "the Met Council has narrowly construed its authority. Under a system of self-imposed restraint, the council will require a plan amendment only when the local comprehensive plan imposes a burden on a metropolitan system that 'threatens its capacity'—a fairly cataclysmic event."

Mills and Lubuele (1997) caution that there are inevitable limits on the ability to move low-income households to the suburbs by ending exclusionary practices. They note that constant-quality housing prices are lower in cities than in suburbs and that households seeking low-cost housing will inevitably find central-city housing cheaper (1997:754): "Poor-quality housing can be built in some suburbs, but old housing cannot, and higher-quality schools and lower crime rates keep land values high in suburbs. The result is that the cheapest housing in the metropolitan area is often found in inner-city slums, even if land use controls impose almost no limits on the supply of low-income housing in the suburbs."

Inclusionary Zoning

Inclusionary zoning specifically includes or requires a range of housing types and densities so that housing opportunities are available to low- and moderate-income households. Calavita and colleagues (1997:110) use the broader term "inclusionary housing" to refer to "a wide variety of techniques that link construction of low- and moderate-income housing to construction of housing for the marketplace, generally by including lower-income units in an otherwise market-driven development. The principal objective . . . is not only to increase the supply of affordable housing, but to do so in a manner that fosters greater economic and racial residential integration."

Inclusionary zoning can involve either state-imposed "fair-share" requirements on local communities (as in Oregon, New Jersey, and California) or publicly imposed requirements that developers, in return for gaining permission for housing development, will agree to provide a share of the units for low- and moderate-income households. In California and New Jersey (but not Oregon) these fair-share requirements are backed up by incentives to developers for the construction of low-income housing. Such incentives include density increases, land write-downs, impact fee waivers, and various other regulatory concessions. In Montgomery County, Maryland, outside Washington, D.C., new subdivisions of more than 50 units are required to include at least 15 percent of housing units at a price suitable for moderate-income families, with the county public housing agency purchasing up to one-third of these units. This program has created more than 9,000 units of moderate- and low-income housing over the past 25 years (Kleit, 1997).

Like Oregon, California has a state statute requiring localities to "make adequate provision for the existing and projected needs of all segments of the community" (Calavita et al., 1997), but, unlike Oregon, the state lacks power to mandate changes in local government plans. Nor does the state have the ability to require local governments to actually construct affordable housing. As Calavita et al. observe (1997:117-118): "Among the 527 cities and counties in the state required to adopt housing elements, the compliance rate at the end of 1992 was only 19 percent. Starting in 1993, HCD [the Department of Housing and Community Development] redoubled its efforts, raising the compliance level to 58 percent by December 31, 1995. . . . It is questionable, however, whether this increase represents a corresponding increase in housing opportunities or is instead little more than the creation of paper documents with little significance for implementation."

In contrast, New Jersey's inclusionary zoning is court imposed. In its 1975 Mt. Laurel decision, the state supreme court ruled that local governments were using a state police power, zoning, to exclude low- and moderate-income households in violation of the state constitution. The original remedy for exclusion was the creation of an obligation for communities to allow "least-cost" housing to be developed. However, as Fischel notes (this volume), newly developed least-cost housing still turned out to be too expensive for low- and moderate-income households. As a consequence, the court imposed a requirement that suburbs must accept a minimum amount of newly constructed low-income housing for any new market-rate housing constructed. The low-income housing is to be paid for by charging developers of the market-rate housing for rezonings.

Fischel (this volume) found little evidence that the inclusionary zoning process brought about by the Mt. Laurel decision has changed the general pattern of suburban housing development. Calavita et al. (1997:130-131) note that, although New Jersey developers were willing to build some units of low- and moderate-income housing as a cost of doing business during the housing boom in the 1980s (particularly as a part of large-scale town house and condominium developments), they have become much less willing to do so during the 1990s. They point to the increasing use of a provision in the law that permits developers to make per-unit cash payments to the municipality in lieu of constructing low- or moderate-income housing; the municipality, generally a suburban jurisdiction, is then permitted to give the cash contribution to another jurisdiction, usually a city, for the construction of affordable housing units that would be credited to the suburban municipality's fair-share account. Calavita et al. contend that the Mt. Laurel decision has had some impact at increasing low- and moderate-income housing units in the state, and they remain supportive of the inclusionary housing approach. However, they acknowledge the limits of the accomplishments as a means of reducing racial segregation, observing that "few projects have substantial minority—particularly African-American—populations and that the minority population is nominal or even nonexistent in many" (1997:129). As evidence they cite a study that sampled new suburban inclusionary housing developments occupied between 1988 and 1996 and found that only 12 percent of the occupants had previously resided in cities, and of these, less than 25 percent were black (Wish and Eisdorfer, 1996).

In the Minneapolis-St. Paul area, the state's Livable Communities Act, enacted in 1995, has created what is in effect a voluntary approach to inclusionary housing. Through a fund administered by the Twin Cities Metropolitan Council, resources to support affordable housing projects (as well as for tax base revitalization and economic and community development) are made available to communities that voluntarily agree to participate in the Housing Incentive Program created by the act. The program requires housing financed under its provisions to include housing at all income levels. In the first year of the program, eight grants totaling $1 million were given for affordable housing projects in seven communities (Metropolitan Council of the Twin Cities, 1997).

Orfield, however, argues (1997) that the Livable Communities Act was a weak compromise that essentially reaffirmed powers the Metropolitan Council already had and, since it was voluntary, would result in little substantive accomplishment. Calling its passage "symbolic," he nonetheless called it "a platform on which a stronger and more enforceable act could be built" (p. 152).

Efforts to Limit or Direct Growth

Another approach is aimed at redirecting growth toward denser, more developed urban and suburban areas. Although containing sprawl is the explicitly stated objective, achieving higher densities should (other things being equal) reduce the land component of housing prices and reduce the price of housing in the suburbs, but higher-density housing could increase construction costs for housing above two or three stories.

Efforts in Portland and Minneapolis-St. Paul have already been discussed. Another initiative is Maryland's Smart Growth Program, designed to "halt suburban sprawl and address its impacts" (Maryland Office of Planning, 1997). The legislation prohibits the provision of state funds for highways, sewer and water construction, and housing and economic development assistance to growth-related projects or developments not located within a "priority funding area," which is an area designated for growth and development. The initial legislation designated the city of Baltimore and suburbs within the Baltimore and Washington beltways (essentially inner and middle-core suburbs) as priority funding areas as well as other major urban areas in the state.

Changes in economic incentives may serve to redirect growth into more compact development as well. It has been argued that requiring automobile users to pay the full, unsubsidized cost of automobile use through higher gasoline taxes will make low-density development on the metropolitan fringe less likely. Similarly, some have argued that, in areas where new suburban developments do not pay the full marginal cost of infrastructure development, they should be required to do so.

Restoring Property Rights and
Requiring Suburbs to Pay the Cost of Exclusion

The restoration of the development rights of owners of undeveloped land and land ripe for development would accomplish the same objective as metropolitan government with respect to reducing the economic stratification of suburban communities and opening up the suburbs to the poor, according to Fischel (this volume). He reasons that owners of such land "are representatives of people not resident in the community who would constitute net additions to the population. . . . Suburban zoning laws regulate the market in part because the market would give existing suburbs more poor people than current residents would like. The owner of undeveloped land, however, does not care whether the high bidder for her 10-acre tract proposes to put 2 mansions or 40 bungalows. In most places, the developer of the higher-intensity use, which will usually serve lower-income people, can outbid others."

Fischel would not simply eliminate land use controls and give landowners and developers the unlimited right to develop what they wanted. Instead, he would give them the right to develop at normal suburban densities, "determined by comparisons to existing well-planned and socially diverse developments at comparable locations within the metropolitan area" (this volume). Communities would be able to purchase lower density for any tract by paying the difference between the land's value at the normal density and its value at the community's desired lower density. Fischel envisions beneficial results: "the existing residents can thus raise the suburban drawbridge if they are collectively willing to pay for it, and I do not doubt that some would. But I also have no doubt that the impassioned pleas by most neighbors who oppose development would be greatly muted if, to get their desires, they would have to pay more in property taxes. Requiring the local governments that want to preserve open space to buy that space (or the development rights) would make existing voters pay attention to the opportunity cost of exclusion and, for the most part, deter inefficient and inequitable low-density zoning."

Subsidies or Cost Reduction

The exclusionary effects of local land use regulation work by increasing the cost of housing beyond the means of low- and moderate-income households. Rather than focusing on the land use regulations themselves, one possible policy option is to attempt to lower the cost of suburban housing through other means or to increase the ability of low- and moderate-income households to pay for such housing through subsidies. Lowering housing costs could be achieved through devices such as improvements in building technology or lowering standards currently incorporated in building and housing codes. Increasing the effective demand of low- and moderate-income households to pay for housing could be achieved through substantially expanding the amount of federal housing subsidies such as Section 8 certificates, or by expanding them into an entitlement program. This approach is discussed in more detail in the section below on household mobility strategies.

REDUCING OUTCOME DISPARITIES

Five major categories of policy alternatives are directed toward reducing unequal opportunity and disparities in outcomes between minorities and whites and city and suburban residents within metropolitan areas:[1]

1. Place-based initiatives, which attempt to bring new resources and opportunities to distressed areas.
2. Worker mobility strategies, which attempt to link residents in cities to jobs in the suburbs, without changing either job or residential locations.
3. Household mobility strategies, which attempt to open up housing opportunities for residents of distressed areas in other areas where housing conditions, employment, and other opportunities are presumably better.
4. Human capital strategies, which attempt to improve the labor market skills of minorities and poor people.
5. Antidiscrimination strategies directed at reducing discrimination in labor markets.

Place-Based Initiatives

Place-based strategies attempt to address unequal opportunity through economic and community development strategies designed to increase employment opportunities in distressed areas and improve them as residential and commercial environments. Targeted approaches aimed at specific geographic sections of a country's regions have a long history in many European countries and are not unknown in the United States (the programs of the Appalachian Regional Commission are the best known). Place-based economic development programs targeted at much smaller, more discrete areas on the sub-city level are more recent, originating with the British enterprise zones in the early 1980s.

Enterprise zones essentially designate a small distressed area as a zone in which various incentives are made available for firms that locate there. Many states have adopted variations of enterprise zone programs; the precise incentives and structure of such programs vary enormously. A federal empowerment and enterprise zone program, embodying some of the original enterprise zone concepts but also differing in important ways, was passed in 1994.

The federal program retains several components of traditional enterprise zone programs, in particular the tax credit for employers in the zone who hire zone residents, but it departs from tradition significantly by including large sums to address a variety of community social issues and issues related to job readiness ($100 million for each empowerment zone and $3 million for each enterprise zone). It thus combines a prior generation of poverty-directed, place-based activities, such as the Model Cities program, with the employer-directed incentives of enterprise zone programs.

The research suggests that enterprise zone programs have been successful in bringing about physical development in distressed areas. However, there is little evidence that they have resulted in additional employment for area residents. Ihlanfeldt (this volume) reviewed the evidence that the number of jobs increases in enterprise zones and found it mixed. However, even if jobs do increase, it appears doubtful that the result will be a net increase in jobs or that the area's residents will be the beneficiaries. After reviewing the literature, Ladd (1994c:208) concluded, "Pure place strategies of the type represented by the English enterprise zone program are not an effective approach to pockets of urban distress. The main effect of the tax and regulatory relief provisions is simply to relocate firms to the zones from nearby locations." Vidal (1995:188) comes to the same conclusion with respect to state enterprise zones: "the information available about the design of state enterprise programs and about performance to date indicates that . . . these programs do not appear to represent a promising strategy for addressing the employment problems of poor inner-city neighborhoods."

Ihlanfeldt (this volume) contends that the fact that jobs are simply relocated from one area to another may not be a bad thing on fairness grounds if they are relocated from suburbs to central city. But this argument is not persuasive if the jobs are simply relocated from other nearby areas of the city, if area residents do not capture the jobs in any case, or, if they do so, but only at the expense of equally poor residents in nearby distressed areas.

More broadly, research by Galster (1997:62-63) casts doubt on the efficacy of place-based initiatives in general as a means of improving the economic condition of central-city residents. On the basis of results from his econometric model, he concludes that "the number of jobs located in the central city . . . did not have a statistically significant path directly to local labor market supply. . . . [T]he empirical estimates here suggest that even if a policy were instantaneously to create 10,000 . . . additional jobs in the typical sample central city, per capita incomes of city residents would rise by only $0.49. . . . The current cross-sectional evidence suggests that merely having more jobs located in the central city (relative to the working-age population) is insufficient to generate significantly more employment for residents."

The proximity of jobs to the local neighborhood (within a two-mile radius) also appears to have a very small effect on neighborhood employment rates in city neighborhoods, casting further doubt on the efficacy of small-area development strategies as a means of employing local residents (Immergluck, 1998). However, if the jobs are of similar occupational categories and skill levels as those of neighborhood residents, the effects are larger.

Another set of place-based strategies advocates building from within rather than attempting to attract jobs to distressed areas through incentives. Community development corporations and community development financial institutions are two such approaches. Community development corporations (called CDCs) are, according to Vidal (1995:204), "nonprofit, community-based organizations whose mission is to make the low- and moderate-income communities in which they work better places to live." Community development financial institutions, Vidal observes (1995: 188-89), "have their genesis in the perception that certain types of communities and credit needs are not adequately served by mainstream financial institutions. Hence, despite their diversity, they have in common a community development mission, a focus on servicing low-income communities or otherwise disadvantaged persons or distressed areas, and direct involvement in lending activities, often accompanied by other services." Peirce (1993:25;303) makes the case for such community-based efforts:

> From Washington's Anacostia to Newark's Central Ward to Chicago's South Side to Miami's Liberty City, CDCs have been the fulcrum of amazing recovery stories. . . . more than 2000 CDCs are operating today across the country. In the last several years, they have built or refurbished 320,000 homes and apartments for low- and moderate-income households and have developed 17.4 million square feet of commercial and industrial space. Through an array of programs for business development and entrepreneurship, they also claim credit for the creation of some 90,000 permanent jobs. . . . Pessimists typically put down promising CDCs and neighborhood revitalization efforts as isolated achievements of charismatic individuals, unlikely to be replicated or spread. But the point is not to replicate precisely; it is to transfer the core ideas and some of the skills of human and economic revitalization under the toughest of circumstances.

Ihlanfeldt (this volume) reviewed the assessment of community development corporations and community development financial institutions by two social scientists, Vidal and Harrison, which, like the more prolific writings of community activists and advocates, is favorable, if more balanced. However, he notes that the evidence reviewed and provided by Vidal and by Harrison and his colleagues is entirely anecdotal and that "there is no statistical evidence on the effectiveness of CDCs as job generators."

Finally, it is possible to devise place-based strategies that target the residents of such places as poor inner-city neighborhoods for assistance, rather than, or in addition to, the jobs or employers that are located there. Thus, Lehman (1994) suggests targeting wage subsidies on the residents of low-income areas, regardless of where they work, a proposal that was originally considered as part of the federal empowerment zone legislation but ultimately rejected. The empowerment zone program does provide, however, for wage subsidies and other services for zone residents who also work within the zone. Another possibility is to target public service employment jobs on low-income neighborhoods and their residents.

Worker Mobility Strategies

Mobility strategies involve linking residents in distressed parts of the metropolitan area such as central cities to opportunities in the suburbs through improved transportation or through improved job information networks. Reverse commuting programs have been tried in many metropolitan areas, but, as Ihlanfeldt notes (this volume), there has been little systematic effort to evaluate their effectiveness. One study, which interviewed the staff members of 20 programs in 15 cities, concluded that there was little evidence that providing transportation had an impact on inner-city unemployment (Drachman Institute, 1992).

Bridges to Work, a demonstration program with a carefully constructed evaluation component by Public/Private Ventures, promises to provide better evidence on the effectiveness of reverse commuting strategies on worker mobility. Funded jointly by the federal government and a variety of philanthropic organizations, it is a four-year project providing reverse commuting services to central-city poor workers in five large metropolitan areas. The project, which will end in December 2000, includes both treatment and control samples, the latter consisting of poor central-city residents who will continue to receive their communities' usual employment-related services but not reverse commuting. Ihlanfeldt (this volume) observes that "this research promises to provide the first reliable evidence on the effectiveness of transportation programs as an anti-poverty strategy."

Improving job information networks and linking socially isolated residents of poor neighborhoods more effectively to them is another means of linking workers to jobs. Ihlanfeldt notes that computerized job opportunity networks are a frequent recommendation, but that "programs that are specifically designed to provide information on suburban jobs to central-city workers are rare and little is known regarding their effectiveness." Another approach, community-based job development, is designed to recreate the various components of informal job networks, including information on job availability, as well as counseling, job readiness, training, and contacts with employers.

Some critics of mobility strategies suggest that they are unlikely to succeed because physical access is only part of the problem; suburban employers will continue to discriminate against central-city residents, particularly black central-city residents, either through racism or through a belief that a central-city address is a proxy for poor education and work readiness. In addition, as Downs notes (1994), a worker mobility strategy, even if successful, would not break up segregated neighborhoods of concentrated poverty in inner cities or the adverse consequences that result from them.

Household Mobility Strategies

Household mobility strategies envision opening up residential opportunities in the suburbs, particularly middle-income suburbs, to poor and minority groups. The expected results would be moving these groups closer to job opportunities, thereby mitigating the spatial mismatch problem; reducing the adverse consequences of residing in areas of high poverty (assuming they are not replicated in the suburbs); and breaking the link between low-income and poor public services as low-income households move to jurisdictions with higher tax capacities.

One set of strategies, described above, involves breaking down existing regulatory barriers and exclusionary zoning devices that currently inhibit low-income households from moving to predominantly middle-class suburbs by increasing the price of housing in these areas. Another set of strategies involves providing housing subsidies to low- and moderate-income households so that they can afford the higher cost of suburban housing. Such strategies might include scattered-site subsidized housing production throughout the metropolitan area or metropolitan-area-wide housing vouchers for low- and moderate-income households that would give them a housing subsidy wherever they found a suitable unit within the area.

An existing federal program, Section 8 certificates, has, since 1989, permitted recipients to search for housing eligible for Section 8 assistance throughout the metropolitan area. However, the potential impact of the program has been muted due to the lack of effective counseling for Section 8 recipients; a disinclination on the part of city public housing agencies who administer the program to lose the federal administrative payment that would result if their client found a house in the suburbs; and, in some cases, fair-market rental ceilings that effectively limit the choice of households searching for Section 8 housing in many suburbs. Prospective tenants also have difficulty finding units in the suburbs as a result of housing discrimination against minorities. An effective program might require metropolitan administration of federal housing programs or, at a minimum, more effective metropolitan coordination.

Such a strategy builds on the successes of the Gautreaux program, discussed in Chapter 3, but also suggests that counseling assistance as well as housing subsidies will be required. Although the results of the Gautreaux program appear promising (see Rosenbaum, 1995), studies in several other locales (Cincinnati, Hartford, Dallas, and Memphis) that are reviewed by Peterson and Williams (1995) appear somewhat more mixed; additional studies in other locales are under way but have not yet been completed.

Other complementary strategies aim at eliminating illegal discrimination in housing markets through more vigorous enforcement of existing laws and random audit-based testing in every metropolitan area (see below). Household mobility strategies do not necessarily imply either stable racially or economically integrated neighborhoods, although they do imply racially and economically mixed jurisdictions. Ihlanfeldt (this volume) discusses the literature on the extent of racially integrated neighborhoods and various policies to achieve them, including the debate over whether integration should be managed—and, if so, how—to foster racially integrated neighborhoods.

Critics of the household mobility approach argue that, if successful, it will further empty out city neighborhoods, exacerbating the problems of concentrated poverty. This will particularly be the case if the low- and moderate-income families who move out are self-selected on the basis of their motivation and are more likely to succeed. Household mobility strategies have political problems as well. At the receiving end, one such effort, the Moving to Opportunity program in Baltimore County, was brought to a halt because of the protests of suburban residents who objected to low-income black households moving into their area. At the sending end, city politicians often do not see losing their constituents to the suburbs as a mark of success; black elected politicians in particular may fear the loss of political power and influence this implies.

In addition, the cost of a full-blown household mobility effort in terms of federal housing assistance could be prohibitive given federal budget fiscal constraints, and the politics of bringing a program such as Gautreaux to scale make it unlikely (Hughes, 1995:285): "simply consider that for African Americans to be represented in the Chicago CMSA suburbs in proportion to their presence in the metropolitan area (which is 27 percent black as a whole), the size of the suburban black population would have to quadruple, from 250,000 (in 1990) to 1 million. Likewise, for poor people to be represented in the Chicago CMSA suburbs in proportion to their presence in the metropolitan area (which is 11 percent poor as a whole), the size of the suburban poor population would have to increase by more than 300,000, from 190,000 (in 1990) to 500,000." Downs argues, to the contrary, that the scale necessary is not implausible (1994:110):

> A simple quantitative analysis of conditions in the Chicago and Atlanta metropolitan areas shows that greater use of household mobility would be feasible. . . . [Assume] that inner-city poverty areas in the two cities contained 15 percent of their 1980 population. . . . If only a small percentage of new housing built during the 1980s in the suburbs of these cities had consisted of subsidized units occupied by inner-city households, the out-movement would have made a notable dent in reducing inner-city populations. In the greater Chicago area, if 5 percent of the suburban housing added from 1980 to 1990 had been subsidized and occupied by inner-city residents, 7.5 percent of Chicago inner-city households could have moved out of the inner-city. In the Atlanta metropolitan area, if 5 percent of added suburban housing had been similarly subsidized and occupied by inner-city residents, 82 percent of these people would have moved to the suburbs. This impact is much greater because Atlanta has a small population compared with its suburbs, and rapid suburban growth added a lot of new housing from 1980 to 1990.

Human Capital Strategies

There are a vast range of potential strategies that might be addressed to improve the human capital of poor and less-skilled people as a means of reducing disparities in outcomes. Taken broadly, these include policies related to early childhood development and preschool education, elementary and secondary education, higher education, job training and school-to-work programs, public health and nutrition, and others. Since the committee's prime concern is with metropolitan governance and its impact on disparities, we have focused attention on human capital policies related to an individual's location in the metropolitan area and, in particular, education.

As discussed, the quality of education and the skills one derives from it are directly related to where one lives in a metropolitan area. Low-income areas and areas of concentrated poverty have, on average, poor-quality schools for a variety of reasons: if the schools are located in low-income school districts, resources are likely to be low relative to need; better-trained and higher-quality teachers are likely to choose to teach in "more pleasant" middle-income districts; students in low-income schools are likely to be attending classes with peers whose education deficits are as large as theirs, so that the potential for learning from peers is reduced.

One approach to this problem is to attempt to improve the quality of existing schools through school-based reforms, efforts to attract better teachers into low-income schools, reducing student-teacher ratios, and reorganizing school management systems (site-based management, decentralization, recentralization). A variety of approaches has been suggested, including "accelerated schools" by Henry Levin, "essential schools" by Ted Sizer, "success for all" by Robert Slavin, and school development projects by James Comer (see Barnett, 1996, for a review and assessment of these programs). Linking district funding to student performance is another type of reform that has been tried in Dallas, South Carolina, and Kentucky (see Clotfelter and Ladd, 1996).

Another approach is to break the link between residential location and the location of schooling through "choice/mobility" strategies, such as metropolitan-area-wide desegregation or a metropolitan education vouchering system that would permit students to attend any public school in the area (some proposals include private schools as well) so long as space is available. Less comprehensive approaches include charter schools (publicly supported institutions chartered by the state but usually run by private or nonprofit institutions rather than the existing school system) open to students without regard to geographic location and, within existing school districts, magnet schools and school choice among any public school in the district. Since 1990, the city of Milwaukee has provided vouchers to low-income students to attend nonsectarian private schools; more recently, voucher programs have been undertaken in a small number of other jurisdictions.

Providing a market proxy mechanism that allows parents to choose the school their child will attend, with the money following the child, should provide a strong incentive for schools to produce outcomes that parents are seeking. However, a choice program, if it is to be practicable in terms of having a large impact, would have to do more than simply allow parents to place their children in more effective schools outside the traditional public school; it would also have to engage the public school system to respond by creating more effective schools within the traditional system.

The research evidence on the effectiveness of efforts to improve the quality of existing schools is to date somewhat inconclusive. However, there is at least some evidence that all of these potential approaches can have positive effects on the performance of poor inner-city students. For instance, Clotfelter and Ladd

(1996) show that performance can rise in districts in which funding is linked to student performance. Barnett (1996) shows that the Levin, Slavin, and Comer approaches have generated positive outcomes for students in particular settings, although questions remain about the extent to which these results can be generalized.

The evidence on the effectiveness of choice/mobility strategies, particularly vouchering strategies, is highly contested. Initial evidence on the performance of inner-city students in the Milwaukee voucher program is conflicting: Witte et al. (1995) and Witte (1997) found no significant effects on test scores, but Greene et al. (1997) found significant effects on both reading and math. Rouse (1997) found that the program had positive effects on math but not on reading. The program is very small (it involves only 1.5 percent of students in the Milwaukee school system), and the results are still unclear. Hoxby (1996b) also found positive effects from school competition on student outcomes.

There is also evidence that inner-city minorities have substantially higher test scores and educational attainment in private parochial schools than in public schools (see Greene et al., 1997). However there have been questions about whether this superior performance merely reflects selection bias: that is, are the results attributable to the effects of the schools or to the characteristics of the students who choose to attend them? Recent evidence from studies by Hoxby (1996a) and Neal (1997) that control for selection bias through more sophisticated instrumental variable modeling techniques (although both are still open to criticism) suggest that the parochial schools do succeed in raising performance.

Two recent reviews of the literature come to quite different conclusions. Levin (1998:378) concludes that "My own reading of the body of studies comparing student achievement in public and private schools is that differences are small." Henig (1998), in contrast, accepts that the existing body of research supports the finding that private schools produce superior outcomes, yet notes that it is still possible that the differences resulted from unmeasured selection biases.

Evidence on the effect of choice or voucher programs on the performance of the existing public school system is scant. A few studies are indicative and encouraging, though hardly definitive. These infer effects from cross-sectional work in which the degree of competition for public schools is proxied through creative means. Hoxby (1997) modeled student achievement as a function of the number of school districts in a metropolitan area and the evenness with which enrollment is spread over these districts. Thus, a district with a large number of school districts and a relatively small share of the area's student population in each district would be one in which a substantial amount of "choice" existed, whereas, at the extreme, a metropolitan area with only one school district or with two districts, one of which enrolled 98 percent of the area's students, would be one with low choice. Controlling for other factors, she found that increased choice results in a slight improvement in the reading and math test scores of public school students in the area and a rather substantial reduction in per pupil expenditure. She also found that the greater the number of private schools providing competition to public schools in a metropolitan area, the better the performance of *public school* students, implying a response of public school systems to competition.

Couch and colleagues (1993) reported that, controlling for a variety of other factors, the performance of public school students on statewide algebra tests in North Carolina was higher in counties in which a larger percentage of county students were enrolled in private schools. This also suggests that public schools are responding to private school competition.

School-to-work programs can also play an important role in improving the skills of inner-city students and linking them to suburban labor markets (Bailey, 1995). At least potentially, the various career academies, tech prep schools, and other programs could serve to raise the incentives of students to improve their basic cognitive skills while in school, if they perceive clearer links between school performance and work opportunities with specific employers. Similarly, training programs for adults like the Center for Employment Training Program in San Jose, California, seem to be effective in providing inner-city minorities with skills that are directly linked to specific jobs and employers located in suburban areas. Although there are some promising models on school-to-work programs and training, it is not yet known how successfully these can be implemented on a wider scale. (For a review of the literature on job training, see Lalonde, 1995.)

Once again, there are also spatial considerations. Not only is school quality highly related to geographic location in the metropolitan area but also, as discussed earlier, the acquisition of human capital relates both to formal schooling and to the family and neighborhood environment. As Galster (1993:1440) observes, "Children first may learn communication and interpersonal skills from family members and neighbors. Schools give children a second chance to learn these skills, however, because students interact with schoolmates from other families and neighborhoods." Thus, policies to reduce concentrations of poverty and achieve at least jurisdictional integration so that poor and middle-class and blacks and whites share the same schools and classrooms, even if not necessarily the same neighborhood, should also be seen as contributing to human capital.

Antidiscrimination in Employment Policies

Some of the differences in labor market outcomes between blacks and whites are due directly to illegal discrimination in the labor market. Stronger enforcement of existing laws is clearly called for. Matched testing employment audits on a random basis in all metropolitan areas might not only result in better enforcement but also act as a deterrent to discrimination if employers perceive that the qualified applicant they are interviewing may actually be testing their compliance with the law.

Special efforts could be made to raise the effectiveness of antidiscrimination policies in the suburbs. To date, these policies have been ineffective and, indeed, more so than they might otherwise seem, since discrimination is frequently measured by the fraction of black employees at firms relative to the fraction of blacks in the local population (rather than in the relevant labor market). Discriminatory companies thus may relocate to the outlying suburbs precisely to get away from black applicants and protect themselves from lawsuits (Bloch, 1994).

It should be noted that, to some extent, worker mobility policies and antidiscrimination employment policies are complements to each other in the suburbs: the former is designed to increase the supply of central-city labor in suburban labor markets, and the latter is designed to increase the demand for central-city minority labor.

REDUCING TAX/SERVICE DISPARITIES

The existing distribution of population across space and jurisdictions in metropolitan areas results in serious tax/service disparities among local governments (see Chapter 3). These tax/service disparities in turn contribute to unequal spatial opportunity in metropolitan areas and to the disparities between residents of central cities and suburbs because they affect the nature of the public services residents receive (particularly education) and the price they pay for them. In this section, we explore alternative strategies for reducing these tax/service disparities or their effects.

There is a distinction between what has been called political stretching strategies and fiscal stretching strategies as means of addressing the tax/service disparity problem (Pagano, this volume). The principal objective of these approaches is either to extend the political boundaries of the city or to stretch its financial reach so that it can encompass the tax base of the broader metropolitan area (or beyond) and thereby lower average expenditure needs.

Political Stretching Strategies

Political stretching strategies attempt, in effect, to reduce or eliminate tax/service disparities by the simple step of eliminating or greatly reducing the multitude of local governments in a metropolitan area and moving to a single unit within which taxes are levied and services are provided as though it were one jurisdiction. Options include aggressive annexation by the central city, reorganization to bring about broader units of government such as single-tier metropolitan government, two-tier federalized metropolitan government, city-county consolidation, and creation of metropolitan-wide, single-purpose special districts.

Annexation

Annexation expands the boundaries of the central city and permits inclusion of the growing suburban population within central-city boundaries, usually adding households with higher incomes and lower service needs. However, annexation is possible (1) only when the central city is not already surrounded by incorporated municipalities, as is already the case in many parts of the country, particularly the older cities of the Northeast and the Midwest, and (2) when state annexation laws are permissive (see Rusk, 1993:20-22).

Governmental Consolidation

Creation of a single general-purpose metropolitan government, a two-tier federalized metropolitan government, or a city-county consolidation have all been suggested and, in some cases, put into place as political stretching reforms (discussed below). Of these, only a single general-purpose metropolitan-area government would in principle completely eliminate tax/service disparities. Two-tier metropolitan government envisions a metropolitan government responsible for some functions, but with an array of local governments, each with its own taxing and spending authority, responsible for other functions. As a consequence, tax/service disparities might be reduced but not eliminated. City-county consolidation would be equivalent to a single metropolitan government in those metropolitan areas that consisted of only one county, but in multicounty metropolitan areas it would simply reduce the number of local governments by eliminating all those previously within the central county, improving the relative fiscal situation for those who previously were city residents.

Within the units created by these reforms, it would seem that differences in tax burdens on residents due to differences in revenue-raising capacity of their previous local governments should be eliminated, assuming fair property assessment practices and administration of tax laws. However, this is not necessarily the case. In city-county consolidations, for example, the county is frequently divided into zones, with outlying areas receiving lower levels of service and tax rates and central-city areas receiving higher levels of services and tax rates (Harrigan, 1993:352). Two-tier metropolitan governments would also retain differences in tax rates and burdens as a result of local taxes imposed by the lower tier. Indeed, Hawkins and colleagues (1991) observe that the term "consolidation" is a misnomer, since in nearly all cases some independent governments with their own taxing authority continue to exist.

Whether differences in service quality would be eliminated, or the extent to which they would be reduced, is even more open to question. It is clear that simply creating a single jurisdiction does not mean that all residents within the component jurisdictions (or, more meaningfully, all neighborhoods) would receive equal services. Pagano (this volume), reviewing the literature on the degree and nature of inequality of service delivery among neighborhoods in the same city, notes that, although studies have consistently shown that levels of service vary among neighborhoods, early studies concluded that these variations were largely due to professional norms and standards applied by service bureaucracies and did not systematically disadvantage low-income or minority neighborhoods. More recent, carefully designed studies by Bolotin and Cingranelli (1983) and Meier et al. (1991) found that levels of service to neighborhoods are correlated with both race and class; minority neighborhoods and low-income neighborhoods systematically receive poorer services than other neighborhoods in the same city.

Metropolitan consolidation efforts would seem to provide the *potential* for reducing tax/service disparities among local governments in metropolitan areas. Do they actually do so? Existing research provides only scant guidance, and most of the findings are little more than anecdotal. In the most systematic study, Gustely (1977) found the net fiscal impact of the Dade County two-tier consolidation was, although modest, in favor of poorer jurisdictions, with the city of Miami and its residents being the biggest winner. Blomquist and Parks (1995) argue that, contrary to expectations, the adoption of Unigov in Indianapolis has not redistributed the area tax base in favor of the central city. This results from the structure of the reform, which retains a variety of municipal functions for the city that must be financed solely from the city's tax base.

In terms of service distribution, Horan and Taylor (1977) found that the Nashville consolidation reduced service disparities between urban and rural areas; Swanson (1996), however, found that consolidation in Jacksonville did little to improve the flow of services to the poor. In a general review of a large number of consolidation efforts, Erie and colleagues (1972:32) conclude that "reformed metropolitan institutions often do not provide services any more equitably than unreformed institutions in the same area."

Using a different approach, Bradford and Oates (1974) tried to estimate the redistributive effects of moving from the present fragmented system of local government in the metropolitan areas of northeastern New Jersey to a unified system with a single area-wide property tax rate and equal per capita expenditures throughout the area. They concluded that, in the long run, a "somewhat more egalitarian" distribution of income would result, but that there would also be some adverse efficiency effects (see also Greene and Parliament, 1980).

In the same vein, Sacher (1993) attempted to model the incidence of local taxes and expenditures and the distribution of income in metropolitan Washington, D.C., under the current fragmented fiscal system and under a hypothetical metropolitan-area-wide system. He concluded that the overall redistributive effects of moving to a metropolitan system would be very modest. A metropolitan system would increase the burden of the suburban well-off relative to the central-city well-off (because the tax burden currently falls heavily on the well-off in central cities), but it would also increase the burden of the central-city poor (who currently receive disproportionate levels of public services) relative to the suburban poor. There would be virtually no change in net incidence between income classes.

The political difficulties involved in bringing about these various forms of greater regionalism through boundary change are well known and are discussed in a later section, along with a variety of considerations concerning their desirability.

Metropolitan-Area-Wide, Single-Purpose Special Districts

Metropolitan-area-wide special districts with their own taxing and spending powers are, in effect, the equivalent of metropolitan governments for a specific purpose. Foster (1997:108) divides regional special districts into two categories: (1) "regionalizing-collectivizing districts" that spread costs across the metropolitan area through region-wide financing mechanisms for services enjoyed throughout the area such as zoos, convention centers, parks, and environmental protection and (2) "regionalizing-privatizing districts" financed directly by users of the service through fees and charges, such as bridge tolls, water consumption charges, and airport fees.

The question of service equalization across areas notwithstanding, creation of single-purpose regional special districts to replace or augment taxing and spending by large numbers of local governments should serve to reduce tax/expenditure disparities for that purpose in metropolitan areas. Unlike other forms of boundary reorganizations in metropolitan areas, special districts, particularly for systems maintenance issues, are not always outside the realm of political feasibility. However, there is almost no empirical evidence on the actual distribution of service for various subregional areas within special districts or on the redistribution of tax burdens within the region as a consequence of moving to regional special-purpose districts. One exception is a study by Hawkins and Hendrick (1997), who found fiscal redistribution in favor of city residents as a consequence of the pattern of taxes and benefits from two special districts in the Milwaukee metropolitan area.

Fiscal Stretching Strategies

Fiscal stretching policies permit existing units of local government suffering from fiscal disparities to gain access to fiscal resources from outside their borders. Such options include metropolitan tax base sharing; county or state assumption of local service responsibilities; the ability to export taxes, particularly through devices such as taxes on income earned within the jurisdiction; and assistance from higher (federal and state) levels of government.

Metropolitan Tax Base Sharing

Tax base sharing involves a redistribution of revenues among local governments in a metropolitan area, with local governments contributing some portion of their tax base or tax base growth into a metropolitan fund, which is then reallocated among the local governments according to need-related criteria. The rationale is both to reduce fiscal disparities among local governments in the metropolitan area and to reduce the incentive for local governments to engage in nonproductive competition with each other to attract property-tax-paying economic activity within their borders. The extent to which fiscal disparities are reduced is dependent both on how much of the area's local tax base is set aside for the pool and the extent to which the distribution from the pool takes local fiscal capacity into account.

The best known example is the tax base sharing system in the Minneapolis-St. Paul area, which was imposed by the state legislature in 1971. All local governments in the seven-county metropolitan area are required to pay into an area-wide pool an amount equal to 40 percent of the growth in their commercial and industrial tax base since 1971. This amount includes growth from any source, including new construction, inflation, revaluation, and appreciation (Bell, 1994:160). The tax base is redistributed from the pool back to local governments on the basis of a fiscal capacity measure,[2] so that jurisdictions with lower fiscal capacity receive relatively higher amounts of per capita tax base. The redistributed portion of the tax base is then taxed at the average area-wide rate. Two other examples of tax-base sharing are the New Jersey Meadowlands area and the Charlottesville, Virginia (Albemarle County), metropolitan area (Bell, 1994:154-55). Pagano (this volume) describes a voluntary tax base sharing program in the Dayton (Montgomery County), Ohio area.

The Twin Cities plan has reduced fiscal disparities among local governments in the metropolitan area from a range of 50:1 to a range of 12:1, according to Orfield (1997). A study for the Minnesota legislature cited by Bell (1994), however, reported that disparities in millage rates have been reduced but the effect in terms of reducing tax burdens has been much less.

Experience has shown that tax base sharing schemes do not inevitably work to the advantage of central cities. Chernick and Reschovsky (1995) report that St. Paul has been a net beneficiary of the process since its inception, but between 1984 and 1994 Minneapolis actually was a net contributor each year. They attribute this to a boom in commercial real estate in Minneapolis during that time period and to the fact that the distribution formula does not take into account the higher costs of providing services in central cities. Nunn and Rosentraub (1996:96) report that Dayton was a net contributor to the Montgomery County (Ohio) tax sharing scheme in 1992, despite the fact that it had a higher poverty rate than many other participating jurisdictions. This results from the distribution formula that allocates money to participating jurisdictions on the basis of population (Pagano, this volume). The extent to which tax base sharing schemes assist central cities is thus critically dependent on the formula by which the pooled funds are distributed.

The relatively small number of such schemes suggests the political difficulty of bringing them into existence. Orfield, however, argues (1997) that a tax sharing program can be structured so that the winners far outnumber the losers, and political alliances can be created within the legislature so that representatives from winning districts outnumber those from losing districts. Even so, Orfield's account suggests how difficult it is to overcome ideological opposition and partisan political position taking, even when measures of objective interests would seem to point to easy victory.

State/County Assumption

The difficulty of financing local services that are either redistributive (and thus cannot be easily financed by a distressed city without further encouraging the out-migration of its tax base; see Peterson, 1981) or region-wide with respect to benefits has led, over time, to a state or county's assuming the responsibility for either financing or both financing and delivering particular services in many areas. For example, there are now only a few states (New York is one) in which city governments are responsible for financing a share of federal welfare or Medicaid services; most city universities have been taken over by the state; and in many places city public hospitals are now the responsibility of the county government. (In some states, there has been a movement for state government to take over failing school systems, although this usually does not imply a complete financial takeover.)

The problem with these approaches is that the incentive for service assumption by county or state government is lacking, except under situations of real stringency. Assuming financial responsibility will affect the fiscal status of these governments, leading perhaps even to unpopular tax increases and, in many cases, overlying county governments are nearly as fiscally distressed as are large city governments. Furthermore, the devolution of federal responsibility for a variety of programs to the states may have the effect of pushing responsibility downward toward local governments rather than upward to the county or state. However, where valued services are near collapse, county or state assumption may still be possible. In many cases, however, the most obvious candidates for assumption have already taken place.

Tax Exporting

All local governments are able to export some portion of their tax burden to nonresidents. The most obvious example is the property tax on commercial and industrial property owned by nonresidents, which in addition is frequently taxed at a higher rate than residential property. Although there is substantial variation among states and even at times among localities within states, Chernick and Reschovsky (1995:153) note that the effective property tax rate on nonresidential property during the 1970s was typically about 25 percent higher than the rate on housing. Differential taxation of nonresidential property sometimes occurs through formal classification schemes and sometimes through de facto differences in assessment rates. However, some states have ruled that such differentials are constitutionally impermissible. In addition, there has been a growth in tax concessions given to businesses by local governments as a means of attracting them into an area or retaining them there, which has probably served to reduce the differential in favor of residential property.

Earnings or commuter taxes are the other major area with potential for tax exporting. For cities that are major tourist attractions, hotel, rental car, and entertainment taxes are also frequently resorted to. Local governments must receive permission from the state government in order to impose an earnings tax; as noted earlier, only 11 states provide local governments with such authority. Chernick and Reschovsky (1995:153) note that 6 of the nation's 24 largest cities make use of an earnings tax, and in 1989 the tax accounted for about 8 percent of total expenditures in these cities. Moreover, Yinger (1996:37) observes that five of the six central cities with the poorest "standardized fiscal health" in 1992 had access to a commuter tax, which served to improve their actual fiscal health.

As the above discussion suggests, the political problems of taxing the earnings of those who work in the city but live in the suburbs, while difficult, appear not to be insurmountable. But there is a question about the economic consequences of such taxes. Chernick and Reschovsky (1995:12) observe: "As with the property tax, the problem with a local earnings or income tax is that while it may be effective at exporting tax burdens and raising revenue in the short run, in the longer run it may hurt the competitive position of the city. In Philadelphia, nonresident earnings are taxed at almost the same rate as resident earnings, while there is no local income tax in the suburbs. Research suggests that the employment impacts of this tax have been quite negative."

To meet this concern, they suggest (1995:165) that suburban residents who work in the city be permitted to take a dollar-for-dollar credit against their residential property tax bill for any wage tax payments they make to the jurisdiction in which they are employed, with the state compensating localities for a portion of the foregone property tax revenues.

Equalization Aid from State and Federal Governments

Equalization aid is designed explicitly to reduce fiscal disparities among local governments by providing disproportionately greater aid to those with lower fiscal capacity and higher needs. Most countries explicitly provide general grants to their subnational governments for this purpose (see Wolman, 1985). However, at the federal level, general revenue sharing was the only program explicitly designed for this purpose, and its distribution formula was poorly designed to do so, resulting in only a very mild equalizing effect. Other intergovernmental aid programs, although not specifically designed for equalization purposes, nonetheless can produce equalizing results. Fiscal assistance from state and federal government plays an important role in moderating the degree of fiscal disparities among local governments. Ladd and Yinger (1991) report that, between 1972 and 1982, much of the decline in the standardized fiscal health of large cities was made up for through grants from the state and federal governments. Nonetheless, in the aggregate, U.S. federal grant programs have a very modest impact on reducing disparities among local governments when compared with those of other countries (Wolman and Page, 1987:88-89).

In addition, federal aid to local governments has fallen precipitously since the late 1970s, from 16 percent of municipal general revenue in 1978 to 5 percent in 1992. State aid as a percentage of local government revenue remained nearly constant over that period, but there was substantial variation among individual states. State aid to local governments has also generally tracked the economic cycle, rising in growth periods and falling during downturns. Between 1978 and 1992, federal and state aid in the aggregate as a percentage of municipal government general revenue fell from 40 to 28 percent. Reductions in intergovernmental aid to local governments have made the equalizing potential of aid more difficult.

State governments provide both general grants for local government operations (about 25 percent of total state aid to local governments in 1992) and categorical grants for specific purposes. In some cases, these grants are explicitly equalizing in intent. Most of the debate about equalization grants has occurred in the context of categorical grants for education purposes, as state court decisions have ruled that gross disparities in fiscal capacity across school districts are impermissible. Although some of these efforts aim explicitly at reducing the actual differences in per capita spending among school districts, the basic principle is that of locational neutrality, i.e., the taxes that individuals bear to support a given level of educational services should not depend on where they reside (Downes and Pogue, 1994:55).

States have responded by designing explicit education equalization grant programs, either through structuring more generous foundation programs or through power equalizing. Foundation programs provide school districts with the difference between a state-set per student amount (the foundation grant) and what they would raise from levying a state-specified tax rate on their property tax base. Power equalizing permits each school district to levy the tax rate it wishes against its property tax base and then provides the district with the difference between a standard yield set by the state for each rate and what the district actually is able to raise at that rate. Districts that raise more from their own base than the state standard receive no state aid (see Pagano, this volume; Downes and Pogue, 1994; Reschovsky and Wiseman, 1994).

Education equalization grants have been criticized from two perspectives: on one hand, because they have not, in fact, resulted in equalization, particularly if the goal is to equalize per pupil spending across school districts. Reschovsky contends (1994:191) that "the limited available evidence suggests that, largely for political reasons, achieving school finance equalization . . . is by and large an elusive goal."

On the other hand, it has been argued that equalization programs may achieve equalization, but at the expense of lower overall spending on education (see Reschovsky and Wiseman, 1994; Hoxby, 1996b). This could result if education financing is transferred in large measure from the local to the state tax base, thus severing the link between local willingness to tax oneself for education and the understanding that the taxpayer will benefit from undertaking the burden with additional education spending in his or her district. By contrast, at the state level, taxpayers may be less willing to tax themselves for education, since it is not obvious that their district will gain the benefit from the tax. Hoxby (1996b) also argues that, although equalization schemes like that of *Serrano* in California, level down, achieving equalization by preventing wealthier districts from spending as much as they wish, and achieving redistribution from property-rich to property-poor districts, at the same time, overall spending on education may be reduced. She concludes that "students from poor households end up experiencing lower school spending under very stringent school finance equalization" (1996b:18).

Others argue that a well-designed equalization program does not inevitably have to reduce expenditure; indeed, if it is so desired, it can be structured to encourage expenditure. Both Chernick and Reschovsky (1995) and Ladd and Yinger (1994) argue for a foundation program that requires local districts to impose a minimum tax rate and then have the state make up the difference between what that rate yields and a generous foundation level (i.e., a minimum per pupil expenditure level for all districts), providing that level accounts for differences in costs. Assuming local districts are not prevented from spending above the foundation level, strict equalization may not result, but disparities will be reduced and the receipt of an adequate standard of education will no longer be dependent on the wealth of the community in which an individual resides.

Ladd (1994b:50) also argues that states could use a program designed to narrow the gap between fiscal capacity and expenditure need, as she and Yinger have defined it, as the criterion for distributing funds to local governments; this has been done in Massachusetts. The problem, as Pagano notes, is more one of political feasibility rather than inability to design a workable program.

Breaking the Link Between Location and Service Quality

In addition to political stretching and fiscal stretching strategies, a third option would be to break the link between residential location and service delivery, so that residents of jurisdictions with high fiscal disparities would be able to receive services throughout the metropolitan area or beyond. Voucher programs or metropolitan or statewide school choice programs (as in Minnesota) are examples, as is the METCO program in the Boston area. METCO enables more than 3,000 minority children in the city of Boston to attend suburban public schools at state expense.

IMPROVING METROPOLITAN GOVERNANCE

This section examines changes in metropolitan governance that might serve to improve the opportunity structure of metropolitan areas. These alternatives can be considered as counterfactuals to the existing metropolitan governance system. The section examines what we know about the potential of these various alternatives for positively affecting the metropolitan opportunity structure and reducing inequality of opportunity, as well as their political feasibility. It also examines the possible adverse consequences of metropolitan reform strategies for other important values, such as efficiency, choice, and local autonomy, as well as the possibility that there is a trade-off between these values and achieving greater equality of opportunity.

Comprehensive Restructuring

Reducing political fragmentation by creating a more encompassing unit or units of government within metropolitan areas has been the subject of long debate. In the context of the committee's concerns, the object of such reform proposals would be to even out the spatial opportunity structure of metropolitan areas.

The argument for reform of metropolitan government structure in this context is that, in a unitary rather than a fragmented system, the incentive to engage in exclusionary zoning practices for fiscal ends would be eliminated, as would the incentive for households to sort themselves based on their ability to pay for high-quality public services. Sorting by race and income might continue to appear at the neighborhood level, but differences in tax burdens among individuals would be reduced and the quality of public services, including services of fundamental importance to equal opportunity, such as education, would no longer be dependent on where in the metropolitan area an individual resided.

The debate about reform, however, has taken place on a much broader canvas. Proponents of metropolitan government reform in the academic and research literature have focused their arguments on efficiency and administrative considerations, such as the need to achieve economies of scale and improved coordination and cooperation, although equity concerns related to fiscal disparities have also been present. They also argue that a metropolitan government structure will allow for expression of interests and development of policies shared by the entire region, such as greater economic growth and development.

Opponents of such centralizing reforms argue that large numbers of governments actually are desirable, both for reasons of efficiency and for those of democratic political participation and accountability. The starting point of these "public choice" arguments is the desire for a government structure that promotes efficiency, as defined by the allocation of resources that best accords with citizen preferences, in metropolitan areas (see Tiebout, 1956; Ostrom et al., 1961).

To that end, public choice proponents propose a market analog: local governments produce and sell public services to consumers (taxpayers) who purchase them. Taxpayers differ among themselves in their taste and demand for public services and in their willingness and ability to pay for them, just as they differ among themselves with respect to other goods. In choosing residential locations, they attempt to match their preferences for tax/service packages with those offered by the large number of local governments in a metropolitan area. In short, they "vote with their feet." The large number of governments providing services in the area promotes competition, thus both ensuring that prices (i.e., the tax price of public services) are driven down and that many specialized niche needs can be satisfied. As a consequence of the large number of relatively small local governments, the tax/service preferences of citizens in any one community are less likely to diverge from the actual tax/service package provided than would be the case if the government covered a larger and more heterogeneous area. This is efficient in the sense of optimal allocation of society's resources.

The public choice argument suggests that the sorting process is actually desirable. Efficiency is conditioned on many small local governments with homogeneous populations in terms of tax/service preferences. If such preferences are also correlated with other characteristics, such as income, class, and race, it also implies homogeneity with respect to these characteristics.

In political terms, the public choice argument is analogous to the proposition that government authority should be exercised at a very local level, where elected officials are close to the people and understand their needs and concerns and where individuals can engage in meaningful political participation and hold their elected officials accountable.

The above discussion suggests the very real possibility that there may be a trade-off between the values associated with equity (in particular, the reduction of unequal opportunity) and values that have undergirded the traditional American system of local government, such as efficiency, choice, and local autonomy. Certainly such a trade-off is perceived by many of the opponents of various proposals for metropolitan reform.

Many of the propositions in this debate have been subjected to the test of empirical research. The literature on the efficiency consequences of consolidated versus fragmented systems of local government (or large versus small units) is particularly extensive (for reviews, see Hirsch, 1968; Parks and Oakerson, 1989; Dolan, 1990; Boyne, 1992a, 1992b; Dowding et al., 1994; Durning, 1995; Foster, 1997; Oakerson, 1998). The preponderance of the evidence indicates that small local governments (and thus metropolitan areas characterized by fragmentation) are more efficient for labor-intensive services, whereas larger units are more efficient for capital-intensive services (because of economies of scale) and for certain overhead functions.

Evaluation of the effects of metropolitan consolidation reforms that have occurred in the post World War II era is disappointing. Most of the studies of these reforms have focused on the politics that brought them about rather than on the consequences of reform for policy (Carl Vinson Institute of Government, 1989). Effects are inherently difficult to assess, since the number of governments that meet the reform criteria are small. City-county consolidations were not uncommon in the nineteenth century (Harrigan, 1993), but only 22 have been approved since 1921 (Pagano, this volume), and, of these, only 3 have involved populations of more than 250,000 people: Nashville, Jacksonville, and Indianapolis. Miami-Dade County is a rare example of two-tier metropolitan government, although incomplete consolidation renders many of the city-county consolidation efforts (such as Indianapolis-Marion County) into a form of two-tier government as well. There is no real example of unitary, general-purpose metropolitan government in the United States.

Evidence on the consequences of comprehensive reform is therefore sparse and impressionistic. Pagano (this volume) observes that "although the evidence on fairness or equity of service delivery tends to be anecdotal, studies on tax equity and service delivery in consolidated counties are nonexistent, focusing instead on residents' satisfaction of services."

There is general agreement that consolidation has not reduced costs (as predicted by some reform advocates) and, in fact, may have even increased total local expenditures (consistent with the literature described above). Gustely (1977) found that expenditures rose after the Dade county consolidation. Benton and Gamble (1984) came to the same conclusions in their study of Jacksonville. Erie and colleagues (1972:30) reviewed a range of consolidation efforts and concluded that "the net effect of restructuring is a per capita increase in service costs," which they attribute to an increase in average service levels.

What are the effects of metropolitan consolidation on the disparities in metropolitan areas between blacks and whites and cities and suburbs with which the committee is concerned? Again, there are no systematic empirical studies. The evidence that does exist, however, suggests that these efforts have had no significant impact on redistributing income or on addressing the problems of the poor or racial minorities (Erie et al., 1972; Carver, 1973; Blomquist and Parks, 1995; Swanson, 1996). Harrigan (1993) concludes that areas that have undergone metropolitan reform have fared no better than multicentered metropolitan areas in dealing with problems that place poor people and minorities at a disadvantage.[3] As has already been discussed, there is little evidence that metropolitan consolidation reforms have actually resulted in reduction in tax/service disparities in metropolitan areas, although they have the potential to do so. And although there appears to be some scope for consolidation schemes to achieve at least a modest degree of income redistribution, there may be a cost to pay in terms of lost efficiency for doing so (Bradford and Oates, 1974; Greene and Parliament, 1980).

How metropolitan governments affect spatial opportunity structures by reducing the ability of localities in the area to control access through local land use decisions is also questionable. Harrigan (1993) notes that in all four of the major metropolitan reformed governments (Indianapolis, Nashville, Jacksonville, and Miami), existing suburban municipalities were allowed to retain their authority over zoning and land use decisions unimpaired. He concludes (1993:361): "Metropolitan governments are uniformly much more successful in dealing with the physical questions such as sewers, water supply, or parks and recreation than they are in dealing with social issues such as fiscal disparities, race relations, open housing, and the location of public, low-income housing in the suburbs. . . . [T]hese governments have not eliminated the biases of the multicentered metropolis on social access issues of zoning, schools, and housing."

The apparently disappointing evaluations of metropolitan reform efforts do not mean that it is impossible to design metropolitan structures that would have the desired impact on spatial opportunity structures, but only that existing ones appear to have failed to do so What is perhaps more relevant, the politics of bringing into being even the weakened forms of metropolitan governments appear nearly insurmountable. With respect to city-county consolidations, Pagano (this volume) notes that less than 20 percent of proposed consolidations have been approved since 1921. Furthermore, most proposed consolidations in recent years have been in smaller metropolitan areas, mostly in the South, and the primary rationale has been efficiency gains and cost savings (Durning, 1995; Pagano, this volume).

Why have these metropolitan forms of government been so difficult to achieve? When the effort is made to bring about these reforms through voter referenda rather than through an act of the state legislature (as was the case in Indianapolis), it typically requires majority approval in both central city and suburbs separately. In their review of voting patterns on 28 consolidation efforts, Marando and Whitley (1972) conclude that black voters oppose consolidation efforts more that whites and suburban residents more than city residents. Suburban residents usually vote against approval, as Harrigan observes (1993:361), because, "suburban voters interpret metropolitan reform as an attempt by central-city officials to 'grab' their tax base" and to increase their taxes. However, recent votes have seen central-city minorities increasingly oppose consolidation as well, fearing a dilution of political influence and of their ability to control political offices. Pagano adds (this volume) that, in states requiring preclearance of electoral changes under the Voting Rights Act, metropolitan government restructuring efforts must first be submitted to the U.S. Department of Justice to demonstrate that minority voting influence is not being diluted.

In general, campaigns for metropolitan reforms are generated at the elite level in response to a specific problem of governance; as Marando and Whitley (1972:200) observe, "consolidation is not basically a grass-roots movement." Furthermore, metropolitan reform campaigns are conducted in an environment of public apathy, ignorance, and misinformation (Marando and Whitley, 1972; Greer, 1963). As Greer (1963:199) observes, "transmitting to the electorate the complex issues of structural change in government is a thankless and near-impossible task." Indeed, there appears to be a tendency for informed voters to be more supportive of consolidation proposals (as Hawkins, 1966, found in his survey of Nashville voters).

Analysis of why some metropolitan reform efforts succeed and others fail tend to focus heavily on idiosyncratic characteristics of each effort. However, it appears that success is much more likely when elite groups are not involved in organized opposition. Greer (1963) compared unsuccessful efforts in St. Louis and Cleveland with the successful Miami referendum. He notes that, in all three areas, reform had at least the nominal support of business groups and the whole-hearted support of area newspapers. However, he points to the active and vocal opposition of central-city mayors in the unsuccessful efforts in contrast to Dade County, where no major elite opposition formed (see also Banfield, 1957). Sofen (1963:214) expands on this: "In other metropolitan areas there were many centers of power or independent pyramids like labor, racial groups, political parties. . . . In Miami, aside from officeholders and municipal and county employees, there were no other strongly organized power groups to oppose the loose coalition of central-city businessmen, area-wide newspapers and 'do-good' organizations that supported Metro. Similar coalitions have, of course, been found in every organized attempt to create metropolitan government. But elsewhere in the nation they invariably met with defeat because of the entrenched position of the countervailing groups who did not want to jettison the status quo for an unproven product."

Most political scientists who have studied the politics of metropolitan consolidation are quite pessimistic about the political feasibility of adoption through the referendum process (Greer, 1963; Horan and Taylor, 1977; Harrigan, 1993). As Greer (1963:199) observes: "When the structure of government is to be decided by a public opinion poll (and this is what a referendum turns out to be) the outlook . . . would appear bleak. The change cannot move far beyond the understanding and normative commitment of the median in the distribution of voters. That, in turn, would seem to be a basically conservative, anti-government position. The alternatives are (1) to manipulate the election through redefining (or misdefining) the issue or (2) to bring about change through fiat."

By fiat, Greer means through the actions of the state government, superimposing a new structure on the metropolitan area, as was the case in Indianapolis and with the less comprehensive metropolitan reforms in the Twin Cities and Portland. Horan and Taylor (1977:200) agree, concluding that "an active state role in the reorganization of local government and the absence of a referendum appear to be the two ingredients that will facilitate, but certainly not guarantee, metropolitan reform."

In short, the evidence of the effect of metropolitan government on reducing disparities and on changing spatial opportunity structures in desirable ways is not compelling, and the political feasibility of achieving comprehensive metropolitan reform of this nature in very many metropolitan areas seems slight.

Partial Restructuring

Comprehensive metropolitanization is not the only alternative for restructuring metropolitan institutions. As discussed, most metropolitan areas engage in various, though limited, single-purpose forms of regional activity. Three of them—Minneapolis-St. Paul, Seattle, and Portland—have developed metropolitan institutions that, since they are multipurpose in nature, represent a form of partial metropolitan government.

In the Minneapolis-St. Paul region, the state legislature established the Twin Cities Metropolitan Council in 1967. The council, whose members are appointed by the governor, covers a seven-county region and is responsible for a wide range of functions, including land use, housing, transit, sewage, parks and recreation, and several other services. However, throughout most of its history, the Metropolitan Council has functioned as a planning and policy-making body rather than as an operating agency. Harrigan (1996) calls it a bifurcated model, in which the Metropolitan Council sets policy and reviews, but the policies are implemented by other local governments, with the exception (since 1994) of transit operations and waste control. He argues that the bifurcated model worked well in some areas (e.g., sewerage), but resulted in a relatively limited impact on important land use decisions: "The more important the project was to development interests, the less the Council seemed to affect the decisions. The result is that the siting of most of these projects resulted from the traditional politics of land use rather than from a guided land use policy directed by the Development Framework" (1996:218).

In 1971, the Minnesota state legislature passed a Metropolitan Council proposal to set up the regional tax base sharing system (described above), which the council administers. In 1975, the Metropolitan Council passed a Development Framework Plan, setting up a regional land use and development plan designed to contain sprawl within a metropolitan urban services area. The state legislature then gave the Metropolitan Council the authority to review the plans of individual local governments in the area and to hold up the plan's approval if it was inconsistent with the growth projected for the area by the Development Framework Plan, thus providing it with considerable power over local land use decisions (Harrigan, 1996).

In Portland, Oregon, the Metropolitan Service District (called Metro), unlike the Twin Cities Metropolitan Council, is an elected body. Metro was authorized by the state legislature in 1977 and created in 1978 by a referendum in the three counties it serves. It is governed by a seven-person board elected on a district basis and an executive officer elected at large. Metro provides services, including the regional zoo, solid waste disposal, and regional tourist development to 3 counties and 24 cities in the Portland area. It is also responsible for coordinating growth management, land use, and transportation planning throughout the region.

Metro actually has a role in delivering only a small number of services (Nelson, 1996:263). Its importance lies with its ability to review local land use plans and its role as a coordinator and convenor in addressing regional issues. In this capacity, it has played a key role in such important issues as arranging the distribution of fair-share housing allocations, creating the urban growth boundary, adjusting the appropriation of transportation funds, and helping to create a consensus for new regional initiatives. Nelson argues that it is the fact that Metro is an elected body that serves to legitimize these functions.

It is difficult to relate the experience of the Twin Cities and Portland to an impact on reducing disparities in outcomes. Harrigan (1996) notes that the Twin Cities Metropolitan Council was highly successful in its first two decades, but has been less successful recently. He attributes this to two factors that are of direct concern to our inquiry (1996:223): "The nature of the most pressing issues had changed from physical development in the 1960s to the much more intractable issues of social deterioration in the 1990s. Economic and demographic change worsened the central-city/suburban disparities." Recently, efforts to restructure the metropolitan council to allow it to better cope with these issues have been undertaken but have yet to be enacted. These include proposals for an elective council, the mandating of low- and moderate-income housing goals for each suburb, with the metropolitan council having the authority to enforce these through denying sewer and highway extensions to noncomplying suburbs, and regional housing reinvestment and poverty reduction efforts.

There is also some debate over how applicable the experience of the Twin Cities and Portland are to other metropolitan areas. Both areas have relatively small minority populations and political traditions and cultures that place a relatively high emphasis on rational discussion and negotiation. As Abbott notes (1997:43), "Portlanders share a political culture that considers policy alliances and team building to be the normal way of doing public business. Nurtured in nonpartisan political institutions for local government, the Portland style prefers protracted discussion and negotiation to ideological battles and electoral confrontation." Despite this, he considers that the Portland experience is, at least to a certain extent, generalizable (1997:39): "Portland in the aggregate is not a unique metropolitan area. Many aspects of its economic base, social geography, and demography certainly set it apart from the typical city of the South or Northeast. However, it is not sui generis, despite its 'whiteness' and its muted class divisions. In particular, Portland bears many similarities to a number of 'middle American' cities, including Indianapolis, Des Moines, Minneapolis-St. Paul, Omaha, Denver, Salt Lake City, Sacramento, and Seattle."

Expansion of Existing Metropolitan Institutions

Most metropolitan areas already have one or more regional institutions for specific purposes. What are the prospects for the evolution of existing regional institutions into multipurpose regional government entities?

Metropolitan planning agencies, most of which exist largely as a result of federal assistance and prodding, frequently provide planning across several functional areas. The most prevalent such entities are councils of governments, which are voluntary associations of local governments that join together for the purpose of engaging in area-wide planning, coordination of activities, review of local applications for state or federal assistance, research, and, in some cases, allocation of federal funds. Most of the metropolitan planning organizations, charged with the responsibility of transportation planning and fund allocation under the Intermodal Surface Transportation Efficiency Act, are councils of governments. Councils of governments have obvious limitations: they lack operating authority in most areas; because they are voluntary they find it difficult to engage in controversial action; and, in most metropolitan areas representation is on a one-jurisdiction/one-vote basis, which implies severe underrepresentation for cities.

Nonetheless, councils of governments and, in some areas, other metropolitan-area-wide planning institutions exist and are accepted. As Harrigan (1993:384) suggests, organic growth of these institutions carries with it the possibility of "metropolitan policy making with teeth." However, he also recognizes that, even if such steps were to occur, it would probably involve metropolitan decision making in systems maintenance rather than life-style issues.

Informal Cooperation, Interlocal Agreements, and Nested Government

Despite the lack of formal metropolitan government structures, interaction does occur among local governments in metropolitan areas. Public choice theorists argue that, when joint action across a fragmented local government system is required, it will occur through activity by overlapping governmental units (such as counties), interlocal agreements, privatization of services across local boundaries, or the creation of special districts. They particularly stress the ability to separate the provision of public services (a public function) from the production of services, which may be undertaken by public or private entities and provides the possibility for delivering services effectively across jurisdictional boundaries (see Tiebout, 1956; Ostrom et al., 1961, 1988; Bish, 1971; Parks and Oakerson, 1989; Oakerson, 1998).

The large number of special districts, including those covering more than one jurisdiction, is well known. The extent of privatization and interlocal arrangements is less well known and understood. Indeed, the number of such arrangements in a metropolitan area can be staggering. Thompson (1997) surveyed municipal governments in the Detroit metropolitan area and found more than 4,000 privatization or interlocal arrangements, an average of 30 for each local government. Of the 2,967 interlocal arrangements municipalities reported, 47 percent involved relationships with other municipalities or authorities that were the joint creations of municipalities.

However, Thompson found that most of the interlocal arrangements were pursued for reasons of efficiency and effectiveness and involved municipalities that had common borders and shared similar populations, particularly with respect to education and race. There were "no obviously redistributive or tax base sharing arrangements between the central city and suburbs that were identified by either side" (1997:15).

Special districts are another means of providing links across a fragmented metropolitan area, at least for a specific service. Indeed, special districts can be tailored to encompass the geographic area most appropriate to the service in terms of relevant economies of scale on the production side and homogeneity of preference on the provision side. As of 1992, there were more than 13,000 special districts (exclusive of school districts) in metropolitan areas, with an average of 43 per metropolitan area. Approximately 25 percent of these are regional, providing services at the county or larger scale (Foster, 1996).

But, like interlocal agreements, special districts are likely to be put in place for reasons of efficiency, and it is not clear what the impact, if any, will be on the spatial opportunity structure with which we are concerned.

Pagano (this volume) notes that, on the ground, interlocal agreements and special districts appear to be the political action of choice as the means of overcoming fragmentation. He observes, however, that most of the services covered through these arrangements "are either 'household' functions, such as garbage collection, fire protection, policing, tax collection activities, payroll, and planning, or infrastructure activities, such as transportation improvement districts, municipal utility districts, metropolitan planning organizations, and the like. They tend not to be social services."

A "nested" arrangement, with larger governmental units overlaying smaller ones, is the most efficient manner of overcoming fragmentation in metropolitan areas, according to Parks and Oakerson (1989:22-23). They observe that "those issues that cannot be effectively addressed by governments of a large number of relatively small, adjacent municipalities can be assigned to overlying special-purpose or multipurpose jurisdictions." Moreover, they contend that such a fragmented and nested system of local government is highly functional, arguing (1989:23) that "local governments tend not to be 'balkanized' in multi-jurisdictional metropolitan areas; rather they are linked organizationally by webs of interlocal agreements and overlaid by larger-scale arrangements for specific purposes."

Within such a nested arrangement, distributional equity concerns can be pursued at an overlying level, without the need of creating a cumbersome and overarching metropolitan government. In this way, Parks and Oakerson suggest an efficient way in which redistribution might be achieved and the spatial opportunity structure altered.[4] They fail, however, to identify the political incentives or conditions that might bring about such redistribution (Keating, 1995). Unfortunately, we have come full circle; under the present system, redistribution appears not to occur or to occur insufficiently to make a difference.

Metropolitan Governance: The Third Wave

There has been a recent resurgence of interest in regionalism, which Wallis (1994) terms the "third wave" of regional governance. He notes that the shift in terminology from metropolitan or regional government to governance is self-conscious (1994:292): "The change in terminology reflects a shift in focus from formal structural arrangements to informal structures and processes for setting policy and mobilizing action. . . . Attempts to achieve regional governance are being led largely by cross-sectoral coalitions or alliances whose interests tend to fall largely within a specific strategic arena. Private corporations, for example, are primarily concerned with economic development, but their interest clearly spills over into concerns over infrastructure, affordable housing, public education, and issues in other areas. Likewise, nonprofit agencies engaged in human service delivery advocacy tend to focus on social equity."

These collaborative efforts reflect an approach that focuses less on authority and more on consensus building as a means of bringing about coordinated activity in a variety of social and political settings (see Innes, 1992, 1996). With respect to regional activity, efforts have tended to focus on specific projects, but there is frequently (Wallis, 1994) substantial stability over time for specific projects and even institutionalization. Peirce calls this cooperation at the regional level "citistate governance." He examines six metropolitan regions in depth and observes, on the basis of his investigations (1993) that "what struck us most was the potential of virtually every citistate to alter its environment to position itself for the new economy. The right civic forces have the potential to coalesce to achieve some form of shared governance" (1993:36).

Nonetheless, Peirce is not convinced that this kind of regional collaboration is sufficient. He notes the impressive degree of informal collaboration among organizations in the Cleveland area to come to grips with the problems of the area economy (1993). Participants include representatives of the city Department of Economic Development, Cleveland Tomorrow, the Greater Cleveland Round Table, Cuyahoga County, local universities, and two community foundations, the George Gund Foundation and the Cleveland Foundation. He concludes, however, that "moving from informal consultations to such tangible regional steps as tax-base sharing, cross-border school enrollment, or formation of a work force preparedness plan for the Cleveland region in the 21st century, is very difficult" (1993:34). Instead, Peirce concludes that "a region simply *must* have some form of umbrella regional governance structure. At a minimum, such an organization needs the power to resolve disputes between individual governments of the region. At a maximum, it would assume direct control of, and coordinate, the major cross-regional functions . . . now performed by independent special authorities" (1993:319).

As Peirce's discussion suggests, there is a debate among proponents of metropolitan governance between those who put great emphasis on consensus building and those who believe that progress requires the building of majority coalitions. There is little disagreement that third-wave metropolitanism is highly desirable. The question is how much an essentially consensus-based approach can do to move toward more equality of opportunity and a reduction in outcome disparities between city and suburbs and whites and minorities. Orfield (1997), for example, lauds the efforts of third-wave regional governance advocates to create coalitions on behalf of a regional perspective or regional interest; however, he is skeptical that such a regional interest will emerge or drive changes in the city's favor.

Federal Actions to Encourage Metropolitan Governance

The federal government has played an important role in encouraging metropolitan activity by providing assistance to metropolitan planning organizations such as councils of governments, and by requiring metropolitan planning and, in some cases, resource allocation within specific programs such as transportation. Federal general aid to agencies such as councils of governments reached its peak in the 1960s and 1970s and has now largely disappeared, but there are actions the federal government could take to encourage greater metropolitan cooperation and activity. It could, for example, make clear that all of its grant programs to local governments are also available to consortia of local governments and to metropolitan-area-wide organizations. It could further encourage regional applications by indicating that it would give a degree of priority to such applications or additional funds for local governments that engage in such regional applications. It could set aside a portion of grant funds for programs such as the community development block grant to be used *only* for metropolitan-area-wide projects. It could create a small program of grants for innovative metropolitan-area-wide initiatives, with an emphasis on those that deal with problems related to unequal opportunity in metropolitan areas.

More radical steps could also be taken. Downs (1994) proposes, for example, that the federal government allocate all federal assistance for local government in metropolitan areas through a regional institution created by area residents or by the state government. This regional allocation agency would have the power to "allocate the federal funds within each program area either to local governments or directly to households, service delivery agencies, or other recipients" (1994:76-177). The Intermodal Surface Transportation Efficiency Act already does something similar to this for federal transportation funding.

State Actions to Encourage Metropolitan Governance

Governance arrangements in metropolitan areas are ultimately a product of state government action. Local governments operate within a framework of state laws and regulations; they are, legally and constitutionally, creatures of the state. State governments could thus bring about forms of metropolitan governance. Indeed, both the Twin Cities Metropolitan Council and the Indianapolis Unigov were the product of state government activity rather than local choice. States may set up special districts within metropolitan areas; they may structure state laws to make municipal incorporation more difficult and to make annexation by cities easier. They can also reduce the power of local governments to engage in exclusionary local zoning behavior and can engage in redistributive tax and expenditure policy that favor more distressed jurisdictions within metropolitan areas.

State governments can also encourage cooperative metropolitan activity among local governments. Recent Virginia legislation, for example, provides state funding for the creation of regional partnerships among local governments and private-sector actors in pursuit of economic competitiveness (Richman and Oliver, 1997). Indeed, state governments could engage in all of the activities suggested in the previous section for the federal government.

NOTES

[1] We do not consider income transfer programs, since these do not address the *causes* of unequal opportunities and disparities.

[2] Fiscal capacity is defined as the per capita equalized market value of all real property in a jurisdiction.

[3] Despite these findings, evidence from citizen satisfaction surveys has frequently indicated strong black support for the results of metropolitan reform (see, for example, Stowers, 1996, in reference to Dade County and Lyons et al., 1992, who find greater satisfaction with services among blacks living in a neighborhood in the consolidated government of Lexington than among blacks living in a socially and economically similar black suburb in the fragmented Louisville metropolitan area).

[4] Only fragmentary evidence exists on whether such redistribution does indeed occur. One study (Hawkins and Hendrick, 1994) found fiscal redistribution between suburban areas and central cities through the tax and expenditure behavior of the overlapping county government in the Milwaukee area; another (Banovetz, 1965) found mixed evidence in the Twin Cities area.

5

Recommendations for Research and Policy Choices

This report has focused on the serious inequalities of opportunity in the nation's metropolitan areas and on the disparities in well-being among residents that result. It identifies multiple causes for these disparities, some of which involve national processes that are not the product of metropolitan phenomena and are unrelated to the system of metropolitan governance. However, the system of metropolitan governance, broadly construed as the committee has defined it, has contributed to unequal opportunity and resulting disparities.

In particular, metropolitan areas are currently characterized by unequal opportunity structures. A key component of these are unequal *spatial* opportunity structures: where one lives greatly constrains (or enhances) one's life chances and affects the notion of equality of opportunity. As the research cited and discussed in this report indicates, unequal spatial opportunity structures are an important contributor to the disparities in outcomes in metropolitan areas between blacks and whites and between city and suburban residents.

Unequal spatial opportunity structures in U.S. metropolitan areas are not solely the inevitable products of markets and technology. They result also from choices about the nature of public institutions and public policies that structure the operations of markets. They result, at least in part, from the existing system of metropolitan governance, a system characterized by fragmented local governments, each of which is largely dependent on its own tax base for financing and delivering public services for its residents and many of which, for those with general-purpose powers, have control over land use regulation within their boundaries. Efforts to bridge this fragmented system through regional mechanisms have been successful in many cases for common-purpose or system-maintenance functions but rarely for purposes that are overtly redistributive or that affect life-style issues.

RECOMMENDATIONS FOR RESEARCH

The committee is impressed by both the importance of the task it undertook and by how much remains to be known about it. It is very clear that additional research is needed, both with respect to causal processes and, even more so, with respect to the effects of policies that have been proposed and undertaken to deal with unequal spatial opportunity structures and unequal opportunity in metropolitan areas. The ability to conduct such research depends on the availability of relevant data, many of which can be gathered only by the federal government acting as a provider of public goods. We strongly urge that the Census Bureau and other related agencies continue to perform their vital role in collecting and providing data on metropolitan areas and their residents and governments. Indeed, such efforts should be expanded. Our recommendations for this research are presented in the sections that follow.

Spatial Distribution of Population and Its Determinants

Social and Geographic Mobility

We have described the spatial distribution of population between central city and suburbs and between poverty and nonpoverty neighborhoods and the extent to which metropolitan-area population is stratified by race and income. We need to know more, however, about both the social and geographic *mobility* of population, particularly with respect to areas of concentrated poverty and areas of racial concentration. The question of social and economic mobility is of critical importance to opportunity structures in general and spatial opportunity structures in particular. High research priority should therefore be given to examining the degree of income, occupational, and status mobility for low-income people in metropolitan areas, particularly for those growing up in areas of concentrated poverty, over their lifetimes and from generation to generation.

Geographic mobility is an additional area of concern. How much geographic mobility is there from areas of concentrated poverty? What types of households move into and out of poverty areas and why? Do the same people live in such areas over time, or is there "churning," with people constantly moving into and out of these areas? What proportion of those who move out move to other neighborhoods of concentrated poverty and what proportion to other types of neighborhoods? How would such churning affect the research literature on neighborhood effects? What is the relationship between how much time a child spends in an area of concentrated poverty and the power of the neighborhood effect? To what extent are areas of concentrated poverty "staging areas" for households moving to better areas and circumstances, and to what extent are they permanent ghettos for those who live there? Is it possible to identify and separate out the staging areas from the ghettos?

Suburbanization and Racial and Economic Stratification

Research has indicated that, although suburbanization is to some extent the product of the forces of markets and technology, the degree of racial and economic stratification that has characterized the suburbanization process has been highly affected by public policy. Another set of research questions builds on the evidence.

Research on the causes of *suburbanization* has been concerned with the extent to which suburbanization has resulted from natural processes, "push" factors related to the condition or characteristics of the central city that movers wish to avoid, and federal policies that have encouraged movement to the suburbs. Additional research is needed to sort out these factors and particularly to identify the nature of these "push" factors and their relative importance. How important to the suburbanization process are factors such as crime, poor schools, and racial avoidance, and what is their relative importance?

Cross-national studies of the pace and extent of suburbanization and its causes would be particularly useful. Such studies would allow examination of the impact of factors frequently cited as causes of suburbanization in the United States, such as racial avoidance and the impact of federal housing and highway programs, since these factors are not present, or are present to a lesser extent, in many other countries.

The highest-priority research, since it relates to ongoing processes that can presumably be affected by public policy, has to do with the *stratification of metropolitan areas by race and income*. There has been considerably more research conducted on the determinants of racial segregation than on economic segregation. Given the committee's interests, the broad question is why households are sorted (or sort themselves) in a manner that results in highly stratified areas.

There is debate about the extent to which stratification by neighborhood is inevitable. Recent research (Ellen, 1996) suggests that neighborhoods that are racially integrated over relatively long periods of time are not uncommon. Research is needed on the extent to which neighborhood racial and economic integration exists in the United States, its causes, and why it varies (if it does) across metropolitan areas. What do we know about the neighborhoods that are able to remain racially or economically diverse over time? What factors help to maintain this diversity? Are the racially integrated neighborhoods stable or transient? To what extent has the rapid increase in residential community associations and "gated communities" affected racial and economic stratification?

Cross-national research would also be useful here: What can be learned from studies of metropolitan area spatial and residential patterns, comparing and contrasting U.S. metropolitan areas to those of other countries? How much variation is there among countries in spatial segregation by income and race and in the location of the poor within metropolitan areas? What are the factors that account for differences in settlement patterns and for variation in the extent of spatial integration by income?

Public Policy Efforts to Affect Spatial Distribution

There have been a scattering of public efforts to attempt to consciously affect the spatial distribution of population through various devices to limit local land use controls. These include state or metropolitan-area review of local land use decisions (as in Portland and the Twin Cities), urban growth boundaries (Portland), state land use guidelines (Florida, New Jersey, and Oregon) and inclusionary zoning policies (New Jersey, California, and Oregon). Since these are possible countereffects to the current system of sorting and stratification, research to assess the effects of each of these approaches on the spatial distribution of population, and particularly on the location of low-income and minority households, is clearly of very high priority.

Outcome Disparities

Available data and research permit us to make relatively easy comparisons with respect to many important outcomes among whites and blacks, Hispanics and non-Hispanic whites (although there is difficulty in comparisons over time), and poverty and nonpoverty neighborhoods. The data are less useful in permitting comparisons among places, forcing us into central-city/suburban comparisons that may not be relevant for many purposes.

Inadequate descriptive data prevent us from gaining a clear understanding of the nature of disparities in metropolitan areas and force us into crude and often unhelpful central-city/suburb dichotomies. Efforts are urgently needed to classify jurisdictions within metropolitan areas on more sensitive dimensions, such as condition or function, and to use these classifications both for descriptive and for research purposes. We need to move beyond simple comparisons of central city and suburb so as to compare jurisdictions by income (poor, middle-income, wealthy), by fiscal capacity (high, medium, low), and by function (residential, commercial, industrial, mixed). This will require not only research on how to classify jurisdictions within metropolitan areas, but also a reaggregation of data into the relevant classification categories.

Fiscal Capacity Disparities

There is substantial research on tax/service disparities among major cities across metropolitan areas, but only scattered research on variation in tax/service capacity among local governments *within* metropolitan areas. A basic task is to compile data on variation in fiscal capacity among local governments in each (or a substantial sample of) metropolitan areas, as well as changes over time. If a summary measure of the extent of variation in fiscal capacity could be derived for each metropolitan area, the measure could then be used as a variable in research. Two such obvious research questions are what kinds of metropolitan areas have substantial variation in local fiscal capacity, and does variation in fiscal capacity contribute to variation in other disparities and outcomes? Research is also needed on the nature of fiscal flows within metropolitan areas (and particularly whether central cities are "exploited" by their suburbs).

Outcome Disparities Across Metropolitan Areas

Disparities in outcomes such as per capita income between central cities and suburbs and between minorities and whites vary, often dramatically, across metropolitan areas. These variations are particularly obvious with respect to regions: the ratio of central-city to suburban per capita income, for example, is much lower in the Northeast and the Midwest than in the South and the West; the ratio of black to non-Hispanic white per capita income is higher in the metropolitan areas of the West than elsewhere, but the ratio of Hispanic to non-white Hispanic income is lower in western metropolitan areas than elsewhere. One thesis holds that these variations reflect the degree to which the central cities of metropolitan areas are "elastic," that is, the extent to which central cities capture a high share of the metropolitan population (Rusk, 1993), but others have contested this explanation (Blair et al., 1996). Research is needed to test this hypothesis in a multivariate context that controls for region, economic structure and performance, and other possibly confounding variables.

Similarly, research is needed to examine the relationship of metropolitan-area density to disparities in outcomes. Although there is now a substantial amount of interest and research on the effect of density ("sprawl") on urban form, behavior, and costs, there has been virtually no research on the contribution, if any, of density to disparities in outcomes among jurisdictions or among groups. Does higher density, controlling for other factors, lead to a more equal income distribution, or to lower disparities between minorities and whites within metropolitan areas? Research on the effects of density on disparities is of particular importance, since density is potentially controllable through traditional land use policies.

Finally, and of critical importance to the mandate of the committee, to what extent does government structure and particularly "fragmentation" contribute to differences in outcomes? There has been some, but inadequate, research on the effect of fragmentation on disparities among jurisdictions, but virtually no research on how fragmentation affects disparities among individuals or groups: Are disparities between blacks and whites, for example, lower, controlling for other relevant factors, in less fragmented metropolitan areas (see Cutler and

Glaeser, 1997, for a preliminary view)? A first step in additional research efforts in this area is to create improved operational definitions of fragmented local government, so that the research results can correspond more directly to the underlying theoretical concern.

Spatial Opportunity Structure

The fundamental question with which this report has been concerned is the extent to which where one lives in a metropolitan area affects the life chances and well-being of individuals and groups. Another way of framing this question is to ask why the disparities among groups exist. The bridging research need is to sort out the portion of inequality of outcomes that is metropolitan in nature from the part that is due to broader causes—differences in human capital, changes in the demand for less-skilled labor, racial discrimination in employment—and is simply manifested in metropolitan areas because that is where most people live.

Metropolitan Place-Related Causes of Outcome Disparities

The broad question that we have asked is what is it that accounts for differences in important outcomes—outcomes such as income, employment, earnings, etc.—among residents of metropolitan areas and particularly between black and white residents and what part of that is due to metropolitan-related explanatory factors and the role of place and location.

At present, research knowledge is partial, fragmented, and often conflicting. It is evident, however, that there is a growing belief that the spatial dimension of job accessibility does contribute to outcome differences, and that neighborhood effects—the adverse consequences of living in a high-poverty neighborhood—do so as well. However, there have been few efforts to try to sort out the relative effects of job accessibility and neighborhood effects on outcomes.

Recent research strongly suggests that racial segregation plays a very important role in contributing to black/white differentials. Additional research on the effects of racial segregation on differences in outcomes between minorities and whites as well as research on the effects of economic stratification on these differences is clearly a very high priority. Research on whites living in conditions of varying economic segregation could effectively isolate the effect of economic segregation from that of racial segregation, which would be a finding of major importance. There has also been little or no research on the effects of factors such as density, population size, or elasticity on outcomes.

There is clearly a need to place all of the various factors in a more comprehensive model in order to assess the *relative* importance of each in accounting for differences in outcomes among groups in metropolitan areas.

Neighborhood Effects

Several recent reviews of the burgeoning literature on neighborhood effects indicate that the negative effects of living in neighborhoods of highly concentrated poverty do matter. Individuals residing in such areas are worse off than are similarly situated individuals living in other neighborhoods. Yet we know little about the causal mechanisms by which neighborhood effects operate. In particular, what are the mechanisms by which adverse peer group effects—such as identifying doing well in school with being "white"—operate and are transmitted, particularly among teenagers? Are neighborhood effects nonlinear, in that they begin to operate at some threshold level? If so, what is that threshold and how does it vary for different outcomes and population subgroups?

Effect of Fiscal Disparities and Jurisdictional Spending Differences on Disparities

Where one lives determines both the local taxes one pays and the level of spending on public services one receives. Do metropolitan areas with greater fiscal disparities among local governments also have greater disparities in outcomes among individuals and groups and, if so, what is the mechanism through which this occurs? We know that fiscal disparities lead to some combination of higher tax burdens and lower expenditures for residents of jurisdictions with low fiscal capacity, but empirically, what is the actual nature of the trade-off made, and how and why does it vary among low fiscal capacity jurisdictions?

The question of whether unequal spending on services among jurisdictions in metropolitan areas contributes to outcome disparities has been the subject of a very substantial amount of research with respect to education. Although the area is contentious, most research appears to find little or no relationship between spending and educational achievement as measured by test scores; however, a parallel body of research does find a positive relationship between educational spending and future labor market outcomes, leading to improved employment and income for those students who received the higher spending. How to relate these findings to each other is an obvious question for research.

There has been considerably less research on the relationship between unequal spending and outcome disparities in noneducational services, and additional research is needed to examine these services. In all cases, we need to know more about the production function or basic processes that are at work by which input resources are transformed into outcomes. What, for example, is the process through which dollars spent on education, or on public health, are transformed into educational achievement, or healthy individuals? In what ways do the resources purchased combine to produce outcomes? How can changes in resources, either in amount or in their organization, improve outcomes? An understanding of these processes is fundamental for directing policy toward changes to improve outcomes and reduce outcome disparities.

Policies to Reduce Disparities

This report discusses a range of strategies that may serve to reduce inequalities in spatial opportunity structures. In many cases, policies have been implemented in at least some places, and, although frequently anecdotal evidence is available, rigorous empirical work evaluating these initiatives with respect to their effects on reducing disparities is urgently needed. Research already exists or is under way in many areas, but the results are frequently partial and contested. Research is particularly needed on the effects of place-based initiatives, such as empowerment zones and community development corporations; on worker mobility and reverse commuting programs, such as Bridges to Work and community-based job development programs; on Gautreaux-type residential dispersion strategies; on the effect of providing housing vouchers on a regional basis; and on the impact of efforts to equalize educational expenditures.

Because of the importance of education and skill development to outcomes, particularly high priority should be given to continuing research on the effect of school organization and governance on educational and labor market outcomes. What are the effects, for example, of school choice programs, charter schools, and standards-based reform, on the educational outcomes of low-income students and students from low-income neighborhoods? How can these programs be structured to protect the interests of these students?

Regarding the equalization of educational expenditures, research is needed on both the extent to which various equalization efforts have actually reduced variations in spending among school districts and also on the effect of these efforts on overall spending. Has equalization been achieved, but at the expense of a reduction of overall spending, including spending on poor and minority students? What has been the effect of equalization efforts on educational outcomes and on disparities in outcomes among students? To what extent have these equalization efforts affected the locational choices of households and reduced their propensity to engage in fiscal sorting?

Research is also needed with respect to the effects on outcome disparities of tax policies to address fiscal disparities. Imposing a commuter tax on wages earned by suburban residents who work in the central city is frequently suggested as a means of increasing the fiscal capacity of the central city. Indeed, several states already permit cities to levy such a tax. Little is known, however, about their effects, particularly on business location decisions. Do such taxes place central cities at a disadvantage as a location for business and end up disadvantaging further city residents?

Metropolitan Governance and Its Effects

We examined the impact of the institutional structure of government on the spatial opportunity structure that produces differences in outcomes among individuals and groups in metropolitan areas. This is an area in which substantial research is needed, both on causal relationships and on policy options.

Fragmentation

We have argued that fragmentation of metropolitan areas into large numbers of local governments with land use and taxing powers results in sorting by race and economic status in metropolitan areas, and that this sorting underpins the unequal spatial opportunity structure we have detailed. Fragmentation, in this argument, plays a critical role in the production of inequalities. Although the argument seems theoretically compelling, it urgently needs to be subjected to the test of additional empirical research. We have already noted the need for a better operational measure for the concept of governmental fragmentation. With such a measure, research on the following two subjects would be of the very high priority:

• Does the extent of governmental fragmentation in metropolitan areas affect the degree of inequality of income or other important outcomes among individuals or groups in those areas?
• Does the extent of fragmentation affect the degree of racial and economic segregation in metropolitan areas?

Regionalism

To some extent, the above questions can be approached by an examination of the effects of existing regionalism in metropolitan areas. Metropolitan areas currently vary in the extent to which they can be characterized as consolidated or fragmented, and thus provide the opportunity for research on the effects of fragmentation. Areas in which the central city is highly elastic—that is, comprises a high proportion of metropolitan area population—can be considered to be examples in some sense of a regional government. Single-county metropolitan areas with strong county governments can also be considered highly regionalized. Nearly all metropolitan areas have some single-purpose authorities that are regional in scope. And in some cases, multipurpose regional government exists through explicit city-county consolidation or through other means.

The broad question is the effect of regionalism on outcomes. Within this framework, there are several important questions for further research:

- To what extent is there greater equalization of service delivery in more consolidated metropolitan areas, or in metropolitan areas with more "elastic" cities, than in more fragmented areas?
- Are the poor and central-city residents better off in metropolitan areas with more consolidated governmental systems?
- What are the redistributive effects of interlocal agreements and regional special purpose districts?

In addition to formal government structure, metropolitan governance encompasses informal efforts to engage in regional decision making through coalitions, alliances, or interaction across the public and private sectors and frequently involving business, nonprofit groups, churches, community groups, and other stakeholders in the metropolitan area. There is now a substantial amount of anecdotal evidence and case studies on these third-wave efforts at regional governance. However, this is another area in which more systematic empirical research is necessary. How widespread is the third wave of regional governance? What determines whether some areas are successful at undertaking regional governance collaborations and others are not? What are the objectives of these efforts and, in particular, to what extent are they concerned with systems maintenance activities, and to what extent at changes involving redistribution and life-style? What are the effects of these public-private sector regional collaborations on the spatial opportunity structure?

Regional approaches, whether through formal restructuring or more informal efforts, have the potential for broadly redistributing resources and power. The fear that such a redistribution will disadvantage various stakeholders has been a major deterrent to efforts to bring about more regional approaches. Research is needed on the extent to which such redistribution will occur and who will be the likely winners and losers. To what extent have central cities and their residents been advantaged or disadvantaged with respect to resource distribution, influence and political control as a result of the existence of metropolitan-area-wide institutions such as councils of governments, metropolitan planning organizations, and region-wide special districts, or as a result of more informal third-wave efforts? Have minorities been adversely affected?

The Role and Function of Cities

Existing knowledge on the continued economic viability and function of the central city and on the relationship of cities to suburbs seems particularly tentative. Research suggests that agglomeration economies continue to exist, but it is less clear that the downtowns of central cities are the necessary repositories of them. Is there still an economic rationale for central cities? Are agglomeration economies still important? To the extent that they are, have they decentralized so that economic activity located anywhere in the metropolitan area can take advantage of them? Or are there some important agglomeration economies (e.g., those that require frequent face-to-face interaction) that can only be taken advantage of through a central-city location?

The relationship between cities and their suburbs is an area of particularly contested research. It is clear that cities and suburbs are interdependent, in that they are part of the same regional economy. But to what extent does the condition and performance of the central city affect that of the suburbs and the metropolitan area as a whole? Initial research relying on simple bivariate correlations with implied causality is not sufficient. More recent research in a multivariate framework needs to be extended.

If the performance of the entire metropolitan area is affected by that of the central city, what are the mechanisms through which this occurs? It is frequently argued that business location decisions throughout the metropolitan area are affected by the image of the central city, but there is little empirical research to back this up. Similar arguments are made for the impact of the condition of central-city infrastructure on regional productivity with similarly scant evidence. Research to test these propositions would be desirable.

Many central cities as jurisdictions suffer from low fiscal capacity, for reasons that have been discussed. However, even within the fiscal constraints they face, it is widely believed that cities are inefficient. The perception that cities are inefficient and wasteful contributes to the belief among many that cities no longer provide a useful function. There is dispute on the extent to which high city costs in fact reflect higher needs as opposed to greater inefficiency. Research on the extent to which city services are efficiently provided after taking into account their higher needs would be useful in resolving this debate.

Many cities have attempted to reduce costs and improve efficiency through adopting new approaches to management and service delivery. These approaches, focusing on competition, performance-based budgeting, and accountability also should be the subject of additional research.

Finally, there is the question of whether effective political coalitions exist for change favorable to the central city and its residents. What are effective political coalitions at the state legislative level on behalf of city interests? Where policy changes favorable to cities have been enacted, what have been the legislative coalitions that have brought these about? How frequently and under what circumstances does a coalition of central city, inner suburbs, and developing middle-income suburbs emerge? What other kinds of (nonplace-based) coalitions of interests have emerged (e.g., civil rights advocates, environmentalists, housing developers), and under what circumstances, that support city interests?

Costs

Perhaps the most important research question of all has to do with the costs imposed by these problems, for the answer determines why, and whether, we consider unequal spatial opportunity structures and declining cities matters worthy of public concern. Throughout this report we have attempted to address this question, but it is clear that research is urgently needed. What are the costs imposed on suburbs and their residents—indeed on the entire metropolitan area and on the nation—of the decline of central cities? What are the costs imposed on the entire metropolitan area—and on the nation—of the disparities in outcomes brought about by unequal opportunity structures and thus unequal opportunity in metropolitan areas? Research should address a wide spectrum of possible costs involving, not only economic costs through lost productivity and lower purchasing power, but also social costs, such as crime and fear of crime, the diminution of individuals' quality of life through reduced enjoyment of amenities foregone, and the cost in terms of social disruption and political disintegration.

THINKING THROUGH THE POLICY CHOICES

The committee examined the range of available policy options with a full recognition of some important constraints. First, as set forth throughout this document, there are limits to the knowledge base about the causes of the problems we address and the likely effects of many of the solutions that have been suggested. The conclusions we draw regarding policy options are based on the existing state of knowledge, with the recognition that it is partial in many important areas.

We also recognize that all levels of government operate under fiscal constraints. Our proposals do not envision vast new expenditures of public funds. Nonetheless, there are areas in which additional spending may be necessary and appropriate, and there are certainly areas in which a reallocation of spending may be desirable.

Finally, we recognize that public attitudes and opinions about the appropriate role and scope of government, although perhaps changeable in the long run, limit the kind of action that is possible. It is an era in which government—and particularly the federal government—is not trusted, devolution is viewed as the most appropriate ordering of political power and authority, and public action is more acceptable at the state and local levels.

The committee's key concern is with reducing severe inequalities in metropolitan areas. We recognize that these inequalities and the disparities that result are not solely the product of metropolitan-level processes. Nonetheless, our primary focus has been on reshaping spatial opportunity structures in metropolitan areas so that life chances are not determined by where people live and so that choice and access to opportunities are maximized. To this end, we discuss the following policy choices as worthy of serious consideration.

Metropolitan Government and Governance

The committee considered two alternatives to the existing system of governance in metropolitan areas. Both are counterfactuals, in the sense that they require us to consider how their implementation would result in differences from the current system and to shape our discussion with these in mind. The first is a change in government structure that would reduce reliance on small-scale local governments and move to a system of more consolidated metropolitan government. The second would largely retain the existing system of nested local governments but would increase the role of the state government in reducing barriers to equal access and opportunity in metropolitan areas.

Metropolitan Consolidation

The committee is skeptical about what reformers typically have in mind by metropolitan government, because, in our judgment, it is both politically unfeasible and not wholly desirable. Instead, we are attracted by the merits of the kind of nested arrangement described in Chapter 4. Such an arrangement would retain the existing set of local governments, but within a changed structure of land use and fiscal powers.

The benefits of the existing system of local government in metropolitan areas are substantial in terms of efficiency, choice, accountability, and broad public support. What is often ignored, however, is that small-scale local governments function best when nested within larger, layered systems of government. This enables them to concentrate on the functions suitable to their scale, enabling the system as a whole to address effectively functions requiring larger scale, such as pollution control, water supply, the construction and operation of major airports, and the like.

Nested Government

The system of government in metropolitan areas in fact displays a highly functional nesting pattern, which has enabled it to respond adaptively to many new challenges. City governments in metropolitan areas are usually nested within county governments that provide many services to city residents, in such areas as public welfare, social services, parks, and environmental control. Counties in many areas have assumed functions previously performed by municipal governments, taking responsibility for such things as public hospitals and aspects of criminal justice administration. State governments, which provide the legal and constitutional framework for the existence of local government (see below), also overlay city governments. States have taken on greater responsibilities for high-way provision, income support and social service provision, educational funding and equalization, and power plant siting. Special districts, many of them regional or multicounty in scope, have been created in great numbers to finance and operate airports, transit systems, water supply and sewage disposal systems, and air and water pollution control. And many problems are addressed cooperatively by formal and informal agreements among individual units of local government and other entitites in metropolitan areas.

As this suggests, when a supra local approach is desirable, existing overlay-ing units of governments can provide services, or special districts can be created to do so. When a regional approach or perspective is more appropriate, creation of such entities as the Portland Metropolitan Service District and the Minneapolis-St. Paul Metropolitan Council is desirable, if locally supported and politically feasible. If such entities are not likely to emerge (i.e., in most metropolitan areas), then we find most appropriate the use and expansion of existing metro-politan forums and agencies, such as councils of governments, metropolitan planning organizations, regional special-purpose authorities, and public-private alliances on the metropolitan level. It is possible that, over time, one or more of these will organically emerge into an institution that has the ability to make decisions for the entire region in several functional areas.

The existing system of nested government in metropolitan areas has proven adaptable and flexible for many purposes, particularly those related to common-purpose concerns and efficiency objectives. It has not, however, been able to address effectively the life-style and redistributional concerns associated with the problem of severe inequality of opportunity on which the committee has focused. Restructuring the existing system of local government to create a consolidated or comprehensive metropolitan government would risk reducing the very real ben-efits produced by the existing system. In addition, it would not, in itself, lead to substantial changes in the metropolitan opportunity structure or to a reduction in unequal opportunity or disparities. Moreover, it clearly is not a solution favored by metropolitan-area residents. Instead, it is the role of the state government that is fundamental to addressing effectively the problem of an unequal spatial oppor-tunity structure.

Restructuring Metropolitan Governance: The Critical Role of the State

Local governments operate within a framework of state laws and regulations. Their very existence is a product of state action; the state is, after all, the locus of constitutional authority with respect to local governments. State laws regulating the behavior and authority of local government and state grants to help finance local government condition every aspect of local government behavior. State governments thus have the power and authority to bring about change in the metropolitan governance system by changing the legal framework within which local governments operate and the set of incentives they respond to.

We support changes in state regulatory frameworks and policies that will, in our judgment, lead to a reduction of severe inequality in metropolitan areas. Much of the discussion that follows involves state action, including state action to inhibit the ability of local governments to exclude low- and moderate-income and minority residents from living within their boundaries and to reduce disparities in fiscal capacity and need among local governments.

Eliminating Barriers to Equal Access and Opportunity

At present, high housing costs prevent low- and moderate-income households from gaining access to many suburban communities. The primary constraints are the exclusionary zoning practices made possible by local government control of land use regulation. These practices drive up the cost of housing beyond the means of low- and moderate-income households.

States have the legal authority to regulate the framework of local land use decisions to prevent exclusionary behavior by local governments; moreover, it is in their self-interest to do so. The state has a crucial interest in promoting metropolitan economies, since it is these economies that largely determine state economic performance. Exclusionary practices in metropolitan areas, to the extent that they reduce the access of workers to jobs, also reduce the state's economic potential and are surely an appropriate object of state concern.

We recognize that local governments are and will continue to be land use regulators. However, in our view, local land use powers should be exercised within the framework of explicit and actively enforced state guidelines and objectives. At a minimum, the state governments should stop being an agent for discriminatory action and a barrier to equal opportunity by failing to exercise oversight over the constitutional authority they have devolved to local government with respect to local land use controls. Beyond that, state oversight of local zoning is necessary to ensure that the exercise of local land use powers does not result in the exclusion of lower-income and minority households.

The committee urges strong consideration of the exercise of local land use control in a state government context so that such exclusionary practices are prevented or highly discouraged. State land use standards and state review of local government land use decisions to ensure compliance with these standards would accomplish this end, as would creation of a metropolitan land use agency operating under state standards and with either land use powers of its own or the ability to review local land use decisions.

Other techniques might also serve to lower housing costs and thus reduce in practice the exclusion of low- and moderate-income households and minorities from suburban areas. These include land use techniques (for example, upzoning, which should serve to lower the land cost of housing) and regulatory reform of housing and building codes. Eliminating these barriers to low- and moderate-income housing throughout metropolitan areas would free the private market and housing developers to meet the housing needs of the entire range of American households. Within this context, expansion of metropolitan-area-wide housing voucher programs (such as Section 8 certificates) would provide low- and moderate-income households with the effective demand to obtain housing in suburban areas, should they choose to do so.

The committee recognizes that reducing the ability of jurisdictions to exclude low- and moderate-income households through exclusionary zoning devices may result in some loss of allocative efficiency, by reducing the homogeneity of preferences among local residents as income segregation is reduced (Mills and Oates, 1975). If so, that would be a cost that we consider worth incurring as a means of reducing inequality of opportunity in metropolitan areas.

Reduce Housing Market Discrimination and Racial Segregation

The research reviewed in Chapter 3 provides strong evidence of the deleterious effects of segregation on outcomes for blacks. More vigorous efforts are required to enforce housing antidiscrimination laws in metropolitan areas and to ensure that access to housing credit is available on an nondiscriminatory basis. Matched-pair housing audits on a random basis, but with enough visibility so that realtors are aware of the possibility that they may be tested, are a particularly good means of both detecting discriminatory behavior and, more importantly, of deterring it through increasing the fear of being caught. In matched-pair audits, a minority and a white with similar credentials use the same realtor or visit the same apartment to determine whether they receive similar treatment.

Positive Action to Reduce Spatial Inequalities and Expand Opportunity

Breaking the Link Between Place of Residence and Access to Opportunity

Widespread movement of people to open up the suburbs to low- and moderate-income and minority households is likely to take a very long time and, in any case, some poor neighborhoods and pockets of poverty are likely to remain. There are two ways to break the link between place and outcome that are of particular importance: educational opportunity and access to suburban jobs.

Expanding the availability of *high-quality educational opportunity* will help to break the link between place of residence and quality of education. There are three main approaches to achieving significant improvement in educational opportunity, all controversial in some respect. One approach is the drive for within-state equalization of educational financial resources. A second approach emphasizes other means to increase educational quality, including the use of standards. A third approach champions choice, for some limited to the public schools and for others inclusive of private choices. None of these three is mutually exclusive; all three need to be carefully evaluated.

With respect to standards and school choice, the committee finds value in a wide range of intense experimentation and careful evaluation. We support continued experimentation with a wide range of school choice schemes, including charter schools, programs to increase the access of central-city children to suburban schools, and various types of voucher programs, including vouchers for private school attendance. Such efforts should be structured to bring about, as much as possible, the access of students currently living in areas with poor public schools to high-quality schools throughout the metropolitan area. This means that choice efforts should be targeted particularly to low-income and minority neighborhoods; special services (such as transportation) should be provided to improve the access of children in these neighborhoods to higher-quality schools; whenever possible, schools that are oversubscribed should admit students on a random basis (thus permitting meaningful evaluations of these programs and also ensuring that minority students are not underrepresented at the better schools). In the longer run, of course, the goal is to enable everyone to have access to quality educational opportunities.

Providing central-city residents with *access to suburban jobs* means efforts to provide them with reliable transportation, but transportation alone is not likely to suffice. Neighborhood-based job development efforts that include provision of job information and link city residents to job networks, provide employment counseling, and make direct contacts with employers are worth supporting at greater levels. Placement efforts that link suburban employers with inner-city workers and provide at least some screens for worker skills appear particularly promising when suburban labor markets are extremely tight. In such an environment, employers are often willing to hire workers whom they might otherwise not consider and whom they may not even know how to recruit.

Finally, access to some jobs in the suburbs is clearly denied because of discrimination. Antidiscrimination in employment legislation needs to be vigorously enforced and matched-pair employment audits on a random basis need to be undertaken.

Reducing the Disadvantages Faced by Cities and City Residents

An emphasis on opening up the suburbs to low- and moderate-income households and ending racial segregation should not be seen as "writing off" the cities or older suburbs. The main disadvantage for cities and city residents with respect to the spatial inequality structure under the current system of metropolitan governance is the problem of tax/service disparities. Residents of the central city, and of suburbs with low tax capacity and high expenditure needs, are faced with the dilemma of shouldering a high tax burden in order to finance an adequate level of public services or accepting poor public services at an average tax burden. City governments, as a consequence, experience chronic fiscal pressure; they are not able to provide adequate levels of service at reasonable tax rates. Efforts to improve services by increasing taxes run up against the openness of city borders: residents and businesses on whom taxes fall most heavily can avoid them by moving from the city to the suburbs.

Local governments should continue to have the responsibility for raising much of their own revenue and for providing public services. They should also be encouraged to continue to engage in new approaches, such as privatization and performance contracting, designed to make their government more efficient. However, greater efficiency, although highly desirable, does not address the problem of disparities in fiscal capacity and need among local governments. To achieve more equal spatial opportunity structures, we support efforts to reduce these tax/service disparities.

There are a variety of potential means for accomplishing this. The most direct is *state fiscal equalization grants* to local governments, similar to those that exist in most developed nations for their subnational governments. These grants would be for general support purposes and would provide cities and other similarly situated local governments with funds sufficient to support an adequate level of services, if they taxed themselves at some standard level of taxation. The grants would take into account the fact that cities not only provide services for suburban communities but also bear the burden of supporting a disproportionate share of people in extreme need, including, in some instances, immigrant groups. Such a system of fiscal equalization grants does not envision that each local government would spend the same amount per capita or that they would all impose the same local tax rate, or that local governments could not raise additional revenues for expenditure by taxing themselves above the standard rate. It is designed, however, so that every local government has the same ability, if it so chooses, to finance an adequate level of public services.

There are also regional mechanisms for dealing with the problem of fiscal disparities. The justification for these is that, since the central city both provides services for suburban commuters and is the source of amenities that benefit the entire region, it is reasonable to ask the entire region to participate in funding some portion of city services. Regional mechanisms as a possible means of reducing fiscal disparities include *metropolitan tax base sharing*, county assumption of selected city government service functions, and state permission for cities to levy a *local income tax,* including a tax on the income earned within the city by employees who reside outside the city.

Improving Human Capital

The committee's charge, as we interpret it, is relatively narrow in scope, focusing on the contribution of spatial opportunity structures in metropolitan areas to unequal opportunity. We therefore did not range widely over the full set of problems, issues, and policies affecting metropolitan areas and their residents. However, we cannot avoid touching on the concern of human capital development. Differences in human capital account for a substantial portion of the disparities in outcomes between minorities and whites and between city and suburban residents. Some of these differences are, in themselves, related to unequal spatial opportunity structures. Our broad conclusion is that increased emphasis is needed on human capital development—early childhood education, elementary and secondary education, increasing the rate of high school graduation and college attendance, and preparing potential workers for employment. Such efforts are particularly important for individuals who are adversely affected by where they live, given the present spatial opportunity structure.

References

Abbott, Carl
    1997   The Portland region: Where city and suburbs talk to each other—and often agree. *Housing Policy Debate* 8(1):11-51.

Abramson, Alan, Mitchell Tobin, and Matthew VanderGoot
    1995   The changing geography of metropolitan opportunity: The segregation of the poor in U.S. metropolitan areas, 1970-1990. *Housing Policy Debate* 6(1):45-72.

Bahl, Roy
    1994   Metropolitan fiscal disparities. *Cityscape* 1(1):293-306.

Bailey, Thomas
    1995   *Learning to Work.* Washington DC: The Brookings Institution.

Banfield, Edward
    1957   The politics of metropolitan area organization. *Midwest Journal of Political Science* 1(May):77-91.

Banovetz, James
    1965   *Governmental Cost Burdens and Service Benefits in the Twin Cities Metropolitan Area.* Minneapolis: University of Minnesota.

Barnett, Steven
    1996   Economics of school reform: Three promising approaches. In *Holding Schools Accountable*, Helen Ladd, ed. Washington, DC: The Brookings Institution.

Bartel, Ann
    1989   Where do the new U.S. immigrants live? *Journal of Labor Economics* 7:371-391.

Bell, Michael
    1994   Tax-base sharing revisited: issues and options. In *Fiscal Equalization for State and Local Government Finance*, John Anderson, ed. Westport, CT.: Praeger.

Benton, J. Edwin, and Darwin Gamble
    1984   City/county consolidation and economies of scale: Evidence from a time-series analysis in Jacksonville, Florida. *Social Science Quarterly* 65(March):190-198.

Bernhardt, Annette, Martina Morris, Mark Handcock, and Marc Scott
    1997   Job Instability and Wage Inequality: Preliminary Results from Two NLS Cohorts. Un-
            published paper, Institute on Education and the Economy, Columbia University.
Berry, Brian
    1973   *Human Consequences of Urbanization: Divergent Paths in the Urban Experience of the
            Twentieth Century.* New York: St. Martin's Press.
Bingham, Richard, and Veronica Kalich
    1996   The tie that binds: Downtowns, suburbs, and the dependence hypothesis. *Journal of
            Urban Affairs* 18(2):153-171.
Bish, Robert
    1971   *The Public Economy of Metropolitan Areas.* Chicago: Markham.
Blair, John, Samuel Staley, and Zhongcai Zhang
    1996   A critical appraisal of Rusk's theory of urban development. *Journal of the American
            Planning Association* 62(3):345-353.
Bloch, Farrell
    1994   *Anti-Discrimination Law and Minority Employment.* Chicago: University of Chicago
            Press.
Blomquist, William, and Roger Parks
    1995   Fiscal, service, and political impacts of Indianapolis-Marion County's Unigov. *Publius:
            The Journal of Federalism* 25(4):37-54.
Bollens, Scott
    1986   A political-ecological analysis of inequality in metropolitan areas. *Urban Affairs Quar-
            terly* 22:221-41.
Bolotin, Frederic, and David Cingranelli
    1983   Equity and urban policy: The underclass hypothesis revisited. *Journal of Politics*
            45(1):209-219.
Boyne, George
    1992a   Is there a relationship between fragmentation and local government cost? *Urban Affairs
            Quarterly* 28(2):317-322.
    1992b   Local government structure and performance. *Public Administration* 70(Autumn):333-357.
Bradford, David, and Wallace Oates
    1974   Suburban exploitation of cities and governmental structure. In *Redistribution Through
            Public Choice*, Harold Hochman and George Peterson, eds. New York: Columbia Univer-
            sity Press
Burns, Nancy
    1994   *The Formation of American Local Governments: Private Values in Public Institutions.*
            New York: Oxford University Press.
Burtless, Gary
    1996   Introduction and summary. In *Does Money Matter: The Effects of School Resources on
            Student Achievement and Adult Success*, Gary Burtless, ed. Washington, DC: The
            Brookings Institution.
Burtless, Gary, ed.
    1990   *A Future of Lousy Jobs? The Changing Structure of U.S. Wages.* Washington, DC: The
            Brookings Institution.
Calavita, Nico, Kenneth Grimes, and Alan Mallach
    1997   Inclusionary housing in California and New Jersey: A comparative analysis. *Housing
            Policy Debate* 8(1):109-142.
Card, David, and Alan Krueger
    1996   School resources and student outcomes: An overview of the literature and new evidence
            from North and South Carolina. *The Journal of Economic Perspectives* 10(4):31-50.

Carl Vinson Institute of Government
  1989   *The Impacts of City-County Consolidations: A Review of Research Findings*. Athens: Governmental Research and Services Division, Carl Vinson Institute of Government, University of Georgia.
Carver, Joan
  1973   Responsiveness and consolidation: A case study. *Urban Affairs Quarterly* 9(2):211-250.
Case, Anne, and Lawrence Katz
  1991   The Company You Keep: The Effects of Family and Neighborhood on Disadvantaged Youths. Working paper no. 3705. Cambridge, MA: National Bureau of Economic Research.
Chernick, Howard, and Andrew Reschovsky
  1995   Urban Fiscal Problems: Coordinating actions among governments. *Lafayette Policy Review*, Fall, 195.
  1997   Urban Fiscal Problems: Coordinating actions among governments. In *The Urban Crisis: Linking Research to Action*, Burton Weisbord and James Wonthy, eds. Evanston, IL: Northwestern University Press.
Chicoine, David, and Norman Walzer
  1985   *Governmental Structure and Local Public Finance*. Boston: Oelgeschlager, Gunn & Hain.
Clapp, John
  1983   A model of public policy toward office location. *Environment and Planning A* 15:1299-1309.
Clotfelter, Charles, and Helen Ladd
  1996   Recognizing and rewarding success in public schools. In *Holding Schools Accountable*, Helen Ladd, ed. Washington DC: The Brookings Institution.
Coleman, James, Ernest Campbell, Carol Hobson, James McPartland, Alexander Mood, Frederic Weinfeld, and Robert York
  1966   *Equality of Educational Opportunity*. Washington, DC: U.S. Government Printing Office.
Corcoran, Mary, and Terry Adams
  1997   Race, sex and the intergenerational transmission of poverty. In *Consequences of Growing Up Poor*, Greg Duncan and Jeanne Brooks-Gunn, eds. New York: Russell Sage.
Corcoran, Mary, Roger Gordon, Deborah Laren, and Gary Solon
  1992   The association between men's economic status and their family and community origins. *Journal of Human Resources* 27(4):575-601.
Couch, Jim, William Shughart, and Al Williams
  1993   Private school enrollment and public school performance. *Public Choice* 76:301-312.
Cutler, David, and Edward Glaeser
  1997   Are ghettos good or bad? *Quarterly Journal of Economics* 112(3):827-872.
Daniel, Kermit
  1994   Fiscal and Political Implications of the Concentration of Immigrants. Working Paper #186. Philadelphia: Real Estate Center, Wharton School of the University of Pennsylvania.
Danielson, Michael
  1976   *The Politics of Exclusion*. New York: Columbia University Press.
Danielson, Michael, and Julian Wolpert
  1992   Rapid metropolitan growth and community disparities. *Growth and Change* 23(4):494-515.
  1994   From old to new metropolis. In *Research in Community Sociology* 4:71-96.
Dodge, William
  1996   *Regional Excellence: Governing Together to Compete Globally and Flourish Locally*. Washington, DC: National League of Cities.

Dolan, Drew
    1990   Local government fragmentation: Does it drive up the cost of government? *Urban Affairs Quarterly* 26(1):28-45.

Dowding, Keith, Peter John, and Stephen Biggs
    1994   Tiebout: A survey of the empirical literature. *Urban Studies* 31(4/5):767-797.

Downes, Thomas, and Thomas Pogue
    1994   Accounting for fiscal capacity and need in the design of school aid formulas. In *Fiscal Equalization for State and Local Government Finance*, John Anderson, ed. Westport, CT: Praeger.

Downs, Anthony
    1994   *New Visions for Metropolitan America*. Washington DC: The Brookings Institution.
    1997   The challenge of our declining big cities. *Housing Policy Debate* 8(2):359-408.

Drachman Institute
    1992   Reverse Commute Transportation: Emerging Provider Roles. Prepared for the U.S. Federal Transit Administration by the University of Arizona.

Durning, Dan
    1995   The effects of city-county government consolidation: The perspectives of United States government employees in Athens-Clarke County, Georgia. *Public Administration Quarterly* 19(Fall):272-298.

Dye, Thomas, and Brett Hawkins, eds.
    1971   *Politics in the Metropolis: A Reader in Conflict and Cooperation*. Columbus, OH: Charles E. Merrill.

Eberts, Randy, and T. Gronberg
    1981   Jurisdictional homogeneity and the Tiebout model. *Journal of Urban Economics* 10: 227-239.

Education Week
    1998   The urban challenge. Jan. 8, 1998.

Ellen, Ingrid
    1996   Sharing America's Neighborhoods: The Changing Prospects for Stable Racial Integration, Ph.D. thesis, Harvard University.

Ellen, Ingrid, and Margery Turner
    1997   Does neighborhood matter? Assessing recent evidence. *Housing Policy Debate* 8(4):833-866.

Ellwood, David
    1986   The spatial mismatch hypothesis: Are there teenage jobs missing in the ghetto? In *The Black Youth Employment Crisis*, Richard Freeman and Harry Holzer, eds. Chicago: University of Chicago Press.

Erie, Steven, John Kirlin, and Francine Rabinowitz
    1972   Can something be done? Propositions on the performance of metropolitan institutions. In *Reform of Metropolitan Institutions*, Lowden Wingo, ed. Washington, DC: Resources for the Future.

Farley, Reynods, Elaine Fielding, and Maria Krysan
    1997   The residential preferences of blacks and whites: A four metropolis analysis. *Housing Policy Debate* 8(4):763-800.

Farley, Reynolds, and William Frey
    1993   Changes in the segregation of whites from blacks during the 1980s. *American Sociological Review* 59(Feb.):23-45.

Farley, Reynolds, Charlotte Steeh, Tara Jackson, Maria Krysan, and Keith Reeves
    1993   Continued racial residential segregation in Detroit: "Chocolate City, Vanilla Suburbs" revisited. *Journal of Housing Research* 4:1-38.

Ferguson, Ronald
  1991   Paying for public education: New evidence on how and why money matters. *Harvard Journal on Legislation* 28(2):465-498.
Ferguson, Ronald, and Helen Ladd
  1996   How and why money matters: An analysis of Alabama schools. In *Holding Schools Accountable: Performance-Based Reform in Education*, Helen Ladd, ed. Washington, DC: The Brookings Institution.
Firebaugh, G., and K.E. Davis
  1988   Trends in antiblack prejudice, 1972-1984: Region and cohort effects. *American Journal of Sociology* 94:251-272.
Fischel, William
  1996   How *Serrano* caused Proposition 13. *Journal of Law and Politics* 12(4):607-636.
  1997   Comment on Carl Abbott's "The Portland region: Where city and suburbs talk with each other—and often agree." *Housing Policy Debate* 8(1):65-73.
Foster, Kathryn
  1996   Specialization in government: The uneven use of special districts in metropolitan areas. *Urban Affairs Review* 31(3):283-313.
  1997   *The Political Economy of Special-Purpose Government.* Washington, DC: Georgetown University Press.
Freeman, Richard
  1992   Crime and the employment of disadvantaged youth. In *Urban Labor Markets and Job Opportunity*, George Peterson and Wayne Vroman, eds. Washington, DC: The Urban Institute Press.
  1996   Why do so many young American men commit crimes and what might we do about it? *Journal of Economic Perspectives* 10(1):25-42.
Frey, William
  1993   People in places: Demographic trends in urban America. In *Rediscovering Urban America*, Jack Sommers and Donald Hicks, eds. Washington, DC: Office of Policy Development and Research, U.S. Department of Housing and Urban Development.
  1995   The new geography of population shifts. In *State of the Union, Volume Two: Social Trends*, Reynolds Farley, ed. New York: Russell Sage Foundation.
Galster, George
  1993   Polarization, place and race. *North Carolina Law Review* 71(5):1421-1462.
  1997   An Econometric Model of the Metropolitan Opportunity Structure. Draft Final Report to the Fannie Mae Foundation. July. The Urban Institute, Washington, DC.
Galster, George, and Mark Keeney
  1988   Race, residence, discrimination, and economic opportunity: Modeling the nexus of urban racial phenomena. *Urban Affairs Quarterly* 24(1):87-117.
Galster, George, and Sean Killen
  1995   The geography of metropolitan opportunity: A reconnaissance and conceptual framework. *Housing Policy Debate* 6(1):7-43.
Garreau, Joel
  1991   *Edge City: Life on the Frontier.* New York: Doubleday.
Gramlich, Edward, Deborah Lauren, and Naomi Sealand
  1992   Mobility into and out of poor neighborhoods. In *Drugs, Crime, and Social Isolation*, Adele Harrell and George Peterson, eds. Washington, DC: The Urban Institute Press.
Green, Richard, and Andrew Reschovsky
  1994   Fiscal assistance to municipal governments. In *Dollars and Sense: Policy Choices and the Wisconsin Budget, Volume III*, Donald Nichols, ed., Madison: Robert M. LaFollette Institute of Public Affairs, University of Wisconsin-Madison.

Greene, Jay, Paul Peterson, and Jiangtao Du
  1997   Effectiveness of School Choice: The Milwaukee Experiment. Occasional Paper 97-1, Taubman Center for State and Local Government, Kennedy School of Government, Harvard University.

Greene, Kenneth, and Thomas Parliament
  1980   Political externalities, efficiency, and the welfare losses from consolidation. *National Tax Journal* 33:209-217.

Greer, Scott
  1963   *Metropolitics: A Study of Political Culture.* New York: John Wiley and Sons.

Gustely, Richard
  1977   The allocational and distributional impacts of governmental consolidation: The Dade County experience. *Urban Affairs Quarterly* 12(3):349-364.

Hamilton, Bruce
  1975   Property taxes and the Tiebout hypothesis: Some empirical evidence. In *Fiscal Zoning and Land Use Controls,* Edwin Mills and Wallace Oates, eds. Lexington, MA: D.C. Heath.

Hamilton, Bruce, Edwin Mills, and David Puryear
  1975   The Tiebout hypothesis and residential income segregation. In *Fiscal Zoning and Land Use Controls,* Edwin Mills and Wallace Oates, eds. Lexington, MA: D.C. Heath.

Hanushek, Eric
  1989   Impact of differential expenditures on school performance. *Educational Researcher* 18(4):45-51.
  1996   School resources and student performance. In *Does Money Matter: The Effect of School Resources on Student Achievement and Adult Success*, Gary Burtless, ed. Washington, DC: Brookings Institution Press.

Harrigan, John
  1993   *Political Change in the Metropolis.* New York: HarperCollins.
  1996   Minneapolis-St. Paul: Structuring metropolitan government. In *Regional Politics: America in a Post-City Age,* H.V. Savitch and Ronald Vogel, eds. Thousand Oaks, CA: Sage Publications.

Hartshorn, Truman
  1986   Suburban Business Centers: Employment Expectations. Final Report prepared for the U.S. Department of Commerce, Economic Development Administration, Washington, DC.

Hartshorn, Truman, and Peter Muller
  1989   Suburban downtowns and the transformation of metropolitan Atlanta's business landscape. *Urban Geography* 10:375-395.

Haveman, Robert, and Barbara Wolfe
  1994   *Succeeding Generations.* New York: Russell Sage Foundation.

Hawkins, Brett
  1966   *Nashville Metro.* Nashville: Vanderbilt University Press.

Hawkins, Brett, and Thomas Dye
  1971   Metropolitan fragmentation: A research note. In *Politics in the Metropolis: A Reader in Conflict and Cooperation*, Thomas Dye and Brett Hawkins, eds. Columbus, OH: Charles E. Merrill.

Hawkins, Brett, and Rebecca Hendrick
  1994   Do county governments reinforce city-suburban inequalities: A study of city and suburban service allocations. *Social Science Quarterly* 75(4):754-771.
  1997   Do metropolitan special districts reinforce sociospatial inequalities? A study of sewerage and technical education in Milwaukee County. *Publius: The Journal of Federalism* 27(1):135-143.

Hawkins, Brett, Keith Ward, and Mary Becker
1991   Governmental consolidation as a strategy for metropolitan development. *Public Adminis-*
tration Quarterly 15(2):252-267.
Hedges, Larry, and Rob Greenwald
1996   Have times changed? The relation between school resources and student performance. In
Does Money Matter: The Effect of School Resources on Student Achievement and Adult
Success, Gary Burtless, ed. Washington, DC: Brookings Institution Press.
Hedges, Larry, Richard Laine, and Rob Greenwald
1994   Does money matter: A meta-analysis of studies of the effects of differential school inputs
on student outcomes. *Educational Researcher* 23(April):5-14.
Heilbrun James
1987   *Urban Economics and Public Policy.* New York: St. Martin's Press.
Henig, Jeffrey
1998   School Choice Outcomes: A Review of What We Know. Discussion paper prepared for
the Conference on School Choice, Law and Public Policy, University of California, Berkeley, April 17-18, 1998. Department of Political Science, George Washington University.
Hicks, Donald
1987   Urban policy in the U.S.: Introduction. *Urban Studies* 24:439-446.
Hill, Edward, and Harold Wolman
1997a   Accounting for the change in income disparities between US central cities and their
suburbs from 1980 to 1990. *Urban Studies* 34(1):43-60.
1997b   City-suburban income disparities and metropolitan area employment: Can tightening labor markets reduce the gaps? *Urban Affairs Review* 32(4):558-582.
1997c   What Lies Behind Changes in Income Disparities Between Central Cities and Their Suburbs from 1980 to 1990? Paper prepared for the Economic Development Administration,
U.S. Department of Commerce, Washington, DC.
Hill, Edward, Harold Wolman, and Coit Ford
1995a   Can suburbs survive without their central cities: Examining the suburban dependence
hypothesis. *Urban Affairs Review* 31(2):147-174.
1995b   Response to straw men, etc. *Urban Affairs Review* 31(2):180-183.
Hill, Richard
1974   Separate and unequal: Government inequality in the metropolis. *American Political Sci-*
ence Review 68:1557-1568.
Hirsch, Werner
1968   The supply of urban public services. In *Issues in Urban Economics*, Harvey Perloff and
Lowden Wingo, eds. Baltimore: Johns Hopkins University Press.
Holzer, Harry
1994   Black employment problems: New evidence, old questions. *Journal of Policy Analysis*
and Management 13(4):699-722.
1996   *What Employers Want.* New York: Russell Sage Foundation.
Horan, James, and G. Thomas Taylor
1977   *Experiments in Metropolitan Government.* New York: Praeger Publishers.
Hoxby, Caroline
1994   Do Private Schools Provide Competition for Public Schools? Working paper, National
Bureau for Economic Research, Cambridge, MA.
1996a   The effects of private school vouchers on schools and students. In *Holding Schools*
Accountable: Performance-Based Reform in Education, Helen Ladd, ed. Washington,
DC: Brookings Institution Press.
1996b   How to do (and not to do) school finance equalization: The legacy and lessons of Serrano.
Proceedings of the National Tax Association.

1997   Evidence on School Choice: What We Learn from the Traditional Forms of School Choice in the U.S. Paper prepared for the Educational Policy and Governance Program, Taubman Center for State and Local Government, Harvard University.

Hughes, Mark
1995   A mobility strategy for improving opportunity. *Housing Policy Debate* 6(1):271-297.

Ihlanfeldt, Keith
1992   *Jobs Accessibility and the Employment and School Enrollment of Teenagers.* Kalamazoo, MI: W.E. Upjohn Institute for Employment Research.
1995   The importance of the central city to the regional economy: A review of the arguments and empirical evidence. *Cityscape* 1(2):125-143.

Immergluck, Daniel
1998   Job proximity and the urban employment problem: Do suitable nearby jobs improve neighborhood employment rates? *Urban Studies* 35(1):7-23.

Innes, Judith
1992   Group processes and the social construction of growth management. *Journal of the American Planning Association* 58(4):440-453.
1996   Planning through consensus building: A new view of the comprehensive planning ideal. *Journal of the American Planning Association* 62(4):460-471.

Jargowsky, Paul
1997   *Poverty and Place: Ghettos, Barrios, and the American City.* New York: Russell Sage Foundation.

Jencks, Christopher, and Susan Mayer
1990   The social consequences of growing up in a poor neighborhood. In *Inner City Poverty in the United States*, Lawrence Lynn and Michael McGeary, eds. Committee on National Urban Policy, National Research Council. Washington, DC: National Academy Press.

Kain, John, and Kraig Singleton
1996   Equality of educational opportunity revisited. *New England Economic Review* (May/June):87-111.

Kasarda, John
1995   Industrial restructuring and the changing location of jobs. In *State of the Union: America in the 1990s: Volume One: Economic Trends*, Reynolds Farley, ed. New York: Russell Sage Foundation.

Kasarda, John, Stephen Appold, Stuart Sweeney, and Elaine Sieff
1997   Central city and suburban migration patterns: Is a turnaround on the horizon? *Housing Policy Debate* 8(2):307-358.

Keating, Michael
1995   Size, efficiency and democracy: Consolidation, fragmentation, and public choice. In *Theories of Urban Politics*, David Judge, Gerry Stoker, and Harold Wolman, eds. Thousand Oaks, CA: Sage Publishers.

Kleit, Rachel
1997   Housing, Social Networks, and Access to Opportunity: Modeling the Benefits of Mixed-Income Housing. Paper presented at the Association of Collegiate Schools of Planning Conference, Fort Lauderdale, FL, November.

Knapp, Gerrit
1989   The political economy of growth management in Oregon: A historical review. *Review of Regional Studies* 18(Winter):43-49.
1990   State land use planning and exclusionary zoning: Evidence from Oregon. *Journal of Planning Education and Research* 10(1):39-46.

Knox, Paul
1997   Globalization and urban economic change. *The Annals of the American Academy of Political and Social Science* 551(May):17-27.

Ladd, Helen

1994a   Big city finances. In *Big-City Politics, Governance, and Fiscal Constraints,* George Peterson, ed. Washington, DC: Urban Institute Press.

1994b   Measuring disparities in the fiscal condition of local governments. In *Fiscal Equalization for State and Local Government Finance,* John Anderson, ed. Westport, CT: Praeger.

1994c   Spatially targeted economic development strategies: Do they work? *Cityscape* 1(1):193-218.

Ladd, Helen, and John Yinger

1991   *America's Ailing Cities: Fiscal Health and the Design of Urban Policy.* Baltimore: Johns Hopkins University Press.

1994   The case for equalizing aid. *National Tax Journal* 47(1):211-224.

Lalonde, Robert

1995   The promise of public-sector sponsored training programs. *Journal of Economic Perspectives* 9(2):149-168.

Ledebur, Larry, and William Barnes

1992   *Metropolitan Disparities and Economic Growth: City Distress and the Need for a Federal Local Growth Package. Research Report on America's Cities.* Washington, DC: National League of Cities.

1993   *All in It Together: Cities, Suburbs and Local Economic Regions.* Washington, DC: National League of Cities.

Lehman, Jeffrey

1994   Updating urban policy. In *Confronting Poverty: Prescriptions for Change,* Sheldon Danzinger, Gary Sandefur, and Daniel Weinberg, eds. New York: Sage Foundation.

Levin, Henry

1998   Educational vouchers: effectiveness, choice, and costs. *Journal of Policy Analysis and Management* 17(3):373-392.

Levy, Frank, and Richard Murnane

1992   U.S. earnings levels and earnings inequality: A review of recent trends and proposed explanations. *Journal of Economic Literature* 30:1333-1381.

Lewis, Paul

1995   Suburban Separation: Political Fragmentation and the Jobs/Housing Mismatch. Paper delivered at the American Political Science Association, San Francisco.

1996   *Shaping Suburbia: How Political Institutions Organize Urban Development.* Pittsburgh: University of Pittsburgh Press.

Logan, John, and Mark Schneider

1982   Governmental organizations and city/suburb income inequality. *Urban Affairs Quarterly* 17:305-318.

Lyons, W.E., David Lowery, and Ruth DeHoog

1992   *The Politics of Dissatisfaction: Citizens, Services and Urban Institutions.* Armonk, NY.: M.E. Sharpe Inc.

Marando, Vincent, and Carl Whitley

1972   City-county consolidation: An overview of voter response. *Urban Affairs Quarterly* 8(Dec.):181-203.

Maryland Office of Planning

1997   *Managing Maryland's Growth.* Baltimore: Maryland Office of Planning.

Massey, Douglas, and Nancy Denton

1993   *American Apartheid: Segregation and the Making of the Underclass.* Cambridge, MA: Harvard University Press.

Mayer, Christopher

1996   Does location matter? *New England Economic Review* (May/June):26-40.

Meier, Kenneth J., Joseph Stewart, and Robert England
    1991   The politics of bureaucratic discretion: Educational access as an urban service. *American Journal of Political Science* 35(1):155-177.

Metropolitan Council of the Twin Cities
    1997   *First Annual Report on the Metropolitan Livable Communities Fund.* St. Paul: Metropolitan Council of the Twin Cities.

Mieszkowski, Peter, and Edwin Mills
    1993   The causes of metropolitan suburbanization. *Journal of Economic Perspectives* 7(3):135-147.

Mills, Edwin
    1992   Sectoral clustering and metropolitan growth. In *Sources of Metropolitan Growth*, Edwin Mills and John McDonald, eds. New Brunswick: Rutgers University Center for Urban Policy Research.

Mills, Edwin, and Luan Lubuele
    1997   Inner cities. *Journal of Economic Literature* 35(2):727-756.

Mills, Edwin, and Wallace Oates
    1975   The theory of local public services and finance: Its relevance to urban fiscal and zoning behavior. In *Fiscal Zoning and Land Use Controls*, Edwin Mills and Wallace Oates, eds. Lexington, MA: Lexington Books.

Morgan, David, and Patrice Mareschal
    1996   Central City/Suburban Inequality and Metropolitan Political Fragmentation. Paper presented at the annual meeting of the American Political Science Association, San Francisco, Aug. 29-Sept. 1, 1996.

Muller, Peter
    1997   The suburban transformation of the globalizing American city. *Annals of the American Academy of Political and Social Science* 551(May):44-58.

National Research Council
    1988   *Urban Change and Poverty,* Michael McGeary and Laurence Lynn, eds. Committee on National Urban Policy. Washington, DC: National Academy Press.
    1990   *Inner-City Poverty in the United States.* Laurence Lynn and Michael McGeary, eds. Committee on National Urban Policy. Washington, DC: National Academy Press.

Neal, Derek
    1997   The effects of Catholic secondary schooling on educational achievement. *Journal of Labor Economics* 15(1) part 1:98-123.

Neal, Derek, and William Johnson
    1996   The role of pre-market factors in black-white wage differentials. *Journal of Political Economy* 104(5):869-895.

Nelson, Arthur
    1996   Portland: The metropolitan umbrella. In *Regional Politics: America in a Post-City Age*, H.V. Savitch and Ronald Vogel, eds. Thousand Oaks, CA: Sage Publications.

Nelson, Michael
    1990   Decentralization of the subnational public sector: An empirical analysis of the determinants of local government structure in metropolitan areas in the U.S. *Southern Economic Journal* 57(2):443-457.

Nunn, Samuel, and Mark Rosentraub
    1996   Metropolitan fiscal equalization: disstilling lessons from four U.S. programs. *Local Government Review* (Fall)195.

Oakerson, Ronald
    1998   *Governing Local Public Economies.* San Francisco: ICS Press.

Oakland, William
    1994   Recognizing and correcting for fiscal disparities: A critical analysis. In *Fiscal Equalization for State and Local Government Finance*, John Anderson, ed. Westport, CT: Praeger.

Oates, Wallace
   1969   The effects of property taxes and local public spending on property values: An empirical study of tax capitalization and the Tiebout hypothesis. *Journal of Political Economy* 77(Nov.-Dec.):957-990.

O'Hare, William, and William H. Frey
   1992   Booming, suburban, and black. *American Demographics* 14:30-38.

O'Regan, Katherine, and John Quigley
   1996   Spatial effects upon employment outcomes: The case of New Jersey teenagers. *New England Economic Review* (May/June):41-59.

Orfield, Gary, with the assistance of Sara Schley, Diane Glass, and Sean Reardon
   1993   *The Growth of Segregation in American Schools: Changing Patterns of Separation and Poverty Since 1968.* Cambridge, MA: Report of the Harvard Project on School Desegregation to the National School Boards Association.

Orfield, Myron
   1997   *Metropolitics: A Regional Agenda for Community and Stability.* Washington DC: Brookings Institution Press.

Ostrom, Elinor
   1983   The social stratification—Government inequality thesis explored. *Urban Affairs Quarterly* 19:91-112.

Ostrom, Vincent, Robert Bish, and Elinor Ostrom
   1988   *Local Government in the United States.* San Francisco: Institute for Contemporary Studies.

Ostrom, Vincent, Charles Tiebout, and Robert Warren
   1961   Organizing government in metropolitan areas: A theoretical inquiry. *American Political Science Review* 55(4):831-842.

Parks, Roger, and Ronald Oakerson
   1989   Metropolitan organization and governance: A local public economy approach. *Urban Affairs Quarterly* 25(1):18-29.

Pastor, Manuel, Peter Dreier, Eugene Grigsby, and Lopez-Garcia Marta
   1997   *Growing Together: Linking Regional and Community Development in a Changing Economy.* Los Angeles: International and Public Affairs Center, Occidental College.

Peirce, Neal, with Curtis Johnson and John Hall
   1993   *Citistates: How Urban America Can Prosper in a Competitive World.* Washington, DC: Seven Locks Press.

Persky, Joseph, and Wim Wiewel
   1998   Suburban Sprawl: The Distribution of Costs and Benefits Due to Employment Deconcentration. Paper presented at the annual meeting of the Urban Affairs Association, Fort Worth, Texas.

Peterson, George, and Kale Williams
   1995   *Housing Mobility: What Has It Accomplished and What Is Its Purpose?* Washington, DC: Urban Institute.

Peterson, Paul
   1981   *City Limits* Chicago: University of Chicago Press.

Quercia, Roberto, and George Galster
   1997   Threshold effects and the expected benefits of attracting middle-income households to the central city. *Housing Policy Debate* 8(2):409-436.

Rafuse, Robert
   1991   Fiscal disparities in Chicagoland. *Intergovernmental Perspective* 17(3):14-19.

Reschovsky, Andrew
   1994   Fiscal equalization and school finance. *National Tax Journal* 47(1):185-198.

Reschovsky, Andrew, and Michael Wiseman
    1994   How can states most effectively meet their school financing responsibilities? In *Fiscal Equalization for State and Local Government Finance*, John Anderson, ed. Westport, CT: Praeger.
Richman, Roger, and James Oliver
    1997   The urban partnership and the development of Virginia's new Regional Competitiveness Act. *The Regionalist* 2(1):3-19.
Rosenbaum, James
    1995   Changing the geography of opportunity by expanding residential choice: Lessons from the Gautreaux program. *Housing Policy Review* 6(1):231-269.
Rouse, Cecilia
    1997   Private School vouchers and Student Achievement: An Evaluation of the Milwaukee Parental Choice Program. National Bureau of Economic Research Working Paper. Cambridge, MA: National Bureau of Economic Research
Rusk, David
    1993   *Cities Without Suburbs*. Washington, DC: Woodrow Wilson Center Press.
Sacher, Seth
    1993   Fiscal fragmentation and the distribution of metropolitan area resources: A case study. *Urban Studies* 30(7):1225-1239.
Savitch, Henry
    1995   Straw men, red herrings, . . . and suburban dependency. *Urban Affairs Review* 31(2):175-179.
Savitch, H.V., and Ronald Vogel
    1996   Perspectives for the present and lessons for the future. In *Regional Politics: American in a Post-City Age*, H.V. Savitch and Ronald Vogel, eds. Thousand Oaks, CA: Sage Publications.
Savitch, Henry, David Collins, Daniel Sanders, and John Markham
    1993   Ties that bind: Central cities, suburbs, and the new metropolitan region. *Economic Development Quarterly* 7(4):341-357.
Schneider, Mark
    1986   Fragmentation and the growth of local government. *Public Choice* 48:255-264.
    1989   *The Competitive City: The Political Economy of Suburbia*. Pittsburgh: University of Pittsburgh Press.
Sellers, Jeffrey
    1998   The Politics of Residential Segregation in Comparative Perspective: Settlement Patterns and Policy Consequences in French, German and U.S. Service Centers. Paper presented at the Urban Affairs Association Annual Meeting, Fort Worth, Texas, April 23-25, 1998.
Sjoquist, David
    1982   The effect of the number of local governments on central city expenditures. *National Tax Journal* 35:79-88.
Sofen, Edward
    1963   *The Miami Metropolitan Experiment*. Bloomington: Indiana University Press.
Stein, Robert
    1987   Tiebout's sorting hypothesis. *Urban Affairs Quarterly* 23(1):140-160.
Stowers, Genie
    1996   Miami: Experiences in metropolitan government. In *Regional Politics: American in a Post-City Age*, H.V. Savitch and Ronald Vogel, eds. Thousand Oaks, CA: Sage Publications.
Summers, Anita
    1997   Major Regionalization Efforts Between Cities and Suburbs in the United States. Working Paper No. 246. Philadelphia: Real Estate Center, Wharton School, University of Pennsylvania.

Swanson, Bert
  1996   Jacksonville: Consolidation and regional governance. In *Regional Politics: American in a Post-City Age*, H.V. Savitch and Ronald Vogel, eds. Thousand Oaks, CA: Sage Publications.
Thompson, Lyke
  1997   The Interlaced Metropolis: Cities in Layered Networks and Confederations in the Detroit Urbanized Area. Unpublished paper, College of Urban, Labor and Metropolitan Affairs, Wayne State University.
Tiebout, Charles
  1956   A pure theory of local expenditures. *Journal of Political Economy* 64(October):416-424.
Turner, Margery, and Ingrid Ellen
  1997   Why Does Neighborhood Matter: Impacts of Neighborhood Environment on the Well-Being of Families and Children. Paper given at the annual meeting of the Urban Affairs Association, Toronto, April 16-19.
Turner, Margery, Michael Fix, and Raymond Struyk
  1991   *Opportunities Denied, Opportunities Diminished: Discrimination in Hiring.* Washington, DC: Urban Institute Press.
U.S. Advisory Commission on Intergovernmental Relations
  1991   *Interjurisdictional Tax and Policy Competition: Good or Bad for the Federal System?* Report M-177. Washington, DC: U.S. Advisory Commission on Intergovernmental Relations.
U.S. Bureau of the Census
  1960   *1960 Census of Population, General Social and Economic Characteristics.* Washington, DC: U.S. Department of Commerce.
  1970   *1970 Census of Population, General Social and Economic Characteristics.* Washington, DC: U.S. Department of Commerce.
  1980   *1980 Census of Population, General Social and Economic Characteristics.* Washington, DC: U.S. Department of Commerce.
  1990a   *1990 Census of Population: Social and Economic Characteristics, Metropolitan Areas.* Washington, DC: U.S. Department of Commerce.
  1990b   *1990 Census Profile: Metropolitan Areas and Cities.* September. Washington, DC: U.S. Department of Commerce.
  1993   *Poverty in the United States: 1992.* Current Population Reports, Series P60-185. Washington, DC: U.S. Department of Commerce.
  1994   *Geographic Areas Reference Manual.* Washington, DC: U.S. Department of Commerce.
  1995   *Statistical Abstract of the United States.* Washington, DC: U.S. Department of Commerce.
  1996a   *1990 Census of Population and Housing Summary Tape File 3C.* CD-ROM. Washington, DC: U.S. Department of Commerce.
  1996b   *Current Population Survey* March 1964-1996. CD-ROM. Santa Monica, CA: Unicon Research Corporation 1996.
  1996c   *Governmental Finances: 1991-92* Series GF/92-5. Washington, DC: U.S. Department of Commerce.
  1996d   *Statistical Abstract of the United States.* Washington, DC: U.S. Department of Commerce.
Vidal, Avis
  1995   Reintegrating disadvantaged communities into the fabric of urban life: The role of community development. *Housing Policy Debate* 6(1):169-230.
Voith, Richard
  1992   City and suburban growth: Substitutes or complements? *Business Review* (Federal Reserve Bank of Philadelphia) Sept./Oct.:21-33.
  1993   Does city income growth increase suburban income growth, house value appreciation and population growth? Working paper no. 93-27, Federal Reserve Bank of Philadelphia.
  1995   Do Suburbs Need Cities? Working paper, Federal Reserve Bank of Philadelphia.

Wagner, Richard, and Warren Weber
  1975   Competition, monopoly, and the organization of government in metropolitan areas. *Journal of Law and Economics* 18:601-684.

Wallis, Allan
  1994   The third wave: Current trends in regional governance. *National Civic Review* 83(3):290-310.

Weicher, John
  1990   How poverty neighborhoods are changing. In *Inner City Poverty in the United States*, Laurence Lynn and Michael McGeary, eds. Committee on National Urban Policy, National Research Council. Washington, DC: National Academy Press.

Weiher, Gregory
  1991   *The Fractured Metropolis: Political Fragmentation and Metropolitan Segregation.* Albany: State University of New York Press.

Weir, Margaret
  1995   The politics of racial isolation in Europe and America. In *Classifying by Race*, Paul Peterson, ed. Princeton, NJ: Princeton University Press.

Williams, Oliver
  1971   *Metropolitan Political Analysis: A Social Access Approach.* New York: Free Press.

Wilson, William Julius
  1987   *The Truly Disadvantaged.* Chicago: University of Chicago Press.
  1996   *When Work Disappears: The World of the New Urban Poor.* New York: Alfred A. Knopf.

Wish, Naomi, and Stephen Eisdorfer
  1996   *The Impact of the Mt. Laurel Initiatives: An Analysis of the Characteristics of Applicants and Occupants.* South Orange, NJ: Seton Hall University, Center for Public Service.

Witte, John
  1997   Achievement Effects of the Milwaukee Voucher Program. Paper presented at the American Economics Association annual meeting, New Orleans, Jan. 4-6.

Witte, John, Troy Sterr, and Christopher Thorn
  1995   Fifth Year Report: Milwaukee Parental Choice Program. University of Wisconsin-Milwaukee.

Wolman, Harold
  1985   National-urban relations in foreign federal systems. In *Urban Policy in a Changing Federal System*, Royce Hanson, ed. Committee on National Urban Policy, National Research Council. Washington, DC: National Academy Press.

Wolman, Harold, and Edward Page
  1987   The impact of intergovernmental grants on subnational resource disparities: A cross-national comparison. *Public Budgeting and Finance* 7(3):82-98.

Yinger, John
  1995   *Closed Doors, Opportunities Lost: The Continuing Costs of Housing Discrimination.* New York: Russell Sage Foundation.
  1996   Fiscal Disparities and Education Finance. Technical paper, Economic Policy Institute, The Maxwell School, Syracuse University.

Zeigler, Donald, and Stanley Brunn
  1980   Geopolitical fragmentation and the pattern of growth and need. In *The American Metropolitan System: Present and Future*, Stanley Brunn and James Wheeler, eds. New York: V.H. Winston and Sons.

PART II

In-Depth
PERSPECTIVES

Does the American Way of Zoning Cause the Suburbs of Metropolitan Areas to Be Too Spread Out?

William A. Fischel
Dartmouth College

Are American metropolitan areas too spread out? I think the answer is yes. Virtually every measure of metropolitan density indicates that U.S. cities are more spread out than those of the rest of the world (Mieszkowski and Mills, 1993:136). Much of American suburbanization can be accounted for by more-or-less market-driven factors, and there is a smattering of evidence that some other countries' metropolitan areas could use some additional suburbanization. These qualifications notwithstanding, I maintain that the peculiarly American system of local land use controls contributes considerably to sprawl.

Although many writers apply the term sprawl to all suburbanization, I employ it only to a normative judgment that the extent of suburbanization is excessive. The normative bases are economic efficiency and the judgment that, if two institutions are (approximately) equally efficient, the one that is more egalitarian should prevail. Efficient suburbanization—and efficient densities—are achieved when owners who wish to increase the intensity of use of their land cannot do so without causing the aggregate value of land in their neighborhood or (small) community to decrease. This criterion is elaborated in Fischel (1990:47-51), and indirect evidence discussed there as well as in this paper strongly suggests that few American metropolitan areas would meet this test.

This paper is organized as follows. In the next section, I treat the issue of income segregation. Income segregated *neighborhoods* are not obviously caused by zoning. However, evidence reviewed in this section strongly suggests that the American pattern of homogeneous, high-income suburbs is at least in part the result of our system of local land use controls. With respect to reforming this problem, however, the best has long been the enemy of the good. Reformers'

insistence that the suburbs must develop new housing for the poor invites municipalities to adopt land use policies that democratically exclude everyone. The
excessively low densities that result probably do more to isolate most of the poor
than would a prodevelopment policy that nonetheless tolerated more-or-less
homogeneous suburbs.

The following section treats the "flight to the suburbs" hypothesis and with it
the question of how much suburbanization is caused by market factors rather than
by urban public policy failures (to the extent that such distinctions can be main-
tained). The consensus among urban economists is that central-city problems do
contribute to additional movement to the suburbs. I take a very rough guess that
perhaps a quarter of modern (post World War II) suburbanization might not have
occurred if central-city public amenities (schools, safety, antipollution) were comparable to that of the average suburb.

Although exodus from central cities contributes to suburbanization, it does
not necessarily cause the *suburbs* to develop at excessively low density. Indeed,
one would expect *higher* densities in suburbs if the only cause of sprawl were
central-city problems. But suburbs are not passive receptors of development. I
describe in the fourth section a process of rational, homeowner-dominated suburban politics that causes their land use controls to become ever tighter in the face
of development. The key to this process is the progressive denigration of the
rights of owners of undeveloped land, who are the most consistent (and often the
only) transmitter of the demands by outsiders to live or work in the community.
The spiral of suburban down-zoning sends development ever farther from the
central city and may contribute to the formation of satellite "edge cities" that
institutionalize the low-density patterns.

The penultimate section considers other public policies and arguable market
failures (other than central-city problems) that contribute to the low-density
patterns in American suburbs. These seem on balance to be relatively minor as
causes of sprawl, although some of them—most notably federal environmental
policies—are important supplements to suburban attempts to exclude development.

The final section frames the public policy issue in terms of micro versus
macro solutions. The macro solution to zoning-induced sprawl is metropolitan
governance. The hazards of this are loss of the desirable features of local self-
government and the possibility that metropolitan governance will result in too
little suburbanization and excessively high densities and even higher housing
prices. The micro solution is to restore the rights of owners of undeveloped land.
I believe that there is a manageable standard called "normal behavior" for judges
to follow that would significantly reduce sprawl. The hazards of the micro
approach are governance by unelected judges and the possible loss of local amenities from too-enthusiastic defense of private property rights.

INCOME SEGREGATION IS NOT THE
SAME PROBLEM AS SPRAWL

Income segregation is a growing problem in American cities. Abramson et al. (1995) studied census tract patterns for the 100 largest metropolitan areas between 1970 and 1990. Their measure of income segregation had increased by 11 percent over that period (1995:70). However, over the same period, their measure of racial segregation declined. This section deals with income segregation issues as they relate to zoning.

The issue of zoning-induced income segregation is often conflated with the question of whether purely market forces in the United States induce high-income people to live predominately in suburban areas. The monocentric urban economics model predicts that, as incomes generally rise (that is, both poor and rich become richer than before), there will be more suburbanization. This is borne out empirically (Mills and Hamilton, 1994:124). But income growth does not necessarily imply that, at any particular moment, high-income people will live in suburbs.

Whether the rich live farther from the center of the city than the poor is an empirical question that involves balancing two offsetting tendencies. Richer people demand more housing (interior space and outside lawns) than poor people, and housing is more cheaply available (per square foot of living space, not per house) in the suburbs. However, people in the suburbs have to commute farther, and time wasted on commuting is more costly for rich people than for poor people. Some evidence suggests that the suburban lure of lower-cost housing offsets the penalty of more commuting time, which means that it is "natural" for wealthier people to settle in the suburbs. But there is questioning of the power of this argument (Wheaton, 1977), and it has been pointed out that it is often not true in other countries and was not true at earlier periods in American history (LeRoy and Sonstelie, 1983).

Historical factors are more likely to account for the pattern of suburbs being settled by the rich in the United States. The stock of housing is both durable and costly to remodel extensively. Housing in central cities was largely constructed for those who in the past were middle- or high-income people. As American incomes generally rose over time, this older housing no longer met the demands of upper-middle-income families. Rather than tear down or extensively remodel older housing to meet the more recent demands, it is cheaper to build from the ground up (Mills and Hamilton, 1994:245). The open ground is in the suburbs.

This long-term filtering process does not necessarily penalize the poor financially. As more people become affluent and move to the suburbs, the price of the older housing in central cities falls. Because of its durability, this housing stock still provides better housing services for a given price than does constructing new housing for the poor (Weicher and Thibodeau, 1988). The problem is that this pattern tends to concentrate the poor in central-city and older suburban neighborhoods. The greater social problems of the poor contribute to declines in neighborhood amenities.

A good deal of American criticism of zoning hinges on the failure of the suburbs to accommodate low-income housing in their midst (Briffault, 1990; Downs, 1973). This focus is valid, but it can create an unrealistic expectation of what would happen if "exclusionary" zoning were somehow eliminated. Most discussions of exclusionary zoning assume that outsiders can distinguish motives for zoning, but few public officials who urge the preservation of open space are stupid enough to say that its chief value is to preclude low-income housing. It is nearly impossible by inference to distinguish more innocent objectives from exclusionary ones (Bogart, 1993; Fischel, 1985:140).

There is little historical evidence that, in the absence of zoning, the rich would be as likely to live next to the poor as to another rich household. Sam Bass Warner's study of Boston's suburban development prior to the use of zoning did not find neighborhood mingling. Land use patterns were income-segregated by neighborhood as independent builders responded to the demands of the market (Warner, 1962:Chap. 6). The same seems to have been true of New Haven. Marketing considerations and informal constraints created uniform housing patterns there well before zoning was even contemplated (Cappell, 1991). Houston, the only large city not to have zoning, is not generally characterized by mixed-income neighborhoods. Houston's suburban development occurs in homogeneous planned communities that are governed by private covenants whose restrictions would be the (unexpressed) envy of the most exclusive municipal planning board (Peiser, 1981).

The problem with misapprehending the settlement patterns that would result in the absence of zoning is that it creates unrealistic expectations for zoning reforms. The state that has carried such reforms the farthest is New Jersey (Haar, 1996). Its supreme court was the first (and, with respect to the vigor with which it pursued the matter, the only) to recognize that zoning desired at the local level is not necessarily desirable for the metropolitan region as a whole. (The case is *Southern Burlington County NAACP* v. *Township of Mount Laurel*, 336 A.2d 713 [N.J. 1975].)

The New Jersey court's initial remedy for exclusion was the creation of an obligation for communities to allow "least cost" housing to be developed (*Oakwood at Madison* v. *Township of Madison*, 371 A.2d 1192 [N.J. 1977]). I think this was a major and largely positive reform, but the New Jersey supreme court six years later did not regard it as going far enough. The reason was that newly built "least-cost" suburban housing was still relatively expensive. The New Jersey court apparently expected, contrary to most economic evidence, that unleashed private developers would build many units for low-income households. This makes little sense for a capital good, housing, that is highly durable. In order to get enough years of use to justify the high construction cost, it is best to start with high-quality construction, which is initially affordable only by the nonpoor (Mills and Hamilton, 1994:251).

As a result of its impatience with what the market for new construction was producing, the New Jersey court hit upon a scheme that required suburbs to accept a quota of new, low-income housing for any "market-rate" housing that would be built (*Mount Laurel II*, 456 A.2d 390 [1983]). These quotas were to be financed by charging developers of market-rate housing for rezonings (required by the courts, not volunteered by the municipalities) that allowed the builders to use more profitable higher densities (Fischel, 1991). This scheme looks generally desirable in terms of mixing population.

An important drawback of *Mount Laurel II* was that the court focused on the *proportion* of low- to high-income housing rather than the overall density of housing. Once a community was certified as having a proportion of new housing that satisfied its "fair share" of low-income housing, it was virtually invited by the New Jersey court to be as exclusive with the rest of its undeveloped land as it wanted to be: "Finally, once a community has satisfied its fair share obligation, the *Mount Laurel* Doctrine will not restrict other measures, including large-lot and open area zoning, that would maintain its beauty and communal character"(456 A.2d at 421). The incentives for the suburbs then became to switch from selective exclusion of the poor to general exclusion of everyone (Fischel, 1991). I have it on local authority that Bedminster Township, for example, has not budged from its multiacre minimum lot sizes since its much-noted (Lamar et al., 1989) quota of *Mount Laurel*-induced housing was constructed.

The new judicial remedy was sufficiently disturbing to New Jersey's large constituency of suburban voters that the state legislature took on the task of administering the court's order. Under the guise of complying with the decision, the legislature's 1985 Fair Housing Act actually subverted most of its goals (Schill, 1991:847). The New Jersey supreme court acceded to this as part of a deal in which the governor agreed to reappoint the chief justice, according to Kirp et al. (1995:142). This extraordinary pressure—reappointment is historically routine in New Jersey—by the executive on the judicial branch and its equally extraordinary acceptance by Chief Justice Wilentz may explain why *Mount Laurel II* has not been emulated by other state courts.

What appears to have most disturbed New Jersey opponents of *Mount Laurel* remedies was not just the fiscal impact of the subsidized housing (although that was certainly important). The more critical issue may have been the neighborhood effects. Many built-up suburbs were actually willing to pay other communities between $10,000 and $20,000 per unit to accept half of their mandated share (Rubin et al., 1990:335). The housing development across the street, not on the other side of town, is most disturbing, and the *Mount Laurel* approach flew in the face of that anxiety. (I infer this both from numerous newspaper articles and my 10 years experience as a zoning board member in my New Hampshire hometown.)

. Although *Mount Laurel* advocates can point to specific projects that have been built (Lamar et al., 1989), my undergraduate student's search for statewide evidence that it had changed the general pattern of suburban housing development was fruitless. For example, the ratio of new apartment to new single-family home development in New Jersey communities singled out as having *Mount Laurel* obligations was not appreciably changed during the 1980s compared with earlier periods and compared with nearby Pennsylvania communities, which did not have a similar obligation (Giovannotto, 1994, summarized in Fischel, 1995:338).

Although I regard neighborhood income segregation as likely to occur under almost any mechanism that operates without a strong dose of coercion, it must be emphasized that income segregation is greatly accentuated by modern zoning. It is one thing to observe that the rich and the poor live in different neighborhoods separated by a thoroughfare, a cemetery, or a railroad track. It is something of a greater order of magnitude to observe that they live in entirely different municipalities separated by miles of low-density development or "natural preserves." The larger-area separation surely discourages economic and social interactions that would otherwise be mutually beneficial and that are the cornerstone of a prosperous, democratic society. The spatial mismatch hypothesis, in which central-city youth are said to be unable to plug into job-finding networks because of excessive distances (Holzer et al., 1994), is just one pathology that emerges from excessive distance between people in metropolitan areas. Low-density counties also have lower output per worker (Ciccone and Hall, 1996).

But does zoning actually cause income segregation by municipality? This is an instance in which the conventional wisdom—that exclusionary zoning is a real issue—is confirmed by evidence. The evidence is necessarily indirect because income segregation by neighborhood would, as mentioned earlier, most likely arise without zoning.

The first bit of evidence is that high-income communities almost invariably have more restrictive zoning regulations than others. They impose more stringent regulations on undeveloped land than those that apply to existing, built-up neighborhoods. If market forces alone were sufficient to create exclusive communities, one would expect to see zoning standards such as minimum lot sizes be more uniform among communities. Rudel's excellent study of the evolution of zoning regulations among Connecticut towns (which jibes with my less-systematic observations) found that settlement by higher-income residents nearly always makes them more restrictive (Rudel, 1989:64-68, 81-137).

It is well established that zoning does not simply "follow the market." The evidence is clear that most suburbs are zoned for minimum lot sizes greatly in excess of what the market would generate (McMillen and McDonald, 1991; Peterson, 1974; Wallace, 1988; White, 1988). The common knowledge among developers that a rezoning to allow greater residential densities nearly invariably raises the value of land indicates that it is zoning, not the market, that constrains the construction of higher-density housing in the suburbs.

Other evidence that is consistent with zoning being an important source of suburban income segregation is a study using a national sample by Hamilton et al. (1975). They found that census tracts within metropolitan areas that had numerous governments—and hence numerous independent zoning authorities— were more homogeneous than the tracts within metropolitan areas that had fewer local governments. Since there is no reason to suppose that the land market operates differently in metropolitan areas with few or many governments, they attributed the sorting of people by income to the existence of independent local governments. This finding is confirmed with different samples by Eberts and Gronberg (1981).

It is theoretically possible for communities to become stratified without zoning, but the conditions for doing so seem unlikely (Epple et al., 1988). Wheaton (1993) found that even under "ideal" conditions for spontaneous in- come segregation, at least a weak form of zoning for minimum lot size was necessary to obtain such stratification. Without fiscal zoning, developers have a strong incentive to build lower-cost housing in affluent districts to take advantage of the higher-quality services and lower tax rates. Doing so would give them a capital gain at the expense of existing homeowners (Hamilton, 1976). Since homeowners are the most politically effective group in small suburbs, they have the means as well as the incentive to pass zoning laws to protect the value of their major asset, their homes (Rossi and Weber, 1996:23). A determinants study by Rolleston (1987) established that the desires of affluent communities to protect their fiscal advantages were significant and large determinants of suburban zon- ing restrictiveness.

The motive is not modern; local governments have been concerned about immigration by the poor since there were local governments (Burns, 1994:35). The incorporation of the many small, independent suburbs in Los Angeles County under the post World War II Lakewood Plan was motivated entirely by the desire of homeowners to preclude the invasion of apartments in residential areas, which had been allowed by the more prodevelopment county government (Cion, 1966). A similar motive seems to have been behind the resistance of Pittsburgh's sub- urbs to annexation by the central city in the 1920s (Lubove, 1969:94-100). The concern that suburban zoning makes low-income housing difficult to develop has been expressed by federal commissions of all political stripes. The National Commission on Urban Problems (1969), chaired by Senator Paul Douglas and commissioned by a Democratic president, regarded local, exclusionary zoning as a major barrier (1969:19). The Advisory Commission on Regulatory Barriers to Affordable Housing (1991), commissioned by a Republican president more than two decades later, came to the same conclusion (1991:2-6). That such similar conclusions should be reached more than two decades later indicates the staying power of localism in zoning.

I think it is important to at least raise the issue of why suburban communities are averse to having low-income residents. Most of the above-mentioned studies have emphasized the desire for fiscal protection and a sense of snobbishness. [The only *legislated* program requiring a modest proportion of new housing in each community to be for low-income residents is Massachusetts' Anti-Snob Zoning Act (Stockman, 1992).] I believe, however, that these factors do not tell the whole story. An important problem, I believe, is fear of crime and other forms of public disorder such as aggressive begging (Segelhorst and Brady, 1984; Ellickson, 1996a). Disorder is worrisome to homeowners not simply because of personal risk, but because it reduces housing values as well (Taylor, 1995).

These fears are only partly controlled by expenditures on police and courts, which are, in any event, costly and uncertain deterrents (Cassell and Hayman, 1996). The least costly way for middle-class people to obtain more safety is to put some distance between themselves and the poor and to use zoning regulations to maintain that distance (Wilson and Boland, 1976:186; Oates, 1977). The rising crime rates of the 1970s and 1980s have been estimated to cause a significant amount of the flight to the suburbs (Cullen and Levitt, 1996; Skogan, 1990:82). Cullen and Levitt estimate that, for the 1976-1993 period, moderate-to-large U.S. central cities lost more than one resident to the suburbs for each crime committed (1996:9). The effects of crime were particularly large on the out-migration of high-income households with children (p. 4) and did not vary by race (1996:20). This may partly explain the divergent trends over the 1970-1990 period observed by Abramson et al. (1995), in which racial segregation fell but income segregation rose. Higher-income blacks as well as whites respond to rising crime by leaving inner-city neighborhoods.

The focus on crime as a cause of excessive suburbanization actually is cause for some guarded optimism. Crime rates in nearly all large central cities have been falling rapidly in the last few years to levels that are nearly those of the 1960s (*New York Times,* December 20, 1996, p. A1.) If this trend continues, middle-class people may reverse some of their out-migration. More important, if crime reduction is a uniform trend (and not simply the result of extraordinary and costly efforts by cities), suburban homeowners may be less inclined to resist development of lower-cost housing.

Reductions in sprawl would reduce the physical distance between people of all income classes and thereby decrease the degree of isolation of the poor from the job market and other forms of social capital (Schill, 1991). Indeed, research on peer group effects in neighborhoods and schools suggests very strongly that social isolation is bad for the economy as a whole, not just the poor (Benabou, 1993; Case and Katz, 1991; Cutler and Glaeser, 1997; Henderson et al., 1978). (For a less pessimistic view of the effects of spatial isolation on income distribution, see Kremer, 1997.) The problem, as Tony Downs has persistently pointed out, is how to get the population as a whole to cooperate to break down the social isolation of the poor (Downs, 1973, 1994). Breaking down the *spatial* isolation of the poor by discouraging excessively low-density suburbs would seem to be an important first start.

FLIGHT FROM CENTRAL CITIES COULD RESULT IN HIGH-DENSITY SUBURBS

The problem of sprawl raises at least two distinct issues related to excessive suburbanization. One asks whether American central cities are being depopulated for reasons besides otherwise benign and probably unstoppable economic trends and technological changes. The second asks whether the population density of suburbs is artificially low. These are not the same issue, nor are they necessarily related. On one hand, central cities could be depopulated as the result of suboptimal public policies, with people moving to the suburbs and causing suburban densities to be too *high*. On the other hand, central-city depopulation trends could be natural, but suburbs could have artificially low densities, spreading the population out too far into the countryside. To put it another way, one trend (city depopulation) does not have to imply the other trend (low-density suburbs).

Although this essay dwells on the possibility of the second trend (unduly low-density suburbs), it may be useful to review what is known about the first (city depopulation). The issue was recently reviewed in the *Journal of Economic Perspectives* by two distinguished urban economists, Peter Mieszkowski and Edwin Mills (1993). Mills in particular has been concerned over much of his career with the causes of suburbanization. He has done this by advancing both theoretical models and empirical evidence that address suburban growth.

As a result of his focus on the standard urban economics model's location predictions (described in the previous section), Mills has emphasized the "natural" causes of suburbanization as being improvements in transportation infrastructure (which reduce the costs of commuting), technological changes that allow employment decentralization, and, most important, long-term increases in household incomes. Even if all households had exactly the same income, city growth in an era of rising personal incomes would be disproportionately located in the suburbs.

Mills's empirical work pushed the date for the beginning of American suburbanization back to the 1880s (Mills, 1972:48). Using the concept of population density gradients (the percentage increase in population density as one moves closer to the center of a city), Mills showed that the decades following World War II were not unusual in their suburbanization trends. Indeed, the major surge of suburbanization (which otherwise seems to have been going on uniformly since 1880) appears to have begun in 1920, not 1950 (Mieszkowski and Mills, 1993:140). It is notable that the number of communities that adopted zoning was very large in the 1920s, but I have argued that suburbanization was more likely a cause of zoning's popularity than vice versa (Fischel, 1995:280).

Because of Mills's long-time emphasis on the "natural market" factors, it came as something of a surprise to me that Mieszkowski and Mills concluded that social (chiefly racial) and political factors accounted for a large amount of American suburbanization: "Our judgment is that both the natural evolution and fiscal-social approaches are important" (1993:144). They did not attempt to quantify the relative importance of each, but an article in the *Journal of Urban Economics* by Robert Margo (1992) does suggest some insights.

Margo used a rough-and-ready version of the urban economics model to estimate how much suburban growth in the 1950-1980 period could be accounted for by the rising household incomes during the period. His method was to estimate metropolitan household location patterns for 1950 and then project 1980 incomes onto this pattern to see how many more households would have lived outside central cities with the higher incomes. His point estimate of how much suburban growth was accounted for by rising incomes was 43 percent (1992:301). That leaves more than half of suburbanization to be accounted for by other factors. I shall speculate in a very rough way about the relative proportions of these other factors.

Aside from growth of personal income, the other "natural evolution" factors of the last century are technological changes and highway building, which is the chief innovation in transportation. [Every society in the world undertakes a system of public transportation (Ellickson, 1993:1381), and in this sense highways are a natural product of American economic development.] The technological changes that most economists believe have contributed to suburbanization are the development of over-the-road truck transport (displacing the railroads, whose intersections once formed the centers of many cities) and the development of continuous-processing manufacturing, which is land-intensive. Large-scale manufacturing is becoming so decentralized that in a few decades it may no longer be classified as an urban activity (Schmenner, 1981). Technical changes in communications also seem to promote decentralization. Examples include telephones, faxes, electronic mail, and rapid package delivery systems.

These other "natural" factors seem unlikely to account for as much suburbanization as long-term growth of personal income. Although it has become decentralized, manufacturing has long been a declining fraction of American (and other high-income nations') employment. The importance of decentralizing inventions likewise seems moderate. Instant communication is nothing new; telephones have been around for more than 100 years. The faster speeds achieved by automobile commuting are partly offset by road congestion and by the fact that higher incomes make the opportunity cost of transportation higher. The reason that Americans complain so much about congestion is not that average automobile trip times have increased (the evidence suggests that they have not—

Gordon et al., 1989), but that people with higher incomes regard even short waits as more costly.

If the foregoing "natural" trends are less important than income in explaining suburbanization, they must account for less than 43 percent (Margo's income effect) of modern suburbanization. Suppose they independently account for 33 percent of suburbanization, so that the aforementioned factors—income growth, transportation development, and technological change—account for three-quarters of American suburbanization. Thus it seems reasonable to guess that perhaps a quarter of Americans' move, beyond the limits of central cities may be accounted for by factors other than mostly benign, "natural" economic trends. I offer this guess solely to attempt to put the issue of excessive suburbanization in perspective on an order-of-magnitude scale. Saying that U.S. cities might be 25 percent too suburbanized means that the problem is not trivial, as it would seem to be if cities were 2.5 percent too suburbanized, and not completely unmanageable, as it would be if cities were 250 percent too suburbanized.

Mieszkowski and Mills describe the alternative factors as social and fiscal, and their examples cover a wide range of items that are predominantly, if not uniquely, American. Primary are the problems of the central cities: high local taxes, high crime rates, poor public schools, racial conflict, automobile congestion, and low-quality environment (1993:137). Mills found in earlier work that race was especially robust in explaining suburbanization (Mills and Price, 1984). These factors suggest that large numbers of households are repelled from central cities as the result of factors that most people would want to discourage by public policies.

As I suggested at the outset of this essay, however, it is logically possible that the suburban development that results from an exodus from central cities could still be highly compact. It is evident from informal observation of privately developed "planned communities" such as Reston, Virginia; Columbia, Maryland; and Foster City, California, that suburbanites are willing to live in relatively high-density communities as long as they get good public amenities, especially safety. Their gross densities—including all land uses, not just housing—range from about 4,000 (Reston and Columbia at its projected completion) to 7,000 (Foster City) persons per square mile. These are on the order of twice the gross density of the suburban parts of most urbanized areas. At the lower-end density—Reston and Columbia—this implies about two-fifths of an acre per household. By the usual rule of thumb that has residential as half of all uses, this works out to a net density of one-fifth acre per household.

The relatively high densities of these very affluent places might, with further investigation, form a useful benchmark for calculating efficient suburban densities. This is because the developers of such communities have a strong incentive to internalize all spillover effects (Fischel, 1994). I am not the only person to have had this thought. Joel Garreau points out that, if the Boston metropolitan statistical area (MSA) were developed at Reston densities, built-up uses would take up less than one-fifth the land area (Garreau, 1991:86). (In support of Garreau's observation, I would add that New England MSAs are delineated by town boundaries rather than counties, so their land area is already much smaller than MSAs in the rest of the United States.) Furthermore, most of the open spaces of Reston, Columbia, and Foster City are actually open to the public, in contrast to the mostly privately owned open spaces in low-density suburbs.

I submit that sprawl is not simply the result of a push of population out from the central cities. It results at least as much from the nearby suburbs' unwilling-ness to accommodate moderate-density housing. Mieszkowski and Mills did mention suburban zoning as a factor contributing to metropolitan suburbanization, but primarily as a device to promote social and income homogeneity, not to control density. That is, they seem to accept that, once people choose to move to the suburbs and find a homogeneous community, suburban densities are not unnaturally reduced. It is here that I part company with them both in description and (implied) prescription.

THE POLITICAL DYNAMICS OF ZONING
CREATE SUBURBAN SPRAWL

The peculiar fact of American metropolitan areas is that many suburbs that are quite close to downtown have preserved large amounts of undeveloped, open space, and most of their residential development has been at relatively low densi-ties. The typical suburban development is not like that of Arlington County, Virginia, which has become a high-rise, high-density suburb of Washington. (The outward push on office development is most likely due to the height limita-tions on buildings in the District of Columbia, which prevent office towers from overshadowing the Capitol.)

The more typical suburb is Marin County, California, the area immediately north of the Golden Gate Bridge from San Francisco. It has large amounts of open space on which development could easily occur but does not (Dowall, 1984:92; Schwartz et al., 1981; Frieden, 1979). Tens of thousands of commuters from far-away suburbs and exurbs pass through the Marin County corridor on U.S. Route 101 on their way to work in San Francisco. Marin's open space is an asset for those who live near it, and it probably provides some pleasures for those who drive through it daily. But it also represents an enormous waste in the form of excessive commuting and displacement of economic activities to less produc-tive areas. (The same might be true of the height limits of the nation's capital, but, in this case, the national benefits of a historically scenic city would have to be weighed against the costs of the height limit.)

Having many close-in suburbs develop at low densities does not necessarily mean that the metropolitan area as a whole will become less dense. It could be— and this seems to be the case for English and European cities—that rendering suburban land off-limits to development would force developers back into the central cities (Cheshire and Sheppard, 1989). A strict policy of low-density (verging on no-density) suburbs could thus result in higher-density cities. (This assumes that would-be suburbanites do not migrate to other cities that have a more permissive policy with regard to suburban development.) The zone-them-back-to-the-city scenario would be most likely to apply in areas in which basic land use regulation was done by a national or regional political body.

The compacting effect of low-density suburban zoning is less likely to occur in the United States. Basic land use controls are undertaken by local governments. In most metropolitan areas with populations in excess of 1 million (which contain about half of the U.S. population), there are scores if not hundreds of independent local governments surrounding central cities (Fischel, 1981). Developers who are frustrated by regulations in one municipality can skip to another.

Municipal choice by itself does not necessarily imply sprawl. Within any given distance from the central city, there could be suburbs with densities that are excessively *high* as well as low. I believe, however, that the political ontogeny of zoning within *any* given suburban community tends toward excessively low-density zoning (Fischel, 1985:Chap. 7). Thus even the relatively accommodating suburbs will not compensate for the zoning in those that are more eager to maintain open space and low-density development. The pervasiveness of this pattern of zoning and the absence of an offsetting impetus toward higher-density development are among the reasons that I strongly suspect that U.S. metropolitan areas are developing at excessively low densities. Land use regulation is pervasive in the suburbs, and its biases are, as I shall describe, almost always in the direction of lower-than-efficient densities.

Most rural townships and villages (or, in much of the West and the South, unincorporated county settlements) at the edge of metropolitan areas are not initially antidevelopment. Many rural residents, even if they are not owners of undeveloped land, stand to gain more from development than they would lose (Rudel, 1989:59). Surveys generally show that rural folk are seldom antigrowth (Hahn, 1970). As a result, the zoning in these communities, when it exists at all, is usually permissive (Siegan, 1976:52; International City Managers' Association, 1960). Rural townships often zone land for agriculture, but only as a kind of holding zone. Rezonings to more intensive activities (housing, industry) are expected to occur when a reasonable proposal comes along.

Once such communities become partially developed with suburban homes, however, a change in the political climate takes place. The new residents eventually become a political majority, and, in such communities, the new homeowner majority rules (Ellickson, 1977:405). They have a different frame of economic reference than that of the traditionally rural, small-town residents. Because suburbanites typically own land only for their own homes, most new residents do not stand to gain directly from further development. Because they work elsewhere in the metropolitan area, further residential development in their own community does not offer spillover wage or employment benefits. Because suburbanites have moved to the area from somewhere else, they are less concerned about jobs, housing, and other local economic advantages for family members and others with whom they have long-term personal ties. [I found that all of these factors— potential land development, job prospects, and family ties—were important among rural New Hampshire residents who favored a pulp mill development in their town (Fischel, 1979).]

This shift in the economic and social profile of the exurban community does not instantly translate itself into political action. But eventually some event galvanizes the new majority to seize the political reins. This change occurs well before the municipality itself is filled up in any meaningful sense. There is much undeveloped land left, and the new majority changes the zoning, usually by stages, to see to it that it will remain undeveloped or developed at far lower densities than the tracts in which they themselves live (Pyle, 1985:43).

Agricultural zoning in the newly suburban areas is converted from a holding zone to a permanent constraint. Of one such farmland preservation program, a suburban county official observed, "We're creating problems for the counties that are just outside the metro area [of Minneapolis/St. Paul]. They don't have this type of ordinance, and we're creating a leapfrog development effect into these counties" (Toner, 1978:14). One might ask why developers do not antici- pate such events and subdivide in advance of the more stringent regulations, thus vesting their right to build. Some developers do anticipate and act (Dana, 1995; Riddiough, 1997), but such foresight is rare.

Although minimum lot size is the workhorse of zoning, many other regula- tions constrain development. One in particular can leave observers of suburban development with the erroneous impression that a community is developing normal-density housing. Many communities with low-density zoning allow or encourage developers to cluster their housing (Whyte, 1964). The owner of a 30- acre tract that is zoned for a minimum of 3-acre lots may be able to cluster the 10 allowable houses in a smaller area of, say, 5 acres. Developers often prefer this because the saving on infrastructure costs exceeds the revenue they could obtain by marketing the larger lot. The net residential density is thus a half acre per home, which appears to be only a moderate constraint. Half-acre residential lot development in fact appears to be the observed norm, as determined by Vesterby and Heimlich (1991:285).

Observing such net residential densities (the 10 houses on 5 acres in my foregoing example), one might conclude that "beyond a doubt, suburban-zoning provisions are consistent with the demands of most of the people who would live there, even in the absence of zoning regulations" (Mills and Hamilton, 1994:414). But the local planning board in my example would not let the remaining 25 acres be developed. To obtain the cluster zoning, the developer would have to agree to keep the remaining acreage in open space. Although local planners might proudly point to the cluster as an example of how they have prevented sprawl-type devel- opment, the effect on *metropolitan-area* development is exactly the same as if each home had been built on a 3-acre lot. There are still only 10 houses on the 30-acre tract. This is why it is important not just to look at the densities in areas in which development is allowed, but to pay attention to the land on which development is entirely precluded (see Box 1).

One might ask how the political system of land use regulation gives rise to the inefficient patterns of sprawl. Modern political economy emphasizes how frequently people with concentrated economic interests manage to prevail over the interests of the majority. With this model in mind, one would expect that owners of undeveloped land and their allies in the development industry would not find their minority status to be any disadvantage (Denzau and Weingast, 1982). But small, local governments are not convincing examples of interest group politics at work. Nearly all empirical evidence on the subject—not just that pertaining to land use controls—indicates that the majority-rule model applies far better in small towns (Bloom and Ladd, 1982; Holcombe, 1989; Holtz-Eakin and Rosen, 1989). Low-density suburban zoning is not the result of the failure of democratic processes. It is a result of its success. The median voter in such places is a homeowner, and elected officials are at considerable pains to pay attention to her concerns about the single largest asset she owns.

A development-minded landowner faced with inefficiently low-density zoning that he cannot change through the political process has two options. One is to attempt to get the courts on his side. The owner could argue that the low-density zoning of his land makes development so uneconomical that most of the economic sticks in his bundle of property rights are missing. Under this premise, his attorney might argue that he has been deprived of his property rights without due process of law. Alternatively, the attorney might invoke the regulatory takings doctrine, arguing that the deprivation of use is tantamount to public acquisition of his property for which just compensation is due (Ellickson, 1977:468).

The chances of either argument succeeding vary by state. On one side is Pennsylvania, whose supreme court has been generally receptive to pro-development due process arguments (Coyle, 1993:54). On the other side is California, where, since the late 1960s, it has arguably been malpractice for an attorney to charge a client for making any such claim (Coyle, 1993:112; DiMento et al., 1980). I suspect such differences account in part for the vast differences in housing prices between California and the rest of the country (Fischel, 1995:Chap. 6). But the rule in most states has been that such claims will help the developer only in unusually stringent circumstances. Most courts defer to the decisions of local government as long as there is some apparent public benefit from the regulation and as long as the landowner has some residuum of value left in the affected parcel. The eyes of the courts are almost always trained on the broadly conceived benefits of the regulation to the community, not on the financial opportunity cost of the regulation to the owner of undeveloped land.

The foregoing observation will seem peculiar to many European observers. In their minds (and in the minds of some American scholars), the United States is

Box 1:   Cluster Zoning and Residential Density

The following stylized sketches summarize my foregoing argument. Suppose the metropolitan area has immutable boundaries that look like this honeycomb:

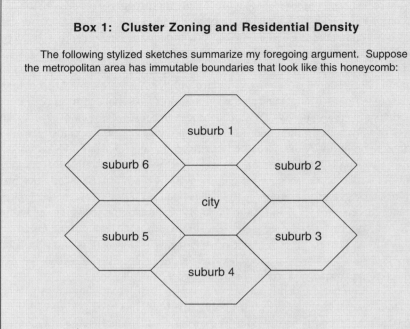

Suppose that the "sprawl" pattern (with large-lot acreage) ends up distributing the population like this pattern:

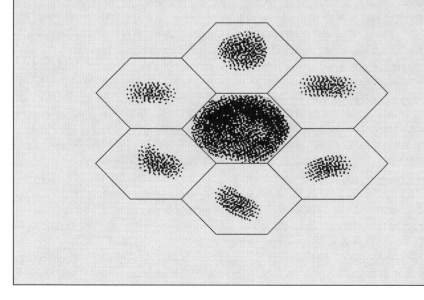

But suppose instead that each suburban town decided to combat sprawl with cluster development, which compacts development but preserves the surrounding area from development. The area then looks like this, which might please the new urbanists such as James Kunstler (1996):

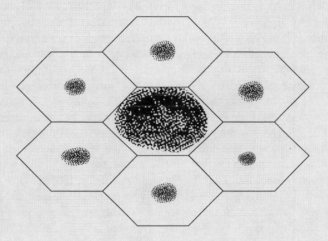

However, the *metropolitan area's* density is not changed by this pattern. Suburbs are as isolated from the central city as before. The results of a true *metropolitan* antisprawl policy would look more like this:

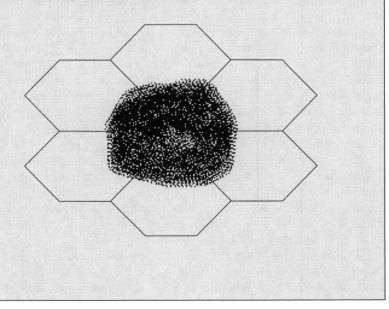

the bastion of property rights, with courts reviewing regulations in ways that never occur elsewhere. They are correct that American courts are unusual in their willingness to review the products of legislative regulation of the economy (Ogus, 1990). But they overlook the fact that the local legislature almost always wins in the United States (Briffault, 1990).

Much has been written (some by myself) about the revival of the regulatory takings doctrine (Fischel, 1995). I shall in the final section of this paper suggest that disinterested institutions can make a useful contribution to the spread of this doctrine in the name of reducing metropolitan sprawl. But it would be remiss of me not to note that regulatory takings have so far barely rumpled the fabric of local land use regulation. By far the greater source of difference between the United States and Europe is that American regulations emerge from more or less autonomous local governments (Cullingworth, 1993). In a few states, a state or regional body can review the products of local regulation (Popper, 1988), but this usually just gives antidevelopment forces another shot at the proposal. Few of the higher-government review bodies tell a local government that it must accept a development it does not want (Healy and Rosenberg, 1979:189).

The other option for the developer who regards his land as excessively regulated is to bargain with the community. Such bargains do occur, but they happen at a rate that is much lower than is optimal (Fischel, 1985:Chap. 4). This is partly because the usual transaction costs of deal-making are greatly increased when they are undertaken in the public sector. Many parties must be satisfied, and judicial hostility to contract zoning is widespread, so that third parties (usually private antidevelopment groups) can upset deals between landowners and the duly elected representatives of the public sector (Fischel, 1985:78; Lassar, 1990).

More important is the sense of entitlement that is promoted by American localism. Localism encourages the newly arrived suburban residents of exurban communities to regard the status quo in land use as their personal property (Nelson, 1979). This has important consequences. It is well known in experimental economics and psychology that it takes much more to persuade people to trade away that which they possess (or have a sense of entitlement to) than to get them to purchase the same thing from a range of choices (Knetsch and Sinden, 1984; Hoffman and Spitzer, 1993). The reluctance to trade that which you already own is called the endowment effect.

Endowment effects are not themselves causes of economic inefficiency. Economic efficiency is simply about voluntary gains from trade, and reluctance to trade is itself a voluntary decision. Hence an important reason that suburban zoning is restrictive has nothing to do with conventional efficiency considerations. Nor does reluctance to trade necessarily favor the rich; the poor may be as attached to what they own as anyone else.

One might respond to this defense of exclusion by noting that the legitimacy of political arrangements might better be posed as an ex ante choice of institutions rather than choices made after the institutions had evolved (Fischel,

1995:198). One might stand in a Rawlsian "veil of ignorance" and ask what constraints on land use should be allowed. A golden rule (of which Rawls, 1971, exposited a sophisticated variation) would ask current suburban residents what sorts of regulations their towns should have if they themselves were outsiders (Fischel, 1995:359). Rather than expand on that rarefied exercise, however, I prefer to invoke a simpler standard invoked in the discussion above: if two systems are (approximately) equally efficient, the more egalitarian system should prevail.

It should be clear that the usual pattern of suburban development regulation favors wealthy people over others. The early suburban residents (as distinct from rural-agricultural old-timers) are usually among the wealthiest stratum in our society (Rudel, 1989:62; Vesterby and Heimlich, 1991:288). They are the voters who remold the local land use laws to favor their interests by demanding lot sizes and other standards that preserve the low-density status quo of the partially developed suburb (Baldassare and Wilson, 1996:467). Thus two powerful economic restraints on trade—transaction costs and the endowment effect—work to perpetuate suburban densities that are "too low" within the standard of efficiency and modest egalitarianism. This standard is modest in that it does not seek to use the public sector to take things from the wealthy; it only asks them to pay for what they get.

In response to the observation that such zoning has been around a long time, so that most current suburban residents have already paid for their exclusivity, I would observe that any status quo, no matter how undesirable, can be capitalized in housing prices. For example, unfair property tax assessments that assess new homebuyers more than long-time residents, are clearly capitalized into property values, thus seeming to equalize total payments from housing and taxes (Yinger et al., 1988:135; Do and Sirmans, 1994). But this in itself is a poor justification for perpetuating an inefficient and unfair system of taxation. Capitalization allows reformers to gauge the depth of opposition and perhaps arrange for transitional relief, but to concede it as a decisive argument against reform is to give up the game entirely.

SUBSIDIES AND SPECULATION ARE NOT IMPORTANT CAUSES OF SPRAWL

I have so far shown that well-informed urban economists think that American central cities are being depopulated as a result of a bundle of social and fiscal ills. I then submitted that the American institution of local zoning has a systematic bias toward low-density residential uses caused in part by a desire to keep new, low-income housing out. The net result of this is a metropolitan area that is excessively spread out. As the close-in suburbs raise the drawbridge, developers vault to municipalities farther away from the city, where the welcome is warmer, at least for a while. It is well known, for example, that San Francisco Bay area growth controls have forced development into the remote Central Valley and induced commuting distances that have become modern legends (Garreau, 1991:310-317).

Some remote but newly developed places in which the jilted developers land recapitulate the experience of the exclusive close-in suburbs. After an initial spate of development, they become more exclusive. Others, oftentimes once-remote satellite cities with a declining economic base, may blossom into "edge city" complexes. These places harden the low-density zoning patterns by making long-distance commutes less necessary for residents of once-remote suburbs (Garreau, 1991:129). The metropolitan patterns of settlement, however, are lower densities of employment and residences than they would have been without this leapfrog process.

As I mentioned in the introduction, the clearest evidence of American sprawl comes from international comparisons. Virtually every measure of metropolitan density indicates that U.S. cities are more spread out than those of the rest of the world. It is not simply higher incomes that account for this. The large urban areas of other high-income countries' are more compact. But it is reasonable to ask whether other American-specific conditions might better explain our tendency to spread out.

Lack of Mass Transit

Whereas other countries have more mass transit (intraurban rail) facilities, the low densities of American metropolitan areas are more likely a cause of our reliance on automobiles than the reverse (Mills and Hamilton, 1994:300). When modern American commuter rail facilities are constructed, ridership is almost always low and less than was projected (Gordon and Richardson, 1989). This is not the result of high fares; all of these rail transit systems are at least as heavily subsidized as the automobile network. The only American metropolitan densities that can support such systems are in cities that have had rail lines for many years (Small, 1992:106).

U.S. Land Area

A factor that is often mentioned as accounting for American sprawl is the greater land area of the United States. Competent urban economists mention this repeatedly, but it seems contrary to economic reasoning. It is not the *amount* of undeveloped land that constrains the outer development of cities, but the *price* of land. The land on which development might occur is owned by people who have to be persuaded to sell it at a price in excess of its value in nonurban uses. The most common nonurban use is agriculture. Of course, much agricultural land on the urban fringe is purchased by speculators—and usually kept in farming—prior to development, but that transaction does not nullify the fact that the speculator must consider the value of competing uses (Peterson, 1978).

It is well established that higher farmland prices cause higher-density residential development (Brueckner and Fansler, 1983; Pyle, 1985). Given the extensive world trade in agricultural products, the cost of farmland (adjusted for crop-growing quality) and hence the opportunity cost of suburban sprawl ought to be about the same in Belgium as it is in Michigan. (Of course, the Belgians may subsidize their farmers and thus keep the price of farmland artificially high, but American subsidies are of a similar order of magnitude—Sanderson, 1990.) Hence the larger amount of land in the United States does not give a convincing account of why our cities should be more spread out. Moreover, Canada offers an obvious counterexample. Its cities are more densely populated by the usual measures than those of comparable size in the United States (Mills and Mieszkowski, 1993:142).

Housing Ownership Subsidy

An alternative reason for sprawl is said to be the special subsidy for single-family housing in the United States. The chief subsidy to housing, which dwarfs all of the rest (including federal mortgage subsidies), is the failure to tax the implicit rent on owner-occupied housing (Aaron, 1972:54, 62). The net value to homeowners from the present system undoubtedly causes them to purchase more housing than they otherwise would, and this has to be regarded as a contributor to suburban sprawl.

But not much. The tax advantages of home ownership are not greatly enhanced by having a multiacre lot. The reason is that, after the first quarter-acre or so, additional land adds very little to the value of a suburban home (Asabere, 1985). The additional tax advantage that a homeowner gets for buying a larger lot is actually quite small. The problem with suburban sprawl is not that residences are mostly owner-occupied, single-family homes. The problem is with the land that is left open as either excess lot size or entirely undeveloped land.

Many of the arguments against urban sprawl take the view that the only cure is to develop multifamily housing. Yet the raw statistics do not give much credence to that. Here is a heuristic calculation that continues to surprise my students (and all other audiences except land developers): take the U.S. population—a quarter of a billion—and divide it into families of four. Give each family an acre of land to live on, an acre being (I tell them) a shade less than the area between the goal lines of a football field. How much of the land area of the 48-contiguous states would be thereby taken up? I poll the students for their guesses (no area figures are given), and the median guess is almost always between 30 and 40 percent. The correct figure is 4 percent.

Since residential land is about half of all urban and built-up land, a half-acre lot size for most households would not cause much sprawl, given that existing urban and built-up areas occupy less than 4 percent of the 48-state land mass (U.S. Department of Agriculture, 1984). A nationally established maximum of quarter-acre lot sizes (which is still not as small as the average of the uncrowded, affluent, planned communities of Reston and Columbia) would result in quite compact suburbs, provided that the area between developments was not excessively large, as noted in the discussion preceding Box 1. This is not an argument against multifamily housing units. It is intended to suggest that restrictions on sprawl densities would still leave most of the population of the United States able to live in single-family homes, an option clearly preferred long before the federal income tax made homeownership especially attractive (Barrows, 1983:398). Antisprawl policies would be more palatable if they did not always conjure up images of high-rise housing in the suburbs.

A neglected factor in the housing-subsidies-cause-sprawl argument is the offsetting effect of agricultural subsidies. The only sector of the economy more favored by government subsidies than homeownership is agriculture (Gardner, 1992). Farmers and other rural landowners barely pay property taxes in most states as a result of various "current-use" assessment programs, in which land is taxed not for its market value, but for its (usually much lower) value as farmland. Inheritance taxes for farmers are also low, and most crops get direct or indirect subsidies from both state and federal governments. The fixed factor that absorbs these benefits is land (Henneberry and Barrows, 1990; Reinsel and Reinsel, 1979). It is thus that much more difficult for developers to purchase exurban land, and this effect offsets at least some of the subsidies to housing.

Land Speculation

Another factor that is often said to cause excessively low densities is land speculation. The story, which is an old one (Fisher, 1933), goes like this. Owners of undeveloped land in the suburbs often decline to develop it, even when there is a bona fide builder at hand. The owner speculates that the land's value will be greater if she waits a few years. As a result, the builders bypass the land and erect houses in locations even more remote from urban centers. This pattern of leap-frog development is said to contribute to suburban sprawl, and a number of land use regulations—some actually put into practice, such as the Portland program, described below—have been devised to discourage it.

The trouble with this scenario is that it ends too soon. It does not ask why the land speculator might reasonably assume that the first offer, which she turns down, will be upped by a later developer. The reason is that the later developer will find it profitable to put up higher-density housing. The eventual pattern is leapfrog-with-infill, in which the infill development has a greater density (Ohls and Pines, 1975; D. Mills, 1981). Thus successful land speculation ultimately causes less suburban sprawl, not more.

If the later, higher-density builder does not materialize with a greater financial offer (which at least compensates for the cost of waiting), the speculator has caused some sprawl. But in that case, the speculator has lost money (in the sense of foregone profits) by waiting too long. Thus the main way by which land speculators contribute to sprawl is by losing money. This may happen, but poor speculators are soon just plain poor and are driven from the market. In any case, empirical studies confirm that later infill development tends to occur at higher densities than that of nearby, earlier-developed subdivisions (Peiser, 1989; Vesterby and Heimlich, 1991).

Land speculators as a group may also find their socially optimal decision rules distorted by taxes (McMillen, 1990). Income taxes raise interest rates, which makes speculators inclined to sell their land too soon. But this is a problem with all investment decisions, not just land. However, the special antispeculation taxes that have occasionally been imposed by some states and provinces (Smith, 1976) are especially distorting. They tend to encourage farmers not to sell to speculators and instead hold the land themselves until a developer arrives. Farmers are not foolish, but one has to assume they are somewhat less sophisticated than professional speculators and so may hold the land too long or sell to developers too soon. (Ironically, these antispeculation taxes are often imposed in order to discourage sprawl.)

Perhaps the strongest evidence that zoning, not the behavior of speculators, causes low density comes from studies of land values. If undeveloped land that has been bypassed by development were simply being held by speculators, its current market value would be nearly equal to that of already-developed land. There would, of course, be some cost to subdividing the land, so vacant land held by speculators would be slightly lower in price than land that was already subdivided and ready to sell. However, even when subdivision costs are taken into account, econometric evidence consistently shows that restrictively zoned, undeveloped land in the suburbs of metropolitan areas has a much lower sale value than land on which development has been permitted (Brownstone and DeVany, 1991; Fischel, 1990:21; White, 1988). Buyers of restrictively zoned, undeveloped land are consistently paying less for it than otherwise comparable land. Such differences can exist only if buyers of the undeveloped land anticipate that there are very large transaction costs to obtaining development permission. Low-density zoning is not a paper tiger, and its existence is pervasive in the suburbs.

Property Taxes and Exactions

The penultimate alternative cause of sprawl (alternative to zoning, that is) is said to be the property tax system. Because of tax uniformity laws, new development with higher infrastructure costs is said to be subsidized by having its cost averaged among all taxpayers in a community (Real Estate Research Corporation, 1974). Under property tax financing, the infrastructure costs of suburban development are said to be perceived as being too low, and developers undertake too much new development rather than using older infrastructure.

This is an example of an argument that is correct in its arithmetic but wrong in its behavioral assumptions. If it really were true that existing residents subsidized new development (without receiving offsetting localized benefits, such as employment), suburban voters and public officials would do even more to stop it. Instead, most communities exact payments from developers that cover at least the difference between the marginal costs of development and its anticipated average property tax payments. (For a collection of articles on this, see Babcock, 1987). These exactions may simply be requirements that the developer put in his own water, sewer, and roads, but, in more sophisticated districts, the developer is asked for cash exactions to compensate the community for any such costs. The legality of this practice was established long ago (Heyman and Gilhool, 1964).

I submit that it is a rare community in which the costs of sprawl are not covered by exactions (cash or in-kind) and anticipated property tax payments. The more controversial issue is whether the community can exact *more* than the actual marginal cost of infrastructure (Altshuler and Gómez-Ibáñez, 1993). A few court decisions have attempted to limit the range of exactions, and some studies have concluded that exactions and impact fees add to the cost of housing (Singell and Lillydahl, 1990), although a nicely nuanced study of California exactions showed that they were passed forward to homebuyers only partially, and then only when housing prices were generally rising (Dresch and Sheffrin, 1997).

Elimination of exactions would make suburban housing even more costly if it caused (as I would predict) the suburbs to retreat to even more exclusive zoning practices (Fischel, 1995:346; Dresch and Sheffrin, 1997:73). The excessive (more than net marginal cost) exactions that some communities are able to extract from developers are enabled in the first instance by highly restrictive zoning. It may be desirable to limit the terms of trade to avoid what some courts regard as legalized extortion, but to restrict trade in discretionary land use permits by sharply curtailing exactions would most likely harm development interests and encourage even more restrictive zoning practices (Gyourko, 1991).

The property tax in most states also finances schools, and it is here that low-income families are most obviously a drag on the local fisc. Although it is true that higher tax rates are capitalized by lowering house values (Oates, 1969), it is exactly that capital loss that most existing suburban residents (poor homeowners as well as rich) seek to avoid. The direction in school finance reform since 1970 has been to reduce reliance on local property taxes (Bahl et al., 1990). To the extent that this is successful, the fiscal motives for excluding low-income housing from communities should diminish (Schill, 1991:851). There is little evidence on this issue as yet, but the fact that exclusionary zoning remains a pressing issue in states like New Jersey, whose supreme court ordered school finance reform decades ago (Harrison and Tarr, 1996), suggests that the effect may be modest.

A third aspect of the property tax system that is said to cause sprawl is its effect on the timing of undeveloped land. Taxing farmland and open space at full market value is said to encourage premature development (Bentick, 1979). The theoretical merits of this proposition continue to be fiercely debated (Tideman, 1982), but in practice the point is moot. Nearly every state authorizes—and often requires—local governments to assess open land (farmland and forests) at its current-use value for tax purposes (Popp, 1989).

State legislatures seem undeterred by research that finds at most a modest effect of current-use taxation on development patterns (Anderson, 1993). The peace treaty has been signed without any evidence of hostility. I suspect that modern current-use programs in fact formalize what local assessors in rural communities always did before property valuation became a more exact science, as the discussion with practicing assessors in Holland (1970) suggests.

Federal Regulation

The last cause of sprawl considered in this section is federal government regulation. Although I think the wellspring of low-density zoning is the preferences of suburban voters, their ability to control large areas of undeveloped land is sometimes limited by political considerations and occasional judicial hostility to multiacre minimum lot size. Federal government environmental regulations (often administered by parallel state programs) have since 1970 added significantly to the weapons by which suburban residents can ward off development (Frieden, 1979).

Federal wetlands preservation is an especially powerful tool to stop development. Most cities are developed along bodies of water, so much of their conveniently located land is arguably wetland. But excluding development from these areas sends it out to rural areas that are not wet but are more remote from central cities. As Garreau observed, "wetlands are also an acute example of how 'insurmountability' [his term for land scarcity] can be created by citizen action" (1991:83). The Endangered Species Act has been a less systematic but often effective tool for suburban antidevelopment interests (Thompson, 1997). This is partly because it takes some political pressure to put the less cuddly creatures on the list, and the local political pressures are greatest in suburban areas. For example, opponents of low-income rental housing in Mount Laurel, New Jersey (still!) raised vague concerns about endangered species and Indian artifacts that might be located at the proposed site (*New York Times, March 3, 1997*, p. A19).

Farmland preservation is likewise a highly selective cause that has been embraced by exclusionary interests, although here the states have been more active, and its effect is tempered by the political influence of farmers. The spurious idea that suburban development is a threat to agricultural production has been a mainstay of exclusionary interests (Fischel, 1982; Kline and Wichelns, 1994:231). Although all of these environmental programs have amenity value (farmland looks pleasant), the legislative hostility to paying attention to their economic costs—benefit-cost analysis being specifically forbidden by much environmental regulation—has made them a potent means of excluding normal-density housing in metropolitan suburbs. It is worth keeping in mind such effects in considering whether federalization of local land use controls would promote more compact development. The Goliath recruited to help your cause can turn into a liability.

METROPOLITAN GOVERNMENTS AND LANDOWNERS CAN REPRESENT THE EXCLUDED

If a major cause of sprawl is, as I have argued, that local governments do not adequately perceive the opportunity cost of excessively low-density zoning, one reform might be metropolitan government. The reason for the excessive low-density zoning that I have dwelt on is that the "insiders" do not include those who are potentially excluded. A government that included all of the metropolitan population would represent the majority of the potential residents who would make use of the undeveloped land. Political pressures might reduce the incidence of exclusionary zoning. Anthony Downs is too much a realist to promote this explicitly, yet his current program for suburban reform recommends steps in that direction (1994:198). (Downs's term is metropolitan *governance*, a more modest term that may evoke less opposition). Metropolitanism in land use is also endorsed by a variety of reformers, such as Jerry Frug (1993) and David Rusk (1993).

There is indirect evidence that larger, more inclusive governments are more prodevelopment than smaller ones. The perennial attempts by state governments to promote employment growth with tax breaks and other policies are one example (Bartik, 1991). Smaller units of government seldom pay much attention to employment issues because most of the benefits of success would be enjoyed by people outside their political borders. Most proindustry local governments, with the exception of depressed central cities, have their eyes trained on fiscal benefits.

Another manifestation of the inclusionary effect of size is that big cities tend to be less exclusionary in their zoning than their suburbs (Clingemeyer, 1993; Linneman and Summers, 1990:22). It is not a coincidence, I submit, that the largest (and virtually only) city in the United States not to have zoning, Houston, is one of the few whose municipal boundaries encompass almost all of its metropolitan population. Judging from the analyses of several plebiscites on zoning, Houston would probably have adopted it if its suburbs were separate from its downtown so that more homogenous groups could be formed. Polls in Houston found that low-income voters and Hispanics generally opposed zoning in part because of their anxiety of being dominated by middle-class suburban interests (McDonald, 1995). Thus there is some reason to believe that shifting land use controls to metropolitan government would make zoning—if it were adopted—more sensitive to the demands of potential homeowners.

The problem with metropolitan government is that it is more likely to be captured by special interests and less likely to respond to legitimate local concerns. Special interests are apt to go too far in either direction. On one hand, special-interest politics can result in excessive development. At the state level, where job creation often dominates political concerns, there are numerous examples of excessive fiscal giveaways to potential employers (Tannenwald, 1996). Large metropolitan cities whose politics are dominated by construction firms and their unions may sometimes discount objections that the megadevelopment stadium or convention center will disrupt traditional neighborhoods (Lassar, 1990:53).

On the other hand, the experience of statewide land use controls in places like Hawaii and Vermont suggests that state-appointed commissions, instead of representing the demands of potential residents and would-be consumers, act as yet another constraint on development in response to local environmental groups (Callies, 1994:Chap 2; Healy and Rosenberg, 1979:Chap. 3). I have observed that Vermont's Act 250 commissions provide a useful lever for entrenched businesses to exclude potential competitors (Fischel, 1985:224). There is also reasonably convincing evidence that larger units of local government in metropolitan areas can function (perhaps inadvertently) as cartel organizers to keep housing prices artificially high (Rose, 1989; Thorson, 1996).

Portland, Oregon, has an interesting (and rare) example of a metropolitan government that has taken over a great deal of land use control (Knaap and Nelson, 1992:51). It is one of the few that is willing to override local zoning to promote infill development. The problem is that Portland shows signs of behaving like an exclusionary suburb with respect to the rest of the world (Fischel, 1997). Its original plan, implemented in the early 1970s, had urban growth boundaries that were intended to contain urban sprawl (Knaap, 1985). This did little harm and perhaps some good as long as growth was moderate and there was plenty of land within the boundaries. (Dresch and Sheffrin, 1997:34, note that Contra Costa County, California, also has urban growth boundaries, but they are drawn sufficiently large that they do not appear to affect housing prices.)

Portland's recent decision not to expand the growth boundary in the face of more rapid immigration to the city, however, seems to account for its sudden and rapid rise in housing prices (Mildner et al., 1996). Portland planners have responded to this with plans to require development at what I would regard as unrealistically high densities within the city. Such housing plans are in principle admirably inclusionary, but for immigrants to Portland who want to live in moderate-density suburban houses, the existing stock is what they must bid for. In a sense, the unrealistically *high*-density development plans are as exclusionary as unrealistically low-density development, since both make accessible but undeveloped land off limits to normal suburban development. Similar situations of metropolitan governance causing housing price inflation by excessively limiting suburban development are Seoul, South Korea (Hannah et al., 1993), Kuala Lumpur, Malaysia (Mayo and Sheppard, 1996), and Reading, England (Cheshire and Sheppard, 1989).

The alternative to metropolitan government as a means of including the demands of outsiders is to restore the development rights of owners of undeveloped land and owners of land ripe for redevelopment (Fischel, 1985:175; 1995:351). These owners are representatives of people not resident in the community who would constitute net additions to the population. Owners of *existing* homes have plenty of incentive to pay attention to the demands of people who want to live in their own houses, but these immigrants would not be net additions to the population.

Attention to the demands of outsiders by owners of developable land is not caused by their beneficence, of course. Outsiders are their most likely customers. In one respect, though, landowners are more democratic than metropolitan governments. Landowners do not care whether their prospective customers currently live and vote within the metropolitan area. Potential immigrants from other parts of the country, or other parts of the world, are as much a part of their market as those existing residents who want to relocate within the metropolitan area.

Although my preferred approach would restore the rights of development-minded landowners, I would not simply give them the right to develop what they wanted. Developers should be allowed the right to develop at normal suburban densities, normal being a reflective standard of what the existing residents of the community actually do. (This standard was developed first by Ellickson, 1977, and I have most recently elaborated on it in Fischel, 1995:Chap. 9.) If nearby land is actually developed on quarter-acre lots, then nearby landowners should be allowed to do the same thing.

This right should not be not absolute. The community can impose exactions to account for higher infrastructure costs, and it can purchase a lower-density development standard for any tract by paying the difference between value at normal density and value at the community's desired density. On the other side of the equation, developers should be able to assert that the pattern of existing development was caused by unreasonably stringent zoning in the past. If this can be proved, development should be permitted at more intensive densities than those that reflect the existing pattern. (This caveat is due to comments from Tony Downs.)

Existing suburban residents can thus raise the drawbridge if they are collectively willing to pay for it, and I do not doubt that some would. But I also have no doubt that the impassioned pleas by neighbors who now oppose development at land use hearings would be greatly muted if, to get their desires, they would have to pay more in property taxes to finance the "just compensation" due the landowner. Requiring the local governments that want to preserve open space to buy that space (or the development rights) would make existing voters pay attention to the opportunity cost of exclusion and, for the most part, deter inefficient and inequitable low-density zoning.

A supposed drawback of restoring property rights as a method of controlling sprawl is that it still excludes the poor. But this is an instance in which the market is probably more accommodating to the poor than the local political process. Suburban zoning laws regulate the market in part because the market would give existing suburbs more poor people than current residents would like. The owner of undeveloped land, however, does not care whether the high bidder for her 10-acre tract proposes to put up 2 mansions or 40 bungalows. In many places, the developer of the higher-intensity use, which will usually serve lower-income people, can outbid others. The major problem for most developers of subsidized, low-income housing units is not the cost of land, but the web of regulatory barriers, as numerous national commissions have amply demonstrated (National Commission on Urban Problems, 1969; Advisory Commission on Regulatory Barriers to Affordable Housing, 1991).

Restoration of landowner rights along the lines I propose can be accomplished along two complementary lines, one by judicial decisions and the other by state legislation. My suggestions here are not for a detailed plan of action but for an educational mission along lines other than changing government structure. (For more details about implementation, see Fischel, 1995:Chap. 9, and Ellickson, 1977.) There is no doubt that these suggestions have some flavor of, as Tony Downs put it in a critique of an earlier draft, "piously urging the world to overcome sin by behaving virtuously." My response is that preachers have in fact urged that for many centuries, and it seems to do at least some good. That there remains much sin after their best work is done is hardly reason for them to stop doing it.

The preaching that social scientists undertake has value largely because of its aspiration for objectivity. Being beholden to one's scientific peers rather than commercial or political interests makes their pronouncements more believable. For this reason, I would urge bodies such as the National Research Council to point out that restoration of landowner rights has social value. The audiences to whom this should be directed are judges (both federal and state) and state legislators. Before discussing what good such information would do for each of these audiences, let me offer an example of the kind of statement that would be useful:

> Owners of developable tracts of land that have reasonable access to metropolitan employment should be accorded legal protection of the right to develop at normal suburban densities. Such densities should be determined by comparisons to what has gone before in the same community and to existing well-planned and socially diverse developments at comparable locations within the metropolitan area. Developing municipalities should not be permitted to use local land use laws or invoke unreasonable environmental review to maintain artificially low densities or exclude a large segment of housing types. Protec-

tion of landowner rights in these situations is consistent with traditional understandings of property rights and prevention of excessive decentralization and social fragmentation of metropolitan areas. Landowner rights should be viewed not as a grudging concession to tradition but as a positive means to promote economical and environmentally sound use of land in metropolitan areas.

Property rights are traditionally a judicial matter, and, as I have noted earlier, most judges are wary of treading on the prerogatives of local governments. Judges are aware that their enterprise has an undemocratic odor to it. For this reason, many judges who are in fact offended by the unfair treatment of owners of undeveloped land are reluctant to intervene, except in the most egregious cases.

This reluctance is gradually changing, however, with the rise of the regulatory takings doctrine and the realization that development-minded landowners are not the social parasites they have often been made out to be. An increasing number of federal and state decisions have made local governments with overly restrictive land use controls liable for monetary damages (Eagle, 1996:Chap. 7). The judiciary is a ready and appropriate vehicle for change in this area.

For these changes to proceed, however, judges need to get objective advice about the social benefits of private property. External sources are needed because one of the litigants who appear before them in local land use disputes is obviously self-interested. Development-minded parties clearly hope to make money by overturning the down-zoning (for instance) that they or their predecessors were subject to. The possibility that they actually represent a larger public interest is, if not entirely absent, easily discounted. This is especially true in land use disputes because the opposing party is usually a local government agency. It is duly qualified to determine the "public interest." That such public interest may be for only a small part of the public may sometimes occur to the judge in the case, but it would be a much larger stretch for her to realize that it is the developer who serves the larger public interest (the demands of outsiders to live in the community).

State legislation is the other means by which landowner rights can be restored. With the demise of the regulatory takings bills in Congress in 1995 (bills that I believe were badly flawed because of overinclusiveness), the action has switched to state legislatures and state courts. Several states have in recent years passed laws that expand the regulatory takings doctrine beyond what most courts of law have traditionally held it to be. (For current information in this rapidly evolving area, see the web site http://www.arin.org/arin/states.html. Useful cautionary information on the design of takings bills is in Ellickson, 1996b.)

Some of the successful bills, most notably Florida's, offer a balanced approach to resolving disputes between landowners and regulators (Powell et al., 1995). Florida's act requires negotiation and mediation between regulators and landowners prior to trial, and, perhaps most important, that the loser at a trial must pay the other party's legal costs. (I was told at a conference in October 1996 that the total number of cases adjudicated during the first year of the law was six, which suggests that negotiation was usually successful.)

Regulatory takings is not the only legal doctrine that might be invoked to help landowners develop at normal densities. Several state courts have continued the substantive review of local legislation that the federal courts nominally discarded in the 1930s (Friedman, 1988). The problem with substantive review is how to set the appropriate standards. If 4-acre minimum lot sizes are unconstitutional, as was decided by the Pennsylvania supreme court in 1965 (Coyle, 1993:54), what about 3-acre minimum lot sizes?

Once again, encouragement of courts and legislatures from bodies other than the obviously (even if usefully) self-interested development industry would have a beneficial effect. The least-cost housing standard initially adopted (and later impatiently abandoned) by the New Jersey supreme court in Oakwood at Madison (cited above) is a good candidate. It appears to be consistent with the writings of Tony Downs, who has spent much of his career grappling with these problems (Downs, 1969; 1991). The *Oakwood* least-cost housing doctrine is more modest in its goals than the *Mount Laurel II* doctrine, but the latter clearly upset voters' sense of established entitlements and proved to be judicially unmanageable.

One might reasonably ask whether, given that a few states are doing something, development interests actually need the endorsement of more neutral bodies. As I have pointed out elsewhere (Fischel, 1995:Chap. 8), state legislatures have been induced to protect specific groups from excessive regulation. For example, siting of mobile homes and group homes has received special protection in many states, and excessive exactions have often been reined in. In the halls of the state legislatures, developers' interests seem not to have fared so badly.

There is a difference, however, between developers' interests and landowners' interests. Developers are often unconcerned with metropolitan location. Many buy only land that is zoned for the use they want. Some large developers have told me that they are indifferent to zoning, except when the rules are changed after they have purchased the land. As a result, the party most sensitive to the *location* demands of otherwise-excluded outsiders are the owners of developable land. But these owners are not easily organized, since their situations differ from one place to another and since their battles over rezoning tend to be episodic rather than ongoing.

Landowning interests are not entirely alone in the political arena, of course. Aside from the developers who do take ownership positions in land not zoned for what they want, a newly vigorous property rights movement has advocated a return to landowner rights (Yandle, 1995). The problem is that much of this movement tends to be driven by a larger ideological agenda that is viewed with suspicion by the mainstream of academics, news media, judges, and legislators. The utilitarian notion that increasing the rights of landowners might lead to net gains for society at large tends to be lost in debates about the welfare state, big government, the New Deal, and the meaning of the Cold War. Some words of endorsement for development-minded landowners in the suburbs by neutral and scientifically responsible bodies might go a long way. It does not seem all that costly to try.

CONCLUSION

American metropolitan areas are both excessively spread out and segregated by income class. This essay has argued that the major cause of both of these problems is the attenuation of market forces by local land use regulation. Demands by outsiders are systematically thwarted by local governments in suburban areas that seek to preserve the status quo. Development-minded landowners, whether for-profit, charitable, or private nonprofit, are often prevented from developing their land at densities and for uses that are considered normal by metropolitan area-wide standards. The better way to open up the suburbs, I submit, is not to have yet another layer of government, but to improve the rights of landowners.

ACKNOWLEDGMENTS

I have benefited from written comments by Anthony Downs and an anonymous referee and from oral comments by members of the committee responsible for this volume.

REFERENCES

Aaron, Henry
    1972   *Shelter and Subsidies: Who Benefits from Federal Housing Policies?* Washington, DC: Brookings Institution.
Abramson, Alan J., Mitchell S. Tobin, and Matthew R. VanderGoot
    1995   The changing geography of metropolitan opportunity: The segregation of the poor in U.S. metropolitan areas, 1970 to 1990. *Housing Policy Debate* 6(1):45-72.
Advisory Commission on Regulatory Barriers to Affordable Housing
    1991   *Not In My Back Yard: Removing Barriers to Affordable Housing.* Washington, DC: U.S. Department of Housing and Urban Development.
Altshuler, Alan A., and Jose A. Gómez-Ibáñez, with Arnold M. Howitt
    1993   *Regulation for Revenue: The Political Economy of Land Use Exactions.* Cambridge, MA: Lincoln Institute of Land Policy.
Anderson, John E.
    1993   Use-value property tax assessment: Effects on land development. *Land Economics* 69(August):263-269.
Asabere, Paul K.
    1985   The relative lot size hypothesis: An empirical note. *Urban Studies* 22(August):355-357.
Babcock, Richard F., ed.
    1987   Exactions: A controversial new source for municipal funds. *Law and Contemporary Problems* 50(Winter).

Bahl, Roy, David Sjoquist, and W. Loren Williams
  1990   School finance reform and impact on property taxes. *Proceedings of the Eighty-Third Annual Conference on Taxation.* Columbus, OH: National Tax Association-Tax Institute of America.

Baldassare, Mark, and Georgeanna Wilson
  1996   Changing sources of suburban support for growth controls. *Urban Studies* 33(April):459-471.

Barrows, Robert G.
  1983   Beyond the tenement: Patterns of American urban housing, 1870-1930. *Journal of Urban History* 9(August):395-420.

Bartik, Timothy J.
  1991   *Who Benefits from State and Local Economic Development Policies?* Kalamazoo, MI: W.E. Upjohn Institute for Employment Research.

Benabou, Roland
  1993   Workings of a city: Location, education, and production. *Quarterly Journal of Economics* 108(August):619-652.

Bentick, Brian L.
  1979   The impact of taxation and valuation practices on the timing and efficiency of land use. *Journal of Political Economy* 87(August):859-868.

Bloom, Howard S., and Helen F. Ladd
  1982   Property tax revaluation and tax levy growth. *Journal of Urban Economics* 11(January):73-84.

Bogart, William T.
  1993   "What big teeth you have!": Identifying the motivations for exclusionary zoning. *Urban Studies* (December):1669-1681.

Briffault, Richard
  1990   Our localism: Part I—The structure of local government law. *Columbia Law Review* 90(January):1-115.

Brownstone, David, and Arthur DeVany
  1991   Zoning, returns to scale, and the value of undeveloped land. *Review of Economics and Statistics* 73(November):699-704.

Brueckner, Jan K., and David A. Fansler
  1983   The economics of urban sprawl: Theory and evidence on the spatial sizes of cities. *Review of Economics and Statistics* 65(August):479-482.

Burns, Nancy
  1994   *The Formation of American Local Governments: Private Values in Public Institutions.* New York: Oxford University Press.

Callies, David L.
  1994   *Preserving Paradise: Why Regulation Won't Work.* Honolulu: University of Hawaii Press.

Cappell, Andrew J.
  1991   A walk along Willow: Patterns of land use coordination in prezoning New Haven. *Yale Law Journal* 101(December):617-642.

Case, Anne C., and Lawrence F. Katz
  1991   The Company You Keep: The Effects of Family and Neighborhood on Disadvantaged Youths. NBER Working Paper No. 3705, Cambridge, MA, May.

Cassell, Paul G., and B. S. Hayman
  1996   Police interrogation in the 1990s: An empirical study of the effects of *Miranda. UCLA Law Review* 43(February):839-931.

Cheshire, Paul, and Stephen Sheppard
    1989   British planning policy and access to housing: Some empirical estimates. *Urban Studies*
            26(October):469-485.
Ciccone, Anntonio, and Robert E. Hall
    1996   Productivity and the density of economic activity. *American Economic Review*
            86(March):54-70.
Cion, Richard M.
    1966   Accommodation par excellence: The Lakewood plan. In *Metropolitan Politics: A
            Reader,* Michael N. Danielson, ed. Boston: Little, Brown.
Clingemeyer, James C.
    1993   Distributive politics, ward representation, and the spread of zoning. *Public Choice*
            77(4):725-738.
Coyle, Dennis J.
    1993   *Property Rights and the Constitution: Shaping Society Through Land Use Regulation.*
            Albany, NY: State University of New York Press.
Cullen, Julie Berry, and Steven D. Levitt
    1996   Crime, Urban Flight, and the Consequences for Cities. NBER Working Paper No. 5737,
            Cambridge, MA, September.
Cullingworth, J. Barry
    1993   *The Political Culture of Planning: American Land Use Planning in Comparative Per-
            spective.* New York: Routledge.
Cutler, David M., and Edward L. Glaeser
    1997   Are ghettos good or bad? *Quarterly Journal of Economics* 112(3):827-872.
Dana, David A.
    1995   Natural preservation and the race to develop. *University of Pennsylvania Law Review*
            143(January):655-708.
Denzau, Arthur T., and Barry R. Weingast
    1982   Forward: The political economy of land use regulation. *Urban Law Annual* 23:385-405.
DiMento, Joseph F., Michael D. Dozier, Steven L. Emmons, Donald G. Hagman, Christopher Kim,
            Karen Greenfield-Sanders, Paul F. Waldau, and Jay A. Woollacott
    1980   Land development and environmental control in the California supreme court: The defer-
            ential, the preservationist, and the preservationist-erratic eras. *UCLA Law Review*
            27(April-June):859-1066.
Do, A. Quang, and C.F. Sirmans
    1994   Residential property tax capitalization: Discount rate evidence from California. *National
            Tax Journal* 57(June):341-348.
Dowall, David E.
    1984   *The Suburban Squeeze: Land Conversion and Regulation in the San Francisco Bay Area.*
            Berkeley: University of California Press.
Downs, Anthony
    1969   Housing the urban poor: The economics of various strategies. *American Economic
            Review* 59(September):646-651.
    1973   *Opening Up the Suburbs: An Urban Strategy for America.* New Haven, CT: Yale
            University Press.
    1991   The Advisory Commission on Regulatory Barriers to Affordable Housing: Its behavior
            and accomplishments. *Housing Policy Debate* 2(4):1095-1137.
    1994   *New Visions for Metropolitan America.* Washington, DC: Brookings.
Dresch, Marla, and Steven M. Sheffrin
    1997   *Who Pays for Development Fees and Exactions?* San Francisco: Public Policy Institute
            of California.

Eagle, Stephen J.
  1996   *Regulatory Takings*. Charlottesville, VA: Michie.
Eberts, Randall W., and Timothy J. Gronberg
  1981   Jurisdictional homogeneity and the Tiebout hypothesis. *Journal of Urban Economics* 10(September):227-239.
Ellickson, Robert C.
  1977   Suburban growth controls: An economic and legal analysis. *Yale Law Journal* 86(January):385-511.
  1993   Property in land. *Yale Law Journal* 102(April):1315-1400.
  1996a   Controlling chronic misconduct in city spaces: Of panhandlers, skid rows, and public-space zoning. *Yale Law Journal* 105(March):1165-1248.
  1996b   Takings legislation: A comment. *Harvard Journal of Law and Public Policy* 20(Fall):75-80.
Epple, Dennis, Thomas Romer, and Radu Filimon
  1988   Community development with endogenous land use controls. *Journal of Public Economics* 35(March):133-162.
Fischel, William A.
  1979   Determinants of voting on environmental quality: A study of a New Hampshire pulp mill referendum. *Journal of Environmental Economics and Management* 6(June):107-118.
  1981   Is local government structure in large urbanized areas monopolistic or competitive? *National Tax Journal* 34(March):95-104.
  1982   The urbanization of agricultural land: A review of the national agricultural lands study. *Land Economics* 58(May):236-259.
  1985   *The Economics of Zoning Laws: A Property Rights Approach to American Land Use Controls.* Baltimore, MD: Johns Hopkins University Press.
  1990   *Do Growth Controls Matter?* Cambridge, MA: Lincoln Institute of Land Policy.
  1991   Exclusionary zoning and growth controls: A comment on the APA's endorsement of the *Mount Laurel* doctrine. *Washington University Journal of Urban and Contemporary Law* 40(Summer/Fall):49-64.
  1994   Zoning, nonconvexities, and T. Jack Foster's city. *Journal of Urban Economics* 35(March):175-181.
  1995   *Regulatory Takings: Law, Economics, and Politics.* Cambridge, MA: Harvard University Press.
  1997   Comment on Carl Abbott's, "The Portland region: Where city and suburbs talk with each other—and often agree." *Housing Policy Debate* 8(1):65-73.
Fisher, Ernest M.
  1933   Speculation in suburban lands. *American Economic Review* 23(March):152-162.
Frieden, Bernard J.
  1979   *The Environmental Protection Hustle.* Cambridge, MA: MIT Press.
Friedman, Lawrence M.
  1988   State constitutions in historical perspective. *Annals of AAPSS* 496(March):33-42.
Frug, Jerry
  1993   Decentering decentralization. *University of Chicago Law Review* 60(Spring):253-338.
Gardner, Bruce L.
  1992   Changing economic perspectives on the farm problem. *Journal of Economic Literature* 30(March):62-101.
Garreau, Joel
  1991   *Edge City: Life on the New Frontier.* New York: Doubleday.
Giovannotto, G. Alessandro (Alex)
  1994   Econometric Analysis of the Mt. Laurel Approach to Providing Affordable Housing in New Jersey. Undergraduate Honors Thesis, Department of Economics, Dartmouth College.

Gordon, Peter, Ajay Kumar, and Harry W. Richardson
    1989   Congestion, changing metropolitan structure, and city size in the United States. *International Regional Science Review* 12(1):45-56.
Gordon, Peter, and Harry Richardson
    1989   Notes from underground: The failure of urban mass transit. *The Public Interest* 94(Winter):77-86.
Gyourko, Joseph
    1991   Impact fees, exclusionary zoning, and the density of new development. *Journal of Urban Economics* 30(September):242-256.
Haar, Charles M.
    1996   *Suburbs Under Siege.* Princeton, NJ: Princeton University Press.
Hahn, Alan J.
    1970   Planning in rural areas. *AIP Journal* 36(January):40-49.
Hamilton, Bruce W.
    1976   Capitalization of intrajurisdictional differences in local tax prices. *American Economic Review* 66(December):743-753.
Hamilton, Bruce W., Edwin S. Mills, and David Puryear
    1975   The Tiebout hypothesis and residential income segregation. In *Fiscal Zoning and Land Use Controls,* Edwin S. Mills and Wallace E. Oates, eds. Lexington, MA: Heath-Lexington Books.
Hannah, Lawrence, Kyung-Hwan Kim, and Edwin S. Mills
    1993   Land use controls and housing prices in Korea. *Urban Studies* 30(February):147-156.
Harrison, Russell S., and G. Alan Tarr
    1996   School finance and inequality in New Jersey. In *Constitutional Politics and the States,* G. Alan Tarr, ed. Westport, CT: Greenwood Press.
Healy, Robert G., and John S. Rosenberg
    1979   *Land Use and the States, Second Edition.* Baltimore, MD: Johns Hopkins University Press.
Henderson, J. Vernon, Peter Mieszkowski, and Yves Sauvageau
    1978   Peer group effects and educational production functions. *Journal of Public Economics* 10:97-106.
Henneberry, David, and Richard Barrows
    1990   Capitalization of exclusive agricultural zoning into farmland prices. *Land Economics* 66(August):249-258.
Heyman, Ira Michael, and Thomas K. Gilhool
    1964   The constitutionality of imposing increased community costs on new suburban residents through subdivision exactions. *Yale Law Journal* 73(June):1119-1157.
Hoffman, Elizabeth, and Matthew L. Spitzer
    1993   Willingness to pay vs. willingness to accept: Legal and economic implications. *Washington University Law Quarterly* 71(1):59-114.
Holcombe, Randall G.
    1989   The median voter model in public choice theory. *Public Choice* 61:115-125.
Holland, Daniel M., ed.
    1970   *The Assessment of Land Value.* Madison: University of Wisconsin Press.
Holtz-Eakin, Douglas, and Harvey S. Rosen
    1989   The "rationality" of municipal capital spending: Evidence from New Jersey. *Regional Science and Urban Economics* 19(August):517-536.
Holzer, Harry J., Keith R. Ihlanfeldt, and David L. Sjoquist
    1994   Work, search, and travel among white and black youth. *Journal of Urban Economics* 35(May):320-345.

International City Managers' Association
  1960   *Urban Fringe Areas: Zoning, Subdivision Regulations, and Municipal Services.* Chicago: ICMA.
Kirp, David L, John P. Dwyer, and Larry Rosenthal
  1995   *Our Town: Race, Housing, and the Soul of Suburbia.* New Brunswick, NJ: Rutgers University Press.
Kline, Jeffrey, and Dennis Wichelns
  1994   Using referendum data to characterize public support for purchasing development rights to farmland. *Land Economics* 70(May):223-233.
Knaap, Gerrit J.
  1985   The price effects of urban growth boundaries in metropolitan Portland, Oregon. *Land Economics* 61(February):28-35.
Knaap, Gerrit, and Arthur C. Nelson
  1992   *The Regulated Landscape: Lessons on State Land Use Planning from Oregon.* Cambridge, MA: Lincoln Institute for Land Policy.
Knetsch, Jack L., and J.A. Sinden
  1984   Willingness to pay and compensation demanded: Experimental evidence of an unexpected disparity in measures of value. *Quarterly Journal of Economics* 99(August):507-521.
Kremer, Michael
  1997   How much does sorting increase inequality? *Quarterly Journal of Economics* 112(February):115-139.
Kunstler, James Howard
  1996   *Home from Nowhere: Remaking Our Everyday World for the Twenty-First Century.* New York: Simon and Schuster.
Lamar, Martha, Alan Mallach, and John M. Payne
  1989   Mount Laurel at work: Affordable housing in New Jersey, 1983-1988. *Rutgers Law Review* 41(Summer):1197-1277.
Lassar, Terry Jill, ed.
  1990   *City Deal Making.* Washington, DC: ULI-the Urban Land Institute.
LeRoy, Stephen F., and Jon Sonstelie
  1983   Paradise lost and regained: Transportation innovation, income and residential location. *Journal of Urban Economics* 13(January):67-89.
Linneman, Peter, and Anita A. Summers
  1990   Patterns of Urban Population Decentralization in the United States 1970-1987. Wharton Real Estate Center Working Paper #76, University of Pennsylvania.
Lubove, Roy
  1969   *Twentieth-Century Pittsburgh: Government, Business, and Environmental Change.* New York: Wiley.
Margo, Robert A.
  1992   Explaining postwar suburbanization of population in the United States: The role of income. *Journal of Urban Economics* 31(May):301-310.
Mayo, Stephen, and Stephen Sheppard
  1996   Housing supply under rapid economic growth and varying regulatory stringency: An international comparison. *Journal of Housing Economics* 5:274-289.
McDonald, John F.
  1995   Houston remains unzoned. *Land Economics* 71(February):137-140.
McMillen, Daniel P.
  1990   The timing and duration of development tax rate increases. *Journal of Urban Economics* 28(July):1-18.

McMillen, Daniel P., and John F. McDonald
  1991   A Markov chain model of zoning change. *Journal of Urban Economics* 30(September):257-270.
Mieszkowski, Peter, and Edwin S. Mills
  1993   The causes of metropolitan suburbanization. *Journal of Economic Perspectives* 7(Summer):135-147.
Mildner, Gerald C., Kenneth J. Dueker, and Anthony M. Rufolo
  1996   Impact of the Urban Growth Boundary on Metropolitan Housing Markets. Portland State University, Center for Urban Studies, May.
Mills, David E.
  1981   Growth, speculation and sprawl in a monocentric city. *Journal of Urban Economics* 10(September):201-226.
Mills, Edwin S.
  1972   *Studies in the Structure of the Urban Economy.* Baltimore, MD: Johns Hopkins University Press for Resources for the Future.
Mills, Edwin S., and Bruce W. Hamilton
  1994   *Urban Economics 5th Edition.* Glenview, IL: Scott, Foresman.
Mills, Edwin S., and Richard Price
  1984   Metropolitan suburbanization and central city problems. *Journal of Urban Economics* 15(January):1-17.
National Commission on Urban Problems
  1969   *Building the American City.* New York: Praeger.
Nelson, Robert H.
  1979   A private property right theory of zoning. *The Urban Lawyer* 11(Fall):713-732.
Oates, Wallace E.
  1969   The effects of property taxes and local public spending on property values: An empirical study of tax capitalization and the Tiebout hypothesis. *Journal of Political Economy* 77(November):957-971.
  1977   The use of local zoning ordinances to regulate population flows and the quality of local services. In *Essays in Labor Market Analysis,* Orley Ashenfelter and Wallace Oates, eds. New York: John Wiley.
Ogus, Anthony
  1990   Property rights and freedom of economic activity. In *Constitutionalism and Rights: The Influence of the United States Constitution Abroad,* Louis Henkin and Albert Rosenthal, eds. New York: Columbia University Press.
Ohls, James C., and David Pines
  1975   Discontinuous urban development and economic efficiency. *Land Economics* 51(August):224-234.
Peiser, Richard B.
  1981   Land development regulation: A case study of Dallas and Houston, Texas. *AREUEA Journal* 9(Winter):397-417.
  1989   Density and urban sprawl. *Land Economics* 65(August):193-204.
Peterson, George E.
  1974   Land Prices and Factor Substitution in the Metropolitan Housing Market. Urban Institute working paper, Washington, DC, November.
  1978   Federal tax policy and land conversion at the urban fringe. In *Metropolitan Financing and Growth Policies,* George Break, ed. Madison: University of Wisconsin Press.
Popp, Terri E.
  1989   A survey of governmental response to the farmland crisis: States' application of agricultural zoning. *University of Arkansas at Little Rock Law Journal* 11(July)515-556.

Popper, Frank
  1988   Understanding American land use regulation since 1970. *Journal of the American Planning Association* 54(Summer):291-301.
Powell, David L. Robert M. Rhodes, and Dan R. Stengle
  1995   A measured step to protect private property rights. *Florida State University Law Review* 23(Fall):255-314.
Pyle, Lizbeth
  1985   The land market beyond the urban fringe. *Geographical Review* 75(January):32-43.
Rawls, John
  1971   *A Theory of Justice.* Cambridge, MA: Belknap Press.
Real Estate Research Corporation
  1974   *The Costs of Sprawl: Environmental and Economic Costs of Alternative Residential Development Patterns at the Urban Fringe.* Washington, DC: U.S. Department of Housing and Urban Development.
Reinsel, Robert D., and Edward I. Reinsel
  1979   The economics of asset values and current income in farming. *American Journal of Agricultural Economics* 61(December):1093-1097.
Riddiough, Timothy J.
  1997   The economic consequences of regulatory taking risk on land value and development activity. *Journal of Urban Economics* 41(January):56-77.
Rolleston, Barbara Sherman
  1987   Determinants of restrictive suburban zoning: An empirical analysis. *Journal of Urban Economics* 21(January):1-21.
Rose, Louis A.
  1989   Urban land supply: Natural and contrived restrictions. *Journal of Urban Economics* 25(May):325-45.
Rossi, Peter H., and Eleanor Weber
  1996   The social benefits of homeownership: Empirical evidence from national surveys. *Housing Policy Debate* 7(1):1-35.
Rubin, Jeffrey, Joseph Seneca, and Janet Stotsky
  1990   Affordable housing and municipal choice. *Land Economics* 66(August):325-340.
Rudel, Thomas K.
  1989   *Situations and Strategies in American Land-Use Planning.* Cambridge, MA: Cambridge University Press.
Rusk, David
  1993   *Cities Without Suburbs.* Baltimore: Johns Hopkins University Press.
Sanderson, Fred H.
  1990   Agricultural protectionism in the industrialized world. *Resources* 100(Summer):6-9.
Schill, Michael H.
  1991   Deconcentrating the inner city poor. *Chicago Kent Law Review* 67:795-853.
Schmenner, Roger W.
  1981   The rent gradient for manufacturing. *Journal of Urban Economics* 9(January):90-96.
Schwartz, Seymour I., David E. Hansen, and Richard Green
  1981   Suburban growth controls and the price of new housing. *Journal of Environmental Economics and Management* 8(December):303-320.
Segelhorst, E., and M. Brady
  1984   A theoretical analysis of the effect of fear on the location decisions of urban-suburban residents. *Journal of Urban Economics* 15(March):157-171.
Siegan, Bernard H.
  1976   *Other People's Property.* Lexington, MA: Heath.

Singell, Larry D., and Jane H. Lillydahl
  1990   An empirical examination of the effect of impact fees on the housing market. *Land Economics* 66(February):82-92.
Skogan, Wesley G.
  1990   *Disorder and Decline: Crime and the Spiral of Decay in American Neighborhoods*. New York: Free Press.
Small, Kenneth A.
  1992   *Urban Transportation Economics*. Chur, Switzerland: Harwood Academic.
Smith, Lawrence B.
  1976   The Ontario land speculation tax: An analysis of an unearned increment land tax. *Land Economics* 52(February):1-12.
Stockman, Paul K.
  1992   Anti-snob zoning in Massachusetts: Assessing one attempt at opening the suburbs to affordable housing. *Virginia Law Review* 78(March):535-580.
Tannenwald, Robert
  1996   State business tax climate: How should it be measured and how important is it? *New England Economic Review* (January/February):23-38.
Taylor, Ralph B.
  1995   The impact of crime on communities. *Annals of AAPSS* 539(May):28-45.
Thompson, Barton H., Jr.
  1997   The endangered species act: A case study in takings and incentives. *Stanford Law Review* 49:601-676.
Thorson, James A.
  1996   An examination of the monopoly zoning hypothesis. *Land Economics* 72(February):43-55.
Tideman, T. Nicolaus
  1982   A tax on land value *is* neutral. *National Tax Journal* 35(March):109-112.
Toner, William
  1978   *Saving Farms and Farmland: A Community Guide*. Chicago: American Society of Planning Officials.
U.S. Department of Agriculture, Soil Conservation Service
  1984   *1982 National Resources Inventory*. Washington, DC: U.S. Department of Agriculture.
Vesterby, Marlow, and Ralph Heimlich
  1991   Land use and demographic change: Results from fast-growth counties. *Land Economics* 67(August):279-291.
Wallace, Nancy E.
  1988   The market effects of zoning undeveloped land: Does zoning follow the market? *Journal of Urban Economics* 23(May):307-326.
Warner, Sam Bass
  1962   *Streetcar Suburbs: The Process of Growth in Boston, 1870-1900*. New York: Atheneum.
Weicher, John C., and Thomas G. Thibodeau
  1988   Filtering and housing markets: An empirical analysis. *Journal of Urban Economics* 23(January):21-40.
Wheaton, William C.
  1977   Income and urban residence: An analysis of consumer demand for location. *American Economic Review* 67(September):620-631.
  1993   Land capitalization, Tiebout mobility, and the role of zoning regulations. *Journal of Urban Economics* 34(September):102-117.

White, James R.
  1988   Large lot zoning and subdivision costs: A test. *Journal of Urban Economics* 23(May):370-384.
Whyte, William H.
  1964   *Cluster Development.* New York: American Conservation Association.
Wilson, James Q., and Barbara Boland
  1976   Crime. In *The Urban Predicament*, William Gorham and Nathan Glazer, eds. Washington, DC: The Urban Institute.
Yandle, Bruce, ed.
  1995   *Land Rights: The 1990s' Property Rights Rebellion.* Lanham, MD: Rowman and Littlefield.
Yinger, John, Howard S. Bloom, Axel Borsch-Supan, and Helen F. Ladd
  1988   *Property Taxes and Housing Values: The Theory and Estimation of Intrajurisdictional Property Tax Capitalization.* Boston: Academic Press.

Spatial Stratification Within U.S. Metropolitan Areas

Ingrid Gould Ellen
New York University

Nearly 80 percent of the U.S. population lives in metropolitan areas. To say this, however, may be to obscure the enormous range of environments found within these metropolitan areas. Typically, they are divided into political jurisdictions and neighborhoods that are highly segregated by class, race, ethnicity, and income and even marked by vastly different physical conditions. In most metropolitan areas, central cities and older, inner-ring suburbs tend to have lower-skilled and less affluent populations, lower tax bases, as well as more deteriorated housing stocks and infrastructures, than their newer, outer-ring suburban neighbors. And the segregation becomes even more apparent if comparisons are made across individual neighborhoods within these jurisdictions.

What makes this especially troubling is the growing body of evidence that these geographic disparities may have serious consequences. Many recent studies suggest that children growing up in deprived communities face substantially greater obstacles in obtaining a sound education, securing a steady job, and otherwise advancing their status than their counterparts in more prosperous environments (Ellen and Turner, 1997; Ihlanfeldt, this volume; Mayer, 1996). Significantly, a few of these studies also suggest that the costs of poverty concentration reach far beyond those poor neighborhoods themselves—that the deprivations of South Bronx and Anacostia resonate in Scarsdale and Chevy Chase. There is some evidence, that is, that certain neighborhood effects are nonlinear, and that a deconcentration of the poor may thus lead to decreased levels of poverty and its consequent problems not only in distressed neighborhoods but also in society overall (Crane, 1991; Hogan and Kitagawa, 1985).

Before any meaningful assessment of the nature and extent of these consequences can take place, however, it is critical to provide a clearer sense of the nature and extent of the spatial disparities themselves. This paper aims to do just this. The first section, in order to set the stage, documents the magnitude of the spatial and jurisdictional disparities within the average metropolitan area and determines how these have changed in recent years. Many researchers go no further and thus overlook the surprising diversity found *across* different metropolitan areas in the magnitude of disparities. This paper, however, makes this variation its central concern. To this end, the second section classifies metropolitan areas on the basis of the magnitude of their central-city-suburban disparities and identifies certain metropolitan-area characteristics (such as population size, the degree of racial segregation, and the elasticity of the central-city boundaries) that are correlated with greater and lesser disparities. The third section then estimates a simple, cross-sectional regression that tests which, if any, of these correlations persist after controlling for other factors. Although more definitive conclusions regarding the precise causes of the jurisdictional disparities would be desirable, they would require further statistical analysis that lies outside the scope of this particular project.

THE MAGNITUDE OF SPATIAL DISPARITIES WITHIN METROPOLITAN AREAS

City Versus Suburb

Most Americans voice a preference for owning a detached, single-family home and view suburban communities as promising better schools, lower crime rates, and less crowding and traffic (Fannie Mae, 1997). Not surprisingly, then, the population of the suburbs continues to swell. In 1940, just over 15 percent of the U.S. population lived in suburban communities. Fifty years later, that proportion had risen to 46 percent (U.S. Bureau of the Census, 1991). As shown in Table 1, however, not everyone is gaining access to the suburban life. Poor and minority households continue to live largely in inner-city communities. In 1990, 57 percent of the black population and 52 percent of the Hispanic population

TABLE 1   Breakdown of Residence by Race and Ethnicity, 1990 (in percent)

Residence	Total Population	Non-Hispanic Whites	Blacks	Hispanics
Metropolitan Areas	77.5	74.7	83.8	90.4
Central Cities	31.3	24.5	57.3	51.5
Suburbs	46.2	50.3	26.4	37.3
Nonmetropolitan	22.5	25.3	16.2	9.6

Source: U.S. Bureau of the Census (1990b).

lived in central cities.[1] By contrast, less than one-fourth of non-Hispanic white households lived in central cities.

The remainder of this section highlights some average differences between central cities and suburbs and examines these differences over time. For the purposes of this paper, attributes of a given metropolitan area's suburbs are viewed in the aggregate, for even though there is substantial variation across individual suburbs in a given metropolitan area, the available census data treat suburbs as a single entity. Nonetheless, neighborhood data are briefly used to reveal some interesting variations across suburban jurisdictions.

The disparities presented in this section may be grouped into three categories: income disparities (median household income levels, per capita income levels, and poverty rates); labor market disparities (employment and unemployment rates for working-age men); and educational disparities (high school and college completion rates). These simple measures do not, of course, fully capture the differences between central-city and suburban residents, but they may provide some sense of the social and economic contrasts.

As shown in Table 2, central-city residents had incomes in 1990 that were considerably lower than those of suburbanites. Compared with their suburban counterparts, the median household income of central-city residents was 74 percent as great, their per capita income was 84 percent as large, and their poverty rate was over twice as high. Disparities in employment and education were somewhat smaller, but central-city residents appear to be more deprived in these realms as well. In particular, compared with suburban communities, 1.7 times as great a proportion of prime-age working men were unemployed in central cities and 94 percent as large a proportion of young men (ages 25-34) had completed high school.

Given the differing racial compositions of central cities and suburbs, much

TABLE 2   Comparison of Selected Outcomes for Central-City and Suburban Residents, 1990

Outcome	Central City	Non-Central City	Ratio of Central-City to Suburban Outcome
Median household income	$26,727	$36,314	0.74
Per capita income	$13,839	$16,527	0.84
Poverty rate, familes	14.1%	6.0%	2.35
Employed,[a] men 25-54	83.3%	90.0%	0.93
Unemployed, men 25-54	6.8	4.0	1.7
High school graduates, men 25-34	80.7%	85.8%	0.94

[a]Members of the armed forces are counted as employed.

Source: U.S. Bureau of the Census (1990b).

of these spatial differences may be largely a reflection of racial differences in income, employment, and education. As shown in Table 3, however, this does not appear to be the case. The group of non-Hispanic whites, blacks, and Hispanics living in the suburbs are all more prosperous than their counterparts in central-city communities. The differences between central-city and suburban minorities—especially blacks—are particularly pronounced. Black households living in central cities, for instance, took home just 68 cents on every dollar brought home by suburban black households. In other words, minorities living in central cities appear to be particularly disadvantaged. This may be because white households of modest means are able to move to suburban areas that are not welcoming to blacks. For blacks and Hispanics to be welcomed to the suburbs, they may need to be more solidly middle-class.

As mentioned above, these comparisons lump together all suburbs as a single entity. Yet as Myron Orfield has pointed out in his analysis of the Twin Cities, suburbia is hardly monolithic (Orfield, 1997). The stereotypical vision of suburbia consists of quiet, affluent, residential neighborhoods made up of single-family detached homes with ample and manicured lawns. Such places of course exist, but they are not necessarily synonymous with the official Census Bureau definition of a suburb (a community within a metropolitan area but outside a central city). Many suburbs today are populated by working-class residents and suffer many of the same social and economic ills found in inner-city communities. In fact, such suburbs have existed for decades. As early as 1960, Bennett Berger challenged the conventional understanding of suburbia in his book *Working Class Suburb*. Unfortunately, despite the widespread acknowledgment that the term "suburb" covers a wide range of metropolitan experience, the Census Bureau offers few alternatives to improve upon it.

To provide some sense of the diversity in suburban America, we have exam-

TABLE 3   Ratio of Selected Outcomes for Central City and Suburban Residents by Race and Ethnicity, 1990

| Outcome | Ratio of Central-City to Suburban Outcome | | | |
	All Persons	Non-Hispanic Whites	Blacks	Hispanics
Median household income	0.74	0.81	0.68	0.73
Per capita income	0.84	0.98	0.8	0.81
Poverty rate, families	2.35	1.66	1.66	1.63
Labor force participation, persons ≥ 16	0.95	0.96	0.9	0.95
Unemployment rate, men ≥ 25	1.56	1.18	1.52	1.27
% high school graduates, persons ≥ 25	0.92	0.98	0.89	0.85
% college graduates, persons ≥ 25	0.96	1.14	0.7	0.78

Source: U.S. Bureau of the Census (1990b).

ined 1990 neighborhood, or census tract, data within suburban areas. As noted above, the median household income in suburban America was significantly larger than that in central cities ($36,314 compared with $26,727). But not all suburban communities were so fortunate. In approximately one-fifth of suburban neighborhoods, the median household income was actually less than the overall central-city median. (And without the commercial tax base of a central business district, these suburbs were arguably even worse off than their central cities.)

The story is similar with the poverty rate. Nationwide in 1990, the poverty rate was 8.1 percent in the suburbs and 18 percent in central cities. But again, high-poverty suburban communities do exist. Approximately 10 percent of suburban census tracts had poverty rates of at least 18 percent. Although we cannot say for sure, it is likely that these are the aging, inner-ring suburbs that Orfield (1997) describes.

Perhaps more significant than the magnitude of these disparities are their trends over time. What has happened to the central-city/suburban gap over recent decades? On the one hand, suburbanization has continued at a rapid pace, presumably leaving behind the increasingly disadvantaged. On the other hand, many inner-suburbs have been "urbanized" (Lineberry, 1975; Masotti and Hadden, 1973; Orfield, 1997; Sternlieb and Lake, 1975).

Table 4 shows, for selected measures, the ratios of central-city to suburban outcomes for 1960 through 1990. With the exception of education, every measure in the table suggests that the relative status of central-city residents has consistently declined over the last three decades. Relative to their suburban

TABLE 4   Ratios of Selected Outcomes for Central City and Suburban Residents, 1960-1990

	Ratio of Central-City to Suburban Outcome			
Outcome	1960	1970	1980	1990
Median family income	.89	.85	.81	.77
Per capita income	NA	.92	.88	.84
Family poverty rate	1.52	1.75	2.08	2.35
% employed, men ≥ 16[a]	0.96	0.93	0.92	.91
Unemployment rate, men ≥ 16 [a]	1.37	1.33	1.34	1.59
% high school graduates, population ≥ 25	0.85	0.86	0.9	.94
% college graduates, population ≥ 25	0.82	0.84	0.94	.96

Note: The number of metropolitan areas differs somewhat from one decade to another, as more metropolitan areas have been defined. In other words, the table is not limited to just those metropolitan areas that existed in all four decades.

NA = not available

[a]For 1960, the employment and unemployment rates correspond to men at least 14 years of age.

Sources: U.S. Bureau of the Census (1960, 1970, 1980, 1990b).

counterparts, that is, central-city residents now have lower incomes, higher poverty rates, and lower employment rates than they did 10, 20, and 30 years ago.[2] The income differences are particularly stark. In 1960, central-city families were taking home 89 cents on every dollar brought home by suburbanites. By 1990, this ratio had fallen to just .77. Per capita income follows a similar pattern, with ratios falling from .92 in 1970 to .84 in 1990. Finally, poverty is becoming increasingly concentrated in central-city areas. In 1960, poverty was 1.5 times as frequent for families living in central cities; by 1990, the ratio had risen to 2.35.

The differences in employment and unemployment ratios are not as dramatic, but the direction is the same—that is, the gap between central-city and suburban residents is growing consistently larger. And, as Ihlanfeldt shows in his paper in this volume, these central city-suburban disparities have grown much more rapidly for blacks than they have for the population as a whole (Ihlanfeldt, this volume).

As noted, education is a marked exception to the general trend of continued central-city decline. The overall rise in educational attainment appears to have led to some convergence between central-city and suburban residents. Because it is easier to increase the proportion of high school and college graduates in a population that has fewer of them to start with, the relative fortunes of central-city residents improved as a result of the overall societal progress. Between 1960 and 1990, for instance, while the high school graduation rate rose by 66 percent in noncentral portions of metropolitan areas, it rose by 79 percent in central cities.

Neighborhood Poverty

To compare central cities and suburbs is hardly to capture all of the segregation in metropolitan areas. To understand its full extent, it is necessary to examine class and racial segregation at the level of the neighborhood, or even the block, as Paul Jargowsky does in his recent analysis (1997). Looking at neighborhood poverty, he forcefully documents that concentrated poverty is growing more prevalent. According to his analysis, 17.9 percent of all poor persons in 1990 lived in high-poverty areas (census tracts in which the poverty rate is greater than or equal to 40 percent). By comparison, the proportions were just 13.6 percent in 1980 and 12.4 percent in 1970. In other words, the proportion of poor people living in high-poverty areas rose by 98 percent over the 20 years between 1970 and 1990.

Another analysis of trends in economic segregation between 1970 and 1990 arrives at a similar, albeit less dramatic, conclusion. In contrast to Jargowsky, Abramson et al. (1995) study the overall segregation of the poor, not simply the prevalence of high-poverty areas. Using the index of dissimilarity, a measure that indicates the proportion of a particular group of households (here, the poor) who would have to move in order to achieve an even distribution of the group throughout the metropolitan area, they avoid the need to set an arbitrary defini-

TABLE 5   Segregation of the Poor in the Central Cities and Suburbs of
Chicago, Los Angeles, and Washington, D.C.

	Poor-Nonpoor Dissimilarity Index	
City	Central City	Non-Central City
Chicago	40.7	32.1
Los Angeles	34.9	33.8
Washington, D.C.	36.2	31.2

Source: Analysis of Urban Institute Underclass Database.

tion of a high-poverty tract, such as 20 or 40 percent poor. Nonetheless, they also find increasing segregation, with the dissimilarity of the poor in the 100 largest metropolitan areas rising by 11 percent between 1970 and 1990, from 32.9 to 36.4.

Like poverty itself, high-poverty neighborhoods appear to be primarily a central-city phenomenon. In 1990, 94 percent of all high-poverty neighborhoods (using Jargowsky's definition of at least a 40 percent poverty rate) were located in central-city communities. (Overall, 52 percent of census tracts were located in central-city jurisdictions.) Most of this difference is of course due to the higher overall rates of poverty in central-city areas. Is it also true that poverty households are more segregated in central cities?

To test this hypothesis, three metropolitan areas are examined: Chicago, Los Angeles, and Washington, D.C. As shown in Table 5, the poor were indeed somewhat less segregated in the suburbs in 1990 than they were in central cities of all three of these metropolitan areas. In Chicago, the central-city dissimilarity index was 40.7 compared with 32.1 in the suburbs, and in Washington, D.C., the dissimilarity index was 36.2 in the central city, compared with 31.2 in the suburbs. Interestingly, the differential was far smaller in Los Angeles, a metropolitan area in which the central city is nearly as prosperous as its suburbs. But more research into the consistency and causes of these central city-suburban differentials in economic segregation is needed before arriving at any firm conclusions.

Neighborhood Racial Segregation

The segregation of the poor seems clearly to have increased over the past two decades, but the segregation of whites and blacks appears to have declined. Massey and Denton, for instance, examine the 30 metropolitan areas with the largest black populations, and their figures suggest that the black-white index of dissimilarity declined from 80.8 in 1970 to 73.3 in 1990, for a decline of 9 percent (Massey and Denton, 1993).[3] As for the shifts over the 1980s, Jargowsky (1997) reports that the average dissimilarity index between blacks and non-Hispanic whites in the full set of metropolitan areas fell from 70 to 66. Farley and Frey (1994) limit their analysis to the 232 metropolitan areas with substantial black populations and uncover a similar decline. Specifically, they estimate that the average index of dissimilarity in these metropolitan areas fell from 69 in 1980 to 65 in 1990.

Nonetheless, the level of racial segregation continues to be quite high, and far higher than the segregation of the poor. Examining the 100 largest metropolitan areas, Abramson et al. (1995) find that the average dissimilarity index for the poor was 36.1 in 1990, and the mean dissimilarity index for blacks was 60.6.

CLASSIFYING METROPOLITAN AREAS

As discussed above, these national averages conceal considerable variation across individual metropolitan areas. Certain central cities, for example, appear to fare far better than others relative to the suburbs surrounding them, and rates of neighborhood poverty vary markedly, too. It is these differences that this section examines.

Data and Method

The analysis here ranks the full set of metropolitan areas nationwide by the degree of their central-city/suburban disparity. To perform this ranking, an index of disparity is calculated from the central-city to suburban ratio of three outcomes: per capita income, employment rate for men between 16 and 64, and the proportion of persons 25 or older who have at least a high school diploma. In order that each of the three measures be weighted equally, they are each standardized to a scale of 0-1 before being averaged to create an overall index of disparity.[4] The higher the number, the better off the central city relative to its suburban counterparts. Significantly and contrary to the conventional wisdom, not all central cities are worse off than their surrounding suburbs. In 1990, central cities were actually more prosperous than their surrounding suburban communities in 101 metropolitan areas (31 percent). With this said, because these metropolitan areas tend to be fairly small, they housed only 14 percent of the total metropolitan population. Thus, the vast majority of metropolitan residents live in areas in which the cities are worse off than their surrounding suburbs.

Although the analysis in the rest of the paper focuses on central-city/suburban disparities, these jurisdictional inequalities are in fact quite correlated with neighborhood-level economic segregation. For example, in 95 metropolitan areas for which data are available, the simple correlation between the neighborhood-level dissimilarity index of the poor and the index of central-city/suburban disparity was a highly significant –.69. Thus, many of the findings below may apply more generally to the extent of neighborhood-level inequalities in metropolitan areas.

As explained above, the general purpose in classifying metropolitan areas by their degree of central-city disadvantage is to further our understanding about the causes and contributors to spatial and jurisdictional disparities. To be sure, the causes of these disparities are complex, and making any definite conclusions about causation would require certain data and data analysis that lie outside the scope of this paper. For example, even where a strong correlation between a certain variable and city-suburban disparity can be demonstrated using the present data, the direction of causality cannot be. Nonetheless, determining which characteristics of metropolitan areas are correlated with greater and lesser disadvantage should enrich our understanding considerably. Toward this end, the remainder of this section hypothesizes a number of possible correlates of greater city-suburban disparity and then presents a simple comparison of means to test these possible correlates.

Hypotheses

There are several possible reasons why certain metropolitan areas might have greater central-city/suburban disparities than others. This paper considers the possible significance of four types of metropolitan attributes: regional location, demographic characteristics, racial segregation, and governmental structure. Future work might also examine the importance of density, industrial structure, and labor market conditions.[5]

Regional Location

One might expect the degree of central-city disadvantage to vary across regions because, among other things, regional location serves as a fairly good proxy for the age of a metropolitan area. Areas in the Northeast and the Midwest, for example, are much older than those in the South and the West. And one might further expect that age, in turn, correlates with central-city disadvantage because, as Massey and Denton (1987) and Farley and Frey (1994) have found, older cities tend to be more racially segregated; it is quite possible that they are more economically stratified as well. As Massey and Denton note, "[c]ities built up before the Second World War have ecological structures that are more conducive to segregation, with densely settled cores and thickly packed working-class neighborhoods" (1987:818). In addition, Hill and Wolman (1997) argue that central cities in younger metropolitan areas may have housing stocks that better match the demands of current consumers and thus that are better able to attract more affluent households.[6]

Different regions also have different local economies that have different consequences for city-suburb disparity. For example, manufacturing jobs have declined disproportionately in the central cities of the Northeast and the Midwest, and thus it may well be that the residents of these central cities have been disproportionately disadvantaged and isolated by such decline. Regions also differ in their overall rates of economic growth, which some have hypothesized should be correlated with lesser disparity as well, the logic being that growth may attract less-skilled, central-city residents into the labor market (Hill and Wolman, 1997).

Another significant regional pattern lies in governmental policies and structure. One example of regional policy differences is that metropolitan areas in the Sun Belt tend to rely less on the property tax as a source of revenue, and thus local suburban communities have less motivation to exclude low-income residents (Bollens, 1986). As for regional differences in governmental structure, metropolitan areas in the West and the South tend to have less fragmented governments; that is, they have fewer local governmental entities, with each entity housing a greater number of people. Consider that, in 1997, the mean number of local governments per 100,000 residents was 14.7 and 12.5 in the West and the South, respectively, compared with 27.2 and 19.9 in the Midwest and the Northeast (Census of Governments, preliminary 1997 estimates). Second, metropolitan areas in the West and the South tend to have what David Rusk has called more "elastic" central cities (Rusk, 1993). Their cities, that is, have been able to grow or perhaps to annex more of their surrounding suburbs and thus to encompass a greater share of the overall metropolitan population. The precise manner in which these distinctive characteristics of governmental structure might impact city-suburb disparity is discussed below.

Finally, regions may differ as well in their racial attitudes, which are plainly linked to some extent to levels of suburban exclusion. After all, regions do differ in their degree of racial segregation. And it would seem that, as suggested above and discussed in more detail below, the more segregated a metropolitan area, the greater the city-suburb disparity.

Demographics

The second category of variables one might expect to correlate with central-city disadvantage are demographic, variables such as metropolitan area size, size of the minority population, and per capita income in the metropolitan area as a whole. In terms of metropolitan area size, it may be that central-city/suburban disparities are greater in larger metropolitan areas simply because of the larger geographic distances involved. If, for instance, some of the central-city/suburban difference is due to a spatial mismatch between suburban jobs and central-city residents, longer physical distances should exacerbate the city's relative disadvantage. It is also likely that political units will be more specialized and competitive in larger, more populous metropolitan areas, leading to greater disparities.

The size of the minority population is examined as well; to the extent that racial considerations contributed to the exclusionary policies of many suburbs, metropolitan areas with larger minority (especially black) populations are likely to have more disadvantaged central cities. Furthermore, to the extent that minorities are highly segregated from whites and also much worse off, metropolitan areas with larger minority populations are likely to be more economically segregated in general. (Abramson et al., 1995, and Jargowsky, 1997, both find some evidence that the poor are more segregated in metropolitan areas with larger black populations.)

As for the overall income in the metropolitan area, there are reasons to believe that it may be related to the magnitude of city-suburban disparity. In particular, if metropolitan-area income is driven largely by the prosperity of high-end, and typically suburban, households, then we would expect city-suburban income disparities to be greater in areas with higher overall incomes. It may be, that is, that central-city residents fare roughly the same across most metropolitan areas, whereas suburban prosperity varies markedly. And indeed, there is some evidence to this effect: the variances of the measures of suburban prosperity are substantially larger than those of the measures of central-city prosperity. Moreover, suburban income, education, and employment are more correlated with overall metropolitan-area prosperity than the corresponding central-city measures.

Racial Segregation

Somewhat surprisingly, researchers appear not yet to have explored the link between racial segregation and city-suburban inequality. Yet there are several reasons to believe that racial segregation, and in particular black-white segregation, should be correlated with central-city/suburban disparities. First, Cutler and Glaeser (1997) have shown that blacks tend to be more disadvantaged relative to whites in more segregated metropolitan areas. And to the extent that blacks tend to live in central cities, greater black-white disparities should lead to greater city-suburban disparities. The hypothesis holds for Hispanics as well, although it is somewhat less persuasive, since there is less evidence that Hispanics are significantly hurt by residential segregation and, moreover, Hispanics are less concentrated in central cities than blacks.

A second possible link between racial segregation and city-suburban inequality is suggested by Massey and Denton's argument that racial segregation concentrates poverty (Massey and Denton, 1993). Again, since blacks, and to a lesser extent Hispanics, tend to live in central cities, racial segregation will tend to concentrate poverty and disadvantage in central cities. The possibility that the causality works in the opposite direction should not be ignored, however. Greater central city-suburban disparities, that is, may encourage a greater proportion of affluent whites to live in suburban communities. Although more affluent blacks may share the same inclination to move to the suburbs, housing market discrimination may discourage their departures.

Governmental Structure

The final and perhaps most critical class of metropolitan-area characteristics considered here relates to the structure of metropolitan government. One of the characteristics is the degree of city elasticity, or the proportion of the metropoli-

tan area's population that resides in the central city.[7]   Consistent with Rusk's
theory about city elasticity, the hypothesis is that central-city/suburban disparities should be smaller in more elastic cities that have been able to expand and
annex their surrounding suburbs.[8]

In addition to this measure of elasticity, the fragmentation of local governments in the metropolitan area is also considered. Specifically, we consider the
number of general-purpose governments per 100,000 persons. The argument,
made by many researchers, is that political fragmentation may heighten spatial
stratification. Their theory is that local governments have an incentive to entice
homogeneous residents with similar incomes and tastes for services, since they
provide services primarily from their own tax base. And they have the means to
do so as well, at least partially, through their regulation of land use. The larger
the number of governments, the greater the competition, and the greater the
pressure on governments to preserve their population. With a greater number of
local governments and thus a broad variety of tax-service packages, there is also
more of an incentive for households to shop for communities.

Results

As a preliminary appraisal, Table 6 displays the ratios between central city
and suburban outcomes for the 10 metropolitan areas with the greatest as well as
the 10 with the least degree of city disadvantage relative to their suburbs. As
shown, the overall index of disparity (described at the beginning of this section)
ranges from a low of 0 in Benton Harbor, Michigan, to a high of .83 in Laredo,
Texas. As for the specific outcomes, the ratio of central city to suburban per
capita income ranges from a low of .43 in Benton Harbor to a high of 2.2 in
Naples, Florida. (Note that Naples is a significant outlier—the next-highest ratio
of per capita income is 1.6 in Laredo, Texas.) The range in employment rate
ratios is far smaller, varying from a low of .49 in Benton Harbor to a high of 1.2
in Yuma, Arizona. (Here it should be noted that Benton Harbor is somewhat of
an outlier, with the next-lowest employment ratio being .72 in Detroit, Michigan.) As for the ratio of the high school completion rate, it varies from .62, again
in Benton Harbor, to 1.46 in Laredo, Texas.

The regional pattern is quite pronounced. With the single exception of Fort
Pierce, Florida, all 10 of the metropolitan areas with the most relatively disadvantaged central cities are located in the Northeast or the Midwest. The metropolitan
areas with the most relatively prosperous cities are all located in the South and the
West. Significantly, these 10 central cities are not necessarily the most well-off
in absolute terms. Some of them may have fairly low per capita incomes and
rates of employment and high school completion but may simply be located in a
metropolitan area that is very distressed overall. Indeed, with the exception of
Naples, Florida, and Midland, Texas, all of the metropolitan areas with the most
relatively prosperous central cities have per capita incomes below the national

TABLE 6   U.S. Metropolitan Areas Ranked by Extent of Central City-Suburban Disparity, Top and Bottom 10 Areas, 1990

Metropolitan Area	Region	Ratio of Central-City to Suburban Outcome			
		Per Capita Income	% Employed, Men 16+	% High School Graduates, persons ≥ 25	Overall Index of Disparity
Greatest Disparity:					
Benton Harbor, MI	MW	.425	.488	.62	0
Newark, NJ	NE	.451	.817	.652	.171
Hartford, CT	NE	.52	.76	.708	.179
Cleveland, OH	MW	.535	.763	.719	.188
Detroit, MI	MW	.562	.717	.795	.202
Middlesex, NJ	NE	.525	.843	.684	.209
Trenton, NJ	NE	.503	.846	.695	.211
Bergen, NJ	NE	.466	.884	.689	.22
Ft Pierce, FL	S	.578	.856	.731	.244
Philadelphia, PA	NE	.63	.803	.775	.246
Least Disparity:					
Laredo, TX	S	1.63	1.08	1.46	.829
McAllen, TX	S	1.52	1.08	1.35	.768
Yuma, AZ	W	1.24	1.2	1.32	.762
El Paso, TX	S	1.58	1.05	1.3	.746
Naples, FL	S	2.24	.917	1.15	.744
Las Cruces, NM	W	1.42	1.06	1.27	.709
Visalia-Tulare, CA	W	1.24	1.06	1.3	.684
Corpus Christi, TX	S	1.29	1.08	1.22	.676
Bakersfield, CA	W	1.27	1.07	1.24	.674
Midland, TX	S	1.43	1.05	1.14	.654

Source: U.S. Bureau of the Census (1990a).

average.   The key point is that "central-city disadvantage" here refers only to disadvantage *relative* to their surrounding suburbs.

To further explore these and other patterns, the full set of metropolitan areas are ranked according to the degree of their central-city/suburban disparity and then subdivided into four quartiles of disparity.[9]   The mean index of disparity ranges from .31 in the most disadvantaged quartile, to .41 in the second, .47 in the third, and .57 in the least disadvantaged quartile.   By comparing the mean of metropolitan-area characteristics across quartiles, we can learn which attributes are correlated with greater and lesser central-city disadvantage.

Table 7 presents the mean characteristics of selected variables for each of the four quartiles of disadvantage.   Once again, the regional pattern is pronounced. In the quartile with the most relatively disadvantaged central cities, 43.9 percent are located in the Northeast, 31.7 percent in the Midwest, 20.7 percent in the South, and 3.7 percent in the West.   In the quartile with the least disadvantaged

TABLE 7 Mean Characteristics of Four Quartiles of Metropolitan Statistical Areas, Ranked by Degree of Central-City Disadvantage Relative to Suburbs

	Quartiles of Central-City Disadvantage Relative to Suburbs			
	Q1: Greatest Disadvantage	2nd Quartile	3rd Quartile	Q4: Least Disadvantage
Region				
Northeast	.439	.256	.085	.036
Midwest	.317	.366	.22	.108
South	.207	.22	.451	.602
West	.037	.159	.244	.253
Demographics				
Population	934,560	537,981	542,056	277,366
% Black	11.7	8.9	9.3	9.3
% Hispanic	5.5	4.2	6.7	11.6
Per capita income	$15,352	$14,238	$13,480	$12,321
Racial Segregation				
Black segregation index	64.2	55.8	51.7	47.0
Hispanic segregation index	43.9	34.2	30.7	29.7
Government Structure				
Elasticity	.35	.445	.494	.473
# of local governments per 100,000 persons	11.3	13.1	11.0	12.0
Population Share				
% of U.S. metropolitan population living in quartile	40.7	23.6	23.6	12.1
Mean Central-City Suburban Ratios				
Per capita income	.705	.864	.99	1.18
% employed, men 16-64	.855	.921	.95	1.00
% high school grads ≥ 25	.848	.934	1.00	1.09

Sources: Number of governments are preliminary estimates from 1997 Census of Governments provided by the Census Bureau; racial segregation taken from author's estimates and Census Bureau Home Page. All other figures are calculated from U.S. Bureau of Census (1990a). Note that neither the measure of Hispanic segregation nor that of government fragmentation was available for the full set of metropolitan areas.

central cites, by contrast, just 3.6 percent are in the Northeast, 10.8 percent are in the Midwest, 60.2 percent are in the South, and 25.3 percent are in the West.

In terms of demographics, the metropolitan areas with greater disparities tend to have larger populations, consistent with the notion that geographic distances play a part in determining the degree of central-city disadvantage. There is some evidence, too, that at least the metropolitan areas with the very highest disparities (or the most distressed central cities) tend to have larger proportions of black residents. It also appears true that central cities fare relatively better in metropolitan areas with lower per capita incomes, which is consistent with the hypothesis outlined above that metropolitan areas with higher overall incomes exhibit greater income and skills disparities, and thus greater spatial disparities as well.

The final demographic characteristic appears to run counter to the hypothesis outlined above, in that metropolitan areas with the relatively strongest central cities tend to have *larger* proportions of Hispanic residents. But given the concentration of Hispanics in the Western and Southern regions of the country, where central cities are strongest, this correlation between central-city prosperity and the size of the Hispanic population may be spurious.

The figures on racial segregation are quite striking. In the areas with the most disadvantaged central cities, blacks appear to be far more segregated at the neighborhood level. In particular, in these highest-disparity metropolitan areas, the mean black segregation index (measured by the index of dissimilarity) is 64.2 in the metropolitan areas with the most disadvantaged central cities compared with 47.0 in those metropolitan areas with the lowest levels of disparity. Similarly, Hispanic segregation also appears to be greater in the metropolitan areas with the relatively weakest central cities.

Finally, one of the two hypotheses regarding governmental structure appears to be supported: metropolitan areas with the greatest city-suburban disparities also tend to be those with the least elastic central cities—with central cities, that is, that contain a smaller proportion of the overall metropolitan-area population. There is little evidence here, however, that the degree of local government fragmentation (measured by the number of county, municipal, and township governments per capita) has any relationship to the level of central-city/suburban disparity.

MULTIVARIATE ANALYSIS

It is not clear of course, whether the simple correlations revealed above between central-city/suburban inequality and metropolitan area characteristics hold up when other variables are held constant. The next step is thus to estimate a regression in which the index of central-city/suburban disparity is regressed on various metropolitan-area characteristics.

Four sets of variables are once again considered: regional location, demographics, racial segregation, and governmental structure. Specifically, the regression includes three regional dummy variables (the Northeast is the reference region); four demographic variables (a measure of metropolitan area size,[10] the per capita income of the overall metropolitan area, the proportion black, and the proportion Hispanic); two measures of racial and ethnic segregation (the black and Hispanic dissimilarity indices); and two key measures of governmental structure—the number of general purpose local governments (county, municipal, and township) per 100,000 people and the degree of central-city elasticity.

In the comparison of the quartiles of central-city disadvantage, central-city

TABLE 8   Regression Results of 1990 Central-City
Suburban Index of Disparity

| | Model 3 | |
	Coefficient	Standard Error
Constant	.532***	.075
Midwest	−.015	.017
South	.09***	.018
West	.053***	.019
Log of MSA population	.007	.007
Per capita income, in MSA	−.009***	.0028
% black, in MSA	−.272***	.065
% Hispanic, in MSA	.158***	.05
Black segregation	−.0013***	.0005
Hispanic segregation	−.0015***	.0005
Elasticity	.197***	.055
Elasticity spline (at 0.45)	−.186**	.09
# Governments per 100,000 people	.0009*	.0005
R-squared	.543	
N	274	

MSA = metropolitan statistical area.

   * = statistically significant at the 10 percent level.

  ** = statistically significant at the 5 percent level.

 *** = statistically significant at the 1 percent level.

elasticity was clearly lowest in the quartile with the most disadvantaged central cities, but approximately the same across the remaining three quartiles. It seemed, in other words, that the degree of elasticity only mattered when the elasticity was very low—that is, when the central city captured only a very small share of the metropolitan-area population. To test this apparent finding, a spline variable (at 0.45) is added to the regression, which effectively allows for the degree of elasticity to matter at low levels, but not at higher ones. More technically, it allows for a kink in the regression line at a threshold of 0.45. For elasticity values below 0.45, the relationship between elasticity and central-city disadvantage remains measured by the coefficient on the elasticity variable. For metropolitan areas with elasticities above 0.45, however, the correct relationship is estimated by the *sum* of the coefficient on elasticity and the coefficient on the spline variable.[11]

Recall that a larger index of disparity implies a more prosperous central city—relative, that is, to its surrounding suburbs. Thus, if a particular variable, say the proportion black, has a negative coefficient, we should interpret this to mean that central cities tend to suffer greater relative disadvantage when the variable in question is larger. If instead a variable has a *positive* coefficient, then this suggests that central cities tend to experience *smaller* relative disadvantage when the variable is larger.

The results from the first regression are largely consistent with the simple comparison of means above. Central cities, that is, tend to fare the worst relative to their suburbs in metropolitan areas located in the Northeast, and the best in the South and the West. Central cities also tend to be more disadvantaged in metropolitan areas with higher overall incomes, larger black populations, more segregated minority populations, and *smaller* Hispanic populations. This final result suggests that the correlation between large Hispanic populations and relatively prosperous central cities is not simply a regional phenomenon and may in fact be more meaningful than at first surmised. With this said, it is difficult to understand just why such a relationship should exist. One notable difference here is that the size of a metropolitan area appears insignificant once its other characteristics are taken into account.

The coefficients on the elasticity variables are indeed what we expect. The coefficient on elasticity is positive and significant, and the coefficient on the spline variable is negative and significant. And the magnitudes are virtually the same. In other words, when a central city's elasticity is below .45, raising its elasticity should improve its relative prosperity. Once a city's elasticity has reached .45, however, subsequent increases appear to have no effect.[12]

Curiously, the coefficient on the number of governments per capita is positive and marginally significant (at the 10 percent level of significance), suggesting that central cities do better in metropolitan areas with *more* fragmented governments. This surprising result is surely the subject for more research, and no definitive conclusions should be made. Indeed, it is quite likely that the simple number of local governments per capita is simply not a good measure of government fragmentation. For although several researchers have found greater inequality in metropolitan areas that rely more heavily on the property tax as a source of revenue, few have found a significant relationship between the number of governments per capita and city-suburban disparities (see Bollens, 1986; Logan and Schneider, 1982; Morgan and Mareschal, 1996). Thus, it may be that government structure can influence residential sorting, but that the count of governments per capita is too simple a measure to capture such structure. Recall, too, that our dependent variable reflects only average differences between cities and suburbs and not differences among what may be highly diverse, individual suburbs.

CONCLUSION

This paper attempts to describe in broad terms the nature and extent of spatial inequality found in contemporary metropolitan areas. It concludes that, although racial segregation is declining modestly, both central-city/suburban and neighborhood-level economic inequality are increasing nationwide. There is, however, considerable variation across individual metropolitan areas in the extent of central-city/suburban disparity. With respect to these variations in inequality, this paper further attempts to test certain key correlates. In general, the results suggest that central cities fare worse relative to their suburbs in the Northeast and the Midwest, in larger and wealthier metropolitan areas, and in areas with larger black and smaller Hispanic populations.

In addition, unlike past studies, this study examined the role played not only by the size of minority populations but by their degree of segregation and found that city-suburb inequality is significantly greater in metropolitan areas with more segregated black and Hispanic populations. As to government structure, the results here confirm Rusk's basic hypothesis that highly inelastic central cities are more deprived than others relative to their suburbs. Interestingly, however, the degree of elasticity does not appear to make much difference once it rises beyond about .45. Finally, the degree of local government fragmentation was also examined, and, contrary to expectations, city-suburban inequality was found to be, if anything, greater in metropolitan areas with less fragmented local government.

These sometimes surprising findings may shed some light on the nature and roots of spatial and jurisdictional disparities in metropolitan areas. But they also raise and leave unanswered many important questions. Thus, this study should also encourage others to further explore the hypotheses generated here as well as to probe other possible links to spatial disparities, such as residential density (known as urban sprawl), industrial structure, and additional measures of local government coordination and competition, including the extent of property tax reliance. Such explorations should not only help us to come to more definitive conclusions regarding spatial inequalities but also guide us ultimately to mitigate them.

ACKNOWLEDGMENTS

The author would like to thank the committee for its direction, as well as Hal Wolman, Alan Altshuler, Tony Downs, Harry Holzer, and the National Research Council's anonymous reviewers for their helpful comments.

REFERENCES

Abramson, Alan, Mitchell Tobin, and Matthew VanderGoot
  1995   The changing geography of metropolitan opportunity: The segregation of the poor in
          U.S. metropolitan areas, 1970 to 1990. *Housing Policy Debate* 6:45-72.
Berger, Bennett
  1960   *Working Class Suburb: A Study of Auto Workers in Suburbia.* Berkeley: University of
          California Press.
Bollens, Scott
  1986   A political-ecological analysis of inequality in metropolitan areas. *Urban Affairs Quar-
          terly* 22(2):221-41.

Crane, Jonathan
 1991   The epidemic theory of ghettos and neighborhood effects on dropping out and teenage childbearing. *American Journal of Sociology* 96(5):1226-1259.
Cutler, David, and Edward Glaeser
 1997   Are ghettos good or bad? *Quarterly Journal of Economics* 112(3):827.
Ellen, Ingrid, and Margery Turner
 1997   Location, location, location: How does neighborhood environment affect the well-being of families and children? *Housing Policy Debate* 8(4):833-866.
Fannie Mae
 1997   *The Fannie Mae National Housing Survey: City Life, Homeownership, and the American Dream.* Washington, DC: Fannie Mae.
Farley, Reynolds, and William Frey
 1994   Changes in the segregation of whites from blacks during the 1980s: Small steps toward a more integrated society. *American Sociological Review* 59:23-45.
Greene, William H.
 1993   *Economic Analysis.* New York: Macmillan Publishing Company.
Hill, Edward W., and Harold L. Wolman
 1997   City-suburban income disparities and metropolitan area employment: Can tightening labor markets reduce the gaps? *Urban Affairs Review* 32(4):558-582.
Hill, Richard Child
 1974   Separate and unequal: Government inequality in the metropolis. *American Political Science Review* 68:1557-1568.
Hogan, Dennis, and Evelyn Kitagawa
 1985   The impact of social status, family structure, and neighborhood on the fertility of black adolescents. *American Journal of Sociology* 90(4):825-855.
Jargowsky, Paul
 1997   *Poverty and Place: Ghettos, Barrios, and the American City.* New York: Russell Sage Foundation.
Lineberry, Robert L.
 1975   Suburbia and the metropolitan turf. *The Annals of the American Academy of Political and Social Science* 422:1-9.
Logan, John R., and Mark Schneider
 1982   Governmental organization and city/suburb income inequality. *Urban Affairs Quarterly* 17(3):305-318.
Long, Larry, and Donald C. Dahmann
 1980   *The City-Suburb Income Gap: Is It Being Narrowed by a Back-to-the-City Movement?* Bureau of the Census. Washington, DC: U.S. Department of Commerce.
Masotti, Louis, and Jeffrey Hadden, eds.
 1973   *The Urbanization of the Suburbs.* Vol. 7 of *Urban Affairs Annual Reviews.* Beverly Hills, CA: Sage.
Massey, Douglas S., and Nancy A. Denton
 1993   *American Apartheid: Segregation and the Making of the Underclass.* Cambridge, MA: Harvard University Press.
 1987   Trends in the residential segregation of blacks, Hispanics, and Asians. *American Sociological Review* 52:802-825.
Mayer, Christopher
 1996   Does location matter? *New England Economic Review* May/June:26-40.
Morgan, David, and Patrice Mareschal
 1996   Central City/Suburban Inequality and Metropolitan Political Fragmentation. Paper presented at the annual meeting of the American Political Science Association, San Francisco.

Orfield, Myron
 1997   *Metropolitics: A Regional Agenda for Community and Stability.* Washington, DC: Brookings Institution Press and the Lincoln Land Institute.
Rusk, David
 1993   *Cities Without Suburbs.* Washington, DC: The Woodrow Wilson Center Press.
Schnore, Leo
 1965   *The Urban Scene.* New York: Free Press.
Sternlieb, George, and Robert W. Lake
 1975   Aging suburbs and black homeownership. *The Annals of the American Academy of Political and Social Science* 422:105-117.
U.S. Bureau of the Census
 1992   *Poverty in the United States: 1992.* Current Population Reports, Series Pp. 60-185.
 1991   *Metropolitan Areas and Cities.* 1990 Census Profile, Number 3.
 1990a   *Census of Population and Housing Summary Tape File 3C.* CD-ROM.
 1990b   *1990 Census of Population, Social and Economic Characteristics for Metropolitan Areas.*
 1980   *1980 Census of Population, General Social and Economic Characteristics.*
 1970   *1970 Census of Population, General Social and Economic Characteristics.*
 1960   *1960 Census of Population, General Social and Economic Characteristics.*
Wilson, William Julius
 1987   *The Truly Disadvantaged.* Chicago: University of Chicago Press.

NOTES

[1] In fact, despite their overrepresentation in central cities, the share of blacks who live in suburban areas has been increasing. In 1960, for instance, just 20 percent of blacks lived in suburban communities, compared with 26 percent in 1990.

[2] Data from the Current Population Survey presented in Ihlanfeldt (this volume) suggest that the city-suburban disparity in family income continued to rise between 1989 and 1995.

[3] Calculated from Massey and Denton (1993:Table 8.1).

[4] The minimum value is assigned 0, the maximum value is assigned 1, and the values in between are standardized according to the following formula: $Z = (X - X_{min})/(X_{max} - X_{min})$.

[5] Hill and Wolman (1997) examine the impact of tight labor market conditions on central-city/suburban differences and find, contrary to conventional wisdom, that economic growth may actually exacerbate disparities.

[6] Several researchers have found the age of the metropolitan area to be correlated with greater central-city/suburban inequality (see Bollens, 1986; Hill, 1974; Logan and Schneider, 1982; Schnore, 1965).

[7] The official Census Bureau definition of central city is used here to construct a measure of elasticity. As Hill and Wolman (1997) point out, the Census Bureau uses a very broad definition of central city, which encompasses more than merely the largest municipality in the metropolitan area and may include as well cities that might be better described as "edge cities." Thus, using the Census definition of central city may not be ideal for constructing a measure of elasticity. Nonetheless, it is consistent with the other data used here, which also rely on the official Census definition for central city. The results remain the same when using a more restrictive definition of central city (at least for the 152 metropolitan statistical areas for which the more restrictive measure of elasticity is available).

[8] Note that this measure of elasticity differs from the more complicated index used by Rusk, but it captures the essence of his concept (see Hill and Wolman, 1997).

[9] Significantly, the quartiles are defined so that each includes an equal number of metropolitan areas, rather than residents. It turns out that the metropolitan areas in which central cities fare worse

are far more populous. Thus, for example, the quartile with the most relatively disadvantaged cities houses a full 41 percent of the total metropolitan population.

10 The natural logarithm is used to smooth the distribution of metropolitan population.

11 Specifically, the regression includes a variable that is equal to the difference between the elasticity and .45 when elasticity is above .45 and takes on the value of 0 when the elasticity is below .45. For more information, Greene includes an excellent discussion of spline regressions (see Greene, 1993:234-238.)

12 Hill and Wolman (1997) find no connection between elasticity and the disparity in per capita income between central cities and suburbs. Their analysis differs in three ways, however. First, they include city-suburban human capital differences as an independent variable, which means that their regression model attempts to explain city-suburban differences in returns to education, rather than overall disparities. Second, most of their estimated models also include the level of disparity existing in 1980 as an independent variable, which means that they test whether elasticity has any effect on the *change* in disparity between 1980 and 1990. Finally, they do not include a spline variable. (When the spline variable is not included here, the elasticity remains significant, but its magnitude is far smaller.)

The Geography of Economic and Social Opportunity in Metropolitan Areas

Keith R. Ihlanfeldt
Georgia State University

Much has been written lately concerning the "geography of opportunity," which most commonly means that "where individuals live affects their opportunities and life outcomes" (Rosenbaum, 1995:231). Although this is certainly not a new idea (see, for example, Kain and Persky, 1969), it has received a revival of interest as the result of the writings of William Julius Wilson (1987, 1996). Wilson maintains that an urban underclass population has grown rapidly in central-city ghettos as the result of an erosion in economic opportunities in these areas and the exodus of working-class and middle-class blacks to better neighborhoods. More generally, there is concern that a continuing high level of racial segregation and increasing income segregation in metropolitan area housing markets have increased the proportion of poor people residing in "bad" neighborhoods, in the sense that the latter offer poor proximity to available jobs, inferior schools, and negative neighborhood effects.[1] If the geography of opportunity has indeed worsened over time for less educated and minority households, this may help to explain growing income inequality among racial and educational groups documented at the national level (Levy and Murnane, 1992).

The purposes of this paper are fourfold. First, I review what is known about the relationships between residential location and the economic and social prospects of individuals. Location both in and among metropolitan areas is considered. Second, policy solutions to unequal spatial opportunities are reviewed in light of considerable new evidence that has surfaced in recent years. Third, scholars have generally overlooked the role that the system of local government may play in influencing the residential location/opportunity nexus; the effects of local government fragmentation on the latter as well as on possible policy solutions are discussed. Finally, since there are major gaps in knowledge in all three of the above areas, suggestions are made regarding future research needs.

SPATIAL INEQUALITY IN ECONOMIC WELFARE

Before considering the hypothesized links between residential location and opportunities, some documentation of the spatial inequalities that these links purport to explain is in order. Table 1 reports unemployment rates and rates of nonparticipation in the labor force for central-city and suburban residents, respectively; Table 2 shows real median family income for these areas.

Unemployment rates were only slightly higher among central-city residents for both blacks and whites in comparison to their suburban counterparts in 1970. However, unemployment rate differences between central-city and suburban residents grew during both the 1980s and the 1990s for both racial groups, but this growth was more than *four* times greater for blacks than whites. In 1990 unem-

TABLE 1   Unemployment Rates and Nonparticipation Rates Inside and Outside Central Cities of Metropolitan Statistical Areas[a]

	Inside Central Cities			Outside Central Cities		
	1970	1980	1990	1970	1980	1990
Unemployment Rate						
All races, both sexes[b]	4.7	7.3	7.8	3.9	5.7	5.0
White, both sexes	4.1	5.7	5.7	3.7	5.4	4.5
Male	3.8	5.9	6.0	3.2	5.3	4.6
Female	4.4	5.4	5.4	4.5	5.4	4.4
Black, both sexes	6.9	12.8	14.4	6.4	9.6	9.5
Male	6.7	13.9	15.9	5.8	9.7	9.8
Female	7.3	11.7	13.2	7.2	9.4	9.1
Rate of Nonparticipation in Labor Force, Workers Aged 25-64[c]						
All races, both sexes[b]	30.0	26.6	22.3	30.8	25.6	19.2
White, both sexes	29.6	25.6	20.3	30.8	25.7	19.7
Male	8.6	11.6	11.8	6.0	8.9	9.4
Female	49.0	39.0	28.7	54.5	41.9	29.8
Black, both sexes	30.0	28.9	27.0	29.4	23.6	21.0
Male	14.3	20.2	22.6	15.7	16.3	18.9
Female	42.9	35.7	30.6	41.8	30.2	23.0

[a]Update of Table 11.6, p. 293, *Urban Economics and Public Policy* by James Heilbrun, St. Martin's Press, 1987.
[b]"All races" includes white, black, and others not shown separately.
[c]Rate of nonparticipation equals the number of persons not in the labor force divided by the total population for the designated age group.

Sources: U.S. Bureau of the Census, *Census of Population: General Social and Economic Characteristics,* 1970, Tables 107, 112, 124, and 126; 1980, Table 144; 1990, Tables 33, 69, and 70.

TABLE 2 Median Family Income by Race Inside and Outside Central Cities of Metropolitan Statistical Areas[a]

	Median Family Income[b] (1985 Dollars)				
	1959	1969	1979	1989	1995
Central Cities					
All races[c]	21,752	27,515	26,801	26,655	24,292
White	23,112	29,472	29,560	30,538	27,303
Black	14,193	19,245	17,183	16,716	16,373
Outside Central Cities					
All races[c]	24,490	32,417	33,992	35,431	33,648
White	24,886	32,895	34,556	37,871	34,315
Black	12,853	20,298	22,294	25,010	24,164

[a]Update of Table 11.7, p. 294, *Urban Economics and Public Policy* by James Heilbrum, St. Martin's Press, 1987.
[b]Income in the year shown for families by place of residence in the following year.
[c]Includes other races not shown separately.

Sources: U.S. Bureau of the Census, *Current Population Reports,* series P-23, no. 37, June 24, 1971, Table 7; series P-23, no. 75, November 1978, Table 17; series P-60, no. 180, November 1992, Table 13; series P-60, no. 193, October 1996.

ployment rates were 4.9 and 1.2 percentage points higher in central cities for blacks and whites, respectively. The central-city unemployment rate was especially high for black males (16 percent).

Rising central-city unemployment rates may illustrate only a portion of the labor market disadvantage associated with a central-city location, since many blacks living in central cities are believed to be "discouraged workers" (i.e., workers who have become so discouraged by their inability to find work that they dropped out of the labor force entirely). Discouraged workers are not counted as being unemployed, because they have stopped searching for work. The rates of labor force nonparticipation, which capture discouraged workers but also those with other reasons for not looking for work, tell a similar story to that of unemployment rates, i.e., there has been little change in the nonparticipation rate difference between whites living in central cities and suburbs, whereas there have been substantial increases in the nonparticipation rates of both central-city black males and black females relative to their suburban counterparts. Finally, as was true for unemployment and nonparticipation rates, there has been a growing gap in real median family income between central-city and suburban residents over time (for income the data cover a longer period, 1959-1995). Although the growth in the gap in dollar magnitude was comparable between whites and blacks, due to the lower average income of blacks the central city–suburban income difference in percentage terms was roughly twice as large for blacks as whites in 1995.

In summary, regardless of the indicator, spatial differences are becoming greater over time for both blacks and whites living in metropolitan areas. But for blacks these differences have grown much more rapidly. The observed growth in spatial differences may reflect two possible phenomena: (1) the labor market outcomes for central-city residents may be worsening relative to those of suburban residents and (2) people with better labor market outcomes may be choosing with greater frequency a suburban over a central-city residential location. Since the data presented in Tables 1 and 2 are consistent with both of these possible scenarios, they suggest but do not demonstrate the existence of a causal link between residential location and opportunity.

RESIDENTIAL LOCATION AND OPPORTUNITY: THE LINKS

Numerous specific hypotheses relate residential location either in or among metropolitan areas to the opportunities and life outcomes of individuals; however, these purported linkages share two assumptions: (1) that there are spatial variations in the resources offered by markets and/or institutions in or across metropolitan areas and (2) that households have unequal ability to reside in locations where they deem these markets and institutions to be most desirable (Galster and Killen, 1995). The various hypotheses that link location and social and economic prospects differ in that they focus on different markets and/or institutions. They can also be distinguished by whether they focus on intra- versus intermetropolitan location. In this section, these hypotheses are first stated and discussed. The empirical evidence related to each hypothesis is then reviewed with an eye toward identifying conclusions for which there seems to be some agreement. Hypotheses dealing with the relationship between intrametropolitan location and opportunity are considered first, followed by those that relate opportunity to intermetropolitan location.

The Spatial Mismatch Hypothesis

Certainly, the most researched hypothesis relating intrametropolitan location to economic opportunity is commonly labeled the "spatial mismatch hypothesis." This hypothesis states that the suburbanization of jobs and involuntary housing market segregation have acted together to create a surplus of workers relative to the number of available jobs in central-city neighborhoods where blacks are concentrated. The spatial mismatch hypothesis, which was first advanced by John Kain way back in 1968, has recently enjoyed a comeback after many years of dormancy. The revival of interest in it can be attributed to a number of factors (Ihlanfeldt, 1994), but probably the most important is Wilson's (1987) and Kasarda's (1989) emphasis on job decentralization as a causative factor in the growth of the underclass.[2] As mentioned above, a common element of all hypotheses that relate residential location to opportunity are the assumptions that resources are spatially nonuniform and residential mobility is differentially constrained. In the case of the spatial mismatch hypothesis as originally formulated, the resource that varies is job accessibility, and the residential mobility constraint is the inability of blacks to follow jobs to the suburbs because of racial discrimination in the suburban housing market. However, Ihlanfeldt and Sjoquist (1989) have argued that spatial mismatch may also affect the labor market opportunities of low-skilled white workers, since they too are constrained in their ability to follow jobs to the suburbs by a relative scarcity of affordable housing units in those suburban areas where job growth is occurring.[3]

The surplus of workers in central-city neighborhoods that results from spatial mismatch may reduce the economic welfare of these workers by making it more difficult to find work, by reducing wage rates in the central city relative to suburban areas, or by increasing commuting costs. All of these possible effects, which may occur alone or in combination, translate into the same outcome— namely, lower net annual earnings for central-city blacks and less educated whites.

From a policy perspective, an important issue is why spatial mismatch would persist in the long run. Spatial mismatch implies a labor market disequilibrium that should be eliminated by market forces. Although racial discrimination in the housing market and high suburban housing costs may permanently keep less educated workers from residentially relocating to the suburbs, disequilibrium can still be eliminated by either labor demand increases in the central city or by workers shifting their labor supply to the suburbs by making a reverse commute. However, both of these adjustment mechanisms may be short-circuited. Regarding the former mechanism, it is frequently argued that the relative magnitudes of taxes, insurance premiums, land costs, skilled workers' wages, and congestion diseconomies may work against businesses selecting a central-city location, even if low-skilled labor costs are lower there than elsewhere due to spatial mismatch. The reverse-commuting mechanism may fail to work for a wide variety of reasons. These include the time and out-of-pocket costs associated with the commute, the possibility that central-city workers do not have knowledge of suburban job openings, greater hiring discrimination in the suburbs, the physical inaccessibility of many suburban job sites by public transit, and blacks' anticipation of being mistreated by suburban whites.

Neighborhood Effects

Under the rubric of "neighborhood effects" falls a variety of mechanisms that link the neighborhood milieu to individual behaviors and opportunities. The nature of these mechanisms are the subject of considerable debate among social scientists. The purpose here is not to provide an exhaustive review of this debate but rather to highlight those channels of neighborhood influence that seem most plausible and susceptible to policy intervention.

One list of possible neighborhood effects is provided by Jencks and Mayer (1990b) in their survey of the empirical literature. Their list includes peer influences, indigenous adult influences, and outside adult influences.

Peer influences refer to the effects that peers have on one another's behavior. To be accepted by one's peer group, the individual adopts the same behaviors, whether good or bad, that characterize the group. Since behaviors considered "bad" according to establishment norms are more prevalent in poor neighborhoods, individuals living in such neighborhoods are more likely to be induced by peers to engage in self-destructive or antisocial activity. The individual's susceptibility to peer group effects is believed to vary with age, with young people, especially teenagers, being most at risk.

Indigenous adults in the neighborhood may also affect individual behaviors by serving either as role models or "enforcers" of public order and decency. Once again, the nature of these effects is thought to vary between poor and affluent neighborhoods, with the former containing fewer positive role models and involved enforcers of community standards.

Among the neighborhood effects identified by Jencks and Mayer, it has been this particular type of effect—the influence of indigenous adults—that has received the most attention in policy discussions. This does not stem from any evidence regarding the strength of this effect relative to others, but rather from the influential writings of Wilson (1987), who argues that the migration of working-class and middle-class blacks from ghettos has left these areas without mainstream role models. He believes that the resulting concentration of poverty has played an important role in the growth of social pathologies in the black community. In addition to serving as role models, Wilson emphasizes that middle-class blacks are the chief supporters of mainstream institutions, such as churches and schools. As successful people have left the ghetto, these neighborhood institutions have undergone a severe deterioration in quality.

The final neighborhood effect identified by Jencks and Mayer is adults living outside the neighborhood who may indirectly influence behaviors and opportunities in the neighborhood. This presumably occurs as the result of more qualified providers of public services preferring to work in better neighborhoods. Hence, this factor may contribute to other possible causes, resulting in the inferior schools, police forces, and other neighborhood institutions found in poorer neighborhoods. Of course, privately provided goods and services in poorer neighborhoods may suffer in quality for this reason as well.

In addition to the neighborhood effects listed by Jencks and Mayer, there are two other possibly important linkages that can be mentioned. First, results from the Gautreaux program (Rosenbaum, 1995) suggest that many ghetto and public housing residents may be unwilling to work out of fear that they will be victimized while traveling to and from work, robbed of their rewards from working, or their unsupervised children will get hurt or get in trouble with gangs. (The Gautreaux program is reviewed in the next major section.) Second, informal sources of job market information, which are heavily relied on by less educated workers in searching for jobs (Holzer, 1987), may vary in quality between good and bad neighborhoods. Wilson (1987) argues that people living in underclass neighborhoods have poor information about legitimate jobs because they lack contact or interaction with individuals and institutions that represent mainstream society. I have argued (Ihlanfeldt, 1997) that Wilson's hypothesis can be couched in terms of the decision to invest in the acquisition of labor market information. In underclass neighborhoods, fewer people make the investment in information about jobs because fewer people choose to participate in the labor force. There is therefore a lower probability that one's neighbors will have accurate information to share on the spatial distribution of available jobs. However, the influence of neighborhood is more complicated than Wilson's hypothesis suggests. Although labor force participation is lower in underclass neighborhoods, among those who do participate there is likely to be a greater investment in obtaining information about jobs that less educated people would be qualified to hold. In affluent neighborhoods, there may collectively be a dearth of information on these types of jobs, simply because the typical resident has some postsecondary education and is employed where few workers are hired into blue-collar or service occupations. It is therefore unclear whether less educated people obtain more useful information about the labor market from their neighbors if they live in better (i.e., more affluent) neighborhoods.

The attention that social scientists have given to these neighborhood effects has increased in recent years, since decennial census data indicate that poor people are increasingly isolated from nonpoor people in metropolitan areas. For example, Abramson et al. (1995) found that poor households became 13 percent more segregated from 1970 to 1990 in the 40 largest metropolitan areas, and Kasarda (1993) shows that in the 100 largest cities the share of the poor living in tracts with a poverty rate over 40 percent increased from 16 to 28 percent over this same time period. The growth in the likelihood that an individual poor person has mostly poor neighbors suggests that negative neighborhood effects are having a greater influence on the opportunities and life outcomes of poor people today than was true in the past (Wilson, 1987).

Educational Opportunity

As alluded to above, all of the neighborhood effects identified by Jencks and Mayer—peer influences, indigenous adult influences, and outside adult influences—may cause differences in educational opportunities between poor and nonpoor neighborhoods. Peer influences may act to reduce learning opportunities in poor neighborhoods by depriving poor students of the possible benefits of being surrounded by smart and motivated students. The adults who reside in poor neighborhoods may devote less time and money toward the support of neighborhood schools and the enforcement of antitruancy laws. Finally, poor neighborhoods may repel more qualified teachers and school administrators.

In addition to educational differences arising from neighborhood effects, educational opportunities may also vary across school districts due to interdistrict fiscal disparities. These disparities are particularly severe between central cities, where the poor are concentrated, and white suburban areas (Bahl, 1994). Moreover, there is evidence that these disparities have grown worse over the past decade (Bahl et al., 1992). The conventional wisdom is that resources spent on education have little effect on observed educational outcomes (Hanushek, 1986), but Card and Krueger (1996) have questioned this conclusion in their recent review of the empirical literature. They note that several meta-analyses—quantitative summaries of the estimates in the literature—suggest that greater resources do in fact lead to higher test scores. More important, they conclude that school resources positively affect long-term outcomes like educational attainment and earnings.

Intermetropolitan Location and Opportunity

In comparison to the linkages that may exist between intrametropolitan location and opportunities, possible effects of intermetropolitan location on opportunity have received far less attention. Nevertheless, a number of new theories suggest that the economic and social prospects of specific groups may vary among metropolitan areas due to differences in growth rates or levels of housing segregation.

Local shifts in labor demand that disturb the steady-state relationship among the unemployment rates of metropolitan areas may cause intermetropolitan differences in the employment and earnings opportunities of indigenous residents. However, the conventional wisdom has been that these differences would be eliminated in the long run because immigration returns all areas to equilibrium. However, Bartik (1991) argues that increases in local labor demand may have beneficial long-run effects on the human capital of indigenous workers, since growth may cause firms to promote their workers to higher-paying jobs more rapidly. Growth may also shorten unemployment durations among local residents, decreasing the likelihood that their human capital will be eroded by inactivity. If blacks or poor people are concentrated in slower growth areas, these so-called hysteresis effects may play a role in explaining the growth in income and racial inequality at the national level.[4]

Neighborhood effects and spatial mismatch imply that blacks living in segregated areas are worse off than blacks living in integrated or predominately white areas. Cutler and Glaeser (1995) have espoused the idea that housing segregation hurts all blacks equally in the same metropolitan area whether they live inside or outside the ghetto. They label their idea "the weak form of the spatial mismatch hypothesis" (1995:3): "This form of the hypothesis does not specify the mechanism relating segregation to poor outcomes, and does not assume that black mobility is constrained. With unconstrained mobility, we would expect outcomes for equivalent people to be equalized across locations in a single city, so that all minorities regardless of location will be hurt by segregation." Cutler and Glaeser's version of the spatial mismatch hypothesis implies that the welfare of blacks residing in more segregated metropolitan areas is worse in comparison to those living in less segregated areas, other things being equal.

Evidence on the Spatial Mismatch Hypothesis

More than 60 studies have provided evidence on the spatial mismatch hypothesis. In the early 1990s, six different reviews of the literature were published (Wheeler, 1990; Jencks and Mayer, 1990a; Moss and Tilly, 1991; Holzer, 1991; Kain, 1992; Ihlanfeldt, 1992). With the exception of Jencks and Mayer, these reviews concluded that the weight of the empirical findings provided either strong (Kain, Ihlanfeldt) or moderate (Wheeler, Moss and Tilly, Holzer) support for the hypothesis. Jencks and Mayer, in contrast, concluded that "support [for the idea that job proximity increases the supply of black workers] is so mixed that no prudent policy analyst should rely on it" (1990a:19).

Since the above reviews were written, roughly a dozen new studies have been completed in this area. In general, these studies use more suitable data and superior methodologies than earlier studies and therefore provide the most reliable evidence to date on the spatial mismatch hypothesis. Since Ihlanfeldt and Sjoquist (1998) have already provided a detailed review of each of these new studies, the approach here will be twofold: (1) to summarize the results of these studies and (2) to highlight a couple of studies that provide particularly noteworthy evidence on the spatial mismatch hypothesis.

Of the new studies providing evidence, only two reject the hypothesis (Taylor and Ong, 1995; Cooke, 1997). However, neither of these studies deals with the endogeneity of residential location, which is the most common methodological error that has plagued empirical investigations of the spatial mismatch hypothesis (Ihlanfeldt, 1992). The hypothesis implies that job accessibility affects labor market outcomes, but both the standard theory of residential location (Muth, 1969) and existing evidence (Ellwood, 1986) indicate that commuting distances rise with earnings.[5] Hence, earnings and proximity to jobs are jointly determined. The failure to account for this simultaneity results in the underestimation of the true effect of job accessibility on labor market outcomes (Ihlanfeldt, 1992).

One approach to handling the simultaneity between employment/earnings and residential location is to focus the analysis on youth still living at home, based on the assumption that for them residential location is exogenously determined by their parents or guardians. The convenience of this approach explains why so many studies of spatial mismatch have focused exclusively on youth.

Among recent studies, Cutler and Glaeser (1995), Holzer et al. (1994), Holloway (1996), O'Regan and Quigley (1996), and Raphael (1998a, 1998b) reinforce the earlier finding of Ihlanfeldt and Sjoquist (1990) that job accessibility has an important effect on the probability that youth have jobs.

In his assessment of the spatial mismatch literature in 1992, Kain concluded that most studies of spatial mismatch have focused on males and that more research was needed on females. Two of the recent studies have responded to this need by providing estimates for females (Thompson, 1997; Kasarda and Ting, 1996). Kasarda and Ting find that spatial mismatch has a stronger effect on the joblessness of women than men, regardless of race. They suggest that this may reflect women's more complex travel patterns and greater domestic responsibilities, both of which make them less able to commute to distant jobs. Although Thompson focuses exclusively on females and therefore provides no gender comparisons, his results are consistent with those of Kasarda and Ting's, in that he finds that job access strongly affects the labor force participation rates of white, black, and Hispanic women.[6]

As noted above, spatial mismatch may affect the employment and earnings of less educated whites as well as blacks. The findings of Holloway (1997), Kasarda and Ting (1996), and Ihlanfeldt and Young (1994) all lend support to this expectation. The last study is of particular interest, since it provides some rare evidence on differences in wage rates between workers employed by central-city and suburban firms. As predicted by the hypothesis, the wage rates of both black and white fast-food restaurant workers are found to be significantly greater in the suburbs than in the central city, after controlling for a lengthy list of individual and establishment characteristics.

Among the recent studies, those by Raphael (1998b) and Rogers (1997) merit special consideration. Using 1990 census tract level data for San Francisco, Raphael regresses male youth employment to population ratios on a set of geographically defined job accessibility measures, a geographically defined competing labor supply variable, and variables describing the demographic composition of the neighborhood. This approach follows the basic methodology employed earlier by Ellwood (1986) and Leonard (1986). The latter two studies have played a major role in the spatial mismatch debate because each finds that racial differences in youth employment rates have little to do with job accessibility.[7] The distinguishing characteristic of Raphael's model is that his access measure, which is obtained by estimating a gravity equation, is based on the change in jobs rather than the number of jobs in a specified commute of each census tract. He persuasively argues that proximity to employment growth comes closer than proximity to employment levels to the ideal measure of job accessibility, namely, the number of job openings per worker.

The estimated effects of his job access variables have the expected signs and are highly significant. Moreover, contrary to the results of Ellwood and Leonard, when Raphael adds his job access variables to an equation that includes the proportion of the census tract's residents who are black, the coefficient on the latter variable falls precipitously. Differential accessibility is found to explain between 30 and 50 percent of the neighborhood employment rate differentials between average white and black male youth. It is remarkable that this range is nearly identical to the one found earlier by Ihlanfeldt and Sjoquist (1990) using 1980 data for Philadelphia.

Raphael presents other results that may go a long way toward resolving the spatial mismatch debate, at least as it applies to youth. When he reestimates his models using Ellwood's and Leonard's employment level-based measures of job accessibility, he reproduces their insignificant results.

Rogers analyzes the relationship between unemployment duration and job accessibility. This study is unique in that her data allow her to address the simultaneity problem between employment and residential location using a sample of males ages 18 to 55 residing in the Pittsburgh area who have submitted unemployment insurance claims. Hence, the results of this study provide some rare and seemingly reliable evidence on the spatial mismatch hypothesis as it applies to the employment of adults. She argues that simultaneity is not a problem for her sample because the residential location of laid-off workers is based on previous job location. Her measures of job access are essentially the same as those employed by Raphael; that is, gravity variables that measure either the worker's proximity to employment change or employment levels. Also consistent with Raphael are her findings that indicate employment change-based measures of access have a statistical effect on unemployment duration, whereas employment level-based measures do not. An increase of one standard deviation in the mean value of her access to job growth variable is found to decrease expected unemployment duration by about five weeks.

In summary, there is now rather convincing evidence that job accessibility plays an important role in explaining the large differences that exist in the employment rates of black and white youth living in large metropolitan areas. Even Jencks and Mayer (1990a) and later Jencks (1992) alone concede this point in their otherwise critical review of the spatial mismatch literature, and this review was written prior to the excellent studies by Raphael (1998a, 1998b).

But what can be concluded concerning the role that spatial mismatch plays in explaining racial differences in youth employment rates in smaller metropolitan areas? These differences are only modestly smaller than those for larger metropolitan areas (Ihlanfeldt, 1992). Unfortunately, none of the recent studies reviewed above addresses this issue. In fact, among all studies, only Ihlanfeldt (1992) provides separate estimates for metropolitan areas of different population sizes. These results suggest that the importance of job access as both a determinant of youth job probability and as an explainer of racial employment gaps is directly proportional to metropolitan area size. In fact, essentially no importance is found for metropolitan areas of less than 1 to 1.5 million people.

As noted above, due to the simultaneity problem between employment/earnings and residential location, it is much more difficult to test the spatial mismatch hypothesis for adults than youth. However, the studies by Thompson and by Rogers appear to adequately handle this difficulty, and their results suggest that spatial mismatch plays some role in explaining the labor market outcomes of adult women and men, respectively, living in large metropolitan areas. Many earlier studies also reach this conclusion (see the reviews of the spatial mismatch hypothesis literature cited above), but the evidence provided by these studies is less convincing due to weaker data and/or methodologies (Ihlanfeldt, 1992).

The role played by spatial mismatch in explaining the employment and earnings of adults living in smaller metropolitan areas has not been studied. But since adults may be more able than youth to overcome poor job accessibility, the insignificant results found by Ihlanfeldt (1992) for youth in smaller areas suggest that spatial mismatch may be strictly a large-city phenomenon.[8]

The Perpetuation of Spatial Mismatch

As first noted by Holzer et al. (1994), it is exceedingly important from a policy perspective to identify the barriers that prevent blacks from shifting their labor supply to suburban areas in response to spatial mismatch. Until very recently, this issue was ignored in the spatial mismatch hypothesis literature. There are now two published studies that provide some evidence.

Ihlanfeldt and Young (1996) use data from a sample of fast-food restaurants in Atlanta to examine the factors that underlie the spatial distribution of black employment between the central city and the suburbs. A model of the racial composition of the restaurant's workforce was estimated that included the following explanatory variables: percentage of white customers, race of manager, whether the restaurant was in walking distance of a public transit stop, miles from the central business district center (a proxy for distance from black residences), chain affiliation, and whether the establishment was franchisee- or company-owned. Of these variables, transit was the most important factor in explaining the lower share of jobs held by blacks in the suburbs. A total of 35 percent of the city-suburban difference in black employment share could be attributed to the tendency of suburban firms not to be in walking distance of public transit. Other important contributors to the city-suburban difference in black employment share were miles from the central business district center (33 percent), race of manager (15 percent), and percentage of white customers (14 percent). These results suggest that the physical inaccessibility of suburban job sites by public transit, the length of the commute (which may proxy either commuting costs or information on job opportunities), and labor market discrimination all represent important barriers preventing blacks from securing suburban jobs.

Holzer and Ihlanfeldt (1996) also investigated the factors that explain the racial composition of the workforce of the individual firm. However, their analysis is based on relatively large (roughly 800 observations per city) and representative samples of firms located in Boston, Atlanta, Los Angeles, and Detroit. Based on estimated equations of the probability that the last worker hired by the firm is black, they decompose central-city/suburban differences in black employment probabilities into the portions accounted for by each explanatory variable. Their results, which strongly parallel those of Ihlanfeldt and Young (1996), indicate that a number of factors play an important role in explaining the lower probability of blacks obtaining suburban in comparison to central-city jobs. These include the tendencies of suburban firms to be located beyond walking distance of a public transit stop, to have mostly white customers and owners, and to be located far away from black residences. Regarding the mechanism underlying the latter effect, they find that distance to black residences has a statistically significant and negative effect on black employment for all recruiting methods (signs, walk-ins, referrals), except for newspaper advertisements. Since newspapers disseminate information over a wider geographical area than the other methods, these results suggest that the distance effect may be attributable to central-city blacks possessing poor information about suburban job openings.[9]

More direct evidence on the possibility that information limits black employment in suburban areas is provided by Ihlanfeldt (1997). As part of the Multi-City Study of Urban Inequality (MCSUI) Household Survey for Atlanta, respondents were asked to look at a map identifying six major employment centers in the Atlanta region and indicate which centers they felt had the fewest and most job opportunities or openings for people without college degrees. Using job vacancy data from the MCSUI employers survey as well as other data, Ihlanfeldt was able to accurately rank the centers based on jobs available for less educated workers. He found that both black and white respondents have very poor knowledge of the spatial distribution of job openings, particularly if they lived in the city of Atlanta. Even among those workers who presumably had the most to gain from acquiring such information—the unemployed with little education—there was a large divergence between actual and perceived rankings.

Evidence on Neighborhood Effects

The effects that neighborhood characteristics have on individual behaviors and opportunities are extremely difficult to estimate reliably. The same problem that has plagued empirical investigations of the spatial mismatch hypothesis—namely, endogenous residential location—confronts with even greater severity empirical studies of neighborhood effects. People who behave in ways that society deems undesirable may self-select bad neighborhoods, either because they prefer to live among others like themselves or because the housing in such neighborhoods is all they can afford. There is therefore always the concern that effects that are attributable to neighborhoods may simply reflect unmeasurable characteristics of individuals or families who end up living in the poorest neighborhoods.

The most comprehensive review of the empirical literature on neighborhood effects is by Jencks and Mayer (1990b). They conclude that "our first and strongest conclusion is that there is no general pattern of neighborhood or school effects that recurs across all outcomes." Regarding specific outcomes, they conclude that the evidence is contradictory and sometimes thin in the areas of educational attainment, cognitive skills, crime, and labor market outcomes. To Jencks and Mayer, the only outcome for which the evidence appears to unambiguously support a neighborhood influence is teenage pregnancy. The reader's impression of the neighborhood effects literature after reading the Jencks and Mayer review is perhaps best expressed by Jencks (1992:138) himself: "Indeed, the list of what we don't know [about neighborhood effects] goes on and on."

Since the Jencks and Mayer review was written, many new studies have been completed that provide evidence that neighborhood effects matter (Crane, 1991; Massey et al., 1991; Corcoran et al., 1992; Case and Katz, 1991; O'Regan and Quigley, 1991; Brooks-Gunn et al., 1993; O'Regan, 1993; Brewster, 1994; Duncan, 1994; Haveman and Wolfe, 1994; Brooks-Gunn et al., 1997). Among these studies, the evidence of Case and Katz is the most convincing, since they explicitly model the possibility of endogenous residential location. Their data come from the 1989 Boston Youth Survey of the National Bureau of Economic Research. For 17- to 24-year-olds they model the following behaviors: criminal activity, illegal drug use, alcohol use, church attendance, idleness (neither working nor in school), friendship with gang members, and parenthood outside wedlock. For all of these behaviors except the last two, they find that the youth's involvement is dependent on the extent to which other youth in the neighborhood evince the same behavior. Case and Katz interpret their results as consistent with the epidemic or contagion model of neighborhood effects, which posits that bad behaviors are spread through peer influence. They conduct a number of sophisticated econometric tests to rule out the possibility that the neighborhood effects they find are just an artifact of the way families sort themselves among communities.

Also new since the Jencks and Mayer review are two papers that highlight the difficulty of reliably estimating neighborhood effects because of the endogeneity of residential location. Evans et al. (1992) show that, if this endogeneity is ignored, teenage women's probability of pregnancy and dropping out of school strongly depends on the quality of their school peer group, measured as the percentage of students who are disadvantaged. However, their results obtained from models that treat residential location as endogenous provide no support for the existence of peer group effects. Manski (1993) theoretically demonstrates the highly restrictive conditions that must obtain before endogenous neighborhood effects can be identified. He believes that satisfying these conditions is so tenuous in statistical models that experimental and subjective data (i.e., statements people make about why they behave as they do) will have to play an important role in future efforts to learn about neighborhood effects.

As is true for the spatial mismatch hypothesis, little is known about neighborhood effects outside large metropolitan areas. However, the results from existing studies may be more applicable to smaller areas with regard to neighborhood effects than spatial mismatch. Neighborhood effects are believed to be highly localized, whereas reachable jobs may extend considerable distances beyond the home neighborhood, even for low-income blacks. In smaller metropolitan areas, reachable jobs may encompass those located in both the city and the suburbs, resulting in unimportant differences in job accessibility between white and black workers.

Studies Comparing Job Accessibility and Neighborhood Effects

Generally, studies of spatial mismatch have focused exclusively on job accessibility as a determinant of labor market outcomes, whereas studies of neighborhood effects have failed to consider the neighborhood's proximity to available jobs. The failure to consider both job access and neighborhood effects together is problematic, since neighborhoods with negative effects are frequently distant from job opportunities for less educated workers.

Two recent studies have included both neighborhood descriptors and a job accessibility measure as independent variables in youth employment models (Cutler and Glaeser, 1995; O'Regan and Quigley, 1996). These studies find that both neighborhood effects and job access are important and that the strength of the former effects is dominant. This regression evidence contrasts with the qualitative evidence obtained from the housing voucher recipients who participated in Chicago's Gautreaux program.[10] As described more fully below, participants who moved to predominately white, middle-income neighborhoods in the suburbs have higher employment rates than those who moved to predominately black, low-income neighborhoods in the central city. When the suburban movers were asked to explain why their suburban location helped them get jobs, both job accessibility and neighborhood influences were emphasized, but the former was ranked consistently above the latter in relative importance.

Evidence on Residential Segregation and Social and Economic Outcomes

Since beliefs are that job access is poorer and neighborhood effects are more negative in segregated neighborhoods, another approach to the question "Does residential location matter?" is simply to relate residential segregation to specific social and economic outcomes. Although this approach is certainly not new (Masters, 1974; Galster, 1987a), the results of recent studies based on the Gautreaux program are of considerable interest, since the use of novel data provides results that are less subject to bias from the endogeneity of residential location. Another reason for the interest in these studies is that, if segregation is not found to matter to black welfare, then there would be support for rejecting both the spatial mismatch and the neighborhood effects hypotheses.

In the minds of many, the Gautreaux program provides the strongest extant support available for the proposition that intrametropolitan residential location matters to social and economic prospects. As a result of a Supreme Court consent decree in 1976, families residing in or on the waiting list for public housing were given Section 8 certificates to rent market rate housing in "revitalized" Chicago-area neighborhoods. The Gautreaux program participants were randomly assigned to move to city or suburban areas, creating a quasi-experimental design. Although some "cream skimming" occurred, selection criteria were not very stringent and eliminated less than one-third of applicants.[11]

Rosenbaum (1995:235) and his various colleagues compared the fortunes of Gautreaux program participants who moved to predominately black, low-income areas in the city of Chicago with those who moved to predominately white, middle-income neighborhoods in Chicago's suburbs. For the adults, who were mostly single mothers originally on public welfare, the results indicate that employment was higher among suburban than central-city movers, but earnings and hours per week were not different, even after extensive controls (Rosenbaum, 1996). Suburban movers were asked to explain why their suburban location helped them get jobs. *All* mentioned the greater number of jobs in the suburbs. Improved physical safety and positive role models were ranked second and third in importance, respectively. There is support, therefore, for both the spatial mismatch and the neighborhood effects hypotheses.

Results for the children of Gautreaux participants showed that suburban in comparison to city movers are more likely to graduate from high school, attend college, and attend a four-year college. Among youth who did not go on to college, suburban movers are more likely to receive higher wages and better job-related benefits.

The social and economic differences between city and suburban movers for both adults and children are all large and statistically significant. This is particularly remarkable since the city movers themselves are probably benefiting from a better neighborhood environment than they had in the housing projects. As Rosenbaum (1995) notes, "city movers are a particularly stringent comparison group."

Evidence Linking Intermetropolitan Location and Opportunity

Neoclassical migration theory maintains that labor and capital flows among regions will, in the long run, equalize expected wages for workers with equivalent amounts of human capital. If this is true, then intermetropolitan location could not cause permanent differences in economic opportunity. However, as noted above, there are two new theories that belie this conclusion; namely, the weak form of the spatial mismatch hypothesis as posited by Cutler and Glaeser and hysteresis effects as hypothesized by Bartik.

Cutler and Glaeser (1995) use data from the 1990 Public Use Microdata Sample on youth living in 204 different metropolitan statistical areas to analyze the following outcome variables: high school graduation, college education, idleness (neither working nor in school), earnings, and (for females) unmarried motherhood. These variables are separately regressed on individual and MSA characteristics, the key variable in the latter group is a dissimilarity index used to measure the degree of housing segregation at the neighborhood level. Recall that Cutler and Glaeser hypothesize that all minorities living in an individual metropolitan area are equally harmed by housing segregation whether or not they live in a segregated neighborhood. To handle the endogeneity of residential location, they measure housing segregation using the following variables: the number of municipalities in the MSA, the share of local government revenue in the state that comes from intergovernmental sources, and the number of rivers. Although anyone's choice of instruments can always be questioned, the results are robust with respect to alternative instruments and show that all of the outcome variables (except college degree) are strongly influenced by housing segregation in a manner that is detrimental to blacks. Moreover, since their results are unchanged when they control for whether the individual resides in the central city or the suburbs, it appears that housing segregation hurts all blacks regardless of where they reside in the metropolitan area. There is, therefore, support for the weak form of the spatial mismatch hypothesis.

Bartik's (1991) book contains extensive empirical research on the various impacts of employment growth in urban areas during the period 1979-1986. He finds considerable evidence of hysteresis effects in local markets. MSA employment growth increases the real earnings of both black and white residents, but the effect is greater for blacks. Stronger effects are also registered for less educated in comparison to more educated workers and younger in comparison to older workers. Increases in local labor demand therefore tend to decrease income and racial inequality in metropolitan areas.[12]

Conclusion

My reading of the studies cited above leads me to the following conclusions:

- Residential location both in and between metropolitan areas affects the individual's social and economic prospects.
- The prospects of minorities and the poor are worse than those of whites and the nonpoor because of racial and income segregation in housing markets.

- Neighborhood effects, job accessibility, and school resources all play some role in the influence of residential locations on opportunities.
- The mechanisms perpetuating spatial mismatch include transportation, information, and discrimination-related factors.
- Black opportunities are richer relative to those of whites in urban areas that are less racially segregated and more rapidly growing in employment.

POLICY ALTERNATIVES

There are many approaches to the categorization of alternative policies that attempt to improve the "geography of opportunity" for disadvantaged groups living in urban areas. The most popular categorization is to lump specific strategies into three types: place-based initiatives, personal mobility programs, and residential mobility strategies. Place-based initiatives attempt to bring new resources and opportunities to distressed central-city areas. Personal mobility programs seek to link central-city workers with suburban jobs *without* changing either job or residential locations. Residential mobility strategies open up housing opportunities in those areas where conditions and opportunities are presumably better.[13]

Numerous assessments of the above types of policies can be found in the literature (see, for example, Ihlanfeldt, 1992; Hughes, 1987).[14] The focus here is to update these assessments by drawing on a substantial amount of new evidence and analyses that have become available, mostly in the last five years.

Another noteworthy development in recent years is that more scholars and policy makers have come to view the above policies as complementing rather than contradicting one another (Yinger, 1995; Downs, 1994; Hughes, 1994; Wilson, 1996). Indeed, as Yinger (1995) notes, former HUD Secretary of the U.S. Department of Housing and Urban Development, Henry Cisneros also holds this position. Clearly, there is little disagreement that minorities should have the opportunity to work and live anywhere in the metropolitan area. But a strong case in favor of inner-city redevelopment can also be made. Minority communities make unique political, economic, and cultural contributions that are worth preserving.

Place-Based Initiatives

A number of strategies fall into the category of place-based initiatives, but the one that has received the most attention and arguably the most use has been the urban enterprise zone. As originally conceived, the zone would encompass an economically distressed area in the central city in which taxes and government regulations would be reduced or eliminated in order to stimulate the origination of small, new enterprises. In practice, the urban enterprise zones established by state governments have offered businesses tax and other financial incentives along with technical assistance.

There is wide disagreement among scholars and policy makers regarding the desirability of urban enterprise zone s as a policy instrument. The critics of UEZs have made three arguments:

- The benefits accruing to individual firms from locating in an urban enterprise zone are insufficient to overcome the many other obstacles associated with a central-city location, namely, crime, inadequate space, and higher wages for skilled employees.
- Growth in jobs may occur as the results of zone inducements, but it will not result from the origination of new firms. Instead, growth will occur if existing firms or new firms that would have started up even without the zone choose to locate in the enterprise area. Hence the zone's employment gain is offset by a loss of jobs elsewhere.
- Regardless of the source of the job growth that occurs in enterprise zones, the expansion in jobs will not help indigent residents, because they do not possess the skills necessary for employers to hire them.

Evidence relevant to the first criticism has been highly mixed. However, the lion's share of this evidence should be disregarded, since it has been compiled using impressionistic or descriptive rather than analytic methods. Deficiencies in the analyses of urban enterprise zones that have focused on employment impacts have been ably inventoried by Vidal (1995:181): "At the most basic level, impact evaluation shortcomings include reporting jobs gained (or 'retained') without netting out job losses, or reporting net job change without establishing a link between employment changes and zone program elements. More thorough analyses that attempt to assess whether observed outcomes are attributable to the program have relied primarily on seriously flawed methods (e.g., before and after studies, employer surveys)."

There are, however, two recent econometric studies that do provide some reliable evidence on whether urban enterprise zones improve conditions in and around their boundaries (Papke, 1994; Boarnet and Bogart, 1996). These studies are unique in that they estimate "fixed effects" models using panel data, which have the important advantage of controlling for permanent differences across areas that are likely to influence zone designation. On the one hand, Papke finds evidence that the program in Indiana increased business investment and reduced employment claims. Boarnet and Bogart, on the other hand, find that the program in New Jersey had no impact on total municipal employment, on employment in various sectors, or on municipal property values. As a possible explanation for the difference in their and Papke's results, Boarnet and Bogart suggest that the specific programs and sites in Indiana were more attractive to firms than those in New Jersey. The possibility that the success or failure of a specific program hinges on an area's inherent potential for growth is frequently empha-sized (Levitan and Miller, 1992; Erickson and Friedman, 1991). Apparently, the question of whether an urban enterprise zone improves economic conditions in targeted areas cannot be given a simple yes or no, but rather the qualified answer that some do and some do not, depending on the circumstances. Unfortunately, we do not know which circumstances are most conducive to success. Levitan and Miller argue that the "other ingredients" required for success include the physical appearance, service, and infrastructure of the area, and Erickson and Friedman emphasize an adequate labor pool with good basic skills. But neither of these positions is based on persuasive evidence.

The evidence on the second criticism of urban enterprise zones, which comes from both British and state experiences, indeed suggests that the incentives offered do not create jobs but instead cause a diversion of activity that would otherwise have occurred elsewhere (Ladd, 1994). Urban enterprise zones are therefore "locational" rather than "generative" (Lehman, 1994). This, however, is not altogether bad. As noted above, the evidence suggests that minorities and whites do not enjoy equal access to jobs. Reshuffling jobs from suburban to central-city areas may be justified on a fairness criterion. In addition, the effects of the job loss experienced outside the enterprise area must be measured against the decline in crime and other antisocial behaviors committed by zone residents as the result of their improved employment opportunities. Finally, as Bartik (1991) has pointed out, individuals living in high-unemployment areas probably place a higher value on getting a job than individuals in low-unemployment areas. Thus the relocation of jobs in favor of zones may enhance net social welfare. At least one state has recognized the validity of one or more of these arguments: the Illinois' program explicitly states as one of its goals moving investment to the urban enterprise zones from elsewhere in the state (McDonald, 1997).

The evidence on the third criticism—that new jobs do not go to residents of the zone—is considerably thinner than that for the first two criticisms. The two studies that do exist are contradictory. A survey of the urban enterprise zones in 17 states conducted by the U.S. Department of Housing and Urban Development indicates that 61 percent of new jobs went to zone residents (Vidal, 1995). How-ever, various analyses of Indiana's program conclude that less than one-third of total new zone jobs went to zone residents (James, 1991; Papke, 1988; Indiana Department of Commence, 1992). This is particularly noteworthy since Indiana's program, unlike those of most states, includes a tax credit for hiring zone resi-dents. This does not augur well for the recently designated urban "empowerment zones," which also include tax credits for hiring zone residents.[15]

In addition to urban enterprise zones, there are other place-based initiatives that have received far less attention, but recent evidence suggests they have generally succeeded in improving opportunities in poor inner-city neighborhoods. These include community development financial institutions and community de-velopment corporations.[16] Vidal (1995) has recently evaluated both, and Harrison et al. (1994) and Stoecker (1997) have evaluated community development corporations. Vidal focuses on five types of community development financial institutions: community development banks, bank-owned community development corporations, community development credit unions, community development loan funds, and microenterprise loan funds. She argues that there is a legitimate need for community development financial institutions since there is overwhelming evidence that conventional financial institutions underserve both households and businesses located in depressed inner-city areas. Performance evaluations of community development financial institutions are sparse, but the information that is available led Vidal to reach the following conclusions:

- Community development financial institutions effectively target their services to people and places with restricted access to capital and services.
- Their operations are too limited to make up for the credit gaps left by mainstream financial institutions in poor inner-city communities.
- Some community development financial institutions are playing a useful role by demonstrating to conventional lenders how to profitably do business in low-income and minority neighborhoods.
- Although community development financial institutions fulfill the needs of an important market niche, the solution to unequal credit and other financial services in poor inner-city communities must come from conventional financial institutions, through stricter community regulations and enforcement.

The three evaluations of community development corporations all have different foci. Vidal (1995) takes a comprehensive look at strategies and records in all three of the areas that community development corporations have traditionally addressed: affordable housing, neighborhood commercial services, and social networks and services. Harrison et al. limit their analyses to the involvement of community development corporations in the employment and training business. Both evaluations are based on findings reported in the literature as well as their own national surveys. Stoecker questions the viability of an urban redevelopment model that relies on community development corporations and proposes an alternative.

Vidal gives community development corporations high marks in each of their three program areas. She cites considerable evidence that they have succeeded as "gap fillers" in the sense that they respond to important community needs that are unmet by other institutions. In her estimation (Vidal, 1995:222): "Resources permitting, community development corporations pursue a diversified agenda aimed at making their communities better places to live and improve the opportunities available to local residents. Available evidence indicates that they have a strong track record in targeting the benefits of their work to needy people and places." Vidal recommends that the capitalization of community development corporations be deepened and that their effective scope be expanded. She sees them as more promising than community development financial institutions or urban enterprise zones as place-based initiatives for improving access to opportunities for residents of poor communities.

Harrison et al.'s review (1994) is also favorable to community development corporations. In their study of the community development corporations located in 10 urban areas around the country, they found many were successfully involved in some manner of job training, placement, and counseling activities. However, the greatest successes were found in activities that connected neighborhood residents with mainstream institutions. Instead of increasing their employment training capacity, the authors recommend that community development corporations network even more extensively with specialized agencies, community colleges, and employers who can train and place their constituents.

In contrast to the evaluations of Vidal and Harrison, Stoecker (1997) is highly critical of community development corporations. He argues that they are too small to have much of an impact on neighborhood revitalization and that they lack community participation. According to Stoecker, the latter reflects the control that is exerted by funders from outside the community. He recommends that community development corporations become high-capacity and multilocal in character and be held accountable through a strong community organizing process.

It is important to note that the evidence reviewed and provided by Vidal and Harrison and his colleagues is entirely anecdotal. In particular, there is no statistical evidence on the effectiveness of community development corporations as job generators. It is therefore unknown whether they are more effective than urban enterprise zones in reducing joblessness in distressed central-city neighborhoods. One approach that future research might take to answer this question is to estimate the same type of fixed effects models that have been used to evaluate urban enterprise zones but allowing for employment shocks from both community development corporations and urban enterprise zones.[17]

A final set of place-based initiatives defines "place" more broadly to include the entire metropolitan area. As discussed above, Bartik's research suggests that economic development policies that increase metropolitan growth can provide significant labor market opportunities for blacks and the poor. There are a plethora of policies currently in use: tax abatements, technology development programs, general tax cuts, improvements in local education, assistance to manufacturers for modernization and exporting, business incubators, and entrepreneurial training programs (Bartik, 1993). Whether and to what extent each of these polices stimulates metropolitan employment growth is not known with any reasonable degree of confidence. However, both theory and extant evidence can be drawn on to develop general principles that economic development programs should seek to satisfy to maximize their cost-effectiveness. A list of 10 such principles appears in Ihlanfeldt (1995).

Personal Mobility Programs

The objective of these programs is to open up more suburban job opportunities to poor central-city residents. As mentioned above, there are three possible barriers that may prevent the central-city poor from obtaining suburban jobs. Although the relative importance of transportation, information, and discrimination-related factors in denying city residents suburban jobs has not been clearly established, the magnitudes of the estimates reported in recent studies suggest that the elimination of any one of these barriers would have nontrivial effects on opening up more suburban jobs opportunities to central-city residents.

Numerous reverse-commuting programs have been implemented nationwide, with almost every large metropolitan area having tried at least some type of service. There are a number of inventories of these programs (American Public Transit Association, 1993; Drachman Institute, 1992; Hughes, 1989; Hughes and Sternberg, 1993), but little evaluation has been done of their effectiveness.[18] Recently, Public/Private Ventures, a research organization located in Philadelphia, was awarded funding from various philanthropic foundations and the federal government to conduct a four-year demonstration. The project, which is entitled, "Bridges to Work," will provide reverse-commuting services to the central-city poor located in five large cities from spring 1997 to December 2000. An important feature of the research is that both treatment and control samples will be drawn. The latter will consist of poor central-city residents who receive their communities' usual employment-related services. This research promises to provide the first reliable evidence on the effectiveness of transportation programs as an antipoverty strategy.

Another demonstration that merits consideration is one in which local transit authorities would give up their current status as monopoly suppliers of services. In recent years, this idea has been promoted as a solution to the chronic deficits experienced by mass transit authorities and as an approach to decreasing the reliance on the private car for the journey to work (Lave, 1985). In addition, in a deregulated environment, creative entrepreneurships providing reverse-commuting services would have an opportunity to develop. Although their completely free entry onto the transportation scene may not be in the offing, reverse-commuting services that would complement rather than compete against existing public transit are a real possibility. For example, an attractive option for getting inner-city workers to suburban jobs would be jitneys that would pick them up at transit stops along major cross-suburban routes and drop them off near their places of employment.[19]

There is other evidence, some optimistic and some pessimistic, regarding the likely success of reverse-commuting programs. One criticism of these programs is that central-city residents would be unwilling to make the lengthy commutes required to get to available suburban jobs. However, Harrell and Peterson (1992) cite evidence by Kasarda (1992) showing that journey-to-work times are only marginally higher for city-to-suburb commuters in comparison to within-city commuters. Black workers who reverse-commuted spent only 2 to 6 minutes more per trip than black workers who lived and worked in the central city. These results are consistent with those of Ihlanfeldt (1992), who found that job accessibility for less educated workers is at its maximum in the inner rather than the outer suburbs. In all but the very largest metropolitan areas, a van traveling from the ghetto against traffic can probably reach jobs located in the inner suburban ring in less than half an hour.

Some pessimistic evidence is reviewed by Rosenbaum (1996) showing that employers consider a housing project address, a central-city address, or attendance at a city public school as signals of poor workers. He is skeptical of transportation programs because they will not fix these residential barriers. Wilson (1996:22) recommends that this problem be addressed by having not-for-profit job information and placement centers certify inner-city workers: "These centers would recruit or accept inner-city workers and try to place them in jobs. One of their main purposes would be to make persons who have been persistently unemployed or out of the labor force "job-ready" so that a prospective employer would be assured that a worker understands and appreciates employer expectations such as showing up for work on time and on a regular basis, accepting the orders of supervisors, and so on. When an information and placement center is satisfied that a worker is job-ready, then and only then would the worker be referred to an employer who has a job vacancy."

Wilson (1996), Kasarda (1988), and Jargowsky (1997) have all advocated the use of a computerized job opportunity network providing up-to-date information on available jobs throughout the metropolitan area. However, programs that are specifically designed to provide information on suburban jobs to central-city workers are rare, and little is known regarding their effectiveness. Once again, a demonstration project can be recommended. Since it is relatively inexpensive to disseminate information, the cost of conducting such a demonstration would be minuscule compared with conducting transportation experiments.

Residential Mobility Strategies

The purpose of residential mobility strategies is to mitigate constraints on residential choice that fall disproportionately on the poor and minorities. The greatest concern is over the inability of the latter two groups to settle in middle-income suburbs, especially those where jobs are available, because of regulatory barriers that artificially inflate the cost of housing and racial discrimination in housing and mortgage markets.

A growing number of social scientists have argued that the use of exclusionary zoning by suburban governments can be curbed only by having state governments pressure local governments to change their behavior (see, for example, Downs, 1993; Salins, 1993). This approach is seen as more politically acceptable than trying to make local governments accept some "quotient" of affordable housing. However, the reality is that states have little incentive to adopt policies that would compel local communities to open up their borders to low-income households. One way to create the necessary incentive is to have the federal government intervene by making housing or other federal assistance conditional on states' adoption of antiexclusionary policies. However, with the movement toward hands-off federalism (Nathan, 1992), this intervention is unlikely to occur any time soon. Moreover, even if the federal government was inclined to become involved, there is concern that the amount of federal assistance required to change states' behavior would be prohibitive in light of current budget realities (Schill, 1992).

Nevertheless, there still may be hope for changes in states' behavior. There is much uncertainty surrounding possible state responses to the recent devolution of welfare responsibilities from the federal government to the states. As welfare recipients are forced off the dole and into the labor market, the resulting increase in labor supply in central cities may exacerbate spatial mismatch to such an extent that central cities become overwhelmed with unemployed and homeless people (Wilson, 1996). States may be forced to step in to alleviate the mismatch. The least costly strategy from the states' perspective would be to pressure suburban governments to allow higher-density housing development in their borders.

There is overwhelming evidence that blacks and Hispanics continue to suffer from housing and mortgage market discrimination (Yinger, 1995). As the result of this discrimination, housing segregation is largely involuntary. Clearly, stronger enforcement of fair housing legislation is necessary to improve the housing and labor market opportunities of minorities. Although there exist differences of opinion on how to best accomplish this, both Downs (1992) and Yinger (1995) provide comprehensive antidiscrimination programs that promise to be cost-effective and politically feasible. An important common element of both programs is random audit-based testing in every metropolitan area at regular intervals.

Successful residential mobility policies would open up suburban neighborhoods to the poor and minorities. If the incumbent households remain in these neighborhoods as previously excluded households move in, greater racial and economic integration will result, which will mitigate both spatial mismatch in the labor market and negative neighborhood effects. Realistically, however, white flight of some magnitude will occur, which may limit any integration that may result.[20]

Little research has been done on policies that may stem white flight from suburban neighborhoods. Policies that merit consideration include urban growth boundaries, government-guaranteed price floors, and scattering housing voucher recipients to keep neighborhoods below the "tipping" point. Urban growth boundaries have been proposed as a solution to urban sprawl and are currently used in a growing number of states for this purpose. But by confining all or most growth to within the established boundary, they may also contribute to integrated neighborhoods by constraining the further decentralization of affluent whites in response to neighborhood infiltration of minorities or low-income households. The efficacy of price floors as a neighborhood integration strategy depends on the extent to which white flight is a panic response to concerns over expected declines in house values (Leven et al., 1976). The scattering strategy has been emphasized as an important reason for the success of the Gautreaux program reviewed above (Rosenbaum, 1995).

The most controversial issue regarding the attainment of stable integrated neighborhoods is whether integration should be achieved by "managing" the entry of blacks into white neighborhoods to keep these neighborhoods below their tipping points. Many authors have expressed opinions on this issue, and the positions of Yinger (1995) and Downs (1992) are representative of those on both sides of the debate. Yinger's objections to quotas are that they are contradictory to free choice and that they are unnecessary, since there are alternative policies that are consistent with both the elimination of discrimination and the promotion of integration. The centerpiece of his Stable Neighborhood Initiatives Program (SNIP) are grants to changing neighborhoods to improve their quality, for example, by boosting public services or increasing housing maintenance.[21]

Downs (1992) believes that controls on black entry into white neighborhoods represent justifiable discrimination, since such controls do result in a socially desirable outcome: stable integrated neighborhoods. Moreover, he argues along with Galster (1987b) that, although controls limit freedom of choice, the absence of integrated living opportunities would also limit people's freedom of choice.

At the center of the disagreement between Yinger and Downs is whether there are indeed policies other than controls that can achieve racially stable neighborhoods. Downs is doubtful, whereas Yinger believes in SNIP. However, as is true for growth boundaries and guaranteed price floors, there is little evidence, either pro or con, that can be drawn on to assess the probable success of SNIP. Research on these alternatives is needed. In addition, much could be learned from conducting comparative analyses of neighborhoods in and across metropolitan areas that have succeeded and failed to achieve lasting integration.

An important first step of comparative analysis has been taken by Ellen (1996). She compared census tracts that remained racially mixed and those that underwent racial succession between the two decennial periods 1970-1980 and 1980-1990. She found that among the tracts that underwent racial transition, racial differences in entry in comparison to exit were more important in explaining the change from white to black residency. This suggests that achieving stable neighborhoods require not only stemming white flight but also encouraging whites to choose mixed neighborhoods. Ellen also found that the tendency of whites to leave racially changing neighborhoods and their reluctance to select mixed neighborhoods appear to be based not on pure prejudice but rather their belief that the entry of blacks will result in the neighborhood's structural decline, which would include such changes as declines in property values and lower school quality.[22] Ellen bases this conclusion largely on results obtained from estimating residential mobility models for white owners and renters. These results show that increases in the percentage of the neighborhood's residents who are black have a stronger influence on the moving probabilities of owners in comparison to renters, owners with children in comparison to childless owners, and owners with children in public school in comparison to those with children attending private school. These results lend support to the use of guaranteed price floors and greater spending for public schools in changing neighborhoods, as recommended by Yinger's SNIP.[23]

SOCIAL AND ECONOMIC OPPORTUNITIES AND THE SYSTEM OF LOCAL GOVERNMENT

The structure of local government may affect the linkages between residential location and opportunity outlined in the earlier discussion as well as the effectiveness and feasibility of the policies discussed above. Unfortunately, theoretical development and empirical evidence having a bearing on these possible effects are extremely thin. In this section I review what little research exists and identify in what ways metropolitan governance may matter.

The Residential Location/Opportunity Nexus and Political Fragmentation

Most of the research that relates the structure of local government to opportunity focuses on the Tiebout (1956) sorting process and its effects on educational opportunities. Under the Tiebout "feet-voting" mechanism for the articulation of preferences for local public goods, higher income households have incentives to sort themselves into school districts that exclude households poorer than themselves. These incentives include the desire to maximize both the fiscal residuum (i.e., benefits received minus taxes paid) received from local government, which requires the exclusion of free riders, and the quality of the student peer group, which is positively related to household incomes. Tiebout sorting by income level therefore results in inequalities in educational opportunity across school districts. Higher-income districts spend more money on schools, since education is a normal good, and provide more favorable peer environments.

Political fragmentation may also exacerbate spatial mismatch and neighborhood effects, although in contrast to the Tiebout literature there are no theoretical models elucidating possible relationships and little relevant empirical evidence. In fact, the only book that explores these relationships—*Cities Without Suburbs* by David Rusk (1995)—was written primarily for a nonacademic audience and contains only tabular evidence. Nevertheless, Rusk's book is of considerable interest for reasons outlined below.

Rusk argues that metropolitan areas with more "elastic" central cities have less racial segregation. Elastic cities are defined by Rusk as those that have developable vacant land in their boundaries and have demonstrated the ability to expand their boundaries outward over time. Operationally, his measure of elasticity places three times as much weight on the latter factor in comparison to the former factor. He divides metropolitan areas into five categories based on the elasticity of their central cities and computes a series of descriptive statistics for each category. His tables indicate that metropolitan areas with more elastic central cities generally have the following features relative to those with less elastic central cities:

- a higher percentage of the area's population is governed by the central city,
- there are fewer suburban governments,
- a smaller percentage of the area's blacks and Hispanics live in the central city,
- both black and Hispanic dissimilarity indexes are lower, indicating less racial segregation at the neighborhood level, and
- schools are less segregated for both blacks and Hispanics.

Rusk provides the following explanation for the tendency for metropolitan areas with more elastic central cities to be less racially segregated (1995): "Does greater socioeconomic integration automatically flow from greater government unity? Probably not. What is clear is that, absent federal or state mandates, a metropolitan area in which local government is highly fragmented is usually incapable of adopting broad integrating strategies. Conversely, a metropolitan area in which key planning and zoning powers are concentrated under a dominant local government has the potential to implement policies to promote greater racial and economic integration if that government has the courage and vision to do so."

Another explanation for why elastic cities are less segregated revolves around the incentives for white flight from the central city and the exclusion of minorities from white neighborhoods. In addition to containing a larger percentage of the region's population, elastic cities encompass a greater share of the region's land area. Hence, moving to the suburbs would entail a longer journey to work for central-city workers. This disadvantage would work against the benefits to whites from living in a segregated suburban community. In addition, central-city whites may expect that the fiscal benefits from moving to the suburbs may be short-lived, since by definition elastic cities have the capacity to capture suburban growth by extending their boundaries outward via annexation or consolidation. Integration may also be greater in metropolitan areas with more elastic central cities because the housing choices of minority households are less constrained by exclusionary zoning.[24]

Obviously, the findings of Rusk require confirmation from estimated models that include a full set of appropriate controls. If it is verified that a nontrivial relationship exists between housing segregation and metropolitan governance, this would be an important result. As noted above, the evidence provided by both Rosenbaum and Cutler and Glaeser, without implicating either neighborhood effects or spatial mismatch, strongly suggests that housing segregation reduces the social and economic opportunities of blacks. In addition, Jargowsky's (1997) results suggest that blacks experience worse neighborhood effects in metropolitan areas where housing segregation, once again measured by a dissimilarity index, is higher.[25]

The Impact of Fragmentation on Policy

All three categories of policies outlined earlier for dealing with spatial variation in economic and social opportunities are affected by local government fragmentation. Residential mobility policies are affected because, as emphasized above, fragmentation results in exclusionary zoning, which frustrates efforts to open up suburban neighborhoods to poor central-city residents. Personal mobility strategies are affected because coordination among a multiplicity of different municipal agencies creates organizational barriers to implementing successful reverse-commuting and job information programs. Since fragmentation complicates effective planning on an area-wide scale, metropolitan area-wide economic development programs are also difficult to initiate. As Rusk (1995:70) has duly noted: "Who speaks and acts for greater Detroit or greater Cleveland, suffering from high political fragmentation, strong racial divisions, sharp income differentials, interjurisdictional competition—in short, from the loss of a shared sense of community and common destiny nationwide?" Place-based policies that focus on central-city economic development are probably least affected by political fragmentation. Yet, even here, fragmentation can have ill effects, since interjurisdictional competition may necessitate that central cities offer greater tax and other incentives than they really can afford.

DIRECTIONS FOR FUTURE RESEARCH

Gaps in our knowledge of the geography of economic and social opportunity in metropolitan areas have been identified throughout this paper. However, thus far suggestions for future research have not been prioritized. In this section I identify the research question from each of the previous three sections that I believe is *most important* among those that can *feasibly* be addressed with existing data. Although I recognize that demonstrations can be more informative than econometric models, the former are not very practical in today's fiscal environment. Besides, the questions I identify are so basic to the topic of this paper that they should probably be answered before proceeding with any new costly social experiments.

Research on Linkages

The policy prescriptions for arresting negative neighborhood effects and spatial mismatch in the labor market overlap but do not coincide. It is therefore important to sort out the relative importance of these alternative linkages between residential location and opportunities. Moreover, as noted above, few studies have modeled neighborhood effects and job accessibility together, which suggests that a large portion of the results reported in the literature may be biased by omitted variables. Now that individual-level data are becoming available that identify the person's neighborhood location, much can be learned by estimating fully specified models of social and economic outcomes.[26]

Research on Policies

There has been great interest, even excitement, among both scholars and policy makers in the success of the Gautreaux program.[27] However, the effectiveness of all residential mobility programs—Gautreaux-type, antidiscrimination, and antiexclusionary—is jeopardized by the possible flight of incumbent suburban residents as their neighborhoods are infiltrated by the poor or minorities. Opening up the suburbs to central-city residents will have little long-run effect on their opportunities if stable, integrated neighborhoods cannot be achieved.[28]

The causal factors that underlie the white flight response (as well as the unwillingness of whites to move into changing neighborhoods) have not been clearly identified. Racial and income prejudice, concerns over property values and student peer group effects, as well as other factors may all play a role and need to be studied. More work, along the lines begun by Ellen (1996) comparing the traits of racially stable and unstable neighborhoods, can be recommended, since such research may point toward policy solutions.

Research on the System of Local Government

Income and racial segregation at the neighborhood level are strong forces limiting the social and economic opportunities of the poor and minorities. The reasons outlined and evidence reviewed above suggest that there may be important relationships between the system of local government and neighborhood segregation. Research is needed that focuses on explaining the substantial differences that exist in the degree of housing segregation across metropolitan areas.[29] Farley and Frey (1994) addressed this issue by regressing the metropolitan area's black-white dissimilarity index for 1990 on the region, the functional specialization of the area, the age of the area, the pace of new construction, and a set of demographic characteristics. Descriptors of the system of local government in the metropolitan area were not included. However, they suggest that their regional results, which indicate that metropolitan areas in the West and the South are far less segregated than those in the Midwest and Northeast, largely reflect the types of local government systems that characterize each region. They point to two differences that may be important. First, zoning and policing decisions tend to be made at the county level in the South but at the municipality level in the Northeast and Midwest. County-level governance may open up more suburban housing opportunities for the poor and minorities. Second, metropolitan areas in the South and the West have more permissive annexation laws than areas located in the Northeast and the Midwest. Annexation by central cities limits the amount of land in metropolitan areas that is governed by suburban governments practicing exclusionary zoning. Moreover, as noted earlier, annexation permissiveness may alter the incentives that higher-income households have to move from central cities to suburban areas.

These hypotheses and possibly others should be honed theoretically and examined empirically by estimating models that include variables fully describing the system of local government in metropolitan areas.

REFERENCES

Abramson, Alan J., Mitchell S. Tobin, and Matthew R. VanderGoot
  1995   The changing geography of metropolitan opportunity: The segregation of the poor in U.S. metropolitan areas, 1970 to 1990. *Housing Policy Debate* 6(1):45.
American Public Transit Association
  1993   *Access to Opportunity: A Study of Reverse Commuting Programs.* Washington, DC: American Public Transit Association.
Bahl, Roy
  1994   Metropolitan fiscal disparities. *Cityscape: A Journal of Policy Development and Research* 1(1):293-306.
Bahl, Roy, Jorge Martinez-Vazquez, and David L. Sjoquist
  1992   Central-city suburban fiscal disparities. *Public Finance Quarterly* 20(4):420-432.
Bartik, Timothy J.
  1991   *Who Benefits From State and Local Development Policies?* Kalamazoo, MI: W.E. Upjohn Institute for Employment Research.
  1993   *Economic Development and Black Economic Success.* Upjohn Institute Technical Report No. 93-001. Kalamazoo, MI: W.E. Upjohn Institute for Employment Research.
  1994   The effects of metropolitan job growth on the size distribution of family income. *Journal of Regional Science* 34:483-501.
Bishop, John H., and Suk Kang
  1991   Applying for entitlements: Employers and the targeted jobs tax credit. *Journal of Policy Analysis and Management* 10(1):24-45.
Boarnet, Marlon G., and William T. Bogart
  1996   Enterprise zones and employment: Evidence from New Jersey. *Journal of Urban Economics* 40:198-215.

Brewster, Karin L.
  1994   Race differences in sexual activity among adolescent women: The role of neighborhood
          characteristics. *American Sociological Review* 59:408-424.
Brooks-Gunn, Jeanne, Greg Duncan, and J. Lawrence Aber
  1997   *Neighborhood Poverty. Volume I: Context and Consequences for Children.* New York:
          Russell Sage Foundation.
Brooks-Gunn, Jeanne, Greg Duncan, Pamela Klebanov, and Naomi Sealand
  1993   Do neighborhoods affect child and adolescent development? *American Journal of Soci-
          ology* 99:353-95.
Burtless, Gary
  1985   Are targeted wage subsidies harmful? Evidence from a large voucher experiment. *Indus-
          trial and Labor Relations Review* 39:105-114.
Card, David, and Alan B. Krueger
  1996   School resources and student outcomes: An overview of the literature and new evidence
          from North and South Carolina. *The Journal of Economic Perspectives* 10(4):31-50.
Case, Anne C., and Lawrence F. Katz
  1991   The Company You Keep: The Effects of Family and Neighborhood on Disadvantaged
          Youths. National Bureau of Economic Research Working Paper No. 3705, May.
Cooke, Thomas J.
  1997   Geographic access to job opportunities and labor force participation among women and
          African Americans in the Greater Boston Metropolitan Area. *Urban Geography*
          18(3):213-227.
Corcoran, Mary, Roger Gordon, Deborah Laren, and Gary Solon
  1992   The association between men's economic status and their family and community origins.
          Journal of Human Resources 27(4):575-601.
Crane, Jonathan
  1991   The epidemic theory of ghettos and neighborhood effects on dropping out and teenage
          childbearing. *American Journal of Sociology* 96(5):1126-1159.
Cutler, David M., and Edward M. Glaeser
  1995   Are Ghettos Good or Bad? National Bureau of Economic Research Working Paper No.
          5163, June.
Downs, Anthony
  1968   Alternative futures for the American ghetto. *Daedalus* Fall:1331-1378.
  1992   Policy directions concerning racial discrimination in U.S. housing markets. *Housing
          Policy Debate* 3(2):685-742.
  1993   Reducing regulatory barriers to affordable housing erected by local governments. In
          Housing Markets and Residential Mobility, G. Thomas Kingsley and Margery Austin
          Turner, eds. Washington, DC: The Urban Institute Press.
  1994   *New Visions for Metropolitan America.* Washington, DC: The Brookings Institution.
Drachman Institute
  1992   Reverse Commute Transportation: Emerging Provider Roles. Prepared for the U.S.
          Federal Transit Administration by the University of Arizona.
Duncan, Greg
  1994   Families and Neighbors as Sources of Disadvantage in the Schooling Decisions of White
          and Black Adolescents. Working paper. Survey Research Center, University of Michi-
          gan.
Eckert, Ross, and George Hilton
  1972   The jitneys. *Journal of Law and Economics* 15:293-325.
Edel, Matthew
  1972   Development vs. dispersal: Approaches to ghetto poverty. Pp. 307-325 in *Readings in
          Urban Economics,* Matthew Edel and Jerome Rothenberg, eds. New York: Macmillan.

Ellen, Ingrid Gould
    1996   The Stability of Racially Mixed Neighborhoods: Revealing New Evidence From 34 Metropolitan Areas. Unpublished manuscript. Harvard.

Ellwood, David T.
    1986   The spatial mismatch hypothesis: Are there teenage jobs missing in the ghetto? Pp. 147-187 in *The Black Youth Employment Crisis,* Richard B. Freeman and Harry J. Holzer, eds. Chicago: University of Chicago Press.

Erickson, Rodney A., and Susan W. Friedman
    1991   Comparative dimensions of state enterprise zone policies. Pp. 155-176 in *Enterprise Zones: New Directions in Economic Development,* Roy E. Green, ed. Newbury Park, CA: Sage Publications.

Evans, William, Wallace Eugene Oates, and Robert M. Schwab
    1992   Measuring peer group effects: A study of teenage behavior. *Journal of Political Economy* 100:967-991.

Farley, Reynolds, and William H. Frey
    1992   Changes in the Segregation of Whites from Blacks During the 1980s: Small Steps Toward a More Residentially Integrated Society. Paper No. 92-257. Population Studies Center, University of Michigan.
    1994   Changes in the segregation of whites from blacks during the 1980s: Small steps toward a more integrated society. *American Sociological Review* 59:23-45.

Galster, George C.
    1987a   Residential segregation and interracial economic disparities: A simultaneous equations approach. *Journal of Urban Economics* 21:21-44.
    1987b   *Federal Fair Housing Policy in the 1980s: The Great Misapprehension.* Working Paper HP 5. Cambridge: Center for Real Estate Development of the Massachusetts Institute of Technology.

Galster, George C., and Sean P. Killen
    1995   The geography of metropolitan opportunity: A reconnaissance and conceptual framework. *Housing Policy Debate* 6(1):7-43.

Hanushek, Erik A.
    1986   The economics of schooling: Production and efficiency in public schools. *Journal of Economic Literature* 24:1141-1177.

Harrell, Adele V., and George F. Peterson
    1992   Introduction: Inner-city isolation and opportunity. In *Drugs, Crime and Social Isolation,* Adele V. Harrell and George E. Peterson, eds. Washington, DC: The Urban Institute.

Harris, David R.
    1997   "Property Values Drop When Blacks Move In, Because . . .": Racial and Socioeconomic Determinants of Neighborhood Desirability. Report No. 97-387. Population Studies Center, University of Michigan.

Harrison, Bennett
    1974   *Urban Economic Development: Suburbanization, Minority Opportunity, and the Condition of the Central City.* Washington, DC: The Urban Institute.

Harrison, Bennett, Marcus Weiss, and John Gant
    1994   *Building Bridges: Community Development Corporations and the World of Employment Training.* New York: Ford Foundation.

Haveman, Robert, and Barbara L. Wolfe
    1994   *Succeeding Generations: On the Effects of Investments in Children.* New York: Russell Sage Foundation.

Holloway, Steven R.
    1996   Job accessibility and male teenage employment, 1980-1990: The declining significance of space? *The Professional Geographer* 48(4):445-458.

Holzer, Harry J.
  1987   Informal job search and black youth unemployment. *American Economic Review* 77:446-452.
  1991   The spatial mismatch hypothesis: What has the evidence shown? *Urban Studies* 28(1):105-122.
Holzer, Harry J., and Keith R. Ihlanfeldt
  1996   Spatial factors and the employment of blacks at the firm level. *New England Economic Review.* Federal Reserve Bank of Boston. May/June, Special Issue.
Holzer, Harry J., Keith R. Ihlanfeldt, and David L. Sjoquist
  1994   Work, search, and travel among white and black youth. *Journal of Urban Economics* May:320-45.
Hughes, Mark Alan
  1987   Moving up and moving out: Confusing ends and means about ghetto dispersal. *Urban Studies* 24:503-517.
  1989   *Fighting Poverty in Cities: Transportation Programs as Bridges to Opportunity.* Washington, DC: National League of Cities.
  1994   Reverse commuting in a policy context. In *Access to Opportunity: Linking Inner-City Workers to Suburban Jobs.* Washington, DC: American Public Transit Association.
Hughes, Mark Alan, and Julie E. Sternberg
  1993   *The New Metropolitan Reality: Where the Rubber Meets the Road in Antipoverty Policy.* Washington, DC: The Urban Institute.
Ihlanfeldt, Keith R.
  1992   *Jobs Accessibility and the Employment and School Enrollment of Teenagers.* Kalamazoo, MI: W.E. Upjohn Institute for Employment Research.
  1994   The spatial mismatch between jobs and residential locations in urban areas. *Cityscape: A Journal of Policy Development and Research* 1(1) (August).
  1995   Ten principles for state tax incentives. *Economic Development Quarterly* 9(4) (November).
  1997   Information on the spatial distribution of job opportunities in metropolitan areas. *Journal of Urban Economics* 41:218-242.
Ihlanfeldt, Keith R., and David L. Sjoquist
  1989   The impact of job decentralization on the economic welfare of central-city blacks. *Journal of Urban Economics* 26 (July).
  1990   Job accessibility and racial differences in youth employment rates. *The American Economic Review* 80(1):267-276.
  1998   The spatial mismatch hypothesis: A review of recent studies and their implications for welfare reform. *Housing Policy Debate* 9(4):849-892.
Ihlanfeldt, Keith R., and Madelyn V. Young
  1994   Housing segregation and the wages and commutes of urban blacks: The case of Atlanta fast-food restaurant workers. *Review of Economics and Statistics* August:425-433.
  1996   The spatial distribution of black employment between the central city and the suburbs. *Economic Inquiry* 64:613-707.
Indiana Department of Commerce
  1992   Indiana Enterprise Zones: A Program Evaluation for 1989 & 1990. October.
Jackson, Jerry
  1979   Intraurban variation in the price of housing. *Journal of Urban Economics* 6:465-479.
James, Franklin J.
  1991   The evaluation of enterprise zones programs. Pp. 225-240 in *Enterprise Zones: New Directions in Economic Development,* Roy E. Green, ed. Newbury Park, CA: Sage Publications.

Jargowsky, Paul A.
1996   Take the money and run: Economic segregation in U.S. metropolitan areas. *American Sociological Review* 61:984-998.
1997   *Poverty and Place: Ghettos, Barrios, and the American City.* New York: Russell Sage Foundation.
Jencks, Christopher
1992   *Rethinking Social Policy: Race, Poverty, and the Underclass.* Cambridge, MA: Harvard University Press.
Jencks, Christopher, and Susan E. Mayer
1990a   Residential segregation, job proximity, and black job opportunities. Pp. 187-222 in *Inner-City Poverty in the United States,* Lawrence E. Lynn, Jr., and Michael G.H. McGeary, eds. National Research Council. Washington, DC: National Academy Press.
1990b   The social consequences of growing up in a poor neighborhood. Pp. 111-186 in *Inner-City Poverty in the United States,* Lawrence E. Lynn, Jr., and Michael G.H. McGeary, eds. National Research Council. Washington, DC: National Academy Press.
Kain, John F.
1992   The spatial mismatch hypothesis: Three decades later. *Housing Policy Debate* 3(2):371-460.
Kain, John F., and Joseph J. Persky
1969   Alternatives to the "gilded ghetto." *The Public Interest* Winter:77-91.
Kasarda, John D.
1988   Jobs, migration, and emerging urban mismatches. In *Urban Change and Poverty,* Michael G.H. McGeary and Lawrence E. Lynn, Jr., eds. National Research Council. Washington, DC: National Academy Press.
1989   Urban industrial transition and the underclass. *Annals of the American Academy of Political and Social Science* 501:26-47.
1992   The severely distressed in economically transforming cities. In *Drugs, Crime and Social Isolation: Barriers to Urban Opportunity,* Adele V. Harrell and George E. Peterson, eds. Washington, DC: The Urban Institute.
1993   Inner-city concentrated poverty and neighborhood distress: 1970-1990. *Housing Policy Debate* 4(3):253-302.
Kasarda, John D., and Kwok-Tai Ting
1996   Joblessness and poverty in America's central cities: Causes and policy prescriptions. *Housing Policy Debate* 7(2):387-419.
Ladd, Helen F.
1994   Spatially targeted economic development strategies: Do they work? *Cityscape: A Journal of Policy Development and Research* 1(1):193-218.
Lave, Charles A.
1985   The private challenge to public transportation—an overview. Chapter 1 in *Urban Transit: The Private Challenge to Public Transportation.* Cambridge, MA: Bollinger.
Lehman, Jeffery S.
1994   Updating urban policy. In *Confronting Poverty: Prescriptions for Change,* Sheldon H. Danziger, Gary D. Sandefur, and Daniel H. Weinberg, eds. New York: Sage Foundation.
Leonard, Jonathan S.
1986   Space, Time, and Unemployment Los Angeles, 1980. Unpublished manuscript. University of California, Berkeley.
Leven, Charles L., James T. Little, Hugh O. Nourse, and R.B. Read
1976   *Neighborhood Change: Lessons in the Dynamics of Urban Decay.* New York: Praeger Publishers.
Levitan, Sar A., and Elizabeth Miller
1992   Enterprise zones are no solution for our blighted areas. *Challenge* May-June:4-8.

Levy, Frank, and Richard J. Murnane
   1992   U.S. earnings levels and earnings inequality: A review of recent trends and proposed explanations. *Journal of Economic Literature* 30:1333-1381.
Manski, Charles F.
   1993   Identification of endogenous social effects: The reflection problem. *Review of Economic Studies* 60(3):531-542.
Massey, Douglas S., Andrew Gross, and Mitchell Eggers
   1991   Segregation, the concentration of poverty, and the life chances of individuals. *Social Science Research* 20:397-420.
Massey, Douglas S., and Mitchell Eggers
   1993   The spatial concentration of affluence and poverty during the 1970s. *Urban Affairs Quarterly* 29(2):299-315.
Masters, Stanley H.
   1974   A note on John Kain's housing segregation, Negro employment, and metropolitan decentralization. *The Quarterly Journal of Economics* 88:505-19.
McDonald, John F.
   1997   *Fundamentals of Urban Economics.* Upper Saddle River, NJ: Prentice-Hall.
Moss, Phillip, and Chris Tilly
   1991   *Why Black Men Are Doing Worse in the Labor Market: A Review of Supply-Side and Demand-Side Explanations.* New York: Social Science Research Council.
Muth, Richard F.
   1969   *Cities and Housing.* Chicago: University of Chicago Press.
Nathan, Richard P.
   1992   *A New Agenda for Cities.* Ohio Municipal League Educational and Research Fund.
O'Regan, Katherine M.
   1993   The effect of social networks and concentrated poverty on black and Hispanic youth unemployment. *Annuals of Regional Science* 27(4):327-342.
O'Regan, Katherine M., and John M. Quigley
   1991   Labor market access and labor market outcomes for urban youth. *Regional Science and Urban Economics* 21(2):277-293.
   1996   Spatial effects on employment outcomes: The case of New Jersey teenagers. *New England Economic Review* Special Issue (May/June).
Papke, James A.
   1988   *The Indiana Enterprise Zone Experiment: Concepts, Issues, and Impact.* Indianapolis: Indiana Department of Commerce.
Papke, Leslie
   1994   Tax policy and urban development: Evidence from the Indiana enterprise zone program. *Journal of Public Economics* 54:37-49.
Picus, Lawrence O.
   1996   Current Issues in Public Urban Education. *Housing Policy Debate* 7(4):715-730.
Raphael, Steven
   1998a   Inter- and intra-ethnic comparisons of the central city-suburban youth employment differential: Evidence from the Oakland metropolitan area. *Industrial and Labor Relations View* 51(3):505-524.
   1998b   The spatial mismatch hypothesis of black youth development: Evidence from the San Francisco Bay area. *Journal of Urban Economics* 43:79-111.
Rogers, Cynthia L.
   1997   Job search and unemployment duration: Implications for the spatial mismatch hypothesis. *Journal of Urban Economics* 42:108-132.
Rosenbaum, James E.
   1995   Changing the geography of opportunity by expanding residential choice: Lessons from the Gautreaux program. *Housing Policy Debate* 6(1):231-269.

1996   Discussion (on "Spatial Factors and the Employment of Blacks at the Firm Level," by Harry J. Holzer and Keith R. Ihlanfeldt). *New England Economic Review* Special Issue (May/June):83-86.

Rusk, David
1995   *Cities Without Suburbs: Second Edition.* Baltimore: The Johns Hopkins University Press.

Salins, Peter D.
1993   Cities, suburbs, and the urban crisis. *The Public Interest* 113:91-104.

Schill, Michael
1992   Deconcentrating the inner city poor. *Chicago-Kent Law Review* 67(3):795-853.

Stoecker, Randy
1997   The CDC model of urban redevelopment: A critique and an alternative. *Journal of Urban Affairs* 19(1):1-22.

Taylor, D. Brian, and Paul M. Ong
1995   Spatial mismatch or automobile mismatch? An examination of race, residence and commuting in U.S. metropolitan areas. *Urban Studies* 32(9):1453-1473.

Thompson, Mark A.
1997   The import of spatial mismatch on female labor force participation. *Economic Development Quarterly* 11(2):138-145.

Tiebout, Charles
1956   A pure theory of local expenditure. *Journal of Political Economy* 64(5):416-424.

Vidal, Avis C.
1995   Reintegrating disadvantaged communities in the fabric of urban life: The role of community development. *Housing Policy Debate* 6(1):169-230.

Wheeler, Laura A.
1990   A Review of the Spatial Mismatch Hypothesis: Its Impact on the Current Plight of Central City in the United States. Occasional Paper No. 137. Metropolitan Studies Program. The Maxwell School of Citizenship and Public Affairs, Syracuse University.

Wilson, William Julius
1987   *The Truly Disadvantaged: The Inner City, the Underclass and Public Policy.* Chicago: University of Chicago Press.

1996   *When Work Disappears.* New York: Alfred A. Knopf.

Yinger, John
1995   *Closed Doors, Opportunities Lost.* New York: Russell Sage Foundation.

NOTES

[1] Evidence on segregation in metropolitan housing markets, on one hand, indicates that racial segregation has declined over time but remains at a high level (Farley and Frey, 1994). Evidence on income segregation indicates that it has been increasing but is not nearly as high as racial segregation (Abramson et al., 1995; Massey and Eggers, 1993; Jargowsky, 1996). The increase in income segregation has occurred in the white, black, and Hispanic groups, but the largest increases were for minorities during the 1980s (Jargowsky, 1996).

[2] Wilson (1987:8) defines the underclass as the heterogenous grouping of families and individuals who lack training and skills and either experience long-term unemployment or are not part of the labor force, individuals who engage in street criminal activity and other aberrant behavior, and families who experience long-term spells of poverty and/or welfare dependency.

[3] In fact, if low-skilled whites can easily shift their labor supply to the suburbs in response to job decentralization, then spatial mismatch is unlikely to be much of a problem, since this may represent enough supply adjustment to eliminate the disequilibrium.

[4] The dependence of long-run effects on short-run events has been labeled "hysteresis," a term

taken from physics that refers to the time lag exhibited by a body in reacting to changes in the forces affecting it.

5   This fact is explained by the standard urban model if the income elasticity of housing demand exceeds the income elasticity of commuting cost. Alternatively stated, higher-income people may have longer commutes because they wish to consume more units of housing at a lower price. This explanation assumes that housing prices on average decline as distances to employment centers increase, which considerable empirical evidence suggests is the case (see, for example, Jackson, 1979). Other models suggest that higher-income workers travel farther to get to work because they are willing to trade commuting costs for either environmental amenities or better government services.

6   Kasarda and Ting find that their measure of job access—commute time of city residents for each racial group—has no effect on their outcome variables for black males, which unlike the rest of their results is inconsistent with the spatial mismatch hypothesis. However, all of their results may be underestimates of true effects, due to the crudeness of their access measure (which they acknowledge) and their failure to address the simultaneity between their endogenous variables and residential location.

Thompson recognizes that simultaneity between labor force participation and job access may affect his results, but be believes the bias will be small, since the women in his sample have uniformly low earnings and household incomes, making it difficult for them to trade higher commuting costs for a more spacious home.

7   To quote Ellwood's often repeated aphorism, "The problem isn't space. It's race."

8   In comparison to adults, youth are less likely to have access to an automobile for commuting to work, they may place a higher value on their commuting time due to their school responsibilities, and have less information on distant jobs because of a greater reliance on informal sources of job information.

9   The results of Holzer et al. (1994) are also suggestive of information limitations. They find that black and white central-city youth do not offset greater job decentralization with greater distances traveled, for either search or work.

10   It should be noted that both of the regression studies use questionable measures of job accessibility. Both use variants of neighborhood mean commute times based on the reasonable assumption that a youth has better job access if he or she lives in a neighborhood where residents have to make only a short commute to get to work. However, neither study standardizes travel times for transportation mode and both use travel times to *all* jobs in computing means. Since there is considerable variation in travel times between public and private carriers and the spatial distribution of youth jobs differs from that of all jobs, the findings of Cutler and Glaeser and O'Regan and Quigley may understate the true effects of job access by a considerable amount.

11   The Gautreaux program does not admit families with more than four children, large debts, or unacceptable housekeeping.

12   More recent research by Bartik (1994) provides further support for this conclusion. He finds that metropolitan-area employment growth increases the income of households in the poorest income quintile by five times as much as the increase experienced by households in the richest quintile.

13   A fourth category of policies includes educational reforms, such as site-based management, charter schools, vouchers, and school choice. These reforms are not discussed here, since adequately covering them would extend this paper to unmanageable length. For a recent review of current issues in public urban education, see Picus, Lawrence O. 1996. Current Issues in Public Urban Education. *Housing Policy Debate* 7(4):715-730 .

14   In fact, the dispersal (category three) versus development (category one) debate has been simmering and at times raging for over 25 years. Early participants in this debate include Kain and Persky (1969), Downs (1968), Edel (1972), and Harrison (1974).

15   Apparently, the problem with tax credits for targeted jobs is that they have a stigmatizing effect on members of the targeted group in the eyes of employers (Burtless, 1985; Bishop and Kang, 1991).

16 Other place-based initiatives that could be listed are business retention and expansion programs focused on areas in central cities where jobs are most needed. Although a number of cities have such programs, no evidence could be located on their effectiveness. Nevertheless, their low cost in comparison to tax incentives and other types of programs designed to attract new firms makes these programs an attractive option. Downs (1994) recommends that city governments survey employers to see what problems they have and what can be done to solve them.

17 This approach is complicated by the heterogeneity of community development corporation employment programs. They may fare more or less well relative to urban enterprise zones depending on the specifics of their programs.

18 There was a series of reverse-commuting demonstration projects funded by the federal government in the 1960s. These projects produced at best only meager benefits. But these results may not be applicable today, since there have been major changes in the spatial distributions of jobs and people in metropolitan areas over the past 30 years.

19 Between 1915 and 1920 jitneys, which were private vehicles (mostly Ford Model Ts), profitably operated in many metropolitan areas throughout the United States (Eckert and Hilton, 1972). They had flexible destinations and carried multiple passengers, generally going to different but nearby locations. Their life in America was cut short by regulations passed by municipalities that made their costs of doing business prohibitive. Jitneys were put down in order to preserve streetcars, which were favored because, unlike jitneys, they were an important source of tax revenue for local governments. It was also believed that competition between streetcars and jitneys would make it impossible for streetcars to subsidize their longer routes from revenues generated by their shorter routes, which were rapidly losing patronage in favor of the faster, more convenient service provided by the jitneys.

20 Even with white flight, residential mobility policies will improve the job accessibility of minorities. Although retailing and personal services will follow whites to more distant suburbs, the immobility of capital will keep manufacturing jobs in those areas that undergo racial transition.

21 Other provisions include race-conscious counseling; housing centers that disseminate information on neighborhood change, provide counseling, and prevent the spread of rumors; and bonuses for metro-based organizations that work with several integrated communities.

22 Some additional evidence that whites' aversion to black neighbors in not based on pure racial prejudice is provided by Harris (1997). He estimates hedonic housing price equations and finds that the racial composition of the neighborhood is not a statistical significant explanatory variable, after controlling for nonracial characteristics of the neighborhood (e.g., percentage poor and percent affluent).

23 There is the possibility that Ellen's results reflect, at least in part, differences in prejudice between owners and renters and families with and without children. To the extent that this is true, policies to arrest structural decline will be less effective in achieving racially stable neighborhoods.

24 Cutler and Glaeser (1995) have also suggested that political fragmentation may impose an added cost on blacks trying to change neighborhoods because a different neighborhood may have different public goods and perhaps even public goods designed to discourage racial integration. Their examples of the latter are racist police officers and schooling designed particularly for white suburban residents.

25 Jargowsky studies the factors that determine what percentage of a metropolitan area's blacks will live in high-poverty census tracts. The latter are defined as tracts that have a poverty rate of 40 percent or higher and are commonly believed to contain the worst neighborhood effects. His regression model includes metropolitan-area mean household income, mean black income relative to overall mean income, measures of income inequality, and dissimilarity indexes to measure economic and racial segregation. The latter variable is found to have a strong and highly statistically significant effect on the percentage of blacks living in concentrated poverty.

26 For example, the Multi-City Study of Urban Inequality data identify respondents' home census tracts. Under special arrangements, tract identifiers can also be appended to the individual

records of the Panel Study of Income Dynamics, the Public Use Microdata Samples, and the American Housing Survey.

[27] The success of this program caused Congress in 1992 to fund a Gautreaux-type program, called Moving to Opportunity, which was initiated in five cities in 1994. The program encountered severe opposition in the suburbs of Baltimore, one of the five cities selected. This was all the fodder needed by opponents in Congress to kill the program after its first year.

[28] Evidence suggests that white flight from inner to outer suburban areas during the 1980s was as virulent as the white flight from central cities to inner suburban areas during the 1960s and 1970s (Ihlanfeldt, 1994).

[29] See Farley and Frey (1992), who report the 1980 and 1990 index of dissimilarity for each of 318 U.S. metropolitan areas.

Metropolitan Limits: Intrametropolitan Disparities and Governance in U.S. Laboratories of Democracy

Michael A. Pagano
Miami University, Oxford, Ohio

BACKGROUND

Defended by its architects as the best defense against tyranny and as the institutional protector of liberties (Hamilton et al., 1961), the federal system of governance in the United States also promises diversity in local government structures and services, revenue access and limits, tax rates and burdens, and outputs and outcomes. By characterizing the role of states in the U.S. federal system as "laboratories of democracy," Justice Louis Brandeis implied that state and local governments, unfettered by central-government rules and regulations, would experiment with a host of public policies—some failing and some achieving desired results. This characterization also implies spatial variations in tax policies, burdens, and services not only across states but also within and between metropolitan areas. The resulting variation in many metropolitan areas has been fragmentation in service delivery and revenue collection and disparities in tax burdens and service quality.

Studies on municipalities in the post-depression era focused on suburban-city (or central city/outside central city) disparities and attendant problems in metropolitan governance (Jones, 1942). White flight and middle-class exodus from the central cities often translated into poorer services in the central cities, higher tax burdens, and inequities resulting from central-city residents covering suburban residents' service costs during the work day. While suburban residents matched their collective preferences (especially for education, safety, and transportation) with an acceptable tax level, central-city residents shouldered the service delivery costs of suburban commuters to the central city (especially police, fire, and transportation services) in addition to the costs of their own collective preferences. More recent studies show that, as the poor are increasingly concentrated in central cities relative to their surrounding suburbs, more own-source revenues are being spent for poverty and social programs by these cities than by smaller suburban cities.[1]

In the past decade, studies have resurrected earlier calls of metropolitan governance as a mechanism for reducing intrametropolitan disparities and have raised questions about the health and vitality of the entire metropolitan region (Wallis, 1994; see also Ledebur and Barnes, 1993; Barnes and Ledebur, 1994; Savitch et al., 1993).[2] One of the more visible advocates of metropolitan government, former Albuquerque mayor David Rusk, contends that "elastic" cities (or cities that are likely to capture surrounding growth that otherwise might have become incorporated suburbs) are more likely to survive economically and politically than are "inelastic" cities (Rusk, 1993). Others argue that the economic and political survival of central cities has a profound effect on the economic and political survival of surrounding communities in the metropolitan region (see, in addition to the references above, Orfield, 1997; Pierce with Johnson and Hall, 1993; Schaefer and Schaefer, 1996; Barnes and Ledebur, 1997).

Recent commentaries on metropolitan regions, central-city poverty surrounded by wealthy suburbs, and efficient service delivery arrangements in extramunicipality regions have created a resurgence of interest in metropolitan governance and regional affairs. The purpose of this paper is to review policies and strategies that have been experimented with and whose goals include mitigating intrametropolitan disparities and enhancing metropolitan governance more generally.

REVENUE AND EXPENDITURE VARIATIONS

Before undertaking a review of those strategies, it is important to sketch briefly the diversity of local governments in the U.S. federal system. Local governments vary both in the composition of their revenue structures and in their service delivery responsibilities. Local governments in a federal system also decide on the appropriate balance between meeting the collective and individual preferences of their citizens. In some local governments, policies are decided that garner a greater share of the community's wealth to meet a comparatively higher level of collective or public needs, and in others the decision is to collect a smaller share of the community's wealth to meet more individual or private needs and demands. The tax burden in the former areas, then, is usually greater than in the latter area, other things being equal (e.g., productivity of public services).[3] As a consequence of this diversity both in access to fiscal powers and in collective needs (both of which create idiosyncratic local government fiscal policies), attempts to compare differential tax burden and services across more than 19,000 U.S. cities and more than 83,000 local governments are, if not impossible, certainly difficult. For example, a property tax rate of 10 mills in one city may generate more revenue than 10 mills in a neighboring city if the assessed value of property in the first city is its fair market value and in the second city only a fraction of fair market value, if the demand for land is greater in the first city than in the second, if the second city is a retirement center that has a circuit breaker for senior citizens, if the first city also includes personal property in the property tax base, and so on.

Moreover, local governments have increasingly turned to user charges and fees to fund their services. Between 1966-1967 and 1991-1992, local government fees and charges have increased from 23.6 percent of general own-source revenues to 36.4 percent (Table 1). At the same time, the composition of general tax revenue has also shifted substantially from little reliance on the sales tax (6.7 percent of general tax revenues) to substantially more (18.2 percent). But it is the user charge that is particularly noteworthy. It has hardly dented school district revenues (Table 2), hovering around 17 percent of own-source revenues for the past quarter-century. Beginning in the late 1970s and early 1980s, user fees and charges have surged in importance for counties from 25-30 to 40 percent of own-source revenues (Table 3), and for cities from 30 to almost 40 percent (Table 4).

Whereas virtually all city governments and most local governments are granted access to a property tax,[4] some states allow their general-purpose municipal governments access to an income tax or a sales tax. Table 5 lists local option taxing authority. According to the latest available data (1994), 4,111 local governments are authorized to levy an income tax, or nearly 25 percent more than in 1976. Yet if one excludes the 2,830 local governments in Pennsylvania, the 615 cities and school districts in Ohio, the 379 school districts in Iowa, and the 140 local governments in Kentucky that are permitted access to a local-option income or wage tax, the remaining 7 states allow only 157 of their local governments the authority to levy an income tax. Few local governments outside those four states, then, have their states' authorization to tax income or earnings. Yet 31 states allowed 6,579 local governments throughout the country access to a sales tax in 1994, up more than one-third from 1976 levels. Whereas local-option income taxes are fairly concentrated, the local-option sales tax is much more pervasive.

Furthermore, some cities and other local governments may not be permitted to increase tax rates or expenditure levels or tax levies because of state- or locally imposed tax and expenditure limitations, such as California's Proposition 13 (approved in 1978) and Proposition 218 (approved in 1996). Thus, given the enormous diversity in potential revenue structures by type of local government, by state, by local ordinances, and by citizen preferences, an unambiguous measure of revenue or tax equity within and between metropolitan areas is clearly difficult to create. Municipalities, for example, are much less dependent on property tax revenues than are school districts; counties are more dependent on

TABLE 1   Local Revenue Sources (in millions)

A. Nonconstant Dollars	1966-67	1971-72	1976-77	1981-82	1986-87	1991-92
Total General Revenue	58,235	105,243	179,045	281,045	410,347	573,255
General Revenue Own sources	38,045	65,549	102,214	164,426	254,062	357,268
—Taxes	29,074	49,739	74,852	103,783	158,216	227,099
	76.4%	75.9%	73.2%	63.1%	62.3%	63.6%
—Property tax	25,186	41,620	60,267	78,952	116,618	171,723
	86.8%	83.7%	80.5%	76.1%	73.7%	75.6%
—Individual income tax	926	2,241	3,752	5,078	7,716	11,106[a]
	3.2%	4.5%	5.0%	4.9%	4.9%	4.92%
—Sales and gross receipts	1,956	4,268	8,278	14,824	24,455	41,263
	6.7%	8.6%	11.1%	14.3%	14.3%	18.2%
—Charges and miscellaneous	8,971	15,890	27,362	60,643	95,846	130,169
	23.6%	24.2%	26.8%	36.9%	37.7%	36.4%

B. Constant Dollars	1966-67	1971-72	1976-77	1981-82	1986-87	1991-92
Total General Revenue	277,441	368,756	439,482	450,392	523,002	573,255
General Revenue Own sources	181,253	229,674	250,893	263,503	323,811	357,268
—Taxes	138,514	174,278	183,731	166,319	201,652	227,099
—Property tax	119,990	145,830	147,931	126,526	148,634	171,723
—Individual income tax	4,412	7,852	9,210	8,138	9,834	11,106[a]
—Sales and gross receipts	9,319	14,954	20,319	23,756	31,169	41,263
—Charges and miscellaneous	42,739	55,676	67,162	97,184	122,159	130,169

[a]1992-1993
Note: Deflated by state and local implicit price deflator.

TABLE 2   School District Revenues (in millions)

A. Nonconstant Dollars	1983-84	1985-86	1987-88	1989-90	1991-92
Total General Revenue	109,645	129,132	149,200	175,570	199,182
General Revenue Own sources	50,492	57,997	67,963	80,970	91,720
—Taxes	41,633 82.5%	48,040 82.8%	56,065 82.5%	65,923 81.4%	76,619 83.5%
—Property tax	40,341 96.9%	46,777 97.4%	54,611 97.4%	64,285 97.5%	74,630 97.4%
—Charges and miscellaneous	8,859 17.5%	9,957 17.2%	11,898 17.5%	15,048 18.6%	15,101 16.5%

B. Constant Dollars	1983-84	1985-86	1987-88	1989-90	1991-92
Total General Revenue	156,279	170,990	181,597	193,125	199,182
General Revenue Own sources	71,997	76,797	82,720	89,066	91,720
—Taxes	53,940	63,612	68,239	72,515	76,619
—Property tax	57,499	61,940	66,469	70,713	74,630
—Charges and miscellaneous	12,627	13,185	14,485	16,553	15,101

Note: Deflated by state and local implicit price deflator.

TABLE 3   County Revenue Sources (in millions)

A. Nonconstant Dollars	1966-67	1971-72	1976-77	1981-82	1986-87	1991-92
Total General Revenue	12,472	23,652	41,441	66,272	101,229	146,495
General Revenue Own sources	7,451	13,697	22,654	38,350	63,989	92,098
—Taxes	5,702 76.5%	10,076 73.6%	15,865 70.0%	22,917 59.8%	37,240 58.2%	54,926 59.6%
—Property tax	5,253 92.1%	8,625 85.6%	12,888 81.2%	17,711 77.3%	27,362 73.5%	40,808 74.3%
—Sales and gross receipts	*a*	*a*	*a*	3,660 16.0%	7,005 18.8%	10,155 18.5%
—Other	449 7.9%	1,452 14.3%	2,976 18.8%	886 3.9%	1,872 5.0%	2,422 4.4%
—Charges and miscellaneous	1,749 23.5%	3,619 26.4%	6,789 30.0%	15,434 40.2%	26,748 41.8%	37,171 40.4%
B. Constant Dollars	1966-67	1971-72	1976-77	1981-82	1986-87	1991-92
Total General Revenue	59,419	82,873	101,720	106,205	129,020	146,495
General Revenue Own sources	35,498	47,992	55,606	61,458	81,556	92,098
—Taxes	27,165	35,305	38,942	36,726	47,464	54,926
—Property tax	25,026	30,221	31,635	28,383	34,874	40,808
—Sales and gross receipts	*a*	*a*	*a*	5,865	8,928	10,155
—Other	2,139	5,088	7,305	1,420	2,386	2,422
—Charges and miscellaneous	8,333	12,680	16,664	24,734	34,091	37,171

a Included in "Other."
Note: Deflated by state and local implicit price deflator.

TABLE 4   City Revenue Sources (in millions)

A. Nonconstant Dollars	1962-63	1966-67	1971-72	1976-77	1981-82	1986-87	1991-92
Total General Revenue	13,127	19,204	34,937	60,921	91,459	130,217	171,618
General Revenue Own sources	10,459	14,121	23,502	36,746	59,823	92,476	123,466
—Taxes	7,934 75.9%	10,445 74.0%	17,058 72.6%	26,067 70.9%	37,077 62.0%	55,366 59.9%	75,486 61.1%
—Property tax	5,807 73.2%	7,629 73.0%	10,988 64.4%	15,657 60.1%	19,502 52.6%	27,163 49.1%	39,706 52.6%
—Sales and gross receipts	1,303 16.4%	1,673 16.0%	3,185 18.7%	5,805 22.3%	10,195 27.5%	15,598 28.2%	20,190 26.7%
—Charges and miscellaneous	2,519 24.1%	3,676 26.0%	6,445 27.4%	10,678 29.1%	22,745 38.0%	37,110 40.1%	47,980 38.9%

B. Constant Dollars	1962-63	1966-67	1971-72	1976-77	1981-82	1986-87	1991-92
Total General Revenue	71,420	91,491	122,414	149,536	146,569	165,966	171,618
General Revenue Own sources	56,904	67,275	82,348	90,196	95,870	117,864	123,466
—Taxes	43,166	49,762	59,769	63,984	59,418	70,566	75,486
—Property tax	31,594	36,346	38,500	38,432	31,253	34,620	39,706
—Sales and gross receipts	7,089	7,970	11,160	14,249	16,338	19,880	20,190
—Charges and miscellaneous	13,705	17,513	22,582	26,210	36,450	47,298	47,980

Note: Deflated by state and local implicit price deflator.

TABLE 5   States with Local Option Tax Authority for Income and Sales,
Selected Years 1976-1994

A. Local Income Taxes: Number and Type of Jurisdiction

State[a]	1976	1979	1981	1984	1985	1986
Alabama						
Cities	6	5	5	8	10	10
Arkansas						
Cities		No cities levy income taxes				
Delaware						
Cities						
(Wilmington)	1	1	1	1	1	1
Georgia						
Cities and Counties		No cities or counties levy income taxes				
Indiana						
Counties	38	37	38	43	44	45
Iowa						
School Districts	3	21	26	57	57	61
Kentucky						
Cities	59	59	59	61	67	78
Counties	—	8	8	9	11	14
School Districts						
Maryland						
Counties						
(and Baltimore City)	24	24	24	24	24	24
Michigan						
Cities	16	16	16	16	16	17
Missouri						
Cities						
(Kansas City and						
St. Louis)	2	2	2	2	2	2
New York						
Cities						
(New York City						
and Yonkers)	1	1	1	2	2	2
Ohio						
Cities	385	417	n.a.	460	467	480
School Districts	0	0	n.a.	6	6	6
Pennsylvania						
Cities, Boroughs,						
Towns, Townships,						
and School Districts	2,553[b]	2,585[b]	n.a.	2,644[b]	2,758[b]	2,777[b]
Virginia						
Cities and Counties		No cities or counties levy income taxes				
Total						
(excludes Pennsylvania)	535	597	n.a.	688	707	740
Total						
(includes Pennsylvania)	3,088[b]	3,182[b]	n.a.	3,332[b]	3,465[b]	3,517[b]

1987	1988	1989	1990	1991	1992	1994
10	10	11	11	11	11	18
1	1	1	1	1	1	1
51	68	79	79	76	80	80
57	60	52	59	144	178	379
85	81	84	83	87	86	94
25	27	26	27	27	29	39
						7
24	24	24	24	24	24	24
17	18	19	19	20	20	20
2	2	2	2	2	2	2
2	2	2	2	2	2	2
482	481	492	506	512	512	523
6	5	5	22	52	76	92
2,782[b]	2,788	2,795	2,809	2,824	2,830	2,830
763	779	797	837	873	1,021	1,281
3,545[b]	3,567	3,592	3,646	3,697	3,853	4,111

TABLE 5 Continued

B. Local Sales Taxes: Number and Type of Jurisdiction

State	1976	1979	1981	1984	1986	1987
Alabama – Total	265	301	321	353	374	382
Municipalities		270	281	310	323	326
Cities		31	40	43	51	56
Alaska – Total	86	93	92	99	97	93
Municipalities		86	85	92	91	87
Boroughs		7	7	7	6	6
Arizona – Total	38	39	59	70	75	77
Municipalities	38	39	59	70	74	75
Counties	–	–	–	–	1	2
Arkansas – Total	1	1	2	60	78	111
Municipalities	1	1	2	44	59	76
Counties		–	–	16	19	35
California – Total [c]	438	441	441	443	444	445
Municipalities		380	380	380	380	380
Counties		58	58	58	58	58
Special Districts		3	3	5	6	7
Colorado – Total	121	165	183	205	222	225
Municipalities		144	159	175	191	193
Counties		20	23	29	30	31
Transit District		1	1	1	1	1
Special District		–	–	–	–	–
Florida – Total [d]						
Counties		–	–	–	0	0
Transit District						
Georgia – Total [e]	16	84	104	133	143	144
Municipalities		3	0	0	0	0
Counties		80	103	132	142	143
Transit District		1	1	1	1	1
Illinois – Total	1,342	1,359	1,359	1,353	1,376	1,375
Municipalities		1,256	1,256	1,249	1,272	1,271
Counties		102	102	102	102	102
Transit Districts		1	1	2	2	2
Water District		–	–	–	–	–
Iowa						
Counties						
Kansas – Total	7	20	40	139	168	168
Municipalities		15	35	87	108	108
Counties		5	5	52	60	60
Louisiana – Total	183	217	251	253	287	302
Municipalities		136	152	158	177	192
Parishes		21	30	30	63	63
School Districts		60	66	65	47	47
Special Districts		7	12	18	23	23
Minnesota						
Municipalities	1	1	1	2	1	3

1988	1989	1990	1991	1993	1994
389	398	403	405	415	421
334	343	344	345	355	359
55	55	59	60	60	62
101	101	101	101	101	98
95	95	95	95	95	93
6	6	6	6	6	5
81	83	85	92	95	100
79	81	82	81	83	86
2	2	3	11	12	14
142	175	185	192	244	261
100	120	131	136	181	192
42	55	54	56	63	69
446	450	460	460	461	465
380	380	380	380	380	380
58	58	58	58	58	58
8	12	22	22	23	27
235	235	236	238	242	250
200	200	198	198	200	201
34	34	37	39	41	42
1	1	1	1	1	1
–	–	–	–	–	6
	11	23	26	39	45
10	10	21	25	38	44
	1	2	1	1	1
155	154	165	158	160	160
0	0	0	0	0	0
154	153	164	157	159	159
1	1	1	1	1	1
1,383	1,348	34	53	74	81
1,279	1,278	31	42	70	70
102	68	0	8	1	8
2	2	2	2	2	2
–	–	1	1	1	1
5	9	12	15	19	27
175	178	180	185	198	211
112	116	119	124	135	142
62	62	61	61	63	69
302	325	325	327	339	340
193	189	193	195	203	203
63	64	63	63	63	63
46	47	48	48	48	50
23	25	21	21	25	24
3	3	3	3	5	5

TABLE 5 Continued

B. Local Sales Taxes: Number and Type of Jurisdiction

State	1976	1979	1981	1984	1986	1987
Missouri – Total	152	215	333	487	556	657
Municipalities	151	214	332	406	458	474
Counties	1	1		81	98	114
Nebraska						
Municipalities	–	4	7	12	16	22
Nevada – Total	12	13	1	1	5	7
Municipalities	1	–	–	–	–	–
Counties	11	12	1	1	5	7
New Mexico – Total	32	99	84	120	134	128
Municipalities		93	76	98	101	100
Counties		6	8	22	33	28
New York – Total	68	70	74	87	81	85
Municipalities		25	29	29	27	26
Counties		45	45	57	53	58
Transit District	–	–	–	1	1	1
North Carolina						
Counties	96	99	99	100	100	100
North Dakota						
Municipalities	–	–	–	–	3	3
Ohio – Total	33	51	55	65	76	81
Municipalities		50	52	62	74	79
Counties		1	3	3	2	2
Oklahoma – Total	356	398	398	447	466	473
Municipalities	356	398	398	441	452	457
Counties	–	–	–	6	14	16
South Carolina						
Counties	–	–	–	–	–	–
South Dakota – Total	18	46	61	82	107	111
Municipalities	18	46	61	82	107	111
Indian Reservations	–	–	–	–	–	–
Tennessee	115	104	105	102	105	105
Municipalities		12	11	8	10	10
Counties		92	94	94	95	95
Texas – Total	854	946	949	1,120	1,032	1,029
Municipalities		921	921	1,117	1,026	1,023
Counties		–	–	–	–	–
Transit Districts		25	28	3	6	6
Special Districts						
Utah – Total	204	230	n.a.	248	248	248
Municipalities		201	n.a.	219	219	219
Counties		29	29	29	29	29
Transit Districts						

1988	1989	1990	1991	1993	1994
674	698	725	780	682	687
479	490	508	563	573	580
120	126	126	126	109	107
25	30	41	44	57	64
7	7	7	7	17	9
–	–	–	–	–	–
7	7	7	7	17	9
132	134	135	134	136	139
101	101	102	101	103	106
31	33	33	33	33	33
83	85	87	89	84	79
28	30	25	27	27	22
54	54	61	61	56	56
1	1	1	1	1	1
100	100	100	100	100	100
4	5	5	10	24	35
88	90	89	95	95	92
83	85	83	86	86	88
3	3	4	7	9	4
479	492	494	495	521	530
458	468	470	470	476	481
24	24	24	25	45	49
–	–	–	6	15	16
120	135	139	144	161	169
117	132	136	141	158	166
3	3	3	3	3	3
106	106	104	103	103	104
11	11	9	8	8	9
95	95	95	95	95	95
1,107	2,610	1,276	1,291	1,276	1,318
1,023	2,521	1,164	1,176	1,157	1,193
78	82	105	105	105	110
6	7	7	7	7	8
			3	7	7
258	260	251	255	260	259
222	225	222	226	228	227
29	29	29	29	29	29
7	6	n.a.	n.a.	3	3

TABLE 5 Continued

B. Local Sales Taxes: Number and Type of Jurisdiction

State	1976	1979	1981	1984	1986	1987
Virginia – Total	133	136	136	136	136	136
Municipalities		41	41	41	41	41
Counties		95	95	95	95	95
Washington – Total	300	302	302	306	305	307
Municipalities		264	264	267	266	268
Counties		38	38	39	39	39
Wisconsin						
Counties	–	–	–	–	2	12
Wyoming						
Counties	5	13	15	15	14	15
U.S. Total	4,893	5,448	5,702	6,492	6,705	6,892

– = not authorized

n.a. = not applicable

[a]Employer payroll taxes are levied in California, New Jersey, and Oregon.

[b]Estimate.

[c]Los Angeles and San Francisco impose a special gross receipts tax.

sales taxes than cities; and municipalities, in general, are diversifying their revenue structures with more income tax revenue than counties.

Ladd and Yinger (1989) propose a measure of cities' fiscal health that is premised on the diversity of city functions and their costs as well as on the variation in city taxes and tax burdens.[5] In order to facilitate comparisons across cities, they develop standardized measures of a city's revenue-raising capacity (measured as the "amount of revenue a city could raise from broad-based taxes at a selected tax burden on its residents"—p. 7) and its expenditure need (measured as the "amount [a city] must spend per capita to provide public services of average quality"—p. 8). The difference between a city's standardized revenue-raising capacity and its standardized expenditure need is a city's standardized fiscal health, which is a comparative measure of a city's fiscal health relative to the average revenue-raising capacity and average expenditure need of all cities. But, because cities operate under both differential service responsibilities and state-restricted access to own-source revenues (as well as differential policies governing state aid to local governments), Ladd and Yinger adjust their standardized measures to create realistic measures of a city's fiscal health. Their "actual fiscal health" measure, then, is the difference between the "restricted" revenue-generating capacity of a city and its "actual" expenditure need.

A city's restricted revenue-raising capacity, then, must account for not only the broad-based tax the city is allowed to levy, but also its ability to export taxes to nonresident users of the city's services in addition to the value of state grants.

1988	1989	1990	1991	1993	1994
136	136	136	136	136	136
41	41	41	41	41	41
95	95	95	95	95	95
307	305	307	307	307	308
267	266	268	268	268	269
40	39	39	39	39	39
18	24	28	40	45	47
16	19	19	23	20	23
6,955	8,814	6,155	6,438	6,431	6,579

[d]Counties may impose a tourist development or impact tax on rentals or leases of living quarters for a term of six months or less.

[e]Local school tax-specified counties are authorized to impose a local sales and use tax for educational purposes.

Source: U.S. Advisory Commission on Intergovernmental Relations, *Significant Features of Fiscal Federalism, 1995, Volume 1* (Washington, DC: U.S. ACIR, 1996).

For example, a city that is prohibited access to an earnings or income tax that can be imposed on nonresident employees who work in the city and receives little state aid will find itself in a poorer revenue-generating position than a city that is permitted access to the exportable income tax and receives generous state assistance. Without acknowledging the state-imposed revenue-generating restriction on the former city, the erroneous conclusion might be reached that both cities have the same revenue-generating capacity if measured in terms of personal income or property value.

Just as cities' (and other local governments') taxing authorities and portfolios vary, so do service delivery costs and responsibilities. States establish the service delivery responsibilities of cities through statutory or constitutional means, requiring local governments to perform certain functional activities (such as public safety) and establishing greater or lesser administrative and reporting flexibility. Provision of these activities is not uniform across the U.S. metropolitan landscape. Only a few city governments, for example, provide education, sanitation, and welfare; in contrast, police, fire, and highway functions are quite common (see, e.g., Liebert, 1976). Ladd and Yinger note the variation in costs of providing services by central cities in creating a measure of expenditure need. Arguing that, even if the outcomes of any function, such as protection, are comparable across cities, they contend that the costs of meeting those outcomes will not be identical because cities' environments differ. A given level of public safety, for example, may cost more in high-poverty cities than in low-poverty cities.

The reach of local government authority, then, is circumscribed first by state constitutional or statutory restrictions (functions and financing) and by territorial jurisdiction (space). The efficacy of city (and other local) governments in redistributive programs is mitigated by residential and firm mobility, although they can influence the growth of cities' underlying economic bases through economic development activities; that is, the effective reach of city governments is circumscribed as primarily a developmental reach (Peterson, 1981; see also Peterson, 1995; Peterson and Rom, 1990). Theory notwithstanding, cities have engaged in redistributive activities and continue to engage in such activities (for a recent study of city redistributive costs, see Summers and Jakubowski, 1996). Consequently, in the U.S. federal system, there is a veritable cornucopia of bundles of services provided by municipal and other local governments, ranging from basic safety functions of police and fire protection to complex arrays of services, including education, welfare, water and sewer, and much more.[6]

POLICY EXPERIMENTATION AND EFFECTIVENESS

Cities, other local governments, and states have experimented with a host of legal or incorporation statutes and revenue-related projects with the intent of minimizing intrametropolitan disparities in services and tax burdens and of enhancing metropolitan governance (U.S. Advisory Commission on Intergovernmental Relations, 1973; see also Bahl, 1980). The principal objective behind these approaches is either to stretch the political (corporation) boundaries of the city or to stretch the financial reach of the city to encompass the growing metropolitan area. Either way, these policies have the effect of capturing urban flight from the center of the metropolitan area and of expanding the economic tax base of the metropolitan area. Some of the more prominent legal or statutory mechanisms include city-county consolidation, annexation, two-tier governments, special-purpose governments, and tax-base-sharing arrangements.[7] Fiscal tools include equalization grants from the state government, state or county assumption of municipal functions, and cost-shifting to nonresident users and beneficiaries of city (or metropolitan) services. These experiments, the attendant impacts, and their political feasibility for other metropolitan areas are discussed in this section.

Political "Stretching" Policies

Proposals designed to alter the political reach of municipalities address issues of managerial efficiency and metropolitan disparities, but also raise important questions about space. As Charles Haar, one of the more outspoken advocates of metropolitanization, so eloquently put it a quarter-century ago (1972:1): "Perhaps the most intractable cause of political strife and misgovernment is the division of the surface of the earth into political jurisdictions. While every new boundary drawn represents the solution to a political problem, once drawn it tends to become as fixed as the constellations in the night sky. The inertia of political boundaries is evident in the enormous energies necessary to alter them and the glacial pace of changes in the jurisdictions of settled political institutions. Social and economic conditions on the other hand can change very rapidly."

In the minds of many reformers, then, metropolitan disparities in addressing social problems could be traced at their core to the artificial and oftentimes arbitrary nature of political-spatial boundaries. Reforms are also of an efficiency and good government nature. Metropolitanization and other proposals have taken aim at the corruption, inefficiency, and service redundancy of fragmented governments (see Jones, 1942; Maxey, 1922; Merriam et al., 1933).

Even if political boundaries could circumscribe metropolitan areas, unless and until those metropolitan areas remain forever static in size, the question of drawing the "best" boundaries will never be answered (see Sharpe, 1995). Only through adjusting these political boundaries at more-than-glacial speed could metropolitan areas ever hope to address the overwhelming local policy problems of transportation, education, health, and safety. Yet Harrigan (1993:358) notes that metropolitan governments are "uniformly much more successful in dealing with the *physical questions* such as sewers, water supply, or parks and recreation than they are in dealing with *social issues*" (italics added). In general, the most popular "political stretching" mechanism is creation of special districts with specific infrastructural responsibilities, which promise efficient, cost-effective service delivery. Several of these policies are examined below.

Consolidation/Fragmentation

As the "wealth" of a metropolitan area escapes the political control of the central city, cities with liberal annexation laws often capture the fleeing tax base. In Texas the designation of land surrounding an incorporated municipality as the city's "extraterritorial jurisdiction" has been instrumental in the growth of the state's municipalities in area and in fiscal capacity.[8] By way of illustration, the physical boundaries of the city of Houston, an "elastic" city according to Rusk, have grown from 328.1 square miles in 1960 to 539.9 square miles in 1990, and the city's per capita own-source revenues have increased 128 percent from $377 (in 1992 dollars) in 1960 to $861 in 1990 whereas Detroit's physical size declined slightly from 139.6 square miles in 1960 to 138.7 square miles in 1990, and its per capita own-source revenues increased 64 percent. Many older central cities are hemmed in by suburban municipalities that incorporated long ago. The political boundaries of Cleveland, Chicago, Pittsburgh, Boston, St. Louis, San Francisco, and other large, older cities have hardly changed in the past half-century, even as out-migration in some of those "inelastic" cities reached double-digit rates between postwar decennial censuses.

Consolidation proposals of the nineteenth and early twentieth century were meant to curb the excesses of corrupt, inefficient, and incompetent city administrations. Hence, consolidation advocates, like reformed city advocates, were the good government reformers who promoted professionalizing governmental administration and removing political considerations from administrators (see, e.g., Studenski, 1930). Efficiency was their calling card, and consolidating services over a broad area was expected to reap economies of scale. The good government concerns of the early reformers gave way to broader concerns in the suburbanization boom of the postwar years. Taxable wealth was fleeing the central cities, and advocates of consolidation fought to extend the noose of the cities' fiscal powers over the growth areas.

City-county consolidation gained considerable academic attention and support until the past three decades, when it was challenged in academic circles and by a nonsympathetic public; only recently has it become a viable option again. It is premised principally not only on capturing externalities of economic growth and ensuring that central-city residents are not burdened by the costs of supporting suburban commuters, but also on achieving economies of scale. Larger production units, according to this theory, can produce a unit of a public good at a lower marginal cost than smaller production units. Consequently, metropolitan-wide service delivery areas are often more efficient, and consolidation of local general-purpose governments or specific services is encouraged. In addition to the efficiency arguments, consolidation is also considered more equitable as cost-shifting to central-city residents is unlikely under uniform, county-wide tax systems. Residents in the far reaches of the county are taxed for city services, just as their central-city counterparts are. And services are to be provided equitably and fairly. Suburban county commuters, then, are to contribute to the cost of the services they consume.

Regardless of the powerful efficiency and equity arguments proffered in defense of consolidation, political acceptance of such arguments as recorded through the ballot box demonstrates a different reality. Willing to sacrifice neither their (local governments') autonomy, nor their tax dollars for perceived inner-city problems, suburban and county dwellers have routinely rejected consolidation proposals for the past four decades. In a 1972 study, Marando and Whitley report that, although there seemed to be very high interest in investigating city-county consolidations (nearly three-quarters of the electorate approved creation of consolidation charter commissions), average voter support fell to under half, and only one-third of the post-World War II proposals were approved (Marando and Whitley, 1972). According to the most recent data compiled by the National Association of Counties and updated by Durning (1995), only 22 city-county consolidations have been approved since 1921, for an approval rate of 17.6 percent. Prior to 1960, 3 of 14 proposals were approved, for an approval rate of 27.2 percent; in the 1960s, 6 of 20 were approved (30 percent); in the

1970s, 8 of 40 (16.7 percent); in the 1980s, 2 of 26 (8.3 percent); and, thus far, in the 1990s, 3 of 17 (17.6 percent)?

Even though central-city residents are often persuaded to vote for consolidation, the non-central-city dwellers usually reject it. In addition to the suburban antipathy for central-city problems, defeat of consolidation proposals also has carried a racial and ethnic dimension, a dimension that is a double-edged sword. Whereas noncity opponents are often discontent over providing more tax support for consolidation than central-city residents, it is also the case that predominantly white county voters dilute minority votes in the central city and their access to city-county government. Diluting minority voters' strength is forbidden under the 1965 Voting Rights Act, which forbids political redistricting that would deny or abridge voting rights on account of race or ethnicity. Consolidation proposals in states for which preclearance is required might contradict the Voting Rights Act if minority voting strength is diluted. For example, in 1988, the proposed consolidation of Augusta and Richmond County, Georgia, was blocked by the U.S. Department of Justice because "the dilution of Black voting strength through consolidation in Richmond County was discriminatory" (State of Texas, Senate Intergovernmental Relations Committee, 1996). In 1995, another consolidation charter for Augusta and Richmond County was precleared and became operational in 1996.

Even though anticonsolidation forces have been chided in the past few decades for the racist or class overtones to the negative suburban and county vote, arguments have been advanced in defense of fragmented metropolitan governments, and in opposition to consolidated governments (see, e.g., Kenyon and Kincaid, 1991; U.S. Advisory Commission on Intergovernmental Relations, 1992; Schneider, 1989). Fragmentation proponents have rested their defense principally on an efficiency argument, that is to say, on the same argument put forward by the proconsolidation forces. The intellectual guiding light behind the fragmented metropolitan government perspective is Charles Tiebout, who in a 1956 article argued that local governments in federal polities have incentives to behave according to market-like principles, an idea that was applied in support of fragmented metropolitan governments by Ostrom, Tiebout, and Warren in 1961 (Ostrom et al., 1961). Because citizens can migrate from jurisdiction to jurisdiction, municipalities (and other local governments) offer competitive bundles of services for a certain price (or tax). These offerings by a number of local governments, then, simulate a market in that the supply or bundle of goods must be provided and produced efficiently or demand (and the threat of migration) will move elsewhere for a more "competitive" bundle of services for a more acceptable tax price.

Empirical studies of consolidation and fragmentation efforts, which measure service delivery effectiveness and equity, are not conclusive (for a rebuttal to the study concerning Allegheny County's fragmentation by the U.S. Advisory Commission on Intergovernmental Relations, see Miller et al., 1995). Consolidation may eliminate duplicate services and improve scale economies, but often at the expense of creating a larger, less-responsive bureaucratic organization. Citizens in fragmented metropolitan areas may be no better informed to make efficient decisions than their counterparts in consolidated counties (Lyons and Lowery, 1989). In a survey of consolidation and fragmentation studies, a recent report concludes, "In all, this skimpy, mixed bag of evidence is inadequate to lead to any firm conclusions about the effect of consolidation on the quality of services provided by local government" (Carl Vinson Institute of Government, 1989:21). A recent test of the fragmentation thesis concluded that "Overall, it is found that the impact of the alternative forms of metropolitan government on the distribution of income are modest, and that the redistribution of metropolitan resources among jurisdictions resulting from fiscal fragmentation is haphazard and bears little relation to a municipality's median income" (Sacher, 1993:1225).

The dissonance between the fragmentation and consolidation forces reached an ironic point when, almost simultaneously with the publication of a study from the U.S. Advisory Commission on Intergovernmental Relations, which documented the efficiency effects of fragmented local governments in Allegheny County and St. Louis County (U.S. Advisory Commission on Intergovernmental Relations, 1993), a report was released by the St. Louis Freeholders urging more integration of the county's local governments (Phares and Louishomme, 1996). And although the evidence on "fairness" or equity of service delivery in consolidated governments tends to be anecdotal, comprehensive studies on intra-metropolitan disparities in tax burden and services are nonexistent, focusing instead on residents' satisfaction with services.

Even though results of consolidation studies appear to be contradictory, most have been undertaken in large counties. Durning notes that scale economies and administrative efficiency are more likely to accrue to fragmented local governments in large counties (> 250,000) and that efficiency gains are more likely in consolidated counties that are small (< 250,000) (Durning, 1995). In recent years consolidation proposals have become important on the political agenda of smaller metropolitan areas. During the 1960s, the average-size county voting on consolidation was 221,995; in the 1970s, it was 193,781; and during the 1980s, it was 132,234 (Durning, 1995:295). In testimony before the Texas Senate Committee on Intergovernmental Relations, Blodgett observed that there is more activity around the country in city-county consolidation in the 1990s than in previous decades and that the motivations behind those consolidation efforts, which tend to be advanced in smaller counties, are primarily for efficiency reasons.[10]

Two-Tier and Special-Purpose Governments

The checkered political success of consolidation strategies, however, does not imply that efficiency arguments have not taken hold. Indeed, the fragmentation studies note that many local governments engage in interlocal agreements for the purpose of efficiency gains from economies of scale of jointly funding and providing certain services, such as garbage collection, policing, and fire protection. Numerous examples of special-purpose governments exist in which interlocal agreements between and among governmental units legitimize their activities. These agreements are negotiated periodically and, as a consequence of continuous oversight by participating governments, are expected to result in their becoming more efficient providers of services.

Rather than wholesale consolidation of a county's local governments, some advocates argue two advantages of a selective consolidation approach. First, the consolidated service can be provided at a more efficient level and a reduced cost than if each local government provided the service independently. And second, consolidating a single function rather than all functions is responsive to citizens' desires to maintain a separate political identity.

Suburban opposition to many of the regional proposals (e.g., city-county consolidations) is partly responsible for leading reformers to consider two-tier governments, consolidating some activities and not others, and to other proposals. Transportation improvement districts, sewer districts, utility districts, and other consolidated services have supplanted wholesale general government consolidations as politically viable regional solutions to service delivery needs (Burns, 1994). One of the most visible two-tier governments is Indiana's consolidation of a few Marion County services with those of the city of Indianapolis. Unigov, as it is called, did not require voter approval by the county's residents; rather, it was created by an act of the state legislature, controlled at the time by the Republican Party. The Democratic Party, which held leadership positions in the "old" Indianapolis council, now became a minority under Unigov. Their political base thus became diluted by suburban Republicans. Yet efficiency of service delivery, the principal reason for Unigov's creation in 1969, was proclaimed its major feat even as school districts and townships (which have relief and fire protection responsibilities) remained unconsolidated, as were the four cities with populations greater than 5,000 that were statutorily excluded from the consolidation. A total of 58 agencies were consolidated into 6 departments and, according to a former director of the Department of Metropolitan Development, "more services now are being delivered per dollar than before Unigov." Further, Unigov streamlined governmental structures and reduced the number of offices developers were required to visit before permits were issued, resulting in more economic development activity (Gorton, 1978).

Nearly a quarter-century after Unigov's creation, Blomquist and Parks (1995) found that, since 1969, the wealthier suburbs have dominated the political landscape of the city-county government and that Unigov "gave suburban leaders access to the central-city base with which to pursue development projects chosen by them, not by city residents" (1995:53). Moreover, they contend that provision and production of "most local services" were unchanged. Their study, however, notes that residents of the "old" city, which still retains education and police functions, are much less satisfied with education services compared with their noncity counterparts in the county; they reach the conclusion that "residents of the pre-Unigov city could be better served by a decentralization of their police and public schools than by any merger with surrounding departments and districts" (1995:46).[11]

Special-purpose regional governments generate greater public support than general-purpose regional (consolidated) governments. Special-purpose governments are usually single-purpose districts with their own governing boards, providing a variety of region-wide services, such as water and sewer services, mass transportation, utilities, and education. The proliferation of special districts and authorities in recent decades can be attributed to both the divisible nature of the services provided and the severity of fiscal controls. With regard to the former, special districts and authorities are often formed to provide a single service, such as water services, that is financed from user charges and not with general tax revenues. These services, it is argued, ought to be self-supporting and not subsidized from the tax revenues of a general-purpose government. They can be operated much like a private business and must be responsive to shifts in consumer demands. With respect to the latter, the creation of special-purpose governments for certain service responsibilities may also be promoted for the simple purpose of removing certain responsibilities from tax and expenditure controls (Sbragia, 1996). The general-purpose government now has more fiscal capacity for the remaining functions because the newly jettisoned service no longer competes with other government functions for scarce resources.

The latest form of special district is the newly invigorated transportation regional district, metropolitan planning organizations (MPO), which were given fiscal powers under the 1991 reauthorization of the federal highway act, the Intermodal Surface Transportation Efficiency Act. Under the act, metropolitan planning organizations are given transportation funds to be disbursed on projects of regional importance. Although the jury is still out on their effectiveness and on the equity of providing transportation services throughout the region, questions have been raised about their autonomy and about the composition of their governing boards. Because representatives are not elected regionally, there still exists the distinct possibility of influencing projects with a clear suburban or anticentral-city flavor. The question, then, is whether or not metropolitan planning organizations are designed and operate with an eye toward reducing intrametropolitan disparities in service delivery and in fiscal burden (see, e.g., Gage and McDowell, 1995; Pagano, 1996; U.S. General Accounting Office, 1993).

Tax Base Sharing

Concerns that local governments within a region outbid each other in offering public subsidies to attract firms and developers, resulting in a destructive competition among municipalities, have prompted proposals that require metropolitan governments to share in the region's tax base growth or in the region's revenue growth. In this way, cities' logic to offer developer incentives is mitigated because other local governments in the region stand to benefit from one city's tax offer. The beggar-thy-neighbor approach to development, it is argued, becomes unimportant in attracting industry and development under tax base sharing.

Probably the most celebrated case of tax base sharing was initiated in 1968 by the Citizens League in the Twin Cities (Minnesota) area and voted into law by the legislature in 1971. According to the Metropolitan Fiscal Disparities Act, each year local governments in a seven-county area calculate changes in the assessed value of industrial-commercial property and contribute 40 percent of the growth to an area-wide pool. Each government receives funds from this pool, according to a formula that takes into consideration the community's population and is inversely related to its fiscal capacity, defined as per capita market value of all real property (i.e., larger cities with lower fiscal capacity receive more funds). In an early study of the Twin Cities' tax base sharing program, Reschovsky (1980) found that "in every year [between 1974 and 1979] tax base sharing has been effective in reducing fiscal disparities" (1980:63). A 1991 study by a state legislative committee concluded that, as a result of the program, fiscal disparity was "reduced to a 4-to-1 ratio of highest to lowest per capita tax base; without the program it would be 22-to-1" (as cited in Nunn and Rosentraub, 1996). Specifically, the study found that "by 1992 tax base sharing had reduced intrametropolitan inequalities in tax base by 28 percent" (cited in Chernick and Reschovsky, 1995:42).

The logic undergirding a tax base sharing approach to metropolitan governance is essentially twofold.[12] First, because communities do not reap the full fiscal benefits of economic development and expansion under tax base sharing, the fiscal imperatives to local governments offering economic incentives (e.g., property tax abatement) are mitigated. Communities within the tax base sharing region, then, do not compete with each other in giving away tax incentives. Second, tax base sharing is expected to benefit the central city of the metropolitan region due, in most cases, to the poorer economic position of the city. A simulation of the efficiency and equity gains of property tax base sharing resulted in "quite small" efficiency gains but a "major redistribution from suburban landowners to city landowners" (Zodrow, 1984:224). Whether or not this equity impact would benefit nonlandowning central-city residents, however, was not examined. But McHone contends that sharing a portion of the industrial property tax base of metropolitan regions could be redistributed without affecting the efficiency of markets for business location (McHone, 1990).

The central principle of tax base sharing is to reduce counterproductive interjurisdictional tax competition and fiscal disparity. In Montgomery County, Ohio, a voluntary tax sharing program was created in 1989 for the purpose of pooling resources for economic development programs and for promoting government equity. The program, the Economic Development/Government Equity program or ED/GE, requires a 10-year commitment from each participating municipal, village, and township government, which is then eligible to apply for economic development funds. The government equity part of the program is funded from tax base sharing. The economic development funds come from a half-cent county sales tax. The complex and politically contentious formula for the tax base sharing pool limits any one local government's contribution to 13 percent of its tax revenues, and the distribution of the pool is based on population (Pammer and Dustin, 1993; see also Nunn and Rosentraub, 1996). Because the GE portion is not distributed according to need, it is questionable whether redistributive impacts were obtained. Nunn and Rosentraub note, "in 1992, the city of Dayton [in Montgomery County] contributed more than it received, yet it had a higher poverty level than many other participating jurisdictions" (1996:96).

Indeed, the question of whether or not intrametropolitan disparities can be reduced through tax base sharing is premised on the distribution formula. In the Twin Cities case, the city of Minneapolis has been a net contributor to the pool since 1984 due to a commercial real estate boom because, like the GE formula in Montgomery County, the Twin Cities' "distribution formula does not at all reflect the higher costs of providing public services in central cities" (Chernick and Reschovsky, 1995:31). Nevertheless, as a mechanism for reducing intrametropolitan disparities between the wealthiest and the poorest communities in the region, and not just for redistributing wealth to the central city, the Twin Cities program has been an unqualified success.

Political Feasibility

Consolidation and annexation tools may enhance regional governance, diminish intrametropolitan disparities, and improve efficient service delivery, but they may also marginalize minority voters in the central city. Cities in states that must submit any alterations in existing political boundaries to the U.S. Department of Justice for preclearance know the importance of not diluting minority voter strength. Eisinger (1980) noted that the first attempt at consolidation in Nashville-Davidson County in 1952 (which eventually was successful in 1962, prior to passage of the Voting Rights Act) was marked by white proponents' claims that black political power in Nashville would be diluted (the same race argument was used by whites in Newport News, Virginia, and the consolidation proposal was overwhelmingly rejected by African Americans a few years later). For minority voters in central cities, there must be a perception that their voice will not be muted by an overwhelmingly nonminority majority council. Suburban voters, especially in states where the U.S. Department of Justice is looking over their shoulders, will need a sufficient incentive to consolidate their tax base with the central city's.

There appears to be a resurgence in interest in consolidation (and in reformed county governments, discussed below) in the 1990s, a resurgence that Wikstrom attributes to the popular reception of Rusk's work (Wikstrom, 1997). The imperative behind these consolidations, especially in smaller counties, does not appear to be a concern for reducing intrametropolitan disparities—except that residents of the consolidated government still expect a "fair" level of services. Rather, the political imperative is to increase efficient and effective service delivery. Augusta-Richmond County and Lafayette City-Parish mergers have recently been implemented, and Florence-Boone County (KY), Durham-Durham County (NC), Las Vegas-Clark County (NV), Gainesville-Hall County (FL), San Antonio-Bexar County (TX) are considering consolidation.

Yet, except for these notable cases, there is greater interest throughout the nation to consolidate specific services, rather than all services, through interlocal agreements that are negotiated periodically or through the process of legally creating special districts. Interlocal agreements and special districts, encompassing areas larger than the central city and often nearly as large as the metropolitan area, appear to be the political action of choice. From 21,264 in 1967, the number of special districts has climbed to 29,532 in 1992. Most of these functions are either "household" functions, such as garbage collection, fire protection, policing, tax collection activities, payroll, cemeteries, drainage and flood control, and planning, or infrastructure activities, such as transportation improvement districts, water supply, municipal utility districts, metropolitan planning organizations, and the like. They tend not to be social services. Whether or not regional governance will ever reduce social disparities within metropolitan areas, Grigsby contends that "as long as [regional governments'] primary function is to provide infrastructure capacity and implement federal or state regulatory mandates, it will receive tacit support from local municipalities and contribute little to the growing problem of regional inequalities" (Grigsby, 1996:57).

Tax base sharing, as another political stretching device, may seem more politically palatable in regions that experience acute intraregional competition. Yet Mikesell counters that tax base sharing implies a surrender of fiscal independence: "if city identity and autonomy of choice are critical elements of city futures, it is no surprise that regional base sharing has not spread beyond its few implementations" (Mikesell, 1993:44). In order to avoid the popular conception of giving away the store to developers and others, the logic of tax base sharing may become persuasive, so long as the political obstacles can be overcome. If the suburbanites' cynicism that they can and should help the cities does not wane, nor does the central-city residents' fears of diminution in their political power, it is unlikely that regional governance will make much headway in the future (although a few successes are noteworthy, precisely because they have been created in smaller counties). And state intervention requiring consolidation without local voter approval, say, in the manner that Unigov was created in Marion County, would certainly be politically contentious. Coordination and cooperation in more circumscribed service delivery arenas of regional governance might be more successful politically than wholesale consolidation.

Fiscal "Stretching" Policies

Although experiments in regional governance have not been attempted uniformly throughout the federal landscape, all states have to a greater or lesser extent engaged in financial support of their local governments for the express purpose of supporting low-income or low-capacity jurisdictions. In 1992, state expenditures to local governments amounted to $197.7 billion, or $777 per capita, ranging from a low of $108 per capita for Hawaii (or 0.5 percent of personal income) to a high of $1,398 per capita for Wyoming (or 7.5 percent of personal income) (U.S. Advisory Commission on Intergovernmental Relations, 1995). States have also assigned a dissimilar set of service delivery responsibilities to their local governments, ranging from, in the case of public education, Hawaii's single statewide school system to the 1,053 school districts in Texas. And local governments, as legal creatures of their respective states, are limited constitutionally and statutorily in the composition of their revenue structures.

In this section, state grants to local government jurisdictions are examined, followed by a brief discussion of state assumption of local services. Finally, an extensive assessment of a regional fiscal policy tool, an earnings or commuter tax, is presented.

Grants-in-Aid, Fiscal Equalization

States provide a substantial portion of local government funding, amounting to $206.1 billion in 1992-1993, or 34.2 percent of total local government general revenues (Bureau of the Census, 1995). Although states often distribute funds without concern for disparities in local government need, variation in revenue generating among a state's local governments has prompted creation of state aid programs, some of which are distributed on the basis of need. Attempts to address fiscal disparities and service delivery inequities are widespread (see Liebschutz, 1989; Bradbury et al., 1984). Disparities in revenue-generating potential derive not only from variations in a local government's underlying economic well-being, but also from its legal access to revenue structures. States establish the constitutional or statutory parameters around tax and fee structures. Some revenue sources are simply unavailable (e.g., local governments in most states do not have access to an income or earnings tax) or constrained (e.g., local governments frequently have their ability to issue debt limited by a dollar amount on debt outstanding or by the tax rate for debt retirement or by a fixed percentage of assessment value). For example, only 13 states do not set limits on local government property taxes; 31 establish rate limits, 14 require revenue rollbacks, and 8 put limits on assessment (Mackey, 1997:Table 7).

Aid to local governments in many states is premised on their expenditure need or resource need and is designed to reduce fiscal disparities among local governments (Gold and Erickson, 1988). In theory, then, a state grant might be based on how much a city or other local government would spend for a given output or workload if it spent at the average level for all cities or local governments. Local governments with a low residential base but a high employee base, then, might be compensated at a higher rate than other governments. Most equalization-like state grants for local governments are designed to target those areas in most "need" as a means to offset fiscal disparities across local governments. These needs are operationalized in a variety of ways, ranging from fiscal definitions of need (e.g., fiscal effort and debt burden) to social definitions of need (e.g., percentage in poverty) (for various definitions of need, see, e.g., Pelissero, 1984; U.S. Advisory Commission on Intergovernmental Relations, 1985).

Oakland, who generally opposes equalization grants, concedes that equity might be addressed through equalization grants but argues that efficiency would be worse (Oakland, 1994a). One reason is that equalization grants and other grants based on need ignore economies of scale (see Ladd, 1994:45). Furthermore, an equalization grant based on revenue or expenditure need sets all points of comparison at the mean, negating the prospects that cities choose to provide a locally distinct bundle of services at a locally determined tax (due to tax and service heterogeneity across cities). And the formulae for disbursing equalization grants ignore the quality of local public services, focusing instead on the costs (Oakland, 1994b).

Most studies on the efficiency and equity impacts of equalization or needs-based grants analyze a single government function, schools. In 1971, the year of the *Serrano* decision in California, 10 states used flat grants to finance public education; today only 1 does. Two-thirds of all states now have adopted public school equalization formulae (or "foundation" grants) for the express purpose of increasing per-pupil state aid to school districts with poor revenue-raising capacity (Evans et al., 1997). The taxable wealth of the school district and the number of recipients (students) rather than the property tax rate determines the state's aid to school districts. Equalization grants are designed explicitly as redistributive grants by linking the value of the grant to the taxable base of the district and to the district's tax effort. Increasing the state's matching rate as a school district's taxable base declines ensures that poorer districts receive higher per pupil grants given a similar tax effort. Reschovsky argues that, although fiscal equalization for school districts via this method achieves taxpayer equity, it does not guarantee adequate spending (Reschovsky, 1994). Differences in the composition of school-age children in a district, such as a higher than average proportion of disadvantaged or disabled students, may require funds to be shifted to meet those needs, rendering less than adequate the total spending levels for students without special needs.

Regardless of the equity merits that underlie equalization grants, even the advocates are skeptical that states will be successful in creating and implementing these redistributive programs for at least two reasons: (1) political obstacles and (2) perverse incentives in some equalization formulae. Ladd argues that any equalization strategy that penalizes wealthy communities (and reduces their aid) lacks political viability (Ladd, 1994). And equalization grants that are designed to supplement locally generated revenues for local government functions may engender a local backlash. Higher-income voters may become less supportive of tax levies for the aided function and may shift their preferences to private services (e.g., higher demand for private education), thereby potentially increasing inequity.[13] Reschovsky likewise concludes that attempts to equalize per pupil spending will fail for political reasons (revolt of the "haves") and that full state funding will lead to equality of spending but will come at the price of the loss of local discretion. The "perverse incentive" reason, especially in equalization grants for education, is that states that reward special needs students may be inefficient because there are no incentives to operate efficiently. If such programs were efficient, it would result in a decline in state funding. In other words, schools receive more per pupil funding for special needs students, encouraging schools not to improve their educational attainment (Reschovsky, 1994).

State/County Assumption

As creatures of their states, local governments' operations can be influenced by state directives but can be controlled by state assumption. Historically, states intervened in the affairs of their local governments when the state concluded that corruption and ineptitude were rampant, especially with municipal police forces, and also when the local governments were experiencing fiscal difficulties. Contemporary state assumption of local government operations is motivated usually by either ineffective administration or poor fiscal capacity (Berman, 1995).

State assumption of local government authority can take the form of direct operation or oversight. Although invoked infrequently in this century, most state takeovers in recent years have been directed at local school districts. As a mechanism for alleviating onerous fiscal demands, especially for cities and school districts with high concentrations of impoverished and low-income populations and with unattractive business sites, some argue that the state ought to assume some local government functions. O'Cleireacain proposed that one mechanism for helping cities in poor fiscal condition is a state takeover of certain responsibilities (welfare, especially) and that a policy modeled on a logical sorting out of government responsibilities be pursued (O'Cleireacain, 1993; for support of the state takeover position, see Ladd and Yinger, 1989). This proposal is premised on Musgrave's and Peterson's framework (Musgrave, 1959; Peterson, 1981), noting that the spillover benefits and costs of redistributive functions ought to be absorbed by another level of government with broader spatial jurisdiction (such as the state or federal government), or at least the costs of such activities should not be the sole province of the city. That some cities—New York is the most notable example—are required by their respective states to assume redistributive responsibilities increases the likelihood of intrametropolitan disparities.

Larger central cities provide more unreimbursed social services to their residents than smaller cities and suburban cities, according to recent studies. The resulting intrametropolitan disparities (primarily in the form of a higher tax burden for residents of larger cities) might be addressed by the state's assuming, or reimbursing the costs of, those redistributive functions that contribute to the disparities. An option short of state assumption is to expand the authority and professionalism of county government. Responsibilities traditionally associated with cities could be shifted to the counties, reducing cities' fiscal burdens and enhancing the county's capacity to deliver certain services to its residents fairly (for a discussion of strengthening county governments, see Harrigan, 1993).

The 1990-1992 recession was an important catalyst for thinking through the "sorting out" issue of which functions ought to be state responsibilities and which functions ought to be local responsibilities. Gold and Ritchie documented these shifts in a series of reports (Gold and Ritchie, 1992, 1993). In 1991, for example, Maryland assumed responsibility for Baltimore's jail, Idaho covered some costs of county indigent health care, and North Dakota expanded state expenses for local courts. The motivation for state assumption of local responsibilities was primarily fiscal, although not necessarily to improve the local fisc. Indeed, states at times devolve responsibilities to local governments as a means of helping the states' fiscal conditions.

States often provide county residents the option of reforming county government, which can mean enhancing the power of the county's chief executive or requiring city-county negotiations for revenue or assuming city functions or exchanging functional responsibilities (see Thomas and Boonyapratuang, 1993; Marando and Reeves, 1993; Sokolow, 1993). While Harrigan considers city-county consolidation problematic in a political sense, he observes that strengthening county governments has become more important over the past few decades and expects it to continue (Harrigan, 1993).

Commuter Tax/Payroll Tax

As proof that city-suburban disparities have increased in the past decade, Chernick and Reschovsky (1995:10-11) found that, "In Chicago in 1960 the ratio of per capita income in the city relative to the income in Chicago's suburbs was 0.86. By 1989 this ratio declined to 0.66. Similarly, in New York, the ratio fell from 0.84 to 0.68. The declining average income of city residents has adverse effects on central city fiscal capacity. As cities' population becomes increasingly poor, cities' tax bases usually shrink."

They also argue that central-city/suburban fiscal differentials are exacerbated because jobs are moving to the suburbs, suburban residents work at high-paying jobs in the cities, and higher-skilled workers are getting paid more relative to lower-skilled workers. Thus, cities that depend on the property tax for their revenues are becoming increasingly more fiscally stressed. This is a true statement, indeed; unless, of course, cities that are becoming increasingly poor are maintaining high-income employment opportunities and those high-income employees can be taxed at their place of work rather than at their place of residence. In other words, a tax on the income or wages of those high-income suburban residents who work in the city might address the problem of fiscal disparity. Indeed, Chernick and Reschovsky conclude that one way to restructure the metropolitan fiscal system would be "to expand reliance on payroll or income taxes which are payable in the jurisdiction where income is earned" (1995:36-37).

Ladd and Yinger conclude their study on fiscal disparities by noting that states can better help their municipalities' fiscal position through fiscal institutional means rather than through grants-in-aid. In particular, they advocate two institutional mechanisms: (1) shift certain service provision responsibilities to the states (as noted above) and, more important, (2) allow cities to export their tax burden through a commuter tax. They argue, "the potential for exporting tax burdens to nonresidents is greater with an earnings tax than with any tax the cities actually employ" (Ladd and Yinger, 1989:300).

The import of their argument is certainly not new to legislators of the nation's capital. Over two decades ago, in 1976, a bill was introduced in Congress allowing the District of Columbia government access to a "commuter tax," a 1.5 percent tax on income earned in the District. Defended as analogous to a state income tax, proponents argued that for tax purposes the Congress should grant the District similar authority that states have; moreover, they argued it should be approved because it was equitable. Stewart McKinney (D-CT), the sponsor of the legislation, argued (U.S. Congress, House, 1976:10): "When the city stops functioning as an economically viable entity, there will cease to be a reason for suburbs to exist. Suburbs exist only because cities do. The jobs which generate the income which supports the suburban community are there because the city is there. I introduced this proposal because I think it is necessary for the well-being of the entire Washington metropolitan area." Then-Mayor Walter Washington lamented that 59 percent of the income earned in the city was earned by nonresidents (approximately $199 million) and 55 percent of the city's real property was tax exempt (approximately $123 million) (U.S. Congress, House, 1976:18, 57).

The idea of a commuter tax is raised frequently and advocated ardently by many scholars (witness the recent call for a D.C. commuter tax 20 years after Mayor Washington's). Gilbert's evaluation of property tax-sharing schemes, for example, concluded that the benefits of shared property taxes would be relatively small and that "the most effective ways to reduce central city fiscal strains are shifting from local property tax financing to personal income tax financing at the regional and especially at the state level" (Gilbert, 1979:688). Based on the Ladd and Yinger measures, the cities with the greatest revenue-raising capacity (measured by the proportion of total revenues that can be exported to nonresidents) are, not surprisingly, in the state with the most progressive municipal earnings tax. Cleveland's actual revenue-raising capacity was 1.41 and Dayton's was 1.59 in 1982, much higher than their potential (Ladd and Yinger, 1989:142-143). Sometimes proposed as part of an "income-with-tax-exporting" scheme (Ladd, 1994), it is a glaring omission in the literature on intrametropolitan disparities that no systematic study has been undertaken of municipalities and metropolitan regions in the only state (Ohio) with nearly unbridled access to the income tax.[14]

In 1957, the Ohio General Assembly passed Senate Bill 133, which was primarily due to the work and support of legislators from urban areas. The bill was proposed by a senator from Cincinnati and support for the legislation seemed to run along urban lines, particularly in the Senate. There the legislation passed 24-5 (with 5 abstentions) with a majority (nearly 60 percent) of the affirmative votes coming from legislators representing urban areas within the state. Ohio's municipal income tax is a 1 percent tax on wages, salaries, and other compensation earned by residents and nonresidents who work in the municipality. The rate may exceed 1 percent only with a vote of the people. A municipality may grant partial or full credit to its residents for income taxes paid to their municipality of work, although it is not legally required to grant credit to residents. As a consequence, in the absence of an interlocal credit agreement, a taxpayer living in a suburb of Cincinnati who works in the city of Cincinnati may pay a 2.1 percent Cincinnati income tax in addition to her 1 percent tax to the suburban municipality. In 1995, 233 cities and 292 villages (under 5,000 population) collected $2,515,317,037 in local income taxes (the city portion was $2.4 billion and the village portion was $163 million) (data from Ohio Department of Taxation).

In an advocacy report published in 1959 by the Research Bureau of Akron's Chamber of Commerce, the authors present a strong case for adopting the income tax (Akron Chamber of Commerce, 1959). The report noted that, if a 1 percent income tax were enacted, the municipal income tax might yield $8-10 million. By 1995, the rate was 2 percent and yielded $80.5 million for the city. The portion attributable to nonresidents, however, is not known. Indeed, nonresident contributions to a city's finances are not collected systematically statewide. The city of Toledo estimates that 25.1 percent of total income tax collections for the city are from nonresidents. In 1995, for example, of the $129 million collected (the tax rate is 2.25 percent), the city shifted $32 million in city government costs to nonresidents. Columbus, which levies a 2 percent income tax, generated income tax revenues of $290 million in 1994 with approximately $72.5 million derived from nonresidents. Unfortunately, neither Toledo nor Columbus can accurately track the personal income or social status of the nonresident contributors for purposes of assessing the distributional impact of the income tax. Like most cities in Ohio, Toledo and Columbus do not have a mandatory city filing system that could identify individual contributors and their total income.

For states that are contemplating the adoption of a local-option income tax that can be exported to nonresidents, a caveat is in order. Substantial differential income tax burdens (or tax burdens more generally) between central-city and suburban locations may create a disincentive to locate or reside in the central city. Cities with the authority to levy an income tax are less likely to be viewed negatively as a place of residence or business if the surrounding suburban municipalities also impose an income tax of similar value, as is the case in Ohio, in which nearly all municipalities over 5,000 population levy at least a 1 percent income tax. Cities that export too much tax burden to nonresidents, however, might be disadvantaged as places of residence and business. However, empirical studies on precisely what is "too much" are lacking.

Political Feasibility

Although there are persuasive theoretical reasons for designing state policies that mitigate intrametropolitan disparities, the empirical evidence shows that state beneficence does not manifest itself in times of economic downturns (see the argument linking state aid and business cycles by Gold and Erickson, 1988). State aid for local governments, especially for general-purpose local governments, tends to decline during times of anemic state fiscal performance. The recession earlier this decade and the severe recession of the early 1980s saw states adjusting their budgets by holding the line or cutting state aid to local governments, at a time when local governments were in need. Furthermore, although state equalization grants for elementary and secondary education are designed with a needs component, in general, "state aid is not very responsive to city need" (Morgan and Shih, 1991:67).

Even though tax base sharing may be more politically palatable than consolidation, the number of metropolitan areas that have experimented with the policy is limited. The conditions under which tax base sharing can be adopted have not been examined except in an ad hoc fashion, and they seem to rest on a perception that destructive competition among local governments has led to unsupportable levels of government subsidy to firms. Once local government officials believe that their municipality or township might be next to see a business migrate to the neighboring jurisdiction, then calls for cooperation through tax base sharing are issued. Nevertheless, it is questionable whether local government need can be designed into the sharing formula in a politically acceptable fashion, that is, defined in a way that would redistribute resources from the more desirable locations in the tax base sharing area to the least desirable (usually the central cities). In the two examples cited above, questions about the distribution formulae were raised by some analysts (definitions of needs in equalization formulae are discussed in U.S. Advisory Commission on Intergovernmental Relations, 1964). In Minnesota, one study noted the high service costs of Minneapolis; in Ohio, the report noted Dayton's high poverty population. Neither formula includes those measures of need. Indeed, although studies demonstrate that the Twin Cities tax base sharing scheme has reduced intrametropolitan disparities, political agreement among local jurisdictions on what to include in the distribution formula can be expected to be difficult if one jurisdiction feels it is ceding too much.

Although a municipal income tax is probably the most effective fiscal stretching policy for reducing intrametropolitan disparities, as long as suburban legislators hold sway in state capitols, a municipal income tax that taxes income at the place of employment has a low probability of being adopted.[15] Until and unless suburban legislators come to the realization that their economic lifeline is dependent in some important and meaningful way on the central city's health and vitality, the prospects of approving municipal income tax legislation that can effectively tax their residents twice is remote. Moreover, if a local income tax is levied by only the central city and not by surrounding municipalities, a locational disincentive may work against the central city, potentially exacerbating, rather than reducing, intrametropolitan disparities.

GAPS IN OUR UNDERSTANDING OF METROPOLITAN DISPARITIES

Policies directed at reducing intrametropolitan disparities are fraught with political difficulties. The key to successful adoption and implementation of any of the policies discussed above is that the participatory process of working through metropolitan area-wide issues must be legitimate, an issue not pursued in this paper (Dodge, 1996). The policies identified above have been designed with an objective of reducing, or at least addressing, intrametropolitan disparities either through stretching the political reach of central cities to a larger metropolitan area or through stretching their fiscal reach.

Future research on reducing intrametropolitan disparities needs to address at least the following issues that have, thus far, been overlooked or slighted in studies: (1) local government revenue structure diversification and changing measures of taxpayer burden, (2) the effect of proliferating residential community associations on service delivery and on taxpayer burden, and (3) defining the territorial limits of metropolitan areas.

Revenue Structures

At a time in the evolution of U.S. local governments when they were highly dependent on a general tax (principally an ad valorem tax on land and structures) to fund their services and activities, a tax measure might have been an appropriate indicator of comparative equity. Revenue structure diversification, especially in user charges over the past two decades, calls into question the public policy utility of such a measure. Efforts to standardize measures of fiscal health certainly move in the direction of cross-metropolitan fiscal comparisons, but the indices often rely on government tax structures (and often the property tax) at a time when local governments have become more independent of the property tax—the major exception is school districts, however. These outmoded measures limit the reach of the analysis. A better measure of fiscal burden, which would necessarily include the full cost of all publicly provided services to each user or resident, adjusted for each citizen's ability to pay, needs to be developed.

Although there is both an equity and efficiency argument for charging non-residents for services consumed in the central city, such as public safety (police and fire), transportation (streets and bridges), parks, and other amenities, the export potential of city revenue structures may need to be reexamined. For example, cities that rely primarily on a property tax to finance their activities may not be shifting the full cost of service delivery to nonresident consumers (employees and visitors), whereas cities that attach a fee or charge to city services may be capturing revenue from nonresidents. Cities with an earnings or commuter tax, however, may be exporting this tax to a low-income nonresident, thus potentially violating horizontal equity among similarly situated income earners who live in separate political jurisdictions in the same metropolitan region. This line of research would build on the already substantial body of literature that examines the mismatch hypothesis (see, among others, the paper by Ihlanfeldt in this volume). The purpose would be to extend the analysis to include the tax equity and service delivery issues in the metropolitan area. Are jobs located in municipalities that impose a fiscal barrier (tax equity) or a service barrier (e.g., transportation systems) on workers?

The Role of Quasi-Local Governments in Intrametropolitan Disparity

Increasingly, residential community associations are created as providers of traditional government services within municipal boundaries (see McKenzie, 1994; Dilger, 1992; U.S. Advisory Commission on Intergovernmental Relations, 1989). Nearly 30 million Americans reside in housing under the control of residential community associations, with an undetermined number who are also citizens of a municipal corporation. The proliferation of residential community associations in the past decade, and the projection that by the year 2000 there will be approximately 225,000 common-interest developments, or CIDs as they are formally known, raise a number of questions for reducing intrametropolitan disparities. First, because residential community associations have quasi-governmental powers to tax (all property owners are required to contribute an annual fee), residents of these communities who reside within the political boundaries of municipal corporations are receiving in many cases a higher level of services than other residents. Studies of metropolitan service delivery levels and tax burdens routinely ignore these "add-on" services, even when they duplicate or add to existing municipal and local government services (e.g., policing, sanitation, street sweeping, zoning enforcement). Without the cost of these "voluntary" contributions, average taxes per capita (a surrogate measure in Ladd/Yinger and other studies for revenue-raising capacity), understate actual contributions for service delivery because these measures do not include contributions to residential community associations. Consequently, without factoring these contributions to a quasi-local government into the measures of fiscal health or disparity, studies that conclude that local services tend to be provided equitably regardless of neighborhood income might not be entirely accurate. Although indicators of tax burden and of service consumption might suggest a pattern of equity, ignoring the nontax contributions to quasi-governmental services (e.g., rental security agencies, additional garbage collection and street sweeping, zoning enforcement) may skew the analysis considerably. The preponderance of residential community associations in suburban municipalities compared with their presence in central cities might make the intrametropolitan disparities in services and in financial burden between central-city and non-central-city residents substantial.

Space and Mobility in a Federal System

Policies on stretching political boundaries and fiscal boundaries are built around the immutable fact that federal republics are layered with overlapping governments, each of which exercises authority within a finite space. Unlike the India model, in which state boundaries change as migratory patterns and settlements change, political boundaries in the U.S. federal system change only at glacial speed, if at all. How a metropolitan region has become defined, then, tends to rely on fixed political boundaries that may or may not reflect any one person's understanding of today's "real" boundary (see also Warren, 1974). As Haar questioned long ago, why should geopolitical service delivery regions be expected to remain static?

Metropolitan reform through consolidation or two-tier governments or tax base sharing may address some concerns over intrametropolitan disparities, but the policies also have a downside, namely, their dependence on fixed political boundaries. Counties were carved out of states as administrative units designed to be accessible to the people, and their boundaries rarely change. But metropolitan development does not confine itself to the niceties of boundary drawings. Migration and settlement patterns can easily step over those boundaries and remove themselves from the control of consolidated service delivery districts. Not only has this happened to nineteenth- and twentieth-century American municipal corporations via railroads, trolleys, buses, and automobiles, but it is also happening in the late twentieth century to regional corporations. Pierce reports that Metro Toronto, the two-tier municipal governmental system in Canada (which became a unified city in 1998 under Bill 103 of the Province of Ontario, The City of Toronto Act of 1997), now contains only slightly more than half the total metropolitan population; ditto for Indianapolis and Unigov. His lament is that "[t]here's no single regional leadership to plot economic advances, to speak out for mass transit or other measures to prepare Indianapolis for the 21st century" (Pierce, 1996:2654). In other words, population growth has already leapfrogged over Metro Toronto's and Unigov's legal boundaries, exacerbating the prospects once again for intrametropolitan disparities.

FINAL NOTE

Municipal government reform movements in the past were motivated by political or economic crisis. The corruption of cities in the late nineteenth and early twentieth centuries provided much grist for the reform mill; the economic and fiscal pressures on central cities in the post-depression era did the same. Nevertheless, the powers to change municipal and metropolitan government boundaries rest with states, which have the power to create and alter local governments, and in some cases with local citizens, who have the voting power to make regional governance a reality or not. The prospects of an affirmative action toward metropolitan governance at either place is remote, so long as state legislatures do not represent cities' interests and so long as suburban residents see no relationship between their corporate welfare and the welfare of their central-city brethren (on this point, see especially Orfield, 1997). Enlightened leadership at the state and local level, coupled with persuasive models of regional governance, might overcome the political resistance to political and fiscal stretching policies designed to reduce intrametropolitan disparities.

Peterson persuasively reminds us that a city's influence is severely circumscribed by the space over which it operates and has legal jurisdiction (Peterson, 1981). His observation on the limits or reach of city government control extends to metropolitan or regional governments as well. Just as states limit the reach of municipalities, so are the spatial and legal limits of metropolitan or regional governments also controlled by the states. Federal systems with inelastic local-government political boundaries will eventually confront the fiscal and economic realities of shifting populations. Mobility within and among metropolitan regions has implications for reducing or exacerbating intrametropolitan disparities. The challenge to policy makers at the state and metropolitan levels is to build public support around political and fiscal stretching policies that address the broad issues of intrametropolitan disparities without compromising the objectives of a federal system.

ACKNOWLEDGMENTS

I am indebted to Hal Wolman, Julian Wolpert, Alan Altshuler, other committee members, and anonymous reviewers for comments on an earlier draft of this paper. I would also like to thank Richard Campbell and Dan Durning of the Carl Vinson Institute of Government at the University of Georgia for contemporary information on consolidation efforts. The research assistance of Pam Van

Zwaluwenburg is gratefully acknowledged, as is the able assistance of Andrew Dudas, who researched the section on Ohio's municipal income taxes.

REFERENCES

Akron Chamber of Commerce, Bureau of Research
  1959   Municipal Income Tax Study: A Revenue Study of the City of Akron, Ohio.
Bahl, Roy
  1980   Alternative approaches to regional financing of urban public services. Pp. 447-469 in *Financing the Metropolis*, Kent Mathewson and William B. Neenan, eds. New York: Praeger.
Bahl, Roy, Jorge Martinez-Vazquez, and David J. Sjoquist
  1992a   Central city-suburban fiscal disparities. *Public Finance Quarterly* (October) 20(4):420-432.
  1992b   City finances and the national economy. *Publius: The Journal of Federalism* (Summer) 22(3):49-66.
Barnes, William R., and Larry C. Ledebur
  1994   *Local Economies: The U.S. Common Market of Local Economic Regions.* Washington, DC: National League of Cities.
  1997   *The New Regional Economies: The U.S. Common Market and the Global Economy.* Thousand Oaks, CA: Sage Publications.
Bell, Michael
  1994   Tax-base sharing revisited: Issues and options. Pp. 151-173 in *Fiscal Equalization for State and Local Government Finance*, John E. Anderson, ed. Westport, CT: Praeger.
Berman, David R.
  1995   Takeovers of local governments: An overview and evaluation of state policies. *Publius: The Journal of Federalism* (Summer) 25(3):55-70.
Blomquist, William, and Roger B. Parks
  1995   Fiscal, service, and political impacts of Indianapolis-Marion County's Unigov. *Publius: The Journal of Federalism* (Fall) 25(4):37-54.
Bradbury, Katharine L., Helen F. Ladd, Mark Perrault, Andrew Reschovsky, and John Yinger
  1984   State aid to offset fiscal disparities across communities. *National Tax Journal* (June) 37(2):151-170.
Bureau of the Census
  1995   Government Finances. Washington, DC: U.S. Bureau of the Census.
Burns, Nancy
  1994   *The Formation of American Local Governments.* Oxford: Oxford University Press.
Carl Vinson Institute of Government, Government Research and Services Division
  1989   *The Impacts of City-County Government Consolidations: A Review of Research Findings.* Athens, GA: University of Georgia.
Chernick, Howard, and Andrew Reschovsky
  1995   *Urban Fiscal Problems: Coordinating Actions Among Governments.* Madison, WI: LaFollette Institute of Public Affairs.
Dilger, Robert Jay
  1992   *Neighborhood Politics: Residential Community Associations and American Governance.* New York: New York University Press.
Dodge, William
  1996   *Regional Excellence: Governing Together to Compete Globally and Flourish Locally.* Washington, DC: National League of Cities.

Durning, Dan
  1995   The effects of city-county government consolidation. *Public Administration Quarterly*
          (Fall):272-298.
Eisinger, Peter
  1980   *The Politics of Displacement.* New York: Academic Press.
Evans, William N., Sheila E. Murray, and Robert M. Schwab
  1997   Schoolhouses, courthouses, and statehouses After *Serrano. Journal of Policy Analysis
          and Management* (Winter) 16(1):10-31.
Fischel, William
  1989   Did *Serrano* cause Proposition 13? *National Tax Journal* (December) 42(4):465-474.
Fuchs, Ester R.
  1992   *Mayors and Money: Fiscal Policy in New York and Chicago.* Chicago: University of
          Chicago Press.
Gage, Robert W., and Bruce McDowell
  1995   ISTEA and the role of MPOs in the new transportation environment. *Publius: The Jour-
          nal of Federalism* (Summer) 25(3):133-154.
Gilbert, D.A.
  1979   Property tax base sharing: An answer to central city fiscal problems. *Social Science
          Quarterly* (March) 59(4):681-689.
Giles, Michael
  1993   The Atlanta Project: A community-based approach to solving urban problems. *National
          Civic Review* 82 (Fall):354-362.
Gold, Steven D., and Brenda M. Erickson
  1988   *State Aid to Local Governments in the 1980s.* Denver: National Conference of State
          Legislatures.
Gold, Steven, and Sarah Ritchie
  1992   State policies affecting cities and counties in 1991. *Public Budgeting & Finance* (Spring)
          12(1):23-46.
  1993   State policies affecting cities and counties in 1992. *Public Budgeting & Finance* (Spring)
          13(1):3-18.
Gorton, Tom
  1978   Unigov: Can a partial merger be a total success? *Planning* (April/May) 44(4):16-20.
Grigsby, J. Eugene III
  1996   Regional governance and regional councils. *National Civic Review* (Spring-Summer)
          85(2):57.
Gyourko, Joseph, and Anita A. Summers
  1997   A new strategy for helping cities pay for the poor. *Brookings Policy Brief 18.* Washing-
          ton, DC: Brookings Institution.
Haar, Charles
  1972   Introduction: Metropolitanization and public services. In *Metropolitanization and Public
          Services*, Charles M. Haar, ed. Baltimore: Johns Hopkins University Press for Resources
          for the Future.
Hamilton, Alexander, James Madison, and John Jay
  1961   *The Federalist Papers.* New York: The New American Library of World Literature, Inc.
Harrigan, John
  1993   *Political Change in the Metropolis 5th ed.,* New York: HarperCollins.
Hill, Edward, and Harold Wolman
  1995   Can suburbs survive without their central cities? Examining the suburban dependence
          hypothesis. *Urban Affairs Review* (November) 31(2):147-183.
Jones, Victor
  1942   *Metropolitan Government.* Chicago: University of Chicago Press.

Kenyon, Daphne, and John Kincaid
1991   *Interjurisdictional Tax Policy and Competition: Good or Bad for the Federal System.* Washington, DC: U.S. Advisory Commission on Intergovernmental Relations.

Ladd, Helen
1994   Measuring disparities in the fiscal condition of local governments. In *Fiscal Equalization for State and Local Government Finance,* John E. Anderson, ed. Westport, CT: Praeger.

Ladd, Helen, and John Yinger
1989   *America's Ailing Cities.* Baltimore: Johns Hopkins University Press.

Ledebur, Larry, and William Barnes
1993   *All In It Together: Cities, Suburbs, and Local Economic Regions.* Washington, DC: National League of Cities.

Liebert, Roland J.
1976   *Disintegration and Political Action: The Changing Functions of City Governments in America.* New York: Academic Press.

Liebschutz, Sarah F.
1989   Targeting by the states: The basic issues. *Publius: The Journal of Federalism* (Spring) 19:(2).

Lyons, W.E., and David Lowery
1989   Governmental fragmentation versus consolidation: Five public-choice myths about how to create informed, involved, and happy citizens. *Public Administration Review* (November/December) 49(6):533-543.

Mackey, Scott
1997   Critical Issues in State-Local Fiscal Policy. Draft report, table 7. Denver: National Conference of State Legislatures, July.

Marando, Vincent, and Carl Reggie Whitley
1972   City-county consolidation: An overview of voter response. *Urban Affairs Quarterly* 8(December):181-203.

Marando, Vincent, and Mavis Mann Reeves
1993   County government structural reform: Influence of state, region, and urbanization. *Publius: The Journal of Federalism* (Winter) 23(1):41-52

Maxey, Chester
1922   The political integration of metropolitan communities. *National Municipal Review* 11(August):229-253

McHone, W. Warren
1990   Highway accessibility, location rents, and the efficiency of metropolitan area tax base sharing. *Growth and Change* (Spring 1990) 21(2):46-55.

McKenzie, Evan
1994   *Privatopia: Homeowner Associations and the Rise of Residential Private Government.* New Haven: Yale University Press.

Merriam, Charles E., Spencer D. Parratt, and Albert Lepawsky
1933   *The Government of the Metropolitan Region of Chicago.* Chicago: University of Chicago Press.

Mikesell, John
1993   *City Finances, City Futures.* Columbus: Ohio Municipal League Educational and Research Fund.

Miller, David, Rowan Miranda, Robert Roque, and Charles Wilf
1995   The fiscal organization of metropolitan areas: The Allegheny County case reconsidered. *Publius: The Journal of Federalism* (Fall) 25(4):19-35.

Morgan, David, and Mei-Chiang Shih
1991   Targeting state and federal aid to city needs. *State and Local Government Review* (Spring):60-68.

Musgrave, Richard
  1959   *The Theory of Public Finance.* New York: McGraw-Hill.
Nunn, Samuel, and Mark S. Rosentraub
  1996   Metropolitan fiscal equalization: Distilling lessons from four U.S. programs. *State and Local Government Review* (Spring) 28(2):90-102.
Oakland, William H.
  1994a   Fiscal equalization: An empty box? *National Tax Journal* (March) 47(1):199-209.
  1994b   Recognizing and correcting for fiscal disparities: A critical analysis. Pp. 1-19 in *Fiscal Equalization for State and Local Government Finance*, John E. Anderson, ed. Westport, CT: Praeger.
O'Cleireacain, Carol
  1993   Cities' role in the metropolitan economy and the federal structure. Pp. 167-186 in *Interwoven Destinies: Cities and the Nation*, Henry G. Cisneros, ed. New York: W.W. Norton & Co.
Orfield, Myron
  1997   *Metropolitics: A Regional Agenda for Community and Stability.* Washington, DC: Brookings Institution and Lincoln Institute of Land Policy.
Osborne, David, and Ted Gaebler
  1992   *Reinventing Government.* Reading, MA: Addison-Wesley Publishing.
Ostrom, Vincent, Charles M. Tiebout, and Robert Warren
  1961   The organization of government in metropolitan areas: A theoretical inquiry. *American Political Science Review* 55 (December):831-842.
Pack, Janet R.
  1995   Poverty and Urban Public Expenditures. Working Paper #197. Wharton Real Estate Center, The Wharton School, University of Pennsylvania (October).
Pagano, Michael A.
  1996   Local infrastructure: Intergovernmental grants and urban needs. *Public Works Management & Policy* (July) 1(1):19-30.
Pammer, William J., Jr., and Jack L. Dustin
  1993   Fostering economic development through county tax sharing. *State and Local Government Review* (Winter) 25(1):57-71.
Peirce, Neil
  1996   Cities beyond their bounds of unity. *National Journal* (7 December) 28(49):2654.
Peirce, Neal R., with C.W. Johnson and John Stuart Hall
  1993   *Citistates: How Urban America Can Prosper in a Competitive World.* Washington, DC: Seven Locks Press.
Pelissero, John P.
  1984   State aid and city needs. *Journal of Politics 46* (August):916-935.
Peterson, Paul E.
  1981   *City Limits.* Chicago: University of Chicago Press.
  1995   *The Price of Federalism.* Washington, DC: The Brookings Institution.
Peterson, Paul E., and Mark C. Rom
  1990   *Welfare Magnets.* Washington, DC: The Brookings Institution.
Phares, Donald, and Claude Louishomme
  1996   St. Louis: A politically fragmented area. Pp. 72-97 in *Regional Politics: America in a Post-City Age,* H.V. Savitch and Ronald K. Vogel, eds. Thousand Oaks, CA: Sage Publications.
Reschovsky, Andrew
  1980   An evaluation of metropolitan area tax base sharing. *National Tax Journal* (March) 33(1):63.
  1994   Fiscal equalization and school finance. *National Tax Journal,* 47:1 (March):185-197.

Rich, Michael
  1993   Riot and reason: Crafting an urban policy response. *Publius: The Journal of Federalism* (Summer) 23(3):115-134.
Rusk, David
  1993   *Cities Without Suburbs.* Baltimore: Johns Hopkins University Press.
Sacher, Seth B.
  1993   Fiscal fragmentation and the distribution of metropolitan area resources: A case study. *Urban Studies* (August) 30(7):1225.
Salins, Peter
  1993   Metropolitan areas: Cities, suburbs, and the ties that bind. Pp. 147-166 in *Interwoven Destinies,* Henry Cisneros, ed. New York: Norton.
Savitch, H.V., David Collins, Daniel Sanders, and John P. Markham
  1993   Ties that bind: Central cities, suburbs, and the new metropolitan region. *Economic Development Quarterly* (November) 7(4):341-357.
Sbragia, Alberta
  1996   *Debt Wish.* Pittsburgh: University of Pittsburgh Press.
Schaefer, David Lewis, and Roberta Rubel Schaefer
  1996   *The Future of Cities.* Lanham, MD: University Press of America.
Schneider, Mark
  1989   The *Competitive City: The Political Economy of Suburbia.* Pittsburgh: University of Pittsburgh Press.
Sharpe, L.J.
  1995   The future of metropolitan governance. Pp. 11-31 in *The Government of World Cities: The Future of the Metro Model,* L.J. Sharpe, ed. New York: John Wiley & Sons.
Sokolow, Alvin
  1993   State rules and county-city arena: Competition for land and taxes in California's Central Valley. *Publius: The Journal of Federalism* (Winter) 23(1):53-69.
State of Texas, Senate Intergovernmental Relations Committee
  1996   Interim Report Pursuant to Interim Charges, Part II-Consolidation (July).
Studenski, Paul
  1930   *The Government of Metropolitan Areas in the United States.* New York: National Municipal League.
Summers, Anita A., and Lara Jakubowski
  1996   The Fiscal Burden of Unreimbursed Poverty Expenditures in the City of Philadelphia: 1985-1995, Working Paper #238. Real Estate Center, The Wharton School of the University of Pennsylvania (August 1).
Thomas, Robert, and Suphapong Boonyapratuang
  1993   Local government complexity: Consequences for county property-tax and debt policies. *Publius: The Journal of Federalism* (Winter) 23(1):1-18.
  1993   Urban growth decision making in the Houston area. In *Metropolitan Governance: American/Canadian Intergovernmental Perspectives,* Donald N. Rothblatt and Andrew Sancton, eds. Berkeley, CA: Institute of Governmental Studies Press.
Tiebout, Charles
  1956   A pure theory of public expenditures. *Journal of Political Economy* 44:416-424.
U.S. Advisory Commission on Intergovernmental Relations
  1964   *The Role of Equalization in Federal Grants.* Washington, DC: ACIR.
  1973   *Regional Governance: Promise and Performance.* Washington, DC: U.S. ACIR.
  1989   *Residential Community Associations: Private Governments in the Intergovernmental System?* Washington, DC: U.S. ACIR.
  1992   *Metropolitan Organization: The Allegheny County Case.* Washington, DC: ACIR.

1993   *Metropolitan Organization: Comparison of the Allegheny and St. Louis Case Studies.*
       Washington, DC: ACIR.

1995   *Significant Features of Fiscal Federalism, 1994.* Washington, DC: ACIR.

1985   *The States and Distressed Communities.* Washington, DC: U.S. Government Printing
       Office.

U.S. Congress, House
1976   Commuter Tax. P. 10 in Hearings and Markup before the Subcommittee on Fiscal Af-
       fairs and the Committee on the District of Columbia, House of Representatives, 94th
       Congress, 2nd session. Washington, DC: U.S. Government Printing Office.

U.S. General Accounting Office.
1993   *Transportation Infrastructure: Better Tools Needed for Making Decisions on Using
       ISTEA Funds Flexibly.* Washington, DC: GAO.

Wallis, Allan D.
1994   The third wave: Current trends in regional governance. *National Civic Review* (Summer-
       Fall):290-310.

Warren, Charles R.
1974   Possible analytical approaches and action models. Pp. 211-219 in *Organizing Public
       Services in Metropolitan America,* Thomas P. Murphy and Charles R. Warren, eds. Lex-
       ington, MA: Lexington Books.

Wikstrom, Nelson
1997   Metropolitan Government: Conceptual Development and Metropolitan Governance. Pa-
       per prepared for the annual meetings of the American Political Science Association,
       Washington, DC, August 28 to 31.

Zodrow, George
1984   The incidence of metropolitan property tax base sharing and rate equalization. *Journal of
       Urban Economics* 15:224.

NOTES

[1] Gyourko and Summers (1997) note that large cities (over 300,000 population) spend 30 percent of their own-source revenues on health, hospitals, and public welfare, compared with only 9.1 percent for smaller cities (under 75,000 population). Pack (1995) found that on average cities spend 3.5 percent of their own-source revenues on unreimbursed "poverty" programs (excluding hospitals), but that Philadelphia spent 7.6 percent in 1995 (see also Salins, 1993).

[2] For an opposing view, see Hill and Wolman (1995).

[3] Much research has centered on the efficient production of local government services, which certainly needs to be factored into any discussion about tax burden. Productivity has received popular attention with the publication of Osborne and Gaebler's *Reinventing Government* (1992).

[4] It should be noted that some special districts, such as sewer and water authorities, mass transit districts, and gas and electric utilities, are usually denied access to any general tax, but rather are restricted to a user charge for revenue generation.

[5] Ladd and Yinger's measures are presented because they are more accurate measures than others. The representative tax structure, developed by the U.S. Advisory Commission on Intergovernmental Relations, is premised on measuring fiscal capacity as equal tax rates, ignoring tax burden (defined as taxes as a percentage of wealth). For a review of other budgetary and economic measures of fiscal health, see Bahl et al. (1992a:420-432 and 1992b:49-66).

[6] This variation in service responsibilities was an important factor in Fuchs's finding that New York City's fiscal condition suffered more than Chicago's (see Fuchs, 1992).

[7] Addressing issues of intrametropolitan disparities, according to some analysts, cannot and should not be left to the local governments in question. Nongovernmental organizations, such as the Atlanta Project, the Providence Plan, and many others, may be more successful in addressing

intrametropolitan inequities than are either formal regional governments or ad hoc interlocal (voluntary) agreements.

The Atlanta Project (TAP) was begun by former President Jimmy Carter and funded primarily from industry and foundations for the purpose of "accomplishing social goals associated with poverty, including teen pregnancy, childhood immunization, school dropout rates, and crime and violence" (Wallis, 1994:304). It provides services to 20 neighborhood clusters in 3 counties in the Atlanta metropolitan region. Each neighborhood cluster has a corporate sponsor and designs programs to address poverty-related problems (e.g., teen pregnancy, violence, school dropout). Rich argues that the solution to municipal social problems, such as Atlanta's, ought to shift from being a responsibility solely of city hall to one that includes the nonprofit sector (see Rich, 1993; Giles, 1993). Nonprofits, unlike municipalities, are usually not constrained by the political boundaries of the municipal corporations. Consequently, they can reach out beyond the central city to the broader metropolis. Moreover, he argues that, in an environment in which the likelihood of substantial federal or state support is remote, partnerships between local governments and nonprofits not only fill the breach, but also, because they spring from local concerns, are more likely to be tailored to local problems. Programs such as the Atlanta Project have spread and have been supported by a number of large foundations, such as the Annie P. Casey Foundation, the Rockefeller Foundation, the Pew Charitable Trusts, among others, and have been implemented in cities and metropolitan regions across the country.

8   Under the state's Municipal Annexation Act, cities over 100,000 population are allowed territorial dominance for five miles beyond the corporate limits. In this extraterritorial jurisdictions, cities "can impose subdivision regulations, approve the creation of MUDs [municipal utility districts], designate tax exempt 'industrial districts,' and prohibit new incorporations" (Thomas, 1993:289).

9   Correspondence with Dan Durning, Carl Vinson Institute of Government, University of Georgia, January 31, 1997 (updated to include two referenda defeated in November 1996). In testimony before the Senate Committee on Intergovernmental Relations, El Paso, Texas, April 1, 1996, Terrell Blodgett, Professor of Urban Management at the University of Texas School of Public Affairs, counted four likely elections for city-county consolidation and eight studies under way in 1996.

10   Testimony of Terrell Blodgett, p. 6 (see note 9).

11   Yet on the basis of their own data of residents' subjective ratings of services, the only substantial discrepancy in ratings is in the education function, which is only one of two services rated (the other was police). One might just as easily speculate that consolidation has reduced the disparity in perception between residents of the pre-Unigov city and the other residents over how well schools were performing because the data are not longitudinal ratings of satisfaction.

12   Bell (1994) argues the purpose is also to rationalize land use planning, an issue not discussed here.

13   In a similar vein, Fischel contends that the *Serrano* decision in California may have actually caused the tax revolt (Proposition 13) by forcing wealthy school districts to raise their own property tax rates even while state equalization grants in response to *Serrano* were redistributing more aid to poorer school districts (see Fischel, 1989).

14   Pennsylvania also allows an income tax, but nonresidents cannot be taxed at more than 1 percent regardless of the city's income tax (excluding Philadelphia).

15   This is an admittedly very tenuous conclusion because no comprehensive study of the effect of Ohio's municipal income tax on intrametropolitan disparities has been conducted.

Regionalism in Transportation and Air Quality: History, Interpretation, and Insights for Regional Governance

Martin Wachs and Jennifer Dill
University of California, Berkeley

Transportation and air quality are areas of public policy in which there is a tradition of thinking, planning, and acting regionally, and we may well ask whether this tradition offers any lessons for public policy makers that go beyond the realms of transportation and air quality. Although it is clear that the locus of most transportation and air quality policy debates is and probably should be at the regional level, it is not at all clear that regionalism in transportation and air quality has resulted in programs that have been so successful as to provide models for other sectors of public policy making. In this paper, we review the evolution of regionalism in transportation and air quality policy making and discuss some of the strengths, weaknesses, and unresolved issues with respect to the regional basis of policy making in these sectors. We close with some observations on the extent to which our impressions may be generalizable to other sectors.

HISTORICAL EVOLUTION OF REGIONALISM IN TRANSPORTATION PLANNING

Transportation policy has been treated as a regional issue for so long that transportation planners and managers would be surprised by proposals to consider transportation in other ways. When the exuberant population and economic growth of the decade immediately following World War I was coupled with even more rapid growth in automobile ownership and use, an extremely progressive federal government took the lead by recognizing that traffic congestion knew few political boundaries. Highways were socially provided and served society primarily by facilitating interjurisdictional flows, so transportation experts in the U.S.

government thought they should be dealt with by creating multijurisdictional plans and programs. Transit at the time was primarily privately owned and generally served local markets, although interurban transit lines were important to regional and interregional growth. Although early efforts at regionalism certainly addressed transit needs, they naturally gave greater emphasis to highways.

When the commissioners of Cuyahoga County, Ohio, in 1927 solicited the help of the Federal Bureau of Public Roads to deal with the growing problems of traffic congestion in Cleveland, they wanted to establish a "scientific plan of highway improvement." The bureau responded that it would cooperate and provide funds for the study only under the condition that it extend to the area principally controlled by the city of Cleveland and surrounding suburban areas *without regard to political boundaries*, and that all governmental agencies in the area having jurisdiction over highways and traffic cooperate in the establishment of a general highway development plan and agree to carry out this plan cooperatively when it is completed. Cleveland was not unique. At exactly the same time, a group in Boston under the direction of Robert Whitten was developing a relatively advanced traffic analysis and forecast based on an origin and destination survey that extended to 39 cities and towns of the metropolitan area (Heightchew, 1979). These early efforts, based on voluntary cooperation among cities and towns, were important precursors to the later metropolitan organizations or special districts with which we are now familiar.

These early plans were regional in scope but relatively narrow in focus in comparison to current concepts of transportation planning. They dealt primarily with the construction of facilities and not so deeply with fiscal or funding strategies, environmental impacts, growth control, or system management, all issues that we today consider critical dimensions in regional transportation planning. The capital investments proposed in many regional plans of the 1920s were mostly highways—conventional streets and boulevards that were often broader than and conceived of more systematically as networks and hierarchies of facilities having far greater capacities than street systems of earlier periods in the American metropolis.

The roads that were planned in these early studies were actually implemented to a rather limited extent, primarily for financial reasons. The shortage of funds needed to construct the regional highways envisioned in the plans of the 1920s was at least in part due to the long and deep depression that followed almost immediately the development of these plans, and to the enormous financial claims of World War II, which followed the depression. The inability of many regions to fund the highways that constituted these early plans was also attributable to the fact that America had not then (and has not yet today) invented ways in which regions could produce their own funds with which to implement their plans. The regional cooperation among transportation agencies that resulted in these early plans was actually a multiyear project that was temporary in nature. It was accomplished without creating any regional governing body and rested entirely on the voluntary participation of cities, counties, and state agencies, although it did set a precedent that later led to arrangements more properly recognized as a kind of regional governance. Fiscal authority for transportation, as for most other types of public expenditures, exists at local, state, and federal levels, and there are few taxing or spending capabilities that are designed to be regionwide. Thus, implementation of the early regional highway projects required commitments of local and state funds. Local funds were, of course, used for those portions of regional networks that clearly benefited the jurisdictions that built them. Funds for state highways at the regional level were scarce because of the competition from intercity highways needed primarily in rural areas in an era when the balance of power in state legislatures was still in the hands of rural representatives.

POSTWAR HIGHWAY PLANNING AND CONSTRUCTION

At the end of World War II, America again turned to regional transportation planning and started to address the enormous backlog of unmet highway needs dating back to the 1920s. Regional transportation study agencies were formed in most large metropolitan areas, some of which were divisions of state highway departments, some of which were cooperative arrangements created by compacts among several agencies—occasionally even involving two or three states—and some of which were independent bodies created by state charter. A few of these were overseen by representative boards or commissions, mainly composed of local elected officials, but many were composed almost entirely of technical staffs who were part of state civil service systems. Their advisory committees and public hearing processes constituted in many cases only the most rudimentary efforts at citizen participation or cooperative governance. Bolstered by improved data collection techniques, the first nonmilitary applications of electronic computers, and planning funds made available by the 1956 and 1962 Federal Highway Acts, metropolitan transportation planners proposed grandiose regional plans featuring systems of radial and circumferential freeways stretching over many jurisdictions.

This time the federal government exerted its leadership by asserting, much as it had in the 1920s, that transportation plans had to be "comprehensive, cooperative, and continuing" and by writing regulations that required regional transportation planning to meet those requirements in a number of specific ways. The federal government also eventually provided a financial basis for implementing the regional transportation plans. It created the interstate highway system, which was first planned to connect major population centers and military bases to one another, leaving the roads within metropolitan areas to the local planners and local financing. But national planners soon realized that the system would carry very light traffic on the rural segments between metropolitan areas. To demonstrate that the interstates would carry sufficient traffic to justify federal funding, the segments within metropolitan areas were included in the system. This gave regional planners access to rather generous federal funding, which provided 90 percent of the cost of constructing many of the freeways that comprised the regional plans, with states and localities responsible only for 10 percent of the initial capital cost plus the majority of the upkeep and maintenance. To ensure that the federal government could provide the vast majority of the funding needed to implement the interstate system, the Federal Highway Trust Fund was created, into which federal gasoline taxes and excise taxes on cars, trucks, tires, and batteries were deposited. These funds were understood to be user fees, really more like tolls than taxes, in that the extent to which a person contributed to the fund was roughly proportional to his or her use of the system. Trust fund monies could be appropriated for the purpose of building the interstate system, thus ensuring that growth in auto use would be paralleled by the further construction of highways to accommodate that growth.

Brian Taylor (1992, 1995) has interpreted the significant role played by funding decisions in determining the course of history of regional transportation plans. He shows that city and county planners in the period just before World War II had developed a highway plan for the Los Angeles metropolitan area that was surprisingly different from the freeway network eventually constructed. The plan included many highway routes that were similar in location to routes eventually adopted, but rather than very broad, access-controlled, and grade-separated facilities, the plan in many instances favored "expressways," which were then conceived of as less than totally grade separated, which had lower design speeds, and which provided for traffic signals at some intersections. The lower design speeds and lesser degree of grade separation meant that the roadways could have sharper turns than the freeways eventually did, and that the roads could be threaded through the urban fabric with far less removal of existing buildings. The high-capacity boulevards or expressways that were planned at the time seem to modern observers to be more fully integrated with local land uses than were the freeways that were eventually built. They featured, for example, direct access to the parking areas at major employment sites and accommodated bus operations, including bus stops on the shoulders of the expressways.

Construction of the network of roadways in this plan, which extended over thousands of miles, required enormous sums of money that proved to be far beyond the resources available within the region. In an effort to actually get some roads built in the face of increasing congestion and very limited resources, regional officials turned to the state and federal governments for the capital investment funds that were needed. In exchange for this support, regional officials accepted the design standards associated with state and federal highway programs, and that meant the construction of freeways having broad shoulders, complete grade separation, and the gentle curves implied by design speeds of 70 miles per hour.

The acceptance of state and federal funding, then, had changed the basic characteristics of the regional highway network. Taylor and others believe that, by adopting the "freeway," which was initially designed for rural areas, Los Angeles accepted a form of highway that was far less suited to its region than the expressways that had been planned there earlier. Ironically, as many urban design critics and environmentalists deride the L.A. freeways as a model not to be emulated elsewhere because of its community impacts and disruption of local circulation patterns, they are hardly aware of the fact that it was a form of network at variance with the hopes and aspirations of regional planners. Rather, it was more or less imposed on the region as the consequence of compromises that were dictated by funding requirements. It is possible that, had Los Angeles been able to more directly pursue its regional highway plans of the late 1930s, the region would today have an entirely different character.

The Los Angeles case indicates that, at an important stage in the evolution of transportation programs, the region was able to articulate a unique and possibly appropriate concept for transportation investment. The absence of a region-wide body having authority to implement this concept and the absence of fiscal independence at the regional level, however, caused compromises that substantially changed the nature of the plans eventually implemented there. We may interpret the Los Angeles freeway system as a regional system, but it is more correct to see it as a regional manifestation of fiscal and political power brought to bear on the region from the state and national capitals.

THE RISE OF PUBLIC TRANSIT

The postwar regional transportation plans in almost all instances emphasized highway construction. Although public transit was given lip service in each regional report, the facilities that were proposed consisted primarily of freeways and expressways. This may reflect the fact that transit was still largely in the hands of private owners and that it was seen to be in a state of decline. Transit technology was seen as outmoded by many planners, public officials, and citizens. Auto ownership and use was continuing to soar, and there was a broad social consensus that autos would become and remain the dominant mode of transportation. The transportation problem was perceived to be one of managing automobile congestion, and transit had a limited role to play.

In political terms, it is also possible to read historical events somewhat differently. The interstate highway building program was funded by the federal government through the states, and at the time neither the federal government nor the states had great interest in public transit, which was primarily of interest in the central areas of the nation's largest cities. By the early 1960s, mayors of large cities and their congressional representatives had realized that their transit systems, mostly privately owned, were going into bankruptcy, that federally financed highways were playing a major role in the decline of transit, and that the cities would face difficult choices without federal help for transit. They would have to take over bankrupt transit operations themselves or face the total elimination of urban transit services. Big-city politicians started to urge that there be a federal transit program, and in 1964 Congress finally enacted the Urban Mass Transportation Act, which provided capital grants to enable cities to take over transit operations or build new rail lines and busways.

Interestingly, federal aid to transit was in the mid- and late 1960s administered in urban areas with little state participation. Transit investment programs were more closely linked with urban renewal programs than they were with the regional highway planning, and the regional highway agencies still played small roles in transit planning, construction, and operation. When, in 1966, Congress added the requirement that transit investments be consistent with regional plans, they *did not* require transit plans to be consistent with the regional highway plans, but rather with the multifaceted metropolitan plans that were being developed by regional councils of government, which had initially been funded under the 1954 Fair Housing Act. Thus, transit plans were to be consistent with planning for urban water and sewer, outdoor recreation, urban renewal and housing, but not necessarily integrated with the regional highway planning process that was described earlier. Highways were funded and overseen by a large state and federal establishment, and transit to be viable and independent was consciously placed under the management of urban political decision-making bodies.

The regional highway planning process of the late 1960s could be characterized as highly technocratic. It involved a great deal of data collection and analysis, used standardized methods of forecasting and evaluation, and relied heavily on computer modeling. Although public hearings were required, this was a planning process carried out by technical experts with relatively little formal participation from local officials and citizens. In contrast, the transit planning process, carried out largely by planners in the employ of cities and of regional councils of government, was overseen by elected representatives of the many cities in each metropolitan area and characterized by a much more open political process of negotiation and bargaining.

MERGING HIGHWAY AND TRANSIT POLICY MAKING

Despite their separate roots and rather different histories, both highway and transit planning were being done at the regional level, and over time the federal government as a condition for continued funding required that the two regional transportation planning processes be merged into one. Major regional highways were most often built and operated by state highway or transportation departments. Facilities included in regional transit plans were most often built and operated by transit authorities that operated at the metropolitan or county level and that in most cases had much less participation by state officials.

During the 1970s and 1980s, after the creation of a U.S. Department of Transportation, a series of highway and transit funding laws gradually pushed transportation planning and investment programs toward a more unified model, in which multimodalism became first the ideal and eventually almost a reality. In the early 1970s, highway and transit planning was most frequently done by separate agencies in most metropolitan areas, but those agencies were first required to create an "intermodal planning group" to coordinate their separate activities, and that group was required to develop a "unified work program" for the planning of transit and highways. Eventually, transit and highway planning were unified under a single metropolitan planning organization in each large metropolitan area. Despite the fact that highway programs had budgets that were orders of magnitude larger than those of transit programs, and although the number of people engaged in highway planning, construction, maintenance, and management was many times greater than those working on transit, the model of regional planning and governance that emerged from the gradual unification of planning for each mode was very strongly influenced by the model that previously characterized transit planning.

Although the transit planning process is technically complex and data intensive, as was the highway planning process, it is today typically conducted by a metropolitan planning organization that is a council of governments or a representative board of elected representatives of different governments within the metropolitan area. In Los Angeles, for example, the Los Angeles Regional Transportation Study (LARTS), an office in the California Division of Highways, prepared the regional highway plans of the 1960s and early 1970s. Its formal planning functions were gradually absorbed by the Southern California Association of Governments (SCAG), the regional council of government, which was overseen by a large board of directors having broad representation of elected officials from several counties and dozens of cities in the metropolitan area. This pattern was repeated in many other metropolitan areas. In fact, during the 1980s as federal funding was decreased for most councils of government, their access to transportation funds prevented many of the weaker ones from closing down, and transportation planning became their dominant function.

There is now in most metropolitan areas a regional body that focuses on transportation funding, planning, and policy making, while major highways continue to be built and operated primarily by state agencies, local streets and highways by cities and counties, and transit services by municipal or county transit authorities.

Over several decades, regional agencies gradually became more and more responsible for planning transportation capital investment programs, but until recently those agencies had relatively little discretion with respect to the allocation of federal and state funds. From the 1950s until the early 1990s, most transportation funds were generally made available by state and federal governments in the form of categorical grants, earmarked for specific programmatic purposes, each having its own particular rules and procedures. Interstate highway construction funds were earmarked for that purpose only, and separate funding was available for bridge replacement, the restoration of older roads, and many other specifically enumerated programs. Transit funds were separate from highway funds and also were categorical, with funding, for example, for new rail system construction, bus purchases, and system operating subsidies made available in separate programs. This complex matrix of different programs for different purposes gave regional authorities relatively little flexibility. Regional transportation plans could be implemented by matching their components with the available federal and state categorical programs, so in reality a regional responsibility for transportation frequently involved adjusting regional preferences and priorities to take advantage of the likely availability of federal and state funds through the mix of available categorical programs. The most successful regional transportation agencies were those that became adept at mixing and matching federal and state categorical funds in order to arrive at a package that enabled them to make reasonable progress toward implementing programs for which there was a high level of regional consensus.

The regional agencies responsible for transportation planning (known widely as the metropolitan planning organizations, or MPOs) differ in structure from one region to another, depending on state laws and idiosyncratic histories. Many, but certainly not all, are councils of government, and most are overseen by policy boards having members who are elected local legislators—city council members, mayors, county supervisors. These people are usually directly elected by the citizens to their offices in local government and then elected to their positions in the metropolitan planning organizations by their peers or appointed by a superior government. A few metropolitan areas provide for the direct election of regional government representatives, but such organizations are certainly in the minority.

Typically, these councils or boards of elected officials meet a few times per year as a "general assembly" to adopt policies and to formally approve elements of work undertaken in response to their formal motions and to approve actions by their staffs and committees. Most of the work, including the preparation of regional transportation plans, is done by committees, task forces, councils, and panels created by action of the larger board, and these groups typically include a few members of the board plus other parties appointed because of their interests or influence. In addition, the regional councils are typified by professional staffs—career civil service professional employees—who do the technical and analytical work, drafting the reports of the committees and of the overall boards. The staffs vary in size from a dozen employees in an agency serving a smaller community in the population range of 100,000 to 250,000, to more than over 100 staff employees in agencies serving larger metropolitan areas with populations in the range of several million. Most metropolitan planning organizations work cooperatively with other agencies, such as the state highway departments, transit districts, and air quality management districts. Sometimes agencies cosponsor and even coauthor regional transportation and air quality documents, but at the very least other units of government are represented on the MPO committees, and representatives of other functional governmental agencies testify before their committees and general assemblies.

TRANSPORTATION POLICY UNDER ISTEA

The passage of the Intermodal Surface Transportation Efficiency Act (ISTEA) in 1991 marked a significant change in the ways in which transportation planning and finance are accomplished. The number of categorical programs was reduced significantly, and at the regional level the designated metropolitan planning organization has for the first time the authority to shift funds from one category to another in such a way that funds may actually be used across several modes. One major funding category, the Surface Transportation Program, makes funds available for roads or transit, and the largest category of highway funding, the National Highway System funds, allows up to half of the allocation to a given area to be shifted to public transit, and even more than half to be shifted with the approval of the secretary of transportation. Under ISTEA, regional officials also have greater authority than existed previously to move funds between new construction projects and the funding of maintenance and operations. Underlining the federal commitment to cleaner air in nonattainment areas, ISTEA also provides a special category of funds (Congestion Management and Air Quality or CMAQ funds) to nonattainment areas that can be used for projects intended to reduce automobile-generated air pollution. In addition, up to 10 percent of the Surface Transportation Funds may be used for what are called transportation enhancements, a much broader array of projects than had typically been funded in past transportation bills. These projects include pedestrian zones, restoration of historic transportation facilities, the provision of recreational bikeways, and similar projects.

It is clearly too soon to judge the full range of impacts that the ISTEA legislation has had on transportation planning, construction, finance, and governance. Although it would appear to have given more authority to regional agencies, much of what has been built in the last few years was planned, designed, and engineered in the years before the enactment of ISTEA, and many new projects conceived under ISTEA have yet to be implemented. It does appear, however, that stronger metropolitan planning organizations, like the Metropolitan Transportation Commission of the San Francisco Bay Area, have welcomed the increased decision authority and have attempted to use ISTEA as justification for more integrated planning for transit and highways. Some observers believe that weaker metropolitan planning organizations, however, have not yet fully mastered the art of increasing their authority to be more creative, and in some metropolitan areas transportation policy making under ISTEA may differ far less from planning in the 1970s or 1980s than the legislation allows.

EVALUATING REGIONALISM IN TRANSPORTATION POLICY

It is crystal clear that planning and systematic resource allocation to accommodate travel should be addressed at the regional level. The vast majority of Americans travel between activities that span many local political jurisdictions, and it is appropriate that highways and transit systems be coordinated across many jurisdictions. It is less clear that construction or the daily management of physical facilities is best addressed at the regional level, since it is possible that a regional system can function smoothly even if some of these functions are carried out by municipalities and counties.

One of the great strengths of transportation planning is that major capital investment programs are and have for some time been planned at the regional level. The views of central-city and suburban constituents are brought to the table and debated as decisions are made regarding investments in new facilities or in the renewal of deteriorated transportation infrastructure. How representative are the deliberative processes that give rise to major transportation policy decisions, such as whether to build a new subway or highway, where it will be routed, whether a facility will be widened or a major bridge reinforced? There is a great deal of debate with respect to this question. Is the distribution of funding undertaken by regional bodies considered to be equitable? Indeed, how shall equity be evaluated from the perspective of a regional body? It is also important to recognize that metropolitan areas differ dramatically from one another, and although some concentrate planning at the regional level, the planning bodies often have little implementation authority, and the effectiveness of regional planning differs from one area to another depending greatly on the extent to which the planning bodies are integrated with implementing and operating authorities.

Central-City Versus Suburban Interests

In most metropolitan areas, the central cities constitute the largest and most influential members of the decision-making bodies that govern transportation and air quality. Yet so large a proportion of the population has shifted to suburban areas that, in total, suburban representation in regional decision-making bodies far exceeds central-city representation. Of course, not every issue pits central cities against the suburbs, and often different central-city communities have conflicting positions, as do suburban communities. Yet many have observed that, on many issues, the political debates are dominated by broad central-city coalitions in contention with broad suburban coalitions. It would appear that over the past 20 or 30 years, most of the need for new capacity in the form of roads or transit routes has been in suburban areas, whereas there is growing need in the central cities for maintenance and renewal of existing facilities. On one hand, many suburban jurisdictions would complain that they have experienced most of the growth in traffic congestion but have not captured sufficient resources through regional decision making to address their burgeoning needs. Central cities, on the other hand, complain that their aging infrastructure is in a state of decline and that their resource needs for upgrading older systems have not been sufficiently addressed. Our own view is that these positions, which are heard often, are both partly true but both are oversimplifications.

Capital Investments Versus Operations and System Maintenance

Most major capital investments in transportation over the past 40 or more years have provided more and more capacity to serve peak-hour commuters from outlying suburban areas to downtown cores. Most major freeway investments have been radial, and circumferential beltways have also been justified on their ability to decrease inner-city congestion. Similarly, most new investments in commuter rail lines and rail rapid-transit lines have served longer trips between outlying residences and inner-city employment areas. Despite this investment pattern, it is clear that most Americans now live and work in the suburbs, and their commutes are made across the grain of transportation system expansions. Central-city employment is a small and decreasing fraction of total regional employment. In newer Sunbelt metropolises, central-city employment is typically below 5 percent of the regional total, and even in established eastern metropolitan areas it is typically in the range of 15 percent. Those who do make long commuting journeys from outlying suburbs to inner-city employment zones are disproportionately people of greater than average wealth: professionals and business people (Pisarski, 1996; Federal Highway Administration, 1993).

Because of limited funds to both build and operate transportation systems, and greater availability of funds for capital projects, many jurisdictions have added new capacity to serve longer-distance peak-hour commuters while decreasing local bus services and decreasing maintenance of local streets and roads. The beneficiaries have been longer-distance upper-income peak-hour commuters. The losers have been both inner-city and suburban communities of more modest income, people making more of their trips at nonpeak times, and people—including the very old and very young—making fewer of their trips for purposes related to work. In a large number of American regions, we have planned and built suburban-to-downtown commuter rail lines and major radial highway facilities while raising fares for local transit service and reducing funds for the filling of potholes.

It is important to recognize that, in the realm of transportation and most other public systems, there is typically a regional agency responsible for long-range planning and for the distribution of federal and state funds, but no regionwide source of revenue and no regional operating authority. Although planning and programming and the allocation of pass-through funds from the state and national governments may take place at the regional level, it is in the nature of regional decision making that policy makers must receive and direct funds made available by others—principally state and federal programs.

Transportation funds have almost always been more available from both state and federal sources for capital investments—new roads and train lines—than for maintenance, repair, or system operations. Thus, we believe that the transportation system has been "overcapitalized." More money has been spent on new facilities and equipment than would have been the case had monies been fungible between capital, operations, and maintenance applications. And capital investments have been allowed to deteriorate to a far greater extent than would have been ideal, since new dollars were being spent on new capital investments rather than maintenance and operations. Many miles of urban freeways were built because federal dollars for construction matched state and local funds by a ratio as high as 10 to 1; subways are today replacing bus operations because federal dollars are more readily available for subway construction than for bus operations. In many cases, regions that are hungry for their share of the federal dollars that create construction contracts and jobs have extended themselves beyond their own abilities to pay the local contribution required as a condition of the receipt of federal capital funds or for the operation and maintenance of the new systems they have constructed (Wachs and Ortner, 1979).

Equity

In the context of political debates, the term "equity" can have many meanings. In fact, explicit tensions between competing concepts of equity have been frequently identified in regional transportation planning. An increasing proportion of the support for transportation, especially public transit, has been raised from local property and sales taxes and a decreasing proportion from federal transfers. This causes participants in the regional transportation policy-making process to seek equity in terms of bringing home to their constituencies at least as many financial resources as are raised there. The bulk of the income derived from transportation-related sales and property taxes is attributable to white suburban taxpayers, and the majority of transit riders are inner-city residents who are poorer and increasingly members of minority groups, so it is not surprising that tensions are growing over the distribution of these subsidies. Suburban officials seek equity in the distribution of resources on the basis of returning those resources to the jurisdictions in which they were raised. Inner-city representatives argue that greater concentrations of poorer people in central cities demand that equity be measured in terms of the degree to which need is satisfied, and that resources should be shifted from communities having higher median incomes to those having lower incomes and greater transportation needs (Wachs, 1997).

Several studies conducted in past decades have concluded that transit subsidies in the aggregate result in a net transfer of benefits from high-income to low-income groups and from white to minority groups. This occurs because low-income inner-city minority groups use transit very much more than others, and it occurs despite greater subsidization, per trip or per vehicle mile of travel, of the types of public transit that suburban, white middle-class people are likely to use, such as express buses on freeways or suburban commuter rail systems (Pucher, 1981, 1982).

Although in the aggregate more resources may be transferred from suburban communities to inner-city transit users, other scholars have focused on the fact that this transfer leaves inner-city transit systems poor in relation to their overwhelmingly larger needs, and that suburban, white commuters are subsidized more highly by transit investment programs on a per capita basis. Brian Taylor (1991) has analyzed the distribution of transit operating subsidies in the San Francisco Bay Area. Examining the distribution of the Bay Area's portion of the proceeds of a statewide sales tax on gasoline, he found, for example, that the larger, inner-city transit operators in the Bay Area carried the overwhelmingly largest share of the passengers and received a dramatically smaller share of the program's resources. Conversely, smaller, more localized suburban transit operators received a far larger proportion of the subsidy dollars under this program than their regional share of transit ridership might suggest they ought to receive. The San Francisco Muni and AC Transit provided about 70 percent of the transit rides in the Bay Area, and their riders paid higher fares than suburban transit users, but they received only about 40 percent of the proceeds of the Bay Area's funds under this program. Although MUNI and AC Transit received more dollars than did smaller, suburban operators, their riders were subsidized by this particular tax at about 40 cents per boarding. And although 10 small suburban transit operators collectively provided 2.1 percent of the transit rides in the Bay Area, their riders were subsidized at a rate of more than $2.00 per ride. Over time, regional politics continues to press for expansions of suburban services and the inner-city transit operators continue to reduce service and raise fares.

In Los Angeles a lawsuit was recently filed alleging that the regional approach to transit funding there violated Title VI of the 1964 Federal Civil Rights Act. The plaintiffs, the Bus Riders' Union, representing poorer, minority, inner-city riders, specifically objected to a proposal by the Metropolitan Transportation Authority to raise fares, eliminate monthly discount fare passes, and decrease local bus service in the inner city. They claimed that at the very same time inner-city service was being reduced and fares increased, commitments were being fulfilled to build new rail lines that connected suburban and predominantly white commuters to downtown job locations. They also claimed that the vast majority of transit security costs were being devoted to policing suburban transit services despite higher crime rates on inner-city bus routes. Before this case went to trial, a settlement was reached in which the regional transit agency committed itself to fully serving the needs of inner-city transit-dependent citizens. The settlement included commitments to increase inner-city bus service, slow the pace of transit fare increases, and experiment with new pricing arrangements, such as off-peak fare discounts on inner-city transit routes. The settlement also included a commitment to provide increased transit security in the inner city. Other groups in Philadelphia, Baltimore, and New York City have raised similar objections to transit funding in their regions.

It is difficult to generalize about equity in the provision of transportation services, to arrive at measures of equity in transportation service delivery that can be widely accepted as appropriate, or to understand the extent to which the existence of regional agencies has increased or decreased equitability in the provision of transportation services. It would appear, however, that political disagreements over the fairness of transit funding are very common and often heated, and that the regional agencies are the locus of much of this debate.

Lack of Integration of Transportation With Land Use

Transportation planning is intimately related to urban form and land use. Economists repeatedly remind transportation planners that the demand for travel is a derived demand, meaning that it is derived from personal needs and desires to participate in activities that are defined in space and in time. Every trip is made from an origin and to a destination that is determined by the spatial distribution of land uses. Transportation planners attempt to manipulate and control transportation facility capacities, but the needs for capacity are the direct result of the spatial distribution of activities. Many planners and environmentalists advocate addressing traffic congestion and air quality problems through land use strategies. By creating higher-density developments of mixed land uses at transit stations, for example, some believe that cities can be created in which people need be less reliant on automobiles and in which they might find transit use more attractive. Similarly, others call for plans to create a greater degree of spatial balance between jobs and housing. By locating new housing developments closer to concentrations of employment, and by locating new employment centers near housing-rich communities, some believe that transportation demand can be managed to reduce traffic congestion and improve air quality.

We have shown that there is a long history of thinking and acting regionally in the realm of metropolitan transportation, but in the United States land use planning, zoning, subdivision regulation, and land taxation remain jealously guarded prerogatives of local governments. Regional bodies make advisory pronouncements about the importance of achieving a jobs/housing balance and transit-oriented development, but local governments ignore these pronouncements to make land use decisions that increase local revenues from property taxes in relation to the costs of local service provision. As long as transportation plans and programs at the regional level remain reactive to strictly local land use decision making, transportation investments will be less effective at directing and determining regional form than could otherwise be the case. There are differences of opinion as to whether the ability to more centrally control land use and transportation policy jointly would create more efficient land use and travel patterns (Gordon and Richardson, 1997; Ewing, 1997), but it is clear that in America regional transportation systems have long had and probably will long have the responsibility to respond to and serve local land use policy making rather than to lead or determine it.

HISTORICAL EVOLUTION OF
REGIONAL AIR QUALITY AGENCIES

As with many aspects of air pollution control, California led the nation in controlling air pollution at the county and regional levels. The California state legislature passed the California Air Pollution Control District Act of 1947, authorizing counties to regulate air pollution, largely in response to the inability of Los Angeles County to control pollution sources in incorporated areas (Bollens, 1957). As a result, the Los Angeles County Air Pollution Control District was formed in late 1947, the first such county agency in the nation. California law also allowed two or more contiguous counties with county air districts to consolidate into a unified district. In 1955, the state took the idea of regional air pollution control further, by passing the Bay Area Air Pollution Control Law, forming the multicounty Bay Area Air Pollution Control District (BAAPCD). The district originally encompassed six counties and expanded to nine in 1971; it was later renamed the Bay Area Air Quality Management District (BAAQMD).

Recognition of air pollution as a regional problem was formalized at the national level starting in 1967. In a message sent to Congress on January 30, 1967, President Lyndon Johnson proposed that "regional air quality commissions should be established, to enforce pollution control measures in regional air sheds which cut across state and local boundaries" (Lieber, 1968:86). In November, Johnson signed the Air Quality Act of 1967, which required the Department of Health, Education and Welfare to designate air quality control regions (AQCRs) on the basis of factors such as jurisdictional boundaries, urban industrial concentrations, and atmospheric areas. The next month President Nixon signed the Clean Air Act Amendments of 1970, which ordered the newly formed Environmental Protection Agency to complete designation of the AQCRs. About 20 percent of the nearly 250 regions crossed state boundaries, and nearly all of the AQCRs included at least one and usually extended beyond a standard metropolitan statistical area (Environmental Protection Agency, 1972; Altshuler, 1979).

California followed a parallel path. In 1967 the state legislature passed the Mulford-Carrell Air Resources Act, which directed the Air Resources Board to divide the state into air basins. The purposes were: "(1) to establish air quality standards that may vary from basin to basin; (2) adopt emissions standards for air pollutants for each basin as found necessary; (3) inventory all sources of emissions for each basin; and (4) provide a mechanism for the establishment of regional air pollution control districts within the basins." The board found that the state was "particularly suited to application of the concept of basins because its large valleys, plains and plateaus are in most instances separated by mountain ranges." Eleven basins were established in November 1968 (California Air Resources Board, 1972).

With the passage of the 1970 Clean Air Act Amendments and the designation of the entire nation into air quality control regions, regional air quality agencies grew in number and authority both inside and outside California. In addition, planning grants helped fund agency activities. By 1973 there were 16 multicounty air pollution control agencies, up from just 2 in 1961. During that same period, the number of city agencies fell from 64 to 49. In Massachusetts, the state established regional air pollution control districts; the localities within the district then paid the state to operate the control program. There are currently four such districts. New Jersey facilitated the joint operation of programs by combinations of local governments. Ohio made arrangements for each major city air pollution agency to provide services to surrounding counties, acting as agents for the state. The state of Washington designated seven air pollution control regions made up of cities and counties. There are currently three multicounty districts in Ohio and four in Washington (Schueneman, 1977; Air and Waste Management Association, 1995). With the 10 multicounty districts in California, there are currently over 20 regional air pollution agencies in the country.

WHY WERE REGIONAL AIR POLLUTION AGENCIES FORMED?

The idea of controlling air pollution on a regional level evolved in the 1950s, as the focus of air pollution control shifted from controlling smoke to other pollutants, including ozone or "smog." Until about 1960, cities operated the vast majority of air pollution control programs. However, debate in the 1950s centered on two weaknesses in city and county control: (1) air pollution crosses political boundaries and uncooperative neighbors could counteract city or county efforts and (2) the high costs of technical personnel, equipment, and facilities were often beyond the reach of individual cities or counties. In addition, state control was "opposed as wielding a heavy hand where a more tactful program based on local sentiment is needed" (Berdahl, 1955).

This first reason was key to the formation of the BAAPCD in 1955. At the time, only one of the nine San Francisco Bay Area counties, Santa Clara County, had formed a county air pollution control district. Area politicians felt that state legislation was necessary to hasten the formation of a regional agency, rather than waiting for each county to form a district and then consolidate, and to streamline the consolidated agency's governing board. There were worries about competition for business between counties; if one or more counties decided not to form a county air district or impose control regulations, businesses might relocate in that jurisdiction.

Acceptance of regional authority was furthered by applying the concept of an air basin. Everyone generally agreed that air quality problems, particularly that of ozone (smog), are regional in nature. Air pollution knows no political boundaries and what is generated in one area usually impacts people in another area within the basin. Furthermore, such a basin, within which most pollution was generated and thought to remain, could be "precisely delineated by scientists. The problem of the administrator and the legislator is also simplified when scientific aids can be brought to bear in determining the appropriate jurisdiction" (Joint Subcommittee on Air Pollution, 1955:8, 29). The region could then be defined based on scientific criteria such as weather and topography, rather than political leanings, demographics, or economics. In California, the legislature had also already divided the state into water pollution control regions based on the watershed concept. In fact, one of the major disagreements in forming the BAAPCD was not the boundaries of the region, but representation on the governing board, with cities wanting to ensure direct representation, rather than a board made up solely of county supervisors.

Support from a wide variety of interests was also necessary. For example, strong support for the BAAPCD came from the more urbanized counties of San Mateo, Alameda, San Francisco, and Santa Clara, where pollution levels were reaching highs of up to three times today's federal standards. In addition, farmers in the region, particularly in southern Santa Clara County, recognized that air pollution generated by northern neighbors was damaging crops (Bay Area Air Quality Management District, 1993). Orchid growers reported large losses that they attributed to air contaminants. The Bay Area Council, a business organization long active in regional issues, had an air pollution committee and called for regional regulations to prevent serious problems from developing. On a statewide level, a majority of delegates at a California State Chamber of Commerce conference on air pollution voted for regional air districts. The League of California Cities adopted a policy in 1955 that recommended mandatory legislation creating multicounty or regional air pollution control districts with all the necessary legal authority to control air pollution (Joint Subcommittee on Air Pollution, 1955). In addition, air quality impacts human health, thus support for controls was also gathered from the general public and political leaders. Health advisories were frequent during the period when air districts were formed and gained much of their power.

Another key to formation of regional districts in California was initiation and support from the regions themselves. Prior to 1955, bills were introduced but failed to give the regional water pollution control boards authority to control air pollution and to establish a parallel system of regional boards for air pollution control throughout the state. There are currently 10 multicounty air pollution control districts in the state, but only 3 of these were established by special state legislation. The remainder were formed by county districts agreeing to consolidate, often in more rural areas such as the north coast, the northern Sierra region, and the Great Basin east of the Sierra Nevada mountains. The need for regional consensus to form an agency covering an entire air basin is evidenced in the Sacramento Valley basin, where 9 separate air districts govern. The state legislature did establish the Sacramento Metropolitan Air Quality Management District, but it currently includes only the County of Sacramento. Neighboring Placer County was given an option to join but declined.

REGIONAL AIR POLLUTION AGENCIES: AUTHORITIES AND ACTIVITIES

In California, most of the regional air districts were formed by combining county districts. Therefore, the governing boards are made up entirely of county supervisors. In the three districts formed by state legislation, the board structure varies. The boards of the BAAQMD and the San Joaquin Valley Air Quality Management District are comprised solely of county supervisors and city council members or mayors. In addition to county supervisors and city council members or mayors, the board of the South Coast Air Quality Management District (SCAQMD) includes one member each appointed by the governor, the state senate, and the state assembly. This has contributed to the highly charged political atmosphere surrounding the SCAQMD. State law also requires each district to have a hearing board made up of one lawyer, one professional engineer, one member of the medical profession, and two members of the public. The hearing boards are a quasi-judicial body and primarily serve to consider variances to district rules.

Funding for air districts in California comes from a variety of sources. Air districts recover a large portion of their operating costs from permit and emission fees and penalties resulting from violations. However, revenue from these fees declines as emissions decline or as the economy stagnates, reducing the number of businesses needing permits. State and federal grants contribute to agency budgets, although that source has declined over the years. A new source of revenue for most urban districts is a $2.00 to $4.00 surcharge on motor vehicle registrations. These funds are used to reduce mobile sources of pollution through demand management measures and alternative fuel vehicles.

The 1970 and 1977 federal Clean Air Act Amendments led to increased activity on the part of the regional agencies in the 1970s and 1980s. For example, prior to 1970, the Bay Area APCD had adopted only 3 regulations in its first 15 years of existence and had not engaged in significant planning activities. In 1979 the agency joined with the Association of Bay Area Governments to develop an air quality management plan for the region, which included measures to reduce pollutants from both stationary and mobile sources. By the end of 1992 the thirteenth regulation was adopted, with numerous rules within each regulation. Staff topped 300 in the early 1990s, with a budget of over $30 million. The SCAQMD had a staff of around 1,000 and a budget of well over $100 million. William Fulton (1996:M6) described the SCAQMD during the 1980s as follows:

"During the boom years of the 1980s, environmentalists, federal bureaucrats, staff members and the public prodded the agency to get tougher on pollution. James Lents, a Tennessee chemist with a nocompromise reputation, took over and declared Los Angeles to be 'the Super Bowl of smog.'"

During this time the state expanded districts' authority and planning requirements. The 1989 California Clean Air Act granted districts the explicit authority to adopt and implement rules to control transportation, indirect, and area sources, in addition to their long-held authority to regulate stationary sources of air pollution. Districts had the authority to seek penalties for violations of their regulations of up to $25,000 per day, and this was increased to $50,000 per day for the most egregious violations. Some violations can result in jail time (California Health and Safety Code, Section 42400 et. seq.). The act also required that air quality plans be prepared and updated every three years to meet stricter state ambient air quality standards. Legislation specific to the BAAQMD and the SCAQMD required the area's metropolitan planning organizations, the Metropolitan Transportation Commission and the Southern California Association of Governments, respectively, to take part in developing the transportation and indirect control measures.

Air districts in California witnessed numerous challenges to their authority in the 1990s. Each legislative session has brought a series of bills to limit the authority of the SCAQMD and air districts in general. Arguments often center on the economic impacts of air regulations and the accountability of the district boards. Two of the leading opponents of the SCAQMD described it as a "monster bureaucracy" that is "accountable to no one" and "crushing businesses with regulatory nightmares" (Hurtt and Lewis, 1996a). Another opponent authored a column in *National Review* entitled "Air Zealots" that led with the statement "The number one killer of business in California is the AQMD" (Hewitt, 1992).

Opponents have succeeded in limiting district authority to some extent. For example, three regional air districts, starting with the SCAQMD in 1987, adopted regulations requiring large employers to impose trip reduction programs aimed at getting their employees to ride share and use transit and other modes to reduce automobile commuting to work. Opposition to the regulatory requirements and the costs of implementing the programs grew, particularly from employers in Southern California. A 1993 *Forbes* article opened "A southern California environmental bureaucracy has become a pioneer in the least efficient ways to clean up the atmosphere" and went on to label the regulation "southern California's most loathed environmental regulation" (Lane, 1993). At that time, the SCAQMD had already imposed over $1 million in fines for this regulation, which affected about 4,000 work sites in the region. As a result of complaints from businesses, a state senator from the region sponsored legislation, signed by the governor in 1995, prohibiting cities, counties, *and* air districts from implementing such regulations.

In 1996 a set of bills introduced by Republican senators in Orange County (within the SCAQMD) sought to overhaul the district's board, require legislative approval of expenditures, and limit its authority to control indirect sources. Prior legislation had already been approved that required some state agency and legislative oversight of the SCAQMD's budget. However, support for the massive changes was not widespread, as two industry groups, including the California Manufacturers Association, spoke against the bills (Cone, 1996). Overall, air district authority remains intact, although agency management and governing boards may be wary of exercising that authority to its full extent.

The change from the 1980s to the 1990s is perhaps summed up best by continuing with Fulton's description of the SCAQMD: "When the recession hit in the early 1990s, political tolerance for anti-smog regulations changed. Though Lents remained in charge, his agency became more flexible, rolling back many regulations. The business community, which had long complained about the anti-smog power wielded by the agency, recognized that this was a two-way street. Throughout, the Clean Air Act did not change. Neither did the technology used to fight smog, nor the computerized-modeling approach used by most air-quality analysts, nor the weather patterns that make Los Angeles susceptible to smog. All that had changed was the political climate" (Fulton, 1996). In response to this change, the SCAQMD adopted the 1996 AQMD Regulatory Reform Initiative, which included policies to reduce its size by 50 percent (staff is now under 800), eliminate permitting requirements for small businesses, and streamline permit processes. However, critics of such actions argue that the SCAQMD is bowing to industry and is not tough enough.

EVALUATING REGIONALISM IN AIR QUALITY PLANNING

Successes

Regional air districts in California are generally viewed as a success in terms of reducing air pollutant emissions and improving air quality. Air quality has improved in all regions despite significant growth in population and vehicle use. Peak ozone levels in the South Coast basin have been cut to less than half of what they were in the 1950s. The same is true in the San Francisco Bay Area, which was declared in attainment of the federal ozone standards in 1995, although a recent action revoked this designation. These improvements are due to a combination of air district controls and improved vehicle emission controls adopted by the state. Several factors contribute to this success at the regional level.

One key factor is that federal legislation and regulation established clear and specific targets for air quality, unlike transportation. The Environmental Protection Agency established the National Ambient Air Quality Standards based on health criteria. The plans that states and air districts develop are designed to meet these standards. In addition, the Clean Air Act and its implementing regulations require specific actions, such as rules requiring the "best available control technology" to reduce emissions. Having a specific goal mandated from above reduces some of the political debate that might otherwise surround air quality agencies and impede action. When developing regulations to meet federal—or in the case of California, state—mandates, regional air districts can place the blame, so to speak, on the EPA or the Air Resources Board. If federal laws are not met, the EPA might come into the region and implement its own plan, or highway funding might be cut. Area interests, including the regulated community, would usually prefer to comply with a regulation developed at the regional level than to deal with state or federal agencies.

Other federal requirements and provisions increase the likelihood of strong regional air pollution control programs. For example, programs must be implemented by agencies with legal authority to enforce the adopted measures. In order to become part of the federally approved state implementation plan, the measures must be enforceable, real, and quantifiable and result in emission reductions in surplus of other measures. The federal Clean Air Act explicitly allows for citizen lawsuits to enforce federal requirements. The possibility, and in some areas the probability, of such lawsuits serves to counteract pressures from the regulated community to weaken plans and regulations. At the same time, there is room for local control. For example, California law allows air districts to delegate implementation of rules, particularly transportation rules, to local cities and counties. This option was exercised by several cities in both the SCAQMD and the BAAQMD with respect to employer trip reduction rules.

Limitations

Air districts are finding it more difficult to continue achieving such substantial improvements in air quality. The agencies have generally succeeded in reducing emissions from stationary sources, ranging from oil refineries to dry cleaners and gas stations. Implementation of these controls has little direct impact on residents' everyday lives or on city and county land use authorities. However, as these sources have been controlled and air quality standards have not yet been met, air districts have turned to more difficult, but significant sources, such as the use of automobiles and consumer products, including barbecues, lawn mowers, paints, and spray cans. Air districts have not been able to significantly reduce emissions from these transportation and area-wide sources. They have had little, if any, impact on the cause of much of today's ozone problem: increasing travel by private automobiles spurred, in part, by current growth patterns. In this area, however, state and federal technology-forcing regulations have been successful; automobile emissions per mile of travel have decreased dramatically since 1970. When the air districts in California entered this arena by adopting employer trip reduction rules, backlash led to a state law forbidding such rules from any level of government. Regulatory controls on automobile use and consumer products are more difficult because they directly impact residents who may not see the benefit to air quality. It is much easier to understand how putting equipment on a refinery will improve air quality than using non-oil-based paints on your house. Similarly, it is much easier to blame pollution problems on Chevron and Exxon than on your and your neighbor's working in the backyard on the weekend or driving to work each day. These types of measures fit into Alan Altshuler's fourth, and least acceptable, level of innovation "those that entail substantial costs or interference with established patterns of behavior, imposed in such a manner that the blame will fall clearly and inescapably upon the public officials who adopt the innovation" (Altshuler, 1979).

Other problems exist with these measures as well, including lack of jurisdiction and authority. Many clean air plans include measures involving improvements in transit service, high-occupancy vehicle lanes, and bicycle facilities. However, air districts are not responsible for these types of facilities that are typically under the jurisdiction of state and regional transportation agencies, cities, and counties. This is even more germane to land use measures that appear in some air quality plans, such as the jobs-housing balance and increased density around rail transit stations. Air districts also struggle to accurately predict the benefits of such measures, unlike traditional stationary source controls. This makes convincing air district boards and other agencies to adopt such measures even more difficult.

Despite the number and impact of rules adopted by air districts and the power given them by the state, air districts have often been at the center of controversy. During the earliest years of the BAAPCD, when adoption of a regulation to limit open burning was debated, opponents burned in effigy a likeness of the agency head. In the late 1980s and early 1990s, the SCAQMD was in the middle of several lawsuits by environmental groups that forced the EPA to develop two federal implementation plans for the region. Given the constraints of the federal Clean Air Act, the EPA's proposals included extremely controversial measures, including high fees on airplanes landing in the region and driving or gasoline purchase restrictions. However, after each proposal was introduced and publicity ensued, agreements were reached to avoid implementation of the plans, with each agency returning to its regular activities.

Overall, regional air agencies face far more difficult challenges today than they did earlier in their 40-year history. Most districts have already adopted the most effective and politically acceptable controls for stationary sources. Getting those last emission reductions needed for attainment are proving to be the most difficult. When adopting air quality plans, California air districts must evaluate the cost-effectiveness of each control measure in terms of dollars per ton of pollutant reduced. Many of the rules that district boards adopted in the past two decades had a cost-effectiveness ranging from cost savings to expenses of $10,000 per ton of reactive organic gases reduced. However, many of the transportation control measures have costs of $50,000 to $100,000 or more per ton of reactive organic gases reduced. New stationary source measures are more costly as well, or call for technology that does not yet exist. Rules adopted today are getting emission reductions of one-tenth of what rules adopted in the 1970s and 1980s achieved. Many of the rules proposed in clean air plans in the 1990s are projected to achieve less than one ton of reactive organic gas reductions per day.

Air districts also struggle in defining their role relative to state and federal agencies. Traditionally, the federal government and California have regulated direct emissions from vehicles. The EPA and the states have also been responsible for programs directly related to vehicle emissions, such as inspection and maintenance programs and fuels, including the formulation of gasoline and the introduction of alternative fuels. However, some air districts have entered this arena by adopting programs to fund alternative fuel vehicles or rules that require or provide incentives to purchase such vehicles. As a result, conflicts may arise between the regional district and the state over how programs might overlap or conflict. In addition, districts often feel constrained by having little or no control over sources such as aircraft, ships, and interstate rail engines. As other sources are controlled, these are becoming a bigger piece of the pie and their control is essential for some areas to meet federal and state standards.

One question that faces regional air quality agencies is their role in reaching attainment of state and federal standards. If the largest sources of pollution remaining, namely cars, trucks, and other mobile sources, cannot be controlled at the local and the regional levels through reducing their use, i.e., if technological changes are the only real solution, will air districts play as large a role in adopting new strategies to clean up the air as they have in the past? In addition, if traditional regulatory strategies are not acceptable, can the agencies adapt by implementing more innovative programs via incentives, public-private partnerships, and market-based measures?

Equity

Issues of equity have not been as visible in air quality debates as in transportation, although they do exist. The lack of debate over equity stems, in part, from the focus of air pollution control on ozone, a pollutant that is formed by chemical reactions in the air over the course of the day. The emissions that cause smog may originate in one area and end up as ozone in another part of the region. The smoggiest areas of a region do not always correspond with income, race, or other demographics. Air districts have traditionally applied their regulations equally throughout the region, believing that emissions from all parts potentially create smog. This is in contrast to providing transportation facilities or services in certain locations that might impact certain neighborhoods or groups differently.

If pollutants other than ozone are considered, particularly toxic air contaminants, effects are often very localized, impacting lower-income ethnic communities. Neighborhoods surrounding refineries and other heavy industrial sites may be subject to higher concentrations of pollutants, in addition to the risks of accidental releases. In many cases they also have active community groups that are often at odds with the air districts, calling for stricter controls. Air quality regulations may also impact income groups differently. Inspection and maintenance requirements for cars and trucks require minimum spending limits that can impact poor families substantially. Critics of the SCAQMD argue that the agency's regulations have eliminated disproportionate numbers of manufacturing jobs and small businesses, although that debate is unresolved. And, although state law requires socioeconomic impact reports for many air district plans and regulations, the required focus of such reports is impacts on businesses and jobs, not residents or neighborhoods.

More recently, the issue of environmental justice, which has its origins in the arena of toxics and waste disposal (Bryant, 1995), has entered into the air pollution arena. Environmental groups in the Los Angeles region are challenging trading rules adopted and proposed by the SCAQMD. These rules allow stationary sources of air pollution to avoid compliance with existing stationary source control rules by reducing pollutants from other sources, such as scrapping high-polluting automobiles. Critics claim that this will result in increased pollution in low-income minority communities. They argue that the programs violate Title VI of the Civil Rights Act. The EPA's National Environmental Justice Advisory Council has recommended postponing federal approval of one such rule, though the EPA staff is divided on the issue (*Inside Cal/EPA*, 1996, 1997). Environmental justice issues are not unique to regional air districts. In this arena the issue is a product of the push toward market-based pollution control measures and the location of noxious sources in low-income areas. Furthermore, it is unclear whether a regional agency will be able to address the issue any better than a county or a city. In fact, with a regional agency, the opportunities for trading between sources are likely to be greater, thereby increasing the demand for and feasibility of such programs. With respect to central cities, the equity impacts of regional air pollution programs are highly dependent on the region in question and whether sources of pollution are concentrated in the central city.

CONCLUSIONS

Transportation and air quality are two sectors of American public policy in which there are today significant regional roles. There are important similarities and differences in regional governance in these sectors, however, and, it is also not completely clear that the evolution of regional approaches to governance and decision making in transportation and air quality offer models of approaches that will be readily applicable to other sectors of public policy making.

A widespread consensus that a problem is regional in extent and in scope does not necessarily lead directly to regional action or to attempted solutions that are regional in scope. Both transportation and air quality are addressed at the regional level in large part because federal legislation and federal regulatory agencies have directed that these problems be attacked regionally. Far less often have effective regional agencies been direct outcomes of progressive initiatives taken entirely within regions that simply recognized the importance of acting collectively to address a serious regional problem. Although many can argue for the potential benefits of collective regional action, they have rarely caused a groundswell of support for councils of government or special districts. Local governments naturally see these forms of regionalism as a threat to their autonomy and financial integrity, and state governments also have seen little to be gained from creating stronger regional bodies. Requirements of the Clean Air Act and its subsequent amendments and those in a series of Surface Transportation Acts have more directly led to the regionalism that we have discussed in this paper.

One of the key differences in regional planning between transportation and air quality is the existence of clearer goals in air quality planning, namely the ambient air quality standards established at the federal level and in California. In addition, the federal and the California Clean Air Acts define specific goals to help reach the ambient standards, such as a 3 percent per year reduction in emissions. Although some may question the reasonableness of the goals, their existence eliminates some of the debate over goalsetting that is typical in planning processes, helps focus efforts, and provides criteria to use in selecting programs and measures. In contrast, the federal government has not set specific, quantitative goals or objectives that define the overall mission of transportation agencies. Rather, transportation planners face several broad goals, such as the reduction of congestion and the provision and enhancement of mobility, which often conflict with each other. The existence of regional authorities does little to clarify the goals of transportation planning, and it is reasonable to conclude that the sharper policy focus associated with air quality does not result from the fact that it is to a great extent addressed at the regional level.

One of the principal arguments that might be given for a regional locus for public policy making is the fact that regions differ dramatically from one another in their economies, demographics, geography, and history. There is little reason to expect, for example, that the type of transportation investment program appropriate for New York or Boston is also likely to be the most appropriate approach for Phoenix or Dallas. Yet in the realms of transportation and air quality, at least, the existence of regional decision-making bodies have not fostered dramatic differences in approaches to regional planning. Because there are few sources of transportation funds at the regional level, and programs at the federal level make transportation funds available for specific types of investments—new rail systems or bridge rehabilitation programs—regional bodies adjust their activities to focus on the capture of federal resources. That focus makes their priorities seem surprisingly similar despite dramatically different regional settings. Rather than finding that one metropolitan area seeks funds for rail system construction, another for express bus operations, and a third for highway network rehabilitation, all seem to compete for their shares of whatever federal programs offer, leading to a surprising similarity in their plans. To fulfill the requirements of air quality regulations, each metropolitan area models its regulatory program after programs that other regions are trying or what the federal government is currently requiring.

It might also appear that the presence of a regional authority for transportation or air quality might lead to greater equity in the distribution of resources within a region. Whereas one school board might have far less to spend on education than another as a function of the wealth of the citizens of their different districts, wouldn't the existence of a region-wide transportation authority suggest the possibility that the needs of less advantaged communities within the region might be more equitably addressed? Unfortunately, there is little evidence that a higher level of distributional equity has been achieved as a result of the existence of regional transportation authorities. Neither transportation nor air quality agencies at the regional level have direct taxing or fund-raising authority, and neither typically has the equitable redistribution of funds as an explicit responsibility within the terms of its charter. In many instances, for example, per capita transportation subsidies for suburban transit services in high-income communities are many times larger than per capita subsidies for inner-city transit networks that serve larger numbers of lower-income, transit-dependent people. In many instances, highways have been built through low-income communities in order to benefit richer suburban commuters despite the fact that a regional authority has reviewed the routing and the funding of the highway construction project. And, as we have noted above, many observers claim that regional air quality goals have led to regulations that have had especially negative impacts on lower-income manufacturing workers.

Governance and policy making at the regional level in transportation and air quality are almost always indirect and derivative. Regional transportation authorities and air quality management districts are not composed of directly elected representatives, but rather are structured so that their boards are composed of locally elected municipal and county officials. These boards and commissions therefore typically include few or no advocates for region-wide interests. Rather, each representative to the regional body or commission is there to serve the interests of his or her home community, seeking to minimize the negative effects of region-wide regulations on the communities they represent, or to maximize the financial gains of region-wide policies for their districts. The policies that are adopted and the compromises that are reached at the regional level rarely redistribute benefits from the haves to the have-nots. They do not result in choices of investments to maximize regional efficiency, but rather they attempt to balance competing interests within the region.

REFERENCES

Air and Waste Management Association
    1995   *1995 Government Agencies Directory.* Washington, DC: Air and Waste Management Association.

Altshuler, Alan
    1979   *The Urban Transportation System.* Cambridge, MA: MIT Press.

Bay Area Air Quality Management District
    1993   *The History of Ozone in the Bay Area (1970-1992).* San Francisco, CA: Bay Area Air Quality Management District.

Berdahl, Robert O.
    1955   Governmental experience in air pollution control. In Joint Subcommittee on Air Pollution, *Air Pollution Control in the San Francisco Bay Area.* Assembly Interim Committee Reports 1953-1955 13(4). Assembly of the State of California.

Bollens, John C.
    1957   *Special District Governments in the United States.* Berkeley, CA: University of California Press.

Bryant, Bunyan, ed.
    1995   *Environmental Justice: Issues, Policies and Solutions.* Washington, DC: Island Press.

California Air Resources Board
    1972   *California Air Basins.* December. Sacramento: California Air Resources Board.

Cone, Marla
    1996   Air board to fight bills curbing power environment. *Los Angeles Times*, p. A20, February 24.

Environmental Protection Agency
    1972   *Federal Air Quality Control Regions.* Washington, DC: Environmental Protection Agency.

Ewing, Reid
    1997   Counterpoint: Is Los Angeles style sprawl desirable? *Journal of the American Planning Association* 63(1) (Winter):107-126.

Federal Highway Administration
    1993   *Journey to Work Trends in the United States and Its Major Metropolitan Areas. 1960-1990.* Washington, DC: U.S. Department of Transportation.

Fulton, William
    1996   The AQMD: A political creature suffers a political fate. *Los Angeles Times*, p. M6, September 1.

Gordon, Peter, and Harry W. Richardson
    1997   Point: Are compact cities a desirable planning goal? *Journal of the American Planning Association* 63(1) (Winter):95-106.

Heightchew, Robert E.
    1979   TSM: Revolution of repetition. *ITE Journal* 48(9) (September):22-30.

Hewitt, Hugh
    1992   Air zealots. *National Review* 44(16) August 17.

Hurtt, Rob, and John Lewis
    1996   Making AQMD more accountable. Letter to editor, *Los Angeles Times*, p. B-6, March 12.

Inside Cal/EPA
    1996   Environmentalists hail EPA move to consider justice in credit trading. *Inside Cal/EPA* 7(51) December 20.
    1997   EPA postpones approval of credit trading plan to focus on justice. *Inside Cal/EPA* 8(5) January 31.

Joint Subcommittee on Air Pollution
    1955   *Air Pollution Control in the San Francisco Bay Area.* Assembly Interim Committee
            Reports 1953-1955, 13(4):8, 29, Assembly of the State of California, February.
Lane, Randall
    1993   The commuter police. *Forbes* 152(14):239 December 20.
Lieber, Harvey
    1968   Controlling metropolitan pollution through regional airsheds: Administrative requirements
            and political problems. *Journal of the Air Pollution Control Association* 18(2):86-94.
Pisarski, Alan E.
    1996   *Commuting in America II: The Second National Report on Commuting Patterns and
            Trends.* Lansdowne, VA: Eno Foundation for Transportation, Inc.
Pucher, John
    1981   Equity in Transit Finance: A Quantitative Assessment of the Impacts of Transit Subsidies
            on Low-Income and Minority Groups. Report Prepared for the Urban Mass Transporta-
            tion Administration, U.S. Department of Transportation, Washington, DC.
    1982   Discrimination in mass transit. *Journal of the American Planning Association* 48(3)
            (Summer):315-326.
Schueneman, Jean J.
    1977   Organization and operation of air pollution control agencies. In *Air Pollution, Third
            Edition, Volume V,* Arthur C. Stern, ed. New York: Academic Press.
Stern, Arthur C.
    1982   History of air pollution legislation in the United States. *Journal of the Air Pollution
            Control Association* 32(1).
Taylor, Brian D.
    1991   Unjust equity: An examination of California's Transportation Development Act, *Trans-
            portation Research Record No. 1297,* pp. 85-92.
    1992   When Finance Leads Planning: The Influence of Public Finance on Transportation Plan-
            ning and Policy in California. Doctoral dissertation, Department of Urban Planning,
            University of California, Los Angeles.
    1995   Public perceptions, fiscal realities, and freeway planning: The California case. *Journal
            of the American Planning Association* 61(1) (Winter):43-56.
Wachs, Martin
    1997   Critical issues in transportation in California. In *California Policy Options:1997,* Xandra
            Kayden, ed. The UCLA Policy Forum and the UCLA Business Forecasting Project,
            School of Public Policy and Social Research, University of California, Los Angeles.
Wachs, Martin, and James Ortner
    1979   Capital grants and recurrent subsidies. *Transportation* 8(1)(March):3-19.

Biographical Sketches of Committee Members and Staff

ALAN ALTSHULER (*Co-chair*) is the Ruth and Frank Stanton professor of urban policy and planning at Harvard University, with a joint appointment in the Kennedy School of Government and the Design School. He is also director of the Kennedy School's Taubman Center for State and Local Government. Prior to joining the Harvard faculty in 1988, he was dean of the Graduate School of Public Administration at New York University (1983-1988), a professor of political science at the Massachusetts Institute of Technology (1966-1971, 1975-1983), and secretary of transportation for the state of Massachusetts (1971-1975). His research interests focus on urban politics and on policy for the built environment. His most recent books are *Regulation for Revenue* (with Jose Gómez-Ibáñez) and *Innovation in American Government* (with Robert Behn and others). He has a Ph.D. in political science from the University of Chicago.

WILLIAM MORRILL (*Co-chair*) is a senior fellow at Mathtech, Inc., an applied research and consulting firm, and formerly its president. Previously, he was president of Mathematica Policy Research, Inc.; assistant secretary for planning and evaluation of the U.S. Department of Health, Education, and Welfare; assistant director of the U.S. Office of Management and Budget; and deputy county executive of Fairfax County, Virginia. He has served as member and chair on a wide range of panels and committees of the National Research Council. His current research is centered on a range of education and human service policy issues. He has a bachelor's degree in government from Wesleyan University and an M.P.A. from the Maxwell School, Syracuse University.

LAWRENCE DAHMS has been executive director for 21 years of the Metropolitan Transportation Commission, which serves as a 19-member governing board that represents nine counties and 100 cities in the San Francisco Bay area. Previously he was employed by the Army Corps of Engineers, the California legislature, BART, Arthur D. Little, Inc., and Caltrans. He has participated on several study committees established by the Transportation Research Board and other units of the National Research Council. In 1996, he was the recipient of the W.N. Carey, Jr., distinguished service award, which recognizes individuals who have given outstanding leadership and service to transportation research. He has a B.S. in civil engineering from San Diego State University and an M.B.A. from Sacramento State University.

MARTHA DERTHICK is the Julia Allen Cooper professor at the Woodrow Wilson Department of Government and Foreign Affairs at the University of Virginia. She teaches courses in American public policy and political institutions, including federalism. She is editor of *Dilemmas of Scale in America's Federal Democracy*, which explores the tradition of local self-government in the United States. She has a Ph.D. in political science from Radcliffe College.

ANTHONY DOWNS is a senior fellow at the Brookings Institution in Washington, D.C. Prior to joining Brookings, he was a member for 18 years and then chairman of Real Estate Research Corporation, a nationwide consulting firm advising private and public decision makers on real estate investment, housing policies, and urban affairs. He has served as a consultant to many of the nation's largest corporations, major developers, and private foundations, as well as to dozens of local, state, and national government agencies. He has a Ph.D. in economics from Stanford University and is the author or coauthor of 20 books and over 400 articles.

JAMES GIBSON serves as project director and president of DC Agenda, a nonprofit community assistance corporation dedicated to addressing issues facing the District of Columbia. He has been a senior associate at the Urban Institute since January 1993, where he focuses on civil rights policies, community development, urban governance, economic and social opportunities, and antipoverty strategies. He was formerly director of the Eugene and Agnes E. Meyer Foundation in Washington, D.C. Other positions he has held include assistant city administrator for planning and development for Washington, D.C., and executive associate of the Potomac Institute.

GENEVIEVE GIULIANO is a professor in the School of Policy, Planning, and Development, University of Southern California. Prior to July 1998, she was professor and director of the Lusk Center Research Institute, School of Urban Planning and Development at USC. Her research interests include relationships between land use and transportation, transportation policy evaluation, impacts of information technology on transportation and travel behavior, and mobility patterns of low-income households. Results of her research have been published extensively, and she has presented numerous papers at conferences both within the United States and abroad. She has participated in several National Research Council committee projects, and is a member of several expert advisory panels and editorial boards. She has a Ph.D. in social sciences from the University of California at Irvine.

STEPHEN GODWIN is director of the Studies and Information Services Division of the Transportation Research Board (TRB) of the National Research Council. He has been with TRB since 1983 and oversees policy studies at the request of Congress and the executive branch dealing with economic, safety, environmental, and research policy issues in transportation. Before joining TRB, he was a research associate at the Urban Institute in Washington, D.C., and also worked in the Policy Studies Office of the U.S. Department of Housing and Urban Development. He has a B.A. in religion and philosophy and an M.A. in regional planning from the University of North Carolina, Chapel Hill.

HARRY HOLZER is chief economist of the U.S. Department of Labor, while on leave from his position as a professor of economics at Michigan State University. His research has focused on the employment problems of disadvantaged workers, particularly urban minorities. More recently he has focused on employer skill needs and hiring practices and how these influence the employment outcomes of unskilled workers. His major publications include *The Black Youth Employment Crisis* (coedited with Richard B. Freeman) and *What Employers Want: Job Prospects for Less-Educated Workers.* He is a research affiliate of the Institute for Research on Poverty at the University of Wisconsin and a national fellow in the Program on Inequality and Social Policy at Harvard University. He has a bachelor's degree and a Ph.D. in economics from Harvard University.

CHRISTOPHER LEINBERGER is a founding partner of the Arcadia Land Company in Santa Fe, New Mexico, which is dedicated to land stewardship and building a sense of community. Since 1979, he has also been managing director and co-owner of Robert Charles Lesser and Company, which is the largest independent real estate advisory firm in the country. His work as a land use strategist and developer combines an understanding of business realities and concern for the nation's social and environmental issues. He has focused on corporate strategic planning for real estate companies and metropolitan development trends. He has been active on several committees of the National Research Council. His research and publications run the gamut of economic, social, and environmental implications of land use patterns; he is author of *Strategic Planning for Real*

Estate. He is a graduate of the Harvard Business School and majored in urban sociology and politics as an undergraduate at Swarthmore College.

FAITH MITCHELL is director of the Social and Economic Studies Division of the Commission on Social and Behavioral Sciences and Education at the National Research Council. From 1993 to 1994, she was senior coordinator for population in the Bureau of Population, Refugees, and Migration of the U.S. Department of State. Previously, she directed the population program of the William and Flora Hewlett Foundation in Menlo Park, California, was a program executive at the San Francisco Foundation, and was assistant professor at the Institute for Health Policy Studies at the University of California in San Francisco. She has a Ph.D. in medical anthropology from the University of California at Berkeley and a B.A. from the University of Michigan.

MYRON ORFIELD is a fifth-term member of the Minnesota House of Representatives, representing southwest Minneapolis. In this capacity, he has authored sweeping legislation for metropolitan reform, creating the nation's most substantial regional government and reforming land use and fiscal equity laws in the Twin Cities area. He has become nationally recognized as an expert in the area of metropolitan planning and policy making. As the executive director of the Metropolitan Area Research Corporation, he has completed studies of regional polarization in 14 of the 25 largest metropolitan areas of the United States. His recent publications include *Metropolitics: A Regional Agenda for Community and Stability*. He has a B.A. from the University of Minnesota and a law degree from the University of Chicago Law School. He has practiced law in both the public and private sectors and currently teaches as an adjunct professor of law at the University of Minnesota Law School.

NEAL PEIRCE is a leading writer about metropolitan regions, their political and economic dynamics, and their emerging national and global roles. He is the lead author of *Citistates*. With Curtis Johnson, he has coauthored the Peirce Reports, on compelling issues of metropolitan futures for leading newspapers in 16 regions across the nation. In 1975, he began—and continues today—the United States' first national column focused on state and local government themes, syndicated by the Washington Post Writers Group. His 10-book series on America's states and regions culminated in *The Book of America: Inside 50 States Today*. He was one of the founders and then a contributing editor of *National Journal* and served in the 1960s as political editor of *Congressional Quarterly*. He is known widely as a lecturer on regional, urban, federal system, and community development issues.

PAUL PETERSON is the Henry Lee Shattuck professor of government and director of the Program on Education Policy and Governance at Harvard University. He is a former director of the Governmental Studies Program at the Brookings Institution. He has a Ph.D. from the University of Chicago, where he was a professor in the Departments of Political Science and Education for many years. He is the author or editor of over 60 articles and 17 books, including *Earning and Learning: How Schools Matter, Learning from School Choice, The Politics of School Reform: 1870-1940,* and *City Limits.* He chaired the Social Science Research Council's Committee on the Urban Underclass and has served on many National Research Council committees.

DEBORAH STONE is the coordinator of intergovernmental affairs for Cook County, Illinois, a local government with a population of over 5 million people. Prior to that, she was executive director of the Metropolitan Planning Council of Chicago, a business-based civic organization. Her past work covers regionalism, transportation planning, health care policy, public housing reform, and tax policy. Currently, she is involved with legislation and policy on juvenile and criminal justice, welfare reform, and public finance. She has an M.A. in public policy from the University of Chicago and a B.A. from Beloit College.

CATHERINE WITHERSPOON is the senior policy advisor to the chairman of the Air Resources Board of the California Environmental Protection Agency. She has worked on air quality issues for the past 18 years in government, consulting, and volunteer positions and at the regional, state, and federal levels. During the study period, she was legislative director at the South Coast Air Quality Management District. She has a bachelor's degree in politics from the University of California at Santa Cruz.

HAROLD WOLMAN (*Consultant*) is professor of policy sciences and director of the Policy Sciences Graduate Program at the University of Maryland, Baltimore County. Prior to that he was a professor of political science and urban affairs in the College of Urban, Labor and Metropolitan Affairs at Wayne State University. His research and publications have been in the areas of urban policy and politics, comparative urban policy, economic and community development, and housing. His current research interests include the impact of sprawl and fragmentation on the poor in metropolitan areas, how local governments learn from one another, and changes in the representation of urban interests in Congress. He has a bachelor's degree in political science from Oberlin College, a master's degree in city planning from the Massachusetts Institute of Technology, and a Ph.D. in political science from the University of Michigan.

JULIAN WOLPERT is the Henry G. Bryant professor of geography, public affairs and urban planning at Princeton University's Woodrow Wilson School. Prior to joining the Princeton faculty, he was professor of geography and regional science at the University of Pennsylvania. He has conducted extensive research on migration, locational issues, and the service sector and has written widely on urban development and nonprofit provision of services. His current research interests include federalism issues and the niche of charity and philanthropy in the nation's three-sector economy. He has a bachelor's degree from Columbia University and M.S. and Ph.D. degrees in geography from the University of Wisconsin.

Index

S